The Genetics of Cognitive Neuroscience

Issues in Clinical and Cognitive Neuropsychology
Jordan Grafman, series editor

The Genetics of Cognitive Neuroscience

edited by Terry E. Goldberg and Daniel R. Weinberger

The MIT Press
Cambridge, Massachusetts
London, England

MIT Press books may be purchased at special quantity discounts for business or sales promotional use. For information, please email special_sales@mitpress.mit.edu or write to Special Sales Department, The MIT Press, 55 Hayward Street, Cambridge, MA 02142.

This book was set in Stone Sans and Stone Serif by SNP Best-set Typesetter Ltd., Hong Kong and was printed and bound in the United States of America.

Library of Congress Cataloging-in-Publication Data
The genetics of cognitive neuroscience / edited by Terry E. Goldberg and Daniel R. Weinberger.
    p. cm. – (Issues in clinical and cognitive neuropsychology)
Includes bibliographical references and index.
ISBN 978-0-262-01307-9 (hardcover : alk. paper) 1. Neurogenetics. 2. Cognitive neuroscience.
I. Goldberg, Terry E. II. Weinberger, Daniel R.
QP356.22.G463   2009
612.8–dc22
                                                                                    2008044259

10 9 8 7 6 5 4 3 2 1

Dedication

We would like to thank the subjects who willingly participated in these sometimes difficult studies and gave their time, effort, and DNA and the scientists, named in this book and unnamed, who thought hard about the issues in this field and then did the work to get the studies done. We also would like to thank our families, who have been patient with us.

Contents

Preface

Cognitive genetics and imaging genetics are emerging fields that seek to combine and integrate advances in capturing the implications of the sequence of the human genome with advances in understanding the neural underpinnings of cognitive architecture, personality dimensions, and affective regulation. This edited, multichaptered volume is designed to give the reader a working understanding of the influence of specific genetic variants on cognition, affective regulation, personality, and CNS disorders. The book can be read as a primer with sections on molecular genetics, statistical approaches, and heritability of cognitive and personality traits, with up-to-the-minute reviews of promising candidate genes for cognition and affective regulation, neurologic and psychiatric disorders, and pharmacogenetic response. We view the book as a how-to manual that should provide a set of principles or "tools" for critically evaluating recent studies and as a compendium of "what's out there" for thinking about and planning one's own studies.

Introduction

It has been known for a century that many aspects of personality run in families. Adoption studies and studies of twin populations have shown that many human characteristics related to cognition, temperament, and other aspects of personality, as well as all major psychiatric disorders, are heritable. Recently, genes for variation in such human characteristics are being discovered, and the mechanisms by which they have an impact on these characteristics is a matter of active investigation. This volume is about one approach to understanding the genetic mechanisms of such inherited traits. We have attempted to maintain a balance between up-to-the-minute understanding of new candidate genes and their relationship to cognition, affective regulation, and neurophysiology and more general methodological points about association studies as they may relate to cognition and their conceptual underpinnings, emphasizing the latter. We have taken this tack because the shelf life of a book on genetics will be an issue in this fast-evolving field. We are hoping that by using a set of judiciously focused and formatted chapters, the book will remain a fresh and a valuable resource even as new discoveries and advances come out around it.

One key aspect of the book is an emphasis on the fundamental conceptual issues regarding experimental designs and their limitations, use of informatic tools, integration of data from different levels of analysis, and basic ideas about validity of findings in a field already notorious for arguments about false positive results. We hope to get across the idea that the genetic endgame is not only about statistical p values but also depends on prior probabilities based on knowledge of a gene's biology; that is, associations must be replicable and placed in a neurobiological context for validation.

Of course, the critical dependent measures in the work presented here will involve cognitive test scores, personality measure profiles, and electrophysiological and neurophysiological responses (the latter driven by various neuroimaging activation paradigms), as opposed to categorical case-control studies of disease. The use of intermediate phenotypes with a putatively simpler genetic architecture (e.g., cognition in schizophrenia), which may be necessary to discern associations between gene and dimensional aspects of disease, will also be discussed.

The strength of associations between genes and cognitive processes and affective regulation will be key to the endeavor's scientific success and will be a function of the paradigm's sensitivity to common genetic variants that affect the gene's product. Many of the paradigms that are being used or will be used to assess gene–cognitive phenotype associations come from cognitive science. However, this is no guarantee that we have parsed cognition in a genetically informed way, and it will take numerous reparsings of cognitive operations that occur iteratively before the field stabilizes around core findings.

The level of the reader of this book may be quite broad, from an advanced post-doctoral fellow or independent researcher who wants to bring himself or herself quickly up to speed in the area and gain a more sophisticated understanding of the field's methods and assumptions to an experienced researcher in genetics or cognitive science who wants to learn about the bridge between these scientific disciplines. The book can be read both as a primer with sections on molecular genetics, statistical approaches, animal models (including "knockout" and transgenic mice), and heritabilities, and as a series of critical, up-to-the-minute reviews of promising candidate genes for cognition, affective regulation, neurologic and psychiatric disorders, and pharmacogenetic response. Our ideal reader should come away with an appreciation that the approach offers a translational and mechanistic approach to higher level information processing and behavior. Demonstrating how DNA sequence or structural differences result in molecular biological differences which result in neurophysiological differences which result in cognitive differences is the goal. Animal work will be reviewed when its relevance to humans at the phenotypic and genetic levels is clear or makes an important conceptual point. It should be appreciated that, at least at this stage, the work is reductionistic in nature as phenotypic development will be oriented to discovering the most basic and elemental information-processing routines.

I Methodologies for Genetic Association Studies of Cognition

1 Molecular Genetics and Bioinformatics: An Outline for Neuropsychological Genetics

Lucas Kempf and Daniel R. Weinberger

In investigating the hereditary transmission of talent, we must ever bear in mind our ignorance of the laws which govern the inheritance even of physical features.
—Francis Galton

There is a beautiful diversity and depth to human thoughts and behaviors. Poets, philosophers, and children alike wonder at the mysteries of why we cry with sorrow, laugh with joy, learn to read, or ride a bicycle. By what mysterious mechanisms do we experience these feelings and develop these abilities? The fundamental governing principles of biology are found in our genes. Human genetics is the study of the biology of inheritance and variability in our human species, and, therefore, neuropsychological genetics is the study of human genetics as it applies to the cognitive and emotive functions of the brain. This is not to say all our brain functions are purely controlled by our genes, but neuropsychological genetics is the study of those components that can be explained by them.

It has long been argued that cognitive and behavioral traits might primarily be the result of either nature or nurture. This time-honored dichotomous argument is gradually dissolving with the discovery that it is ultimately the interaction between our biology and our experiences that determines how we think and feel. While the concept of a phenotype's equaling the combined effects of genetic and environment components ($G + E$) is taught in basic biology classes, the popular conception of this reality has lagged when we point the microscope at our own thought processes. Neuropsychological genetics has emerged as a discipline focused on the interaction between our genetics and our experience within the context of processing cognitive and emotional information. This new focus has led to a revolution in the understanding of our basic thought processes.

One of the key concepts underlying the role of genetics in any complex human trait such as cognition is that of heritability. A trait's heritability is the variance in its expression that can be accounted for solely by variation in genetics. The total variance in the expression of a phenotype is the combination of the variance that is genetically determined and that which is environmentally determined. A person's height is determined by both genetic predispositions and nutrition. It is important to note that the term "heritability" does not mean whether something is inherited or not. For example, having a head is obviously a genetically determined human trait, but its heritability is zero, because the phenotype does not vary in viable human beings. Conversely, religion shows considerable variability of expression in humans, but it is not accounted for by genetics and is therefore not inherited. The heritability of a trait can be determined from studies of twin populations, comparing the similarity of expression of a phenotype (e.g., height, asthma, diabetes, etc.) in identical (i.e., monozygotic) versus fraternal (i.e., dizygotic) twins, who share all of their genetic variance in the first case, and, on average, only 50% in the second, but also mostly the same environment in both. Such studies have shown that many complex aspects of human cognition, temperament, and personality are relatively highly heritable; in most instances more than 50% of the variance in these characteristics is accounted for by genetic variance (Plomin et al. 1994). The term "heritability" also should not be confused with the concept of familiality. Characteristics may run in families because they are inherited (e.g., hair or eye color), but they also may be familial because they are "cultural" (e.g., going to school at Oxford or Harvard or eating with chopsticks). Thus, while aspects of cognitive functions are clearly under biological control, the impact of the environment may reflect familial components that are not genetic.

The cognitive processes that we will discuss below arise from the nervous system, which is made up of networks of nerve cells that operate as molecular machines that are designed and maintained by intricate and elegant principles determined by our genes. Therefore, a brief review of the basics of molecular genetics, recent developments in the field, and strategies for investigating the association between our genetics and our neuropsychological functions is of value.

A Brief History of Medical Genetics

For centuries, people have recognized the heritable nature of variable traits and have even explicitly used this knowledge on a limited scale in the breeding of domesticated plants and animals. The diversity and varieties of domestic dog breeds and the size and bountiful production of domestic crops compared to the wild varieties illustrate the use of controlled breeding programs for mutable traits. Ancient cultures had a keen interest in the inheritance of selected physical attributes of animals, and genetic anthropology illustrates the extent of these relationships. For example, modern comparative genomics studies have shown that all common species of domestic dogs are the result of selective breeding from a Chinese wolf ancestor, and the existing various domestic dog breeds are closer genetically to that wolf than other wild dog species (e.g., coyote, jackal) are to each other (Savolainen et al. 2002). This implies that the complete spectrum of dogs seen at the Westminster Dog Show has been selectively bred after wolves, coyotes, and jackals diverged evolutionarily. Even the Old Testament makes reference to selective breeding programs in the story of Jacob and Laban, where Jacob was to inherit the spotted sheep from Laban's herd and Jacob artificially influenced the breeding so the majority of the new generation was of the color he desired. Though the move away from mystical explanations for manipulation of variable characteristics began relatively recently in human history, it is only in the last hundred and fifty years that we have developed a scientific approach to understanding differences between inherited traits such as eye color and familial traits such as attending Oxford.

Two major observations greatly influenced the science of inheritance. The first was Charles Darwin's theory of evolution, revealed in *The Origin of Species* in 1859. He pointed out that variable traits of a species were heritable and evolving due to repeated matings under selective pressure for "fitness," with the environment's being the predominant selective pressure for shaping a trait. Darwin believed that the offspring of individuals with a specific variation of a trait that improved their survival, even if the improvement was marginal, would also have an improved chance of reproducing. Over several generations of mating of the fittest specimens of a *population* (here defined as a group of individuals that are breeding together), the result would be a new species with special characteristics to fit the environmental niche. Since the environment was changing, species were constantly under selective pressure, and therefore new species were continuously evolving. Darwin also recognized that, within a species, it was important for the entire population to contain large amounts of minor variation to serve as a reservoir for possible adaptive processes. He also believed that the minor variation seen in a population contains evidence of the evolutionary trail the species has taken through its history. As such, traits that no longer serve a current biological advantage, such as light skin pigmentation for enhanced vitamin D production in Northern Europeans, may still exist. Indeed, the skin cancer protection of darker skins in our now vitamin D–rich environment may currently have a selective advantage that was once a disadvantage in light-poor northern climates.

Darwin's theory was quickly applied to human cognitive and behavioral traits by his half-cousin, the noted eugenicist Francis Galton. Galton authored the article "Hereditary Talent and Character" in 1865 and founded the Anthropometric Laboratory in London, which, as part of its scientific studies, included one of the first attempts to show the heritability of cognitive and behavioral "biometrics." This branch of study in London fathered many of the founding luminaries of the statistical method for measuring traits, most notably Karl Pearson and Charles Spearman.

In the same year that Galton wrote the first paper on neuropsychological genetics, a monk and high school teacher in the natural sciences in Austria, named Gregor Mendel, was breeding peas hybrids at his monastery and made a series of seminal observations that forever changed the field of genetics (Mendel 1865). He noted that some simple traits, such as pea color or plant height, followed simple laws of inheritance across plant generations. At the time it was believed that hybrids were always an intermediate phenotype between the parents—for example, a pink-colored flower would result from the mating of a red and a white flower. Mendel made the fundamental observation of a *special* case of inheritance of traits in hybrids that provided the first insights into the fundamental mechanisms of genetics. When he mated (i.e., cross-pollinated) yellow peas with green peas, he discovered that these matings resulted in a predictable pattern of pea color in the next generation (F1); all were yellow. However, when this new all-yellow generation (F1) self-pollinated, the result was a 3 : 1 ratio of yellow:green peas in the F2 generation. Mendel recognized that this unexpected result implied that traits were being passed silently from one generation to the next. In this example, the simple *Mendelian trait* of yellow pea color is referred to as *dominant* and green color is called *recessive*. This distribution of effects can easily be seen in a Punnet square (see table 1.1), in which b refers to the heritable unit accounting for green and B relates to yellow.

Mendel formulated that each individual pea had a combination of two basic units of inheritance, one from each parent, and that the male and female sex cells, the sperm and the egg in humans, contain only one unit from each parent and combine in mating to form a new offspring. This concept is one of the fundamental principles of heredity. While Mendel's conceptualization is credited with being the first description of a gene as being the fundamental functional unit of heredity information, the term "gene" was not used until 1909 by Wilhelm Johannsen. The term "gene" itself has gone through a complex evolution as the basic biological understanding of the structure and function of genes has changed.

Chromosomes and Meiosis

Further testing of Mendel's observations by other scientists brought new insight that these units of inheritance did not sort independently with each mating. Some of these simple traits tended to segregate together with matings and were not found in off-

Table 1.1
Punnet square of a Mendelian trait crossing two heterozygotes (F1 generation), showing there would be a 3:1 distribution on traits in the resultant population (F2)

		Maternal	
Paternal	B	b	
B	BB	Bb	
b	Bb	bb	

spring according to a random distribution. In other words, it might be observed that short leaves and yellow peas tended to be found in the same offspring more than expected by chance. Long before the discovery of DNA and the visualization of the chromosome under the microscope, it was recognized that genes were lined up in series and were passed on in the egg or sperm in linked units. Our genome comprises two copies of twenty-two chromosomes (autosomes) and a pair of sex-determining chromosomes, XY for males and XX for females, contained in the nucleus of the cell. Each member of a pair of matching chromosomes is called a homologous chromosome. Each chromosome is made of a linear string of double-stranded DNA, composed of the four component nucleotides, and a complex of chromosomal proteins that provide structure and regulatory control. Chromosomes can be seen clearly under a microscope with special staining in the nucleus of dividing cells when the DNA strand is packaged tightly. The chromosome pairs are numbered from one to twenty-two for the autosomal chromosomes, and the order of their numbering corresponds roughly to their physical length, from the longest to the shortest. Chromosomes are further characterized by their physical structure, with each having a long arm, called the *q arm* (for *queue*, or tail, in French), and a short arm, the *p arm* (for *petit*, or small, in French), separated by a centromere. By using specific stains to label the appearance of chromosomes under the microscope, the arms can be further subdivided by patterns of stained bands, which have numbering designations. Thus, physical locations within a chromosome are designated by arm and band identity (e.g., 22q11 corresponds to the 11 (pronounced "one–one") band of the long arm of the twenty-second chromosome). The visualization of chromosomal structure is called *cytogenetics* and is the oldest molecular method for studying human genetic disorders.

The evidence that there are exceptions to the law of random assortment of inherited traits led to the observation that, in general, the more tightly two genes are linked, the more physically close they tend to be along a chromosome. Unlinked genes (e.g., those on different chromosomes) are sorted together 50% of the time, because any offspring has a 50–50 chance of getting any individual chromosome from the chromosome pair. On the other hand, genes lined up on a chromosome should be inherited as an intact chromosomal unit. However, even genes that are close together on a chromosome can be segregated in a mating. This exception to the rule of chromosomal linkage was first observed by Thomas Morgan in his studies of traits in fruit flies. He noted that genes that were on the same chromosome were not always passed together, and he devised a unit of measure, the morgan, representing the probability that two linked genes would end up being separated in a mating. Thus, a centimorgan (1 cM) denotes a genetic distance corresponding to the likelihood that two traits on the same chromosome will be separated once every hundred matings.

Separation of linked genes on a chromosome occurs because homologous chromosomes of a pair exchange genetic material, that is, they recombine during *meiosis*, the process in cell division that is critical for forming gametes: sperm and egg. The first step in meiosis involves alignment of the homologous pairs of chromosomes in the center of the nucleus. At this stage, homologous chromosomes can exchange portions of their q or p arms. This is called a *crossover event*, and it happens at least once for every pair of chromosomes for each meiosis. The exact location of the crossover is theoretically random, so genetic distance can be calculated as the probability that two linked loci will be separated by a crossover. The further apart two loci are on the chromosome, the more probable it is they will be separated by a crossover, because of the increased likelihood that the obligate crossover event will happen between them. Thus, if loci are close, they may only be separated once every ten meioses (corresponding to 10 cM of genetic distance), whereas if they are further apart, they may be separated half the time (50 cM), analogous to their being on separate chromosomes. This is the concept of genetic distance. Genetic distance is a rough estimate of physical distance measured in nucleotide base pairs (1 cM is about one million base pairs), although recent population analyses have discovered that this is not a precise measure of physical distance because crossovers do not occur at random; instead, there are so-called recombination hot spots and regions of relative sparing of crossover events. This has led to recent speculation that genes of evolutionally relative importance map to hot spots.

Errors can occur at all stages of the meiosis machinery, producing a variety of chromosomal abnormalities, many of which result in nonviable zygotes or clear developmental abnormalities. For example, whole chromosomes can be missorted during meiosis, creating some of the most commonly recognized genetic causes of mental retardation, such as Down's syndrome, or trisomy 21, and Edwards syndrome, or trisomy 18. The crossover events of meiosis can lead to mismatches of base pairing, causing DNA deletions, insertions, duplications, inversions, and translocations of sequence. Each of these errors has provided insights into the discovery of genes that impact cognition. For example, the observation that patients with Down's syndrome develop Alzheimer's dementia was one of the first clues to a gene for Alzheimer's disease, the amyloid precursor protein gene on chromosome 21. Similarly, a family with a rare translocation of a chromosomal block from 1q to 11q led to the discovery of DISC1, a pleiotropic gene implicated in mood and psychotic disorders and related to memory and hippocampal function.

Gene Structure and Function

Identifying the genetic bases of cognitive and emotional traits involves an approach called *statistical association*. We know that genes do not code directly for complex phenomena like the experience of hallucinating a voice commenting on how you comb your hair or the belief that aliens have implanted a chip in your head or for more mundane cognitive experiences like memory or language. Rather, genes code for the molecular machinery that carries out the functions of a cell. Historically, Beadle and Tatum (1941) proposed a theorem that one gene was responsible for one enzyme, but now we know that genes can code for many proteins and RNA structures. We now know that genes are responsible for a diverse array of proteins that extends beyond those related only to metabolism and includes those related to the structure and physiology of the cell. Therefore, genes for memory or intelligence or for complex medical disorders such as schizophrenia are genes associated with the underlying physiological processes that each individual genetic polymorphism alters through its role in the molecular machinery of the cell. Together, susceptibility genes and environmental factors combine to impact these basic cellular mechanisms and cause variance in expression of cognition or of a behavioral disorder.

The human genome project has provided us with a nearly complete sequence of the entire human genome. Most of the DNA sequence is nongenic, meaning it is does not contain genes sequences and does not code for proteins. In fact, less than 5% of the human genome is thought to contain "genes" (Gerstein et al. 2007). However, the concept of what a gene is is still evolving: currently, a gene is considered to be a sequence of DNA that is transcribed into messenger RNA (mRNA) and further translated into a protein. A gene consists of multiple elements, including sequences called *exons* that are transcribed into mRNA and transported out of the nucleus for processing into protein as well as sequences called *introns* that are not part of the mature mRNA. Introns often contain regulatory domains—for example, regions involving specific instructions in the splicing together of exons. Genes vary enormously in size and in their composition of exons and introns. Some genes are only a few thousand nucleotide bases in length, and others are over a million bases long. The common functional structure of a gene is that it starts transcription from the 5′ end with an untranslated sequence of mRNA that typically contains the signals for the transcriptional machinery. Sequences of DNA that control whether the gene is transcribed are called *promoter*, *inducer*, or *inhibitor* sites. They are typically found close to the beginning of the 5′ end of a gene, but sometimes they reside in sequences that are a great distance from the transcription start site. (It should be noted, however, that, due to coiling of the DNA strand itself, "a great distance" as laid out in a linear sequence in a textbook or on a Web site may be a distance that is quite short when measured in the three-dimensional space of DNA in vivo.) Researchers have even found some promoters and inhibitors 2 million bases distant from the 5′ transcription start site of a gene. The 3′ end of the gene also usually contains an untranslated region, which is important for mRNA stability, translational efficiency, and mRNA degradation. While the vast majority of mammalian genes encode for proteins, some do not. For example, some genes encode ribosomal and transfer RNAs, which are involved in the translation of the genetic code into peptides. Some genes encode antiRNAs, or small interfering RNAs (siRNAs), a recently discovered family of genes involved in regulation of the processing of other RNAs. Very recent evidence indicates that much more of the human genetic sequence is involved in gene regulation than was previously thought and that most DNA is transcribed as non-protein-coding regulatory elements (ENCyclopedia Of DNA Elements (ENCODE) pilot project 2007).

DNA codes for the construction of a protein via several intermediate steps. First, a section of the DNA sequence is copied or transcribed into an mRNA which is further processed or spliced and then translated into proteins. This is initiated by transcriptional regulatory machinery, including factors that drive transcription, factors that inhibit it, and factors that modify both of these processes. The exact protein structure can also be modified at the level of the mRNA, a process called *splicing*, which refers to the editing of expressed elements in the DNA sequence (exons), where some elements are added and others are subtracted. The final mature mRNA, from which the protein is translated, may represent the full gene or only a portion of it. These are called *slice variants*. Splicing is a level of genetic variation that is especially important in the brain. It is thought that approximately 20,000 genes are expressed in the brain, but over 2 million proteins are estimated to be derived from these relatively few genes (Gerstein et al. 2007). With the addition of posttranslational modifications, the proteins themselves can go through other modifying steps to change the function of the protein in the cell, its packaging, how and where it is shipped, its final placement in or outside the cell, whether or not it is imbedded in the membrane or released as an extracellular messenger, or even specification of a particular time in development for the gene to be active.

Principles of Genetic Variation

If the genomic sequence was exactly alike in every human, we would know that all human variation is a result of variation in each individual's environment, but that is not the case. It has been estimated that unrelated humans are 99.9% the same as each other based on sequence variance. Humans are 96% to 97% genetically the same as the chimpanzee. That little difference in sequence makes a vast difference in phenotype. The human genome sequence that appears in the databases is actually a composite sequence that resulted from the sequencing of several separate individuals. When variations between individuals were discovered, they were classified and recorded as known variations and given numbered designates. Several private and public databases exist to catalogue these variations, the most commonly used database being dbSNP, sponsored by the U.S. government (see the Web site links at the end of this chapter).

The variation that we see in the human genome is largely the result of evolutionary changes based on the diversity of responses to our uniquely complex environment. Variation that impacts the brain is a key ingredient in the diversity of reactions to mental experience. Some people are thrilled with a multivariate linear algebra problem that others find to be the dullest thing imaginable; some of us love jumping out of airplanes with only a silk cloth and rope for protection, while others will find that to be the most horrifying thing imaginable. Similarly to how a species benefits from variable traits to survive changing environmental pressures, our human species benefits from an enormous variety of cognitive and emotional capacities. As a society or population of humans, we benefit from having among us people who enjoying climbing mountains, people who remember exactly what happened many rainy seasons ago, and people who can fight the neighboring tribe for water in times of drought. Without this cognitive and social diversity, our species would have difficulty surviving the changing demands of the environment. Variations that have environmental advantage will increase in frequency over time in our species, those that are neutral will likely remain at a low frequency unless they are carried along by other variations that are linked to them, and variations that are deleterious will be selected out over time and become rare.

What is the form of this variation? Since our genome is made up of a double strand of 3 billion base pairs of DNA, the genetic variation takes place mostly in the sequence itself. This can be in the substitution of something as small as a single nucleotide for another (a single nucleotide polymorphism; SNP) to larger structural variations involving duplications or deletions of large segments of sequence. SNPs are the most frequent polymorphism, occurring approximately every 500 base pairs in the human genome, with simple short repeated sequences being the next most common. Repeated sequences are classified by the number of repeating nucleotides, which can range from small repeats of only two nucleotides (*dinucleotide repeats*) to ones of quite some length. They are also characterized by the number of repeating elements, sometimes called *variable number tandem repeats* (VNTRs).

A recently discovered common genetic variation is in copy numbers of DNA sequences, so-called *copy number variations* (CNVs). While large cytogenetic deletions or duplications of sequence can be seen through the microscope, it has only recently been revealed that there are a surprising number of small deletions and duplications of DNA throughout the entire genome. Recent estimates are that CNVs, currently defined as being at least a kilobase in length, may actually be as common as SNPs (Sebat et al. 2004). Several well-known large deletions are relevant to neuropsychology. One is the deletion of a portion of 22q11, that is, the first subband of the first major band on the long arm of the 22nd chromosome, leaving affected individuals with only one copy of that genetic region. This hemideletion encompasses approximately thirty genes, one of which is the gene catechol-O-methyltransferase (COMT), whose function has been instrumental in elaborating the genetic contributions to variation in the physiology of the working memory network through its modulation of dopamine levels (Egan et al. 2001). Likewise, the Williams–Beuren syndrome, caused by a smaller deletion on chromosome 7, has led to an understanding of genetic regulation of visual spatial cognitive networks and to the facial emotion processing networks, as these patients have unique visual construction deficits and a lack of social anxiety with people, but phobias related to threatening nonhuman objects such as sharks and barking dogs (Meyer-Lindenberg et al. 2006).

Another form of genetic variation that has been explored only superficially to this point is epigenetic control of gene function. Epigenetic regulation refers to genetic-like effects that are not related to changes in the DNA sequence. These effects may be inherited, or they may be spontaneous and arise in the genome after conception. Epigenetic mechanisms include changes in the histone proteins that package DNA into chromosomes and in the methylation of promoter–inhibitor regions in genes. For genes to be effectively transcribed, their promoters must be unmethylated and histones need to be appropriately unraveled so that the transcriptional machinery has access to the DNA molecule. One example of epigenetic regulation is the modification of a chromosome inherited from one parent that effects gene transcription in the offspring. This is called *imprinting*, a term borrowed from the behavioral psychology literature. Angelman syndome is a classic example of genetic imprinting caused by deletion or inactivation of critical genes on the maternally inherited chromosome 15. Angelman syndrome is characterized by seizures, severe mental retardation, inappropriate laughter, and a characteristic face that is small with a large mouth and prominent chin. The sister syndrome is called Prader–Willi syndrome and is caused by paternally derived deleted or inactivated genes. Prader–Willi syndrome is characterized by developmental delay, mild retardation, cryptorchidism (small or undescended testes), short stature, and hyperphagia and obesity (fatness due to overeating in an attempt to reach satiety). The phenotypes for each syndrome are vastly different, while genetic region is the same but depends on the paternally versus maternally different methylation patterns.

Variation Can Affect Gene Function

We have discussed several forms of genetic variation. Such variations can be coincidental, that is, accounting for sequence variation in human beings but not accounting for variation in gene function, or they can be functional, that is, resulting in a change in the biology of a gene and its product. The mechanisms by which genetic variation affects gene function are numerous and can occur at every stage of gene processing, that is, at transcription, translation, and posttranslational modification. For some examples that relate to brain function see table 1.2. To begin with, variations can affect the *structure* of the DNA or the transcribed mRNA. The genetic variations we discussed above are of the *primary* structure of DNA, simply the linear sequence of nucleotides. Genetic variation also can impact on the secondary structure, that is, how the DNA or RNA sequence loops around and interacts with itself. DNA and RNA are not stiff noodles; the sequence curls and can bind to itself in looping formations.

Table 1.2

Examples of functional polymorphisms that affect neuropsychological function

Gene	Location	Polymorphism	Function
COMT	22q11.2	Leu13Lleu	Increased stability of mRNA and decreased translation
		Val108/158Met	50% change in enzymatic activity
BDNF	11p14.1	Val66met	Impaired intracellular transport
5-HTT	17q11	5-HTTLPR	Altered transcription rate
NRG1	8p12	rs6994992	Promoter binding

Note. COMT, catechol-O-methyltransferease; mRNA, messenger RNA; BDNF, brain-derived neurotrophic factor; 5-HTT: serotonin transporter; 5-HTTLPR, a common polymorphism in the promoter region of the serotonin transporter; NRG1, neuregulin 1.

Changes in mRNA secondary structure may even involve sequence variations that appear functionally inert at the level of protein structure. For example, recent findings have identified a coding SNP in the COMT gene that changes both the primary and the secondary structure of the mRNA, but not the sequence of amino acids in the protein (Nackley et al. 2006). The SNP changes the DNA primary sequence in exon 4 of the gene. Because the amino acid code is redundant (sixty-four trinucleotide codons code for the twenty amino acids), this nucleotide switch does not change the protein structure (i.e., it is a synonymous SNP). It encodes for leucine regardless of the SNP allele. Since there is no change in protein sequence, such SNPs have traditionally been thought to be functionally neutral. However, this SNP is not functionally neutral; it affects the translation of the gene by changing mRNA secondary loop structure and the ability of the translational machinery to have access to a more stable looping variant of the mRNA. Tertiary structure is the three-dimensional structure of the sequence, the coiling and bundling of the structure much like the classic description of the old desk telephone cords. Quaternary structure is the dynamic coiling and uncoiling and vibratory nature of the sequence. This can be varied by the binding of proteins to the sequence or the sequence itself. Different polymorphisms can alter all of these aspects of DNA and mRNA structural biology.

While genetic variation in noncoding parts of genes will not affect the amino acid sequence, they can still effect the *transcription* phase. By changing promoter or inhibitor binding sites for various transcription regulatory factors, an allele can change the likelihood and amount of the gene that is transcribed. One example is the serotonin transporter gene polymorphism in which the promoter sequence is moved further from the start sequence of the gene physically by a VNTR (14), or the example of a SNP in neuregulin 1 (NRG1), a psychosis susceptibility gene, that changes the short sequence of a promoter–inhibiter binding site, thereby altering the binding of a transcription factor that turns the gene on or off (Tan et al. 2007). The effects of sequence variations that impact on transcription are typically quantified by the amount of the mRNA measured in the cell. Other things that can alter the amount of mRNA transcripts found in the cell are CNVs that deviate from the typical two copies of any autosomal gene.

Once transcribed to mRNA, sequence variations in the mRNA sequence can affect the *splicing* of the transcript into different isoforms that are used differentially in specific cell types or at different developmental stages. This might be a more frequent source of variation than previously appreciated. Since these forms of variation tend to impact the timing and spatial characteristics of gene function, they are less likely to be as generally deleterious to the brain as alleles that cause widespread change in the gene by alteration of the amino acid sequence or disruption of the gene product completely. While the human genome project has given us the sequence of the human genome, the finer points of the human transcriptome are barely known. Expression-level databases have been created that quantify the relative expression levels of different genes by tissue type, development stage, or organism. These give helpful clues as to which genes may be involved in specific brain regions and, by inference, in the specific cognitive and behavioral functions mediated by these regions. For example, if a cognitive process requires hippocampal function, then testing genes that are expressed in the hippocampus would be a good start.

mRNA and protein translation levels can be altered also by variations that affect mRNA degradation. After DNA is transcribed into mRNA, a tail of multiple adenines is added to its "downstream" 3′ end. The length of the polyadenylated tail determines the stability of the message and how long the transcript can exist in the nucleus. Sequences in the 3′ end of the mRNA can bind a special set of ~20 base pair sequences of RNA called siRNAs, which lead to more rapid degradation of mRNA. This recently discovered mechanism of mRNA regulations appears to have evolved from a protective mechanism that helped to degrade double-stranded RNA commonly found in viruses. This mechanism can greatly reduce the translation levels of an mRNA due to the lack of transcript available for translation. This mechanism is used by the cell to have ultrafast translational control of mRNA. This recent discovery of transcript regulation by microRNAs led to the awarding of the 2006 Nobel Prize in medicine.

SNPs in exons, called coding SNPs, may change the amino acid sequence and thus the primary, secondary, and tertiary structure of the protein. In the primary sequence, different amino acids each have different chemical and charge properties that influence the complex three-dimensional structures of the protein products. Coding nonsynonymous SNPs can twist and bend the protein out of its usual shape. These effects usually change the physiology of the protein, and such SNPs are called functional. In the brain, there are examples of functional polymorphisms that alter protein sequence and cause ion channels to be leaky (Hahn and Blakely 2007) or result in changes in an enzyme's reaction sites (Bender et al. 2005) and, thus, its dynamics (Chen et al. 2004).

The simplest form of protein sequence change and the first to be investigated in human genetics are changes in the activity of enzymes. Sir Archibald Garrod, one of the forefathers of medical genetics, identified at the turn of the 20th century a metabolic change in urine that led to the discovery of the metabolic disease alcaptonuria, a genetic deficit caused by a mutation in the enzyme homogentisic acid oxidase (Childs 1970). Changing a single amino acid has been shown to alter the activity of the enzyme COMT, a gene extensively studied recently in behavioral genetics that degrades catechole molecules like caffeine, estrogen, and also the neurotransmitter dopamine. A simple valine-to-methionine change alters the active of this enzyme by approximately 50% and therefore changes the dynamics of the dopamine system in the brain (Chen et al. 2004).

Changes in the amino acid sequence can also affect the trafficking of the protein within the cell. There are signals embedding in the protein sequence that control how proteins are processed by the cellular machinery. Signal sequences determine whether a protein is trafficked to a dendrite, to a vesicle for release as a neurotransmitter, or provides a structural support. The right part in the wrong place is just as bad as having a broken part in the right place. An example of a functional polymorphism in a signaling sequence that disrupts the normal processing of a protein is the val66met functional polymorphism in brain-derived neurotrophic factor (BDNF) (Egan et al. 2003). In this case, the mature protein is normal and functions normally but is not transported to the right location within the cell, so it is no longer able to perform its normal plasticity-enhancing effects.

Posttranslational modification of the gene's protein product can also be altered by genetic variation. This can be the splicing of the protein or addition of specialized molecules to the protein chain. The cell is not just a series of proteins but a complex of organic and inorganic materials such as fats, sugars, ions, and more exotic substances. Simply attaching a fatty acid tail to a protein can anchor the protein in the cell membrane, or adding trees of branching sugars can extend a protein out into the extracellular matrix as a signal to the exterior world. Thus, changes in a gene based on genetic variation may result in changes in the molecular modifications that the protein engages.

It is important to remember that variations in genetic sequence are common. Most such variations are not likely to be functional. In searching for associations with genetic variations at the level of protein function, or metabolism, or brain function or behavior, the prior probability of any SNP's showing real association to brain-related phenotypes is low and many positive associations will be spurious and not make sense. However, such variants have neighbors, variations that are in linkage disequilibrium (LD; see below) with them, and associations to changes in brain function related to nonfunctional variations may be clues to functional variants in their neighborhood. These alternative interpretations of positive results represent complexities that often require additional experiments and other levels of analysis. In the meantime, as novel candidate genes for behavioral phenotypes are identified, new doors open that may lead to the expanded molecular system through which the phenotype of interest (e.g., an illness, a brain phenotype, and cognition) arises.

About Complex Phenotypes

Neuropsychological genetics is the discipline of characterizing the genetic contribution to variation in human cognition and emotion. This involves characterizing human behavior as a phenotype that will show variation based on genetic variation, that is, genotype. It is assumed that many genes will be implicated in the various human cognitive capacities and that final phenotypic variation will reflect the contributions of these genes, the effects of their interactions with each other, the impact of the nongenetic environment, and the interactions of the genes with the environment. The first task in studying the genetic contribution to this complexity is to characterize the phenotype as completely as possible. The next step is to identify relevant genes.

There are an estimated 20,000 genes in the human genome, and the majority of these genes are expressed in the brain in one way or another, so how do we pick one to investigate? Single-locus categorical Mendelian medical disorders were the first to be investigated due to the relative ease of identification in simple family studies, but most mental traits and mental illnesses are complex traits that do not represent the effects of a single major gene. In large part, the answer to this question involves a full understanding of the phenotype and its likely genetic and neurobiological complexity.

The term "complex trait" refers to a phenotype that is determined by multiple variables. These phenotypes can be dimensional or categorical. Dimensional traits like height, weight, and IQ commonly have a Gaussian distribution in the population and are called quantitative traits. Individuals can be plotted in a multidimensional space based on the measurement of their distribution of traits in every measurable dimension. The first major quantifying measure of general cognition was by Alfred Binet, who published his general intelligence test in France (Binet 1905). Binet did not advocate his test as a measure of a singular factor for intelligence. In London, however, Charles Spearman introduced a measure of general intelligence, called "g," in 1904, and advocated for the concept that most neuropsychological measures were proxies for this single determinant. This continuing argument has since spawned an industry of tests that attempt to parse different aspects of cognition. The general concept of intelligence has been dissected in scientific ways using statistical means to subdivide the concept into possibly divisible brain functions. Now there are measures of verbal IQ, performance IQ, immediate memory, short-term memory, long-term memory, working memory, attention, visual construction, motor performance, and many more. Generally, a proper test contains questions or measures that maximally differentiate from each other and has a normal population distribution. These principles are discussed in detail elsewhere in this volume. Several attempts have been made to dissect these cognitive constructs by means of genetics from the gross construct of g to more narrowly defined constructs.

Similarly, the desire to dissect quantifiable dimensional aspects of personality and temperament is almost as old as recorded history. From the zodiac signs to the four humors, we have attempted to derive systems to better define personality types. While most ancient forms used a categorical method, modern personality research has also focused on dimensional traits. For example, Hans Eysenck and his associates enumerated a set of independent personality characteristics based on a factorial analysis of personality measures (Eysenck 2001). In the field of personality dimensional research, the most widely used of such factor-based inventories is the "Big Five," or NEOAC (also called NEO). This instrument consists of five factors, dubbed Neuroticism, Extroversion, Openness to Experience, Agreeableness, and Conscientiousness (Costa and McCrae 1985). The Axis II diagnostic scale of the *Diagnostic and Statistical Manual of Mental Disorders*, fourth edition, approaches the concept of personality with a categorical description of behaviors that, interestingly, have been shown to overlap with the NEOAC mappings of personalities and that typically are two standard deviations from the mean in one or several factor dimensions Eysenck 2001).

From a genetic perspective, however, categorical descriptions of human neuropsychological and temperamental characteristics are problematic, because they attempt to represent a complex and likely quantitative trait as a binary state. Either you have it or you do not. However, the genes associated with these complex traits are not about the behaviors, per se, but reflect the underlying neurobiology. Fisher argued at the turn of the twentieth century that Gaussian distributed complex polygenic human traits are probably made up of multiple additive or multiplicative effects of several genes (Fisher 1918; see figure 1.1).

Another example of this complex genetic phenomenon is the observation that quantitative traits in offspring typically regress to the mean of the two parents. Initially, categorical diseases were thought not to be complex disorders but rather examples of simple Mendelian genetic disorders. How, then, is one to conceptualize something like schizophrenia as a categorical but complex disorder? One formulation is based on a proposal by Fisher, who advanced the notion of a threshold genetic effect. In other words, a quantitative accumulation of risk factors (e.g., multiple genes for a purely genetic trait) is required before a biological threshold is crossed that results in clinical expression (see figure 1.2).

Threshold disorders theoretically have the predicted prevelance rate in first-degree relatives that is the square root of the population rate. This appears to be the case for

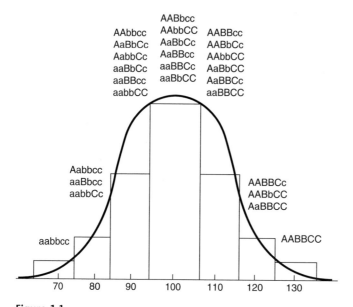

Figure 1.1

A theoretical complex trait derived from three independent genes with each polymorphism contributing in an equal and additive fashion.

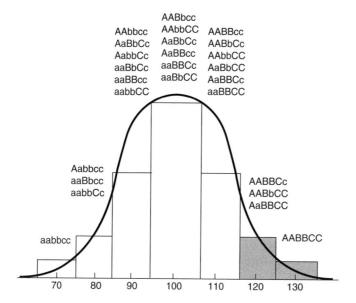

Figure 1.2

A theoretical complex trait in which a threshold of five risk alleles are needed to exhibit the categorical trait.

schizophrenia, where the first-degree relatives have a prevalence rate of 1/10 whereas the population rate is 1/100. Using these polygenic disorders as a target phenotype based on a threshold categorical model, large association studies have helped identify the first neuropsychiatric genes from patient categories of schizophrenia, bipolar disorder, major depression, and anxiety disorder. Interestingly, these disease and behavior disorder susceptibility genes have a strong impact on neuropsychological measures.

Likewise, direct large population association studies have led to the discovery of several neuropsychological genes that directly impact quantitative dimensional traits. That such genes have been found is somewhat surprising, since genetic polymorphisms that impact complex mental traits are subtle and of small effect. If they were otherwise, they would probably be dramatically disabling. The phenotypes that we can observe at the level of behavior are remote from the cells in which the genes operate, and common polymorphisms in genes typically explain only a relatively small amount of the variance in quantitative traits or increase the relative risk for categorical traits minimally. This increases the need for targeted strategies for picking the genes we investigate. Because of the vast number of polymorphisms in the genome, if we indiscriminately pick them to test against the myriad of phenotypes related to behavior and cognition, then the likelihood of spurious associations is high. Therefore, it is important that the genes investigated meet a standard of biological plausibility and the methods be statistically rigorous.

How to Pick Genes for Neuropsychological Genetic Studies

Many of the first disease susceptibility genes for complex disorders such as mental illness were localized in the genome through linkage mapping. This statistical method is a family-based strategy that exploits the likelihood of multiple affected family members sharing DNA markers in regions of the genome in which causative genes reside. Linkage is a fairly easy exercise in Mendelian disorders of simple categorical traits and requires only a handful of families. For complex traits, however, substantially larger numbers of families are needed. The first wave of linkage studies in psychiatric and neurological disorders provided neighborhoods in the genome for more intensive study of individual genes that reside in the identified regions. There was some confusion about inconsistencies in several of the early linkage studies. Differences from one study population to another are not surprising considering the heterogeneity of these disorders. An informative illustration of the impact of heterogeneity on the consistency of linkage and, for that matter, association findings is the case of blindness. If one were looking for genes for blindness, specific genes for macular degeneration in the elderly, multiple sclerosis affecting the optic radiations in young women, retinoblastoma in children, retinal microvascular change in diabetics, and susceptibility to infectious onchocerciasis from the black fly in Africa would vary greatly in their impact depending on the composition of the samples studied. Stratifying populations by more biologically distinct subgroups is an important strategy to reduce heterogeneity. Further success in dissecting meaningful subtypes will come from bottom-up stratifications based on genotype, though this assumes a relative independence of subtypes in these heterogenic disorders.

Candidate gene approaches have also been successful as a direct means to investigate cellular and neural systems mechanisms when we know something about the biology of the trait. If we know, for example, that medications used to treat major depression impact the serotonin system, then investigating genes involved in the serotonin system for their impact on emotion-processing neuronal systems is biologically plausible. Candidate genes are investigated through statistical association. Genetic association tests whether a specific allele of a gene has an increased frequency in the disease population relative to a normal population or predicts the relative mean scores of quantitative traits. A significant increase in genotype or allele frequency or in mean score based on genotype is evidence for association.

Candidate gene associations have become the staple of the gene discovery field, though they are frequently inconsistent across different populations and susceptible to problems in study design and interpretation as well as heterogeneity. Association may be spurious for a number of reasons, particularly stratification and admixture, measures of the substructure of the populations studied. These artifacts refer to the instance in which different alleles appear to be associated with a trait because, coincidentally, the populations that vary in the expression of the trait have unrelated background allele frequency differences. The human population is made up of several subpopulations that are the result of restrictions on random breeding, based on factors such as geography, religion, politics, and so forth. This is most obvious in terms of race. Because modern humans are descendents of an original African population, the variability seen in the African population today is only partially represented in the branches of the subpopulations that migrated to Europe or across Asia and down into the Americas. Additionally, some new mutations have arisen in the subpopulations since the human diaspora from Africa. Allele frequencies in the subpopulation reflect the alleles in their founders. Neil Risch of Stanford University offered a useful illustration of how ancestral structure in a study sample derived from the population in San Francisco would lead to a spurious case–control association between genes and chopstick use. Alleles that are overrepresented in Americans of Asian descent would be erroneously associated with the genetics of chopstick use. This example illustrates the importance of controlling for ancestral variation that may corrupt genetic association. Databases now frequently report differing population allele frequencies for many genetic markers to help avoid these problems.

Since population structure can confound genetics research, methods have been developed to adjust for this effect. A human-genome-wide-mapping study of thousands of SNPs across the entire genome for several populations, called the International HAPMAP Project, has recently been completed (2003). The allele frequencies of each of the SNPs and the frequencies of haplotypes made up of linked SNPs is available from four ethnic populations, including Europeans, Nigerians, Japanese, and Han Chinese. A statistical haplotype is a set of two or more SNPs whose alleles are highly correlated with each other. In other words, if one knows the allele at one SNP in a haplotype, there is a high probability of knowing the status of its neighbor, and runs of these SNPs can be treated as one block of a chromosome that are inherited together. This relationship between SNPs is called linkage disequilibrium, or LD, reflecting that in a population the two markers do not randomly assort but are linked DNA markers. The reason for LD is that recombination has not occurred between the markers over the ancestral history of the particular chromosome in which they reside. Haplotypes are very useful for selecting SNPs to genotype in a sample. Haplotypes make it possible to assay genetic variation more specifically than individual SNPS, and they allow for a reduction in the total number of SNPs that must be typed to survey a region of a gene. SNPs that mark haplotypes and serve as proxies for other SNPs are called *tag* SNPs. If the SNP tested is in a haplotype but is not a known functional SNP, it could reside in the same haplotype block as the causative allele. It therefore serves as a proxy for the functional allele. For a candidate gene or mapping approach, researchers can simply chose the subset of "tag" markers to run their association test and reduce problems of multiple testing and the financial expense of wasteful genotyping.

While candidate gene association studies have been marginally successful with complex behavioral traits, remarkable advances in our understanding of the underlying mechanisms have rapidly expanded by investigation of quantitative intermediate phenotypes. This term, while historically used to describe phenotypes derived by the mating of extreme phenotypes for polygenetic complex traits, is now also used to mean a phenotypic trait making up one of the variables of the complex trait. Being one level down in complexity in this multidimensional space, one can more clearly see the impact of individual alleles. Currently, the most common approach to intermediate phenotypes in neuropsychological research is brain imaging and more narrowly defined neuropsychological measures rather than broad concepts like *g*. Additionally, brain imaging provides a means to visualize and quantify the mechanism of the genetic variation associated with behavior.

Beginners' Guide to Gene Picking and Bioinformatics

The most important thing to do when starting an analysis of the impact of a gene on a neuropsychological phenotype is to ground it in a solid understanding of biology. As we previously discussed, biological plausibility is the most important consideration in picking a gene. There are many ways to approach the plausibility issue. One could start from existing association studies of psychiatric or neurological diseases, or from gene or protein expression data from brain regions of interest, interactions with known neuropsychological genes, medication–drug site of action, known critical biological systems, and so forth. Once one picks a gene to interrogate, it is important to thoroughly understand the literature about the gene. Reading the published papers on the gene and the OMIM article about it are good starting points. There may be a previously reported functional variant to examine with your phenotype of interest that was discovered or possibly associated with another disorder. It is generally advisable to make known functional variants top-priority polymorphisms to study in a given gene. After one has a good idea what is known about the gene and what it does, then it is important to see how it is expressed in the brain. Browsing the gene expression Web sites and the animal literature is valuable. One should download the *Allen Brain Atlas* mRNA expression data and display it in *Brain Explorer* to see if there is further evidence that this gene is expressed in the brain and that it is expressed in a regionally relevant manner. For example, if one is studying declarative memory and hippocampal function, then it is not plausible to examine association if a gene not expressed in the hippocampal formation.

The next step is to pick variants in the gene, usually SNPs, to genotype in your sample. First go to the genome.ucsc.edu genome browser and search for the gene map of the gene. There is a specific "track" on the browser that shows all SNPs in the gene, their locations, and their potential functions. Since the causative variants in a gene are ultimately functional variants by definition, you should pick polymorphisms based on increasing probability of their being functional. A polymorphism that interrupts or changes any of the functions discussed above should be considered, that is, a non-synonymous SNP that changes the amino acid may be fairly significant and even more so if the change is in the active site of the protein product or if it is a "distant" change like a hydrophilic amino acid for a hydrophobic amino acid. The modeled protein shape can be visualized for many genes using ModBase, NCBI cd3d structures, or similar programs and will give you a good idea of how the protein looks and where the variations lie if there is not already a crystal structure done. You can predict the relative effect of a coding polymorphism from the structure. If you are looking at a synonymous SNP then one would then looking at the secondary structure of the mRNA through a variety of programs that predict whether the polymorphism greatly changes the free energy of the mRNA. Mfold is a popular program for this analysis, and an alternate program for calculating this is linked through the genome.ucsc.edu browser. Outside of the coding variations, one can consider splice site variations that may affect the isoforms that are created. One should look for known splice site motifs in intronic regions. In general, splice sites are found within fifty nucleotides of the start and end of exons. An alternative strategy, if this information is not known, is to identify intronic regions within the gene that are highly conserved across species. This can be visualized by turning on the conservation track in the UCSC genome browser.

SNPs that fall into these regions may be interesting and have occult functions. For the possibility of SNPs that have an impact on epigenetic or transcription mechanisms, one can also examine SNPs that lie in CpG islands, which are typically methylated sequences. There is a CpG track in the browser that allows inspection of these sequences. If one has access to transcription site analysis software, looking at these predictions in relation to the polymorphisms that may lie in promoter–inhibitor regions is important. The same is true for all other forms of regulation such as microRNAs binding sites.

Currently, not all variations are known or represented in the databases. Since the databases of genetic variation are not fully annotated, one must sometimes make an educated guess concerning whether a polymorphism may be functional and concerning how best to capture all important genetic variation within a gene. One screening method is to pick *tag* SNPs. The HAPMAP site has a public downloadable program called Haploview, which provides a semi-automated routine for selecting tag SNPs across a region, though there are an ever growing number of programs to pick tag SNPs. The SNPs are selected from the HAPMAP catalog and are only as good as the catalog is complete, which varies by gene. The selection of tag SNPs also helps with the multiple testing problem that occurs when testing many polymorphisms, especially when some of them are neither truly independent nor functional. Haploview also allows you to force the inclusion of SNPs with putative functional significance during the tagging process. This is helpful if you want to increase the likelihood of picking a functional SNP as a tag SNP. Since regulatory SNPs exist both upstream and downstream of regions of genes, one should attempt to include variants found within a region about 5 kB upstream and about 2 kB downstream from the start and stop sites of transcription, respectively.

Now you are ready to run your association analysis with these SNPs. The use of tag SNPs is also the basis of genome-wide association studies, which involve genotyping upwards of 500,000 SNPs on a chip for a single individual. This industrial-scale genotyping method is an agnostic search strategy, which identifies association based on a brute-force genetic algorithm. Because SNPs are typed across the genome, the likelihood of association is not limited by the validity of a candidate gene hypothesis. Early experience with this technique has been mixed, as there have been important discoveries of novel genes for common medical disorders, but correction for the large number of tests required limits the findings to common genes that are relatively uncorrupted by heterogeneity and that tend to account for small increments in risk across the whole sample. One study that applied this approach to finding genes for episodic memory by typing 500K SNPs across in genome in normal subjects stratified by episodic memory performance (Gerstein et al. 2007) has appeared. The gene KIBRA was found using this approach, and it strongly predicted variation in normal human memory and hippocampal function studied with functional magnetic resonance imaging.

All of these steps are purely limited by your financial resources and the technological advances in this field. Several private human genomes have been sequenced at the cost of $1 million U.S., and the goal is to get whole genome sequencing to a cost of under $1,000. While the option to have the complete sequence and all the variation in your subjects is out of reach for now, our understanding of the genome is rapidly expanding one variation at a time.

The characterization of neuropsychological genes is opening up a new understanding of brain mechanisms. It is important to remember, however, that reductionist interpretations of genetic variations as being good or bad are no longer realistic. A good variation for working memory may be a bad variation for cancer prevention. Also the genomic and environmental background greatly influences gene expression and the impact of a polymorphism. While we are acquiring the ability to know one's entire genome, our understanding of the interaction of genetics with our environment is just beginning. The neuropsychological genetics of our population allows an interesting view of our species's genetic anthropology. We have been uniquely selected for a variety of complex cognitive and social abilities. The shadows of our species's history are reflected in our own biology as it plays out in the current pressures of our environment.

Our natural constitution seems to bear as direct and stringent a relation to that of our forefathers as any other physical effect does to its cause. Our bodies, minds, and capabilities of development have been derived from them. Everything we possess at our birth is a heritage from our ancestors.

—Francis Galton

References

Beadle GW, Tatum EL (1941). Genetic control of biochemical reactions in Neurospora. *Proc Natl Acad Sci USA*, 27:499–506.

Bender HU, Almashanu S, Steel G, Hu CA, Lin WW, Willis A, et al. (2005). Functional consequences of PRODH missense mutations. *Am J Hum Genet*, 76:409–20.

Binet A (1905). New methods for the diangnosis of the intellectual level of subnormals. *L'Annee Psychologique*, 12:191–244.

Chen J, Lipska BK, Halim N, Ma QD, Matsumoto M, Melhem S, et al. (2004). Functional analysis of genetic variation in catechol-O-methyltransferase (COMT): effects on mRNA, protein, and enzyme activity in postmortem human brain. *Am J Hum Genet*, 75:807–21.

Childs B (1970). Sir Archibald Garrod's conception of chemical individuality: a modern appreciation. *N Engl J Med*, 282:71–7.

Costa PJ, McCrae RR (1985). The NEO personality inventory manual. Odessa, FL: Psychological Assessment Resources.

Darwin C (1859). The origin of species: by means of natural selection or the preservation of favored races in the struggle for life. London: J Murray.

Egan MF, Goldberg TE, Kolachana BS, Callicott JH, Mazzanti CM, Straub RE, et al. (2001). Effect of COMT Val108/158 Met genotype on frontal lobe function and risk for schizophrenia. *Proc Natl Acad Sci USA*, 98:6917–22.

Egan MF, Kojima M, Callicott JH, Goldberg TE, Kolachana BS, Bertolino A, et al. (2003). The BDNF val66met polymorphism affects activity-dependent secretion of BDNF and human memory and hippocampal function. *Cell*, 112:257–69.

Eysenck HJ (2001). Bibliography. *Pers Indiv Diff*, 31:45–99.

Fisher R (1918). The correlation between relatives on the supposition of Mendelian inheritance. *Trans Royal Society Edinburgh*, 52:399–433.

Galton F (1865). Hereditary talent and character. *Macmillan's Magazine*, 12:157–66, 318–27.

Gerstein MB, Bruce C, Rozowsky JS, Zheng D, Du J, Korbel JO, et al. (2007). What is a gene, post-ENCODE? History and updated definition. *Genome Res*, 17:669–81.

Hahn MK, Blakely RD (2007). The functional impact of SLC6 transporter genetic variation. *Annu Rev Pharmacol Toxicol*, 47:401–41.

Identification and analysis of functional elements in 1% of the human genome by the ENCODE pilot project (2007). *Nature*, 447:799–816.

Johannsen W (1909). Elemente der exakten Erblichkeitslehre. *Science*, 30:851–3.

Lesch KP, Bengel D, Heils A, Sabol SZ, Greenberg BD, Petri S, et al. (1996). Association of anxiety-related traits with a polymorphism in the serotonin transporter gene regulatory region. *Science*, 274:1527–31.

Mendel G (1865). Versuche über Pflanzen-Hybriden. Vorgelegt in den Sitzungen. Feb. 8 and March 8; 8.

Meyer-Lindenberg A, Mervis CB, Berman KF (2006). Neural mechanisms in Williams syndrome: a unique window to genetic influences on cognition and behaviour. *Nat Rev Neurosci*, 7:380–93.

Nackley AG, Shabalina SA, Tchivileva IE, Satterfield K, Korchynskyi O, Makarov SS, et al. (2006). Human catechol-O-methyltransferase haplotypes modulate protein expression by altering mRNA secondary structure. *Science*, 314:1930–3.

Plomin R, Owen MJ, McGuffin P (1994). The genetic basis of complex human behaviors. *Science*, 264:1733–9.

Savolainen P, Zhang YP, Luo J, Lundeberg J, Leitner T (2002). Genetic evidence for an East Asian origin of domestic dogs. *Science*, 298:1610–3.

Sebat J, Lakshmi B, Troge J, Alexander J, Young J, Lundin P, et al. (2004). Large-scale copy number polymorphism in the human genome. *Science*, 305:525–8.

Spearman C (1904). "General Intelligence," objectively determined and measured. *Am J Psychology*, 15:201–93.

Tan W, Wang Y, Gold B, Chen J, Dean M, Harrison PJ, et al. (2007). Molecular cloning of a brain-specific, developmentally regulated neuregulin 1 (NRG1) isoform and identification of a functional promoter variant associated with schizophrenia. *J Biol Chem*, 282:24343–51.

The International HapMap Project (2003). *Nature*, 18:426.

Bioinformatics Web Sites

Collection of links updated by GCAP/NIH: http://cbdb.nimh.nih.gov/~max/binf/list.html

Allen brain: http://www.brainatlas.org/aba/

Genome databases: http://ihg.gsf.de/ihg/databases.html

UCSD genomic maps: http://genome.ucsc.edu

U.S. government integrated genetics query Web site: http://www.ncbi.nlm.nih.gov/gquery/gquery.fcgi?itool=toolbar

Hapmap: http://hapmap.org/

Gene name database: http://www.gene.ucl.ac.uk/nomenclature/

Jackson Labs: http://www.jax.org/

Ensembl: http://www.ensembl.org/index.html

Interactome: http://humgen.med.uu.nl/~lude/genenetwork/

Reactome: http://www.reactome.org

Gene ontology GO: http://www.geneontology.org/

GEO Expression Sites: http://www.ncbi.nlm.nih.gov/geo/

Statistic sites: http://portal.litbio.org/Registered/Menu/, http://www.biostat.harvard.edu/~fbat/default.html, http://www.sph.umich.edu/csg/abecasis/GOLD/index.html, http://www.sph.umich.edu/csg/abecasis/, http://pritch.bsd.uchicago.edu/software.html

Variation site: http://www.hgvs.org/dblist/dblist.html

Signaling pathways: http://www.signaling-gateway.org/molecule/

2   Statistical Methods in Neuropsychiatric Genetics

Kristin K. Nicodemus and Fengyu Zhang

Many *phenotypes*, or observed characteristics, are influenced by the interplay of genetic and environmental factors and thus are considered *complex traits*. Phenotypes that are studied in psychiatric genetics range from binary characteristics, such as presence or absence of a disease, to categorical ones, such as severity of disease (e.g., mild, moderate, or severe), to continuous ones, such as scores on cognitive tests, for example, the Wechsler Adult Intelligence Scale (WAIS). Given that complex traits are the product of both genetic and environmental factors, how do we know if a trait is hereditary or if it is largely the product of environment? Further, how do we decide which phenotypes should be evaluated by genetic studies along with studies of environmental factors?

Overview of the Statistical Genetics of Neuropsychiatric Traits

Researchers can use several study designs to determine whether a trait is under the control of genetic versus environmental influences, including *familial aggregation, twin,* and *migrant* studies. Once the trait has been shown to be genetic, researchers may want to determine how much of the variance of the trait is under genetic control using *variance component* methods to estimate *heritability* (h^2) in both the *broad* and *narrow* sense. To ascertain genomic regions that may contain genes that influence a trait, family-based analyses such as *parametric* or *nonparametric linkage* that trace chromosomal regions that segregate with values of a phenotype are conducted; alternatively, a more recent approach is to use either a family-based or case–control study of *genome-wide association* (GWA) to find areas of association between a marker and a trait. Once regions of interest are determined or genes are selected based on known function, *fine mapping* via *association studies* is performed to determine the causal variants within the gene that contribute to the phenotype. Once the putative causal variant(s) are determined, functional studies are used to delineate the mechanism by which the variant influences the phenotype and, if appropriate (such as in the case of studies of disease states), ways in which to alter the pathology to improve human health. We give a general overview of each type of study below; more in-depth discussion of components of genetic variance, population genetics, linkage analysis, and association studies follow.

Familial aggregation studies compare rates of disease between the relatives of individuals with a disease versus rates observed in relatives of individuals who do not have the disease. If a trait is under genetic influence, the rate of disease among relatives of affected individuals would be expected to be higher than among relatives of disease-free individuals. Indeed, the degree of relationship (e.g., full siblings, first cousins) should be predictive of disease rates if a trait is under strong genetic control because, on average, full siblings share 50% of their genomes, whereas more distantly related relatives such as first cousins share 25%. However, because family members share environments, familial aggregation can suggest both shared genetic and environmental factors. *Twin* and *migrant* studies are used to untangle the correlation between genes and environment. Because monozygotic (MZ) twins share 100% of their genomes, we expect any trait greatly determined by genetics to show more similar phenotypes in MZ twins than in dizygotic (DZ) twins or full siblings, both of whom share, on average, 50% of their genomes. Migrant studies assess differences between, for example, the rate of disease in individuals who have migrated to a new environment–lifestyle versus that observed in the migrants' source population, with differences in rates often interpreted to be reflective of environmental factors if the migrants are representative of the source population. A related paradigm is the *adoption* study, in which the rate of illness in individuals adopted at birth who have biological relatives with illness is compared with that of control adoptees that have illness-free relatives.

Linkage analysis is used to localize genomic regions that may contain genes that influence the outcome of interest. In general, linkage analysis scans hundreds to thousands of markers across the genome to find chromosomal regions that segregate with disease status or other phenotypes within families. Linkage studies have been responsible for successfully mapping many *monogenic* or single-gene disease genes such as the CF gene that causes cystic fibrosis. There are two main types of linkage analysis: parametric and nonparametric. Parametric linkage analysis requires large, multigenerational *multiplex* families, or families with many individuals carrying the trait of interest, such as a particular disease. When this paradigm is used, the finding that a genetic locus marker segregates with illness in a predictable pattern of inheritance within these families more often than would be predicted by chance indicates that the marker locus is in linkage with the disease locus. Ascertainment of multiple members of the same family across generations who carry the phenotype of interest, especially if the phenotype manifests itself in later life, such as Alzheimer's disease, or if the phenotype leads to a higher probability of death, such as familial breast cancer, can be time-consuming, expensive, and sometimes impossible. Nonparametric linkage, on the other hand, requires only pairs of relatives and assesses the deviation from expected allele-sharing values given the relationship between the relatives. For example, full sibling pairs are expected to share no alleles at a locus at approximately 25% of their genomes, share one allele at a locus approximately 50%, and share both alleles at a locus 25%. When relative pairs show excess allele sharing at a locus, it can be said that the locus shows linkage with the phenotype providing the phenotype is shared between relatives.

There are two broad categories of genetic association studies: candidate gene and GWA. The candidate gene approach is used if a gene has a known function that is plausibly related to the trait and is often used to follow-up regions of interest discovered during a linkage study. GWA studies use markers covering the genome to test for association, similar to a linkage scan, and may be followed up with a candidate gene approach. Designs for association studies may include nuclear family based (sometimes used on samples of families ascertained for linkage analysis), case–control, and/or a combination of the two, such as a set of families with an affected proband and a set of unrelated healthy controls. The statistical methods used for each type of study and to combine studies are similar and generally differ in the type of control sample. Family-based studies generally are analyzed using some form of the *transmission disequilibrium test* (TDT) (Spielman et al. 1993), which considers the alleles carried by the parents of a proband to be the unit of analysis and compares the distribution of alleles transmitted to a proband versus those carried by the parents but not transmitted to the proband. Under the null hypothesis of no association (and/or no linkage; cf. Laird and Lange 2006 for a review), the expected values for transmission of a single nucleotide polymorphism (SNP) with two alleles would be 50:50, and the statistical test is testing for distortions in transmission from the expected values. In fact, the TDT can be considered to be a matched case–control study and can be analyzed using methods appropriate for such studies such as the McNemar χ^2 or conditional logistic regression. However, there are many extensions to the basic formula of the TDT to handle general pedigrees (including multiple probands and extended families), to handle missing data (e.g., a missing parent), to estimate parent-of-origin effects (useful for detection of *imprinting*), and to conduct genotype-based analyses, to name a few; the selection of which method to use should be based on the characteristics of the data at hand and the most statistically powerful method should be applied (Nicodemus et al. 2007). Case–control data may be analyzed using a Pearson χ^2 test, Fisher's exact test (especially for rare alleles or small sample sizes) and/or unconditional logistic regression. In addition, methods have been developed to combine families, unrelated cases, and unrelated controls from the same study and also to combine independent samples across studies via meta-analysis. The combination of samples is an important issue, since the effect size of individual genes in any complex trait is likely to be modest, and increasing the sample size often increases the statistical power to detect association.

Determination of a Genetic Component for a Trait

The determination of evidence of a genetic component for a trait is an important step for planning a molecular genetic study. Once a phenotype, which can be a disease, subphenotype, or a quantitatively measured trait, is defined, one needs to assess whether or not the phenotype of interest has any genetic component by conducting a series of statistical analyses.

Heritability is one of common measures for determining the genetic component. In quantitative genetics, phenotypic variance (V) of a trait can be decomposed into additive genetic variance (V_a), dominant genetic variance (V_d), and environmental variance (V_e) due to nongenetic factors. Most practical applications have been concerned with only the additive genetic component of the phenotypic variance, with remaining components being treated as random error. The ratio V_a/V is known as the *heritability* (also called the *narrow sense heritability*). The proportion of the total phenotypic variance that is attributable to genetic factors, that is, defined as ratio $(V_a + V_d)/V$, is known as *broad sense heritability*. Variance components are the key elements in estimating the heritability of a trait. Determination of these variance components can be estimated in families, based on degree of relatedness of family members as a function of phenotypic variance. The classic strategy, however, is to compare phenotype variance in MZ versus DZ twins, who share both variable genetic and environmental components.

Familial aggregation measures whether or not a potential genetic trait tends to aggregate in families. In practice, twin studies are optimal for estimating heritability, but such studies are sometimes difficult to implement. Familial aggregation can provide evidence for a genetic component by examining how the phenotype correlation changes with genetic relationship. Genetic relationship or relatedness is an important concept in statistical genetics, particularly for linkage analysis. It is defined by the probability that two members of a pedigree share one or two alleles from the same ancestor at any autosomal locus. Two alleles are *identical by descent* (IBD) if they are derived from a common ancestor.

Familial correlation measures the family aggregation for a quantitative trait. If we randomly sample or enroll a certain number of families, examine the pattern of correlation in a trait between different types of relatives (sib–sib, parent–offspring, etc.), then, in principle, the Pearson's correlation coefficient can provide a measure of the correlation between pairs of relatives. When there are multiple sibs in the family, the *intraclass correlation coefficient* (ICC) from variance components can be used. Suppose we have trait (Y_{ij}) data from families; the trait can be expressed as $Y_{ij} = \mu + \mu_i + e_{ij}$, where μ is the overall mean, μ_i is the random effect from family, and e_{ij} is the deviation of an individual j from the family mean. The variance of Y_{ij} can be decomposed into variance from family (σ_u^2) and variance from individuals (i.e., within family; σ_e^2). These variances can be obtained by fitting a one-way analysis of variance model. The ICC can be calculated as follows:

$$\rho = \frac{\sigma_\mu^2}{\sigma_\mu^2 + \sigma_\varepsilon^2}.$$

The interpretation of ICC is intuitive; it directly depends on the variance from family (σ_μ^2), that is, heterogeneity at family level. A large ρ may imply that a trait has a familial aggregation. One should keep in mind that this measurement may be affected by individual and shared environmental factors at the family level.

Familial risk is used to measure familial aggregation for a disease (or binary trait). It is defined as the probability that an individual will be affected by a disease, given that he or she has an affected family member or a family history of the disease. The ratio of the familial risk to the risk in general population or to the risk in those without an affected family member is known as *familial relative risk*. Similarly, for a disease trait, when we randomly select families from a population, we can conduct variance component analysis for a binary trait using a random-effect logistic model. Assume that the likelihood of an individual in a family j having a disease follows a binomial distribution (n_j, p_j). When using logistic regression (or other models such as a probit model) to fit the relationship between the probability and predictors, we can use a random-effect logistic regression. When there is no predictor in the model, a logistic variance component or variance partition model can be $log\,it(p) = \alpha + \mu_j$, where μ_j is random effect at the family level (Browne et al. 2005). We can calculate the ICC for a disease as follows:

$$\rho = \frac{\sigma_\mu^2}{\sigma_\mu^2 + \pi^2/3},$$

where σ_μ^2 is random effect at the family level and $\pi^2/3$ is the variance at the individual level for a standard logistic distribution (Snijders and Bosker 1999). When the random effect at the family level (heterogeneity between families) is very large, it is less likely that the disease has familial aggregation. However, this type of analysis often requires that families are randomly selected from a population. Where the disease is rare, it may require a very large sample size.

Regressive Model   Although variance components can be used to provide evidence for familial aggregation, they may be affected by individual or family environments. For example, when sampling multiple people from the same family, we may extend the variance component to a random-effect regression model to control some observed environmental factors. When sampling parental data, parent–offspring may have a natural order. Bonney (1986) proposed a regressive model for a binary trait to include an individual's covariates (Bonney 1986). With this approach, one may regress an offspring's trait on parental traits, that is, using parental traits as independent variables, while controlling for some other covariates, to examine how the individual's trait status depends on the parental trait. For quantitative traits, one can regress the individual's phenotype on midparent (i.e., the average of parental) phenotypes. The regression slope provides an estimate of the proportion of phenotype variance due to additive genetic factors and is also known as the narrow sense heritability (Lynch and Walsh 1998).

Marker Statistics in Population Genetics

Marker statistics are important for understanding of properties of a single locus before starting a genetic data analysis. A genetic marker is a known DNA sequence which can be described as variation that may arise due to mutation or alteration in the genomic loci that can be observed. It may be a short DNA sequence, such as a tri- or dinucleotide repeat, a tandem repeat element (so-called variable number of tandem repeat or VNTR), or a single base-pair change (SNP). Microsatillites and SNPs are the two most common markers for genetic studies of human disease. At a given single locus, we observe a genotype, the pair of alleles that a (diploid) individual carries. Individuals that have two identical alleles are called *homozygotes*, whereas those that have different alleles are *heterozygotes*. If we denote the alleles at a particular diallelic locus as A and a, there are three possible genotypes: AA and aa homozygotes and Aa heterozygotes.

Allele frequency measures how a known DNA sequence varies at the observed genomic locus. It is defined uniquely by genotype frequencies, which are denoted as P_{AA}, P_{Aa}, and P_{aa} and represent the proportions of the population that are homozygotes AA, aa, and Aa heterozygotes (here, $P_{AA} + P_{Aa} + P_{aa} = 1$). If there are N individuals in the population, then $P_{AA}N$ individuals have two A alleles and $P_{Aa}N$ contain a single A allele. Since there are a total of $2N$ alleles in the populations for each locus, the frequency of allele A1 is $(2P_{AA}N + P_{Aa}N)/2N$, which is the observed frequency of observed homozygotes plus one-half the observed frequency of all heterozygotes containing allele A. This is a general rule of estimating allele frequency for diploids. The estimate is mathematically equivalent to a maximum likelihood estimate.

Hardy–Weinberg equilibrium (HWE) is an important measure in population genetics. It states that the genotype frequencies in a population remain constant or are in equilibrium from generation to generation. Consider alleles A and a, with frequencies p and q, respectively, in the population; under random mating, the offspring will have the proportions of p^2, $2pq$, and q^2 for three possible genotypes AA, Aa, and aa, respectively. These proportions, called Hardy–Weinberg proportions, are the same as their parental proportions.

Departure from HWE may occur in a population where nonrandom mating is taking place or in a case-control study where population stratification exists, whereas new mutations, random genetic drift, and sampling error due to genotyping error also may disturb the HWE in a population. A number of methods for genetic data analysis including allele frequency estimation, linkage analysis using relative pairs, and haplotype analysis require that genetic markers analyzed are in HWE.

A test for HWE is generally performed using the chi-square test. If, for example, we observed at a locus that 200 (N) individuals have genotype counts of 60 (n_{AA}), 120 (n_{Aa}), and 20 (n_{aa}) for three possible genotypes AA, Aa, and aa respectively, allele frequencies can be calculated as follows: $p = (2*n_{AA} + n_{Aa})/2N = (2*60 + 120)/2*200 = 0.6$ for the frequency of allele A, and $1 - p = 1 - 0.6 = 0.4$ for allele a. Based on these allele frequencies and assuming that the sample is from a population that is in HWE, we can calculate the expected genotype counts as follows: $E(AA) = p^2N = 0.6*0.6*200 = 72$, $E(Aa) = 2*p*q = 2*0.6*0.4*200 = 96$, and $E(aa) = q^2N = 0.4*0.4*200 = 32$. Pearson's chi-square test states

$$\chi^2 = \sum \frac{(O-E)^2}{E} = (60-72)^2/72 + (120-96)^2/96 + (20-30)^2/32$$
$$= 2 + 6 + 4.5 = 12.5;$$

with 1 degree of freedom, the p value $= 0.000407 < .05$, which suggests that the locus we observed is not in HWE. When HWE tests need to be performed for a small sample with a low minor allele frequency, the Fisher's exact test can be applied.

Linkage disequilibrium (LD) is defined as the *association of alleles* between two or more loci, which can be either on the same or on different chromosomes. It is different from linkage, which describes the *association of two or more loci* on a chromosome with limited recombination between them. Since LD is the nonrandom association of alleles from different loci, it can provide valuable information on the structure of *haplotypes*, or alleles on the same chromosome, in the human genome. LD can help to characterize markers from within a gene to a large chromosomal region. Based on the LD between markers, we can understand genomic structure in populations.

LD provides an important concept that leads to the large-scale genomic association study including GWA. Suppose there is an observed disease-risk allele in a gene or a chromosomal region, but it is unknown. Through LD, however, we can genotype a SNP that is in LD with the disease SNP and use this SNP as a proxy to perform association analysis. This is the beauty of LD for genetic association studies. Moreover, if there are a number of SNPs or markers that are in LD, we may perform haplotype-based association to localize the gene to a small chromosomal region.

Among several LD measures, Delta (Δ) is the most widely implemented LD measure for association study (Devlin and Risch 1995). Assuming two diallelic loci A and B, and $\pi_{A_1B_1}$, $\pi_{A_1B_2}$, $\pi_{A_2B_1}$, and $\pi_{A_2B_2}$ are frequencies for possible haplotype A_1B_1, A_1B_2, A_2B_1, and A_2B_2, resepctively, the corresponding frequencies for allele A_1, A_2, B_1, and B_2 are π_{A_1+}, π_{A_2+}, π_{+B_1}, and π_{+B_2}, and the LD measure delta is defined as

$$\Delta = \frac{\pi_{A_1B_1}\pi_{A_2B_2} - \pi_{A_1B_2}\pi_{A_2B_1}}{\left(\pi_{A_1+}\pi_{A_2+}\pi_{+B_1}\pi_{+B_2}\right)^{1/2}}.$$

Delta is commonly squared to remove the arbitrary sign. In practice, Δ^2, also known as r^2, is often used. Another commonly used LD measure is D', introduced by Lewontin (1964), a normalized measure of D by dividing it with theoretical maximum (D_{max}) for the observed allele frequency, where $D_{max} = \min(\pi_{A_1+}\pi_{+B_2}, \pi_{A_2+}\pi_{+B_1})$ when $D > 0$, or $\max(-\pi_{A_1+}\pi_{+B_1}, -\pi_{A_2+}\pi_{+B_2})$ when $D < 0$ (Jorde 2000). Both r^2 and D' range between 0 and 1. However, there is no statistical test for LD based on these measures. In general, $r^2 = 1$ indicates complete LD, or allelic identity between two loci, and $r^2 > 0.3$, which is equivalent to $r > 0.55$ or $r < 0.55$, indicates a moderate LD. $D' = 1$ indicates a complete LD between two markers, however; $D' = 0$ indicates a complete equilibrium, but unlike r^2, typing one SNP provides no information on the other SNP.

Linkage Analysis

Linkage analysis is an important tool for localizing genetic loci for human disorders by applying molecular biology techniques in combination with statistical linkage analysis. It examines whether individuals affected with a disease within the same family have likely received chromosomal material from a common ancestor who possessed a disease-causing DNA sequence variation. This chromosomal material is likely to be measured by variations at neighboring loci inherited together with disease (Schork et al. 2007). By looking at the number of recombinants between two loci (disease locus and marker locus) in families, we can decide whether or not two loci are linked.

The *LOD score* is a statistical method for linkage analysis. It was defined to represent the logarithm of the odds (to the base 10) for linkage. Suppose we observed a particular relationship between a disease and a marker locus in a family or pedigree; we can calculate the likelihood of having this configuration when assuming there is no linkage between a disease and a marker locus. Then, we compare this likelihood with the likelihood of observing the same family assuming different degrees of linkage, that is, recombination fraction (a value ranging from 0 to 0.5) between two loci. It can be expressed as

$$LOD = \log_{10}(L(pedigree|\theta = x)/L(pedigree|\theta = 0.5)).$$

Assuming that a recombination occurs during meiosis between two loci and the number of individuals in the family, the probability of observing this in the pedigree (i.e., r, the number of recombinants at a locus) follows a binomial distribution, and the likelihood is

$$\Pr(R|N) = \binom{n}{r}\theta^r(1-\theta)^{n-r}.$$

We can appreciate this calculation in the pedigree shown in figure 2.1. The affected and unaffected individuals are denoted as D‖d and d‖d, respectively, and the genetic

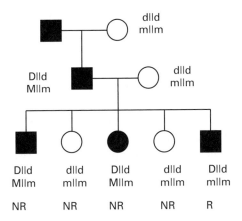

Figure 2.1

A pedigree with information on two genetic loci, where an open circle and square are unaffected female and male; black fill stands for affected; D||d, d||D are genotype information for affected and unaffected at disease locus; and M||m, m||m are genotype information for affected and unaffected at a marker locus. Non-recombinants, NR; recombinants, R.

marker alleles are M and m. It is evident that the first four offspring are nonrecombinants, having a consistent relationship between M alleles and illness status, but the last one is recombinant. When there is no linkage $\theta = 0.5$ between two loci, the likelihood (L_0) of the observed pedigree structure is

$$\Pr(R = 1 \mid N = 5) = \binom{5}{1} 0.5^1 (1 - 0.5)^{5-1},$$

and assuming $\theta = 0.05$, the likelihood (L_1) of the observed pedigree structure is

$$\Pr(R = 1 \mid N = 5) = \binom{5}{1} 0.05^1 (1 - 0.05)^{5-1};$$

therefore, the LOD can be directly calculated as: $LOD(x = 0.05) = L_1/L_0 = 10*0.07673 = 0.7673$. In practice, we can use a maximum likelihood method to directly estimate the recombination fraction θ where the maximum LOD score is obtained. This LOD score, based on one disease and one locus, therefore is known as a two-point LOD score.

Linkage analysis examines the "within-family association." When there are multiple families for linkage study, a total LOD score can be obtained by summing over the LOD scores from all individual families. This is intuitive because likelihoods of independent families are multiplied to form a total likelihood for a sample population. A LOD score of 3 or greater is usually considered to be strong evidence for linkage. Unfortunately, there is no formal statistical test to perform. The LOD score analysis requires a specified disease model (e.g., dominant or recessive model) and penetrance function, which are in practice difficult to define. The necessity for defining these terms, or parameters, is why this is referred to as *parametric linkage analysis*.

As we described above, in determining the genetic components of a disease or trait, one of the important concepts is that the relative risk of a trait or disease is changing with genetic relationship. IBD is often used to measure genetic relatedness at a specific locus. DNA at the same locus on homologous chromosomes in individuals is said to be IBD if it originated from the same ancestral chromosome. If two homologous chromosomes from *different* people are IBD at some locus, the people are *related*. Two people, neither of whom is inbred, can share DNA IBD at a particular locus on either 0, 1, or 2 chromosomes.

The *relative pair linkage method* examines whether relative pairs with similar phenotypes tend to share marker alleles more than would be expected by chance given the nature of their relationship. Instead of using unaffected individuals in relative pairs, an affected individual is more likely to carry a risk allele than an unaffected individual. When a disease is rare, affected relative pairs are more informative.

Affected sib pairs (ASP) is the most commonly used relative pair linkage method. ASP is based on the probability of sharing alleles IBD. In general, a random pair of siblings would be expected to share two alleles IBD with probability $\pi_2 = 1/4$, to share one allele IBD with probability $\pi_1 = 1/2$, and to share no allele IBD with probability $\pi_0 = 1/4$. This would be true for a diallelic marker between two sibs. If a marker is linked to a disease, an affected sib pairs would be expected to share more alleles IBD than expected at the locus. If , for example, we observe N affected sib pairs for linkage analysis, the number of pairs sharing 0, 1, and 2 alleles IBD is n_0, n_1, and n_2, respectively. As noted above, the expected number of affected sib pairs for sharing 0, 1, and 2 alleles IBD would be $0.25N$, $0.5N$ and $0.25N$. As we stated in the HWE test, a chi-square statistic with 2 degrees of freedom (d.f.) can be constructed to test whether or not the observed alleles shared IBD is significantly different from expected. Since the number of allele sharing 0, 1, and 2 has an ordinal nature, the *trend test* with degrees of freedom (*d.f.*) of 1 can be applied and provide more power due to the reduction in *d.f.*

In general, the LOD score is powerful, and it is especially powerful for testing linkage with Mendelian disorders, but sometimes it is difficult to specify the related parameters that may affect the LOD score calculation. When the two-point LOD score indicates a linkage signal, multipoint analysis and haplotype analysis can be performed to define the disease-associated flanking markers and refine localization of a linkage region. ASP is a nonparametric method, but it offers statistical validation and does not require any assumption of penetrance function or disease model. This is particularly useful for screening a large number of markers for linkage evidence. Markers for linkage analysis are also required to be in HWE.

Quantitative trait linkage analysis is another important method in mapping genes for complex human diseases. Many complex diseases such as neuropsychological and cardiovascular diseases have some intermediate subphenotype that can be used for facilitating gene mapping. The *Haseman–Elston regression* is one of the methods for quantitative trait linkage analysis using sib pairs, based on regressing the squared trait difference between sib pairs and shared allele IBD. Sib pairs sharing two alleles IBD would tend to have greater similarity in traits if the trait is related to the genetic marker (Haseman and Elston 1972). Based on sib pairs, Fulker et al. proposed a multipoint linkage analysis method using variance components, and it was later extended to use general pedigrees (Fulker et al. 1995; Almasy and Warren 2005). *Solar* (sequential oligogenic linkage analysis routines) software provides both two-point and multipoint linkage analysis for quantitative traits based on general pedigrees.

Candidate Gene Association Analysis

The *candidate gene association study* design is efficient in terms of time and cost. In general, one tends to find candidate genes in under a chromosome region defined by a linkage study peak or based on a known function and its potential relevance to the phenotype of interest. We can also find some genes for candidate gene association studies based on possible molecular pathways. Recently GWA studies have emerged as an important tool for searching for genes associated with disease. One may use GWA results to select candidate genes for follow-up.

The chi-square test is generally performed to examine association between a genetic marker and disease in a study using a population-based case–control design. It simply analyzes a 2-by-3 contingency table to compare the genotype differences between cases and controls. For example, we observed a sample at a locus based on a case–control design (see table 2.1). When we perform a Pearson's chi-square test, $\chi^2 = 7.40$, with 2 degrees of freedom, p value = 0.025, which implies that the genotype distribution is different between cases and controls. One should keep in mind that the chi-square test requires computing expected genotype frequency by using allele frequency. As we stated above, estimation of allele frequency requires the assumption that the marker is in HWE. We should check for HWE for this marker before performing the statistical test. In addition, we can test the association under dominant (*AA + Aa* vs.

Table 2.1

Genotype distribution in cases and controls

	AA	Aa	aa
Case	143	203	91
Control	110	225	68
Total	253	428	157

aa) or recessive (*AA* vs. *Aa* + *aa*) models, or whether or not heterozygote (*Aa*) is associated with disease.

The chi-square test is unable to tell which allele is associated with disease and what the effect size is. Assuming an additive genetic model, we can perform the *trend test* by coding a SNP genotype as an ordinal variable (0, 1, 2) to test whether or not the association has a linear trend with the number of alleles. The trend test is believed to have more power to detect significant association than the chi-square test, and it does not require that markers are in HWE.

When covariates or known genes need to be controlled for analyzing the genotype–phenotype association, *logistic regression* can be used by coding genotype as a categorical variable or an ordinal variable. One of the advantages for the population-based case–control study is that it is easier to recruit participants and collect samples than in the family-based study, but it is well-known that the association may be confounded by genomic structure (discussed later in the chapter) and potential environmental confounders. Depending on the scale of a candidate gene study, we may need to genotype extra ancestry informative markers to control for genomic structure. Meanwhile, when there are a number of markers that are in LD, that is, markers are highly correlated with each other, we may need to perform haplotype analysis to reduce multiple testing.

Haplotype analysis in case–control studies is problematic because *phase*, or the assignment of alleles to each chromosome, is unknown. There are two ways to perform haplotype analysis under these circumstances. The first is to infer phase for each haplotype and to use the inferred haplotypes as observed predictors, which can introduce bias (Mensah et al., 2007). A more sophisticated but unbiased way to perform haplotype analysis in case–control data is to weight phase assignment probabilistically for each individual and use those weights as the observed predictors when assessing association between haplotypes and phenotype, such as the score-statistic-based method implemented in the R package haplo.stats (Schaid et al. 2002).

Family-based association studies are an ideal design to reduce the population structure problem. For the genetic association study of a disease, the TDT can be used (Spielman et al. 1993). The TDT considers parents heterozygous for a certain allele (*A*) at the marker locus and counts the number of times that such parents transmit *A* to their affected offspring. The ideal design for the TDT test needs an affected offspring and their parents genotyped at the marker locus.

It often happens, however, that parental genotypes are missing when the disease of study is more prevalent in older adults. *Sib-TDT* can be used in these circumstances. It constructs probabilities of association by comparing the observed number of *A* alleles in affected children with the number expected with no linkage, conditioned on the observed distribution of marker genotypes in the whole sibship (Spielman and Ewens 1998). This test does not require parental marker genotypes but uses marker genotypes of both affected and unaffected siblings. Several other versions of the TDT test, such as *combined TDT* and *reconstruction combined TDT*, have been derived to accommodate a variety of family data.

Family-based association test (FBAT) is one of the most widely used tests for analyzing family-based association data (Laird et al. 2000). Based on offspring in each nuclear family, the test statistic (S) is constructed to be the sum of the product of trait (T) and a function of offspring genotype (X) across each family, that is, $S = \sum TX$. Traits can be disease status, quantitative traits, or censored traits, that is, time to event such as age of onset of the trait where only individuals with the disease have a complete observation and others have a censored age of onset at the time of study completion. When it is applied to study a disease trait, the S statistic is equivalent to the test statistic used in TDT. However, FBAT can be extended to test quantitative traits, using nuclear families and/or sibships. It allows using multiple nuclear families from a large pedigree, testing multi-allelic markers, considering additive, dominant, or recessive models, and it can adjust for covariates. FBAT also has been implemented to perform haplotype-based association analysis, and recently it has been developed to test multiple markers.

Genome-Wide Association Analysis

The advent of high-throughput genotyping platforms has ushered in the current era of GWA studies, which allow the examination of association between thousands to millions of SNPs and a phenotype, which may be binary (e.g., disease status) or quantitative (e.g., WAIS scores). GWAs may be family-based, case–control, or a combination of both. The same types of analyses described for candidate gene association studies may be performed for single SNPs and/or haplotypes, given the type of study sample. Because genotyping in the larger SNP (100,000 and larger) sets is dense, fairly strong LD is found in most regions of the genome, allowing *imputation* of both missing (observed) genotypes and ungenotyped SNPs (Marchini et al. 2007). The ability to impute genotypes in GWA studies facilitates pooling of data across studies either directly or via meta-analysis, thus increasing sample size and subsequent ability to detect modest association signals. A major challenge of GWA studies is analyzing and summarizing a large volume of data, which has led to the development of genome-wide software packages that range from open source (e.g., PLINK; Purcell et al. 2007) to proprietary (e.g., Biocomputing Platforms Ltd., Espoo, Finland).

In large-scale association studies, *multiple testing* is an important issue that has to be addressed. In searching for a genetic variant associated with a disease or trait, one may genotype a large number of SNPs and perform thousands to millions of statistical tests. Thus, for example, when we test 100,000 SNPs for association, 5,000 SNPs will be expected to be significant at the level of 0.05 by chance alone, even though there is no SNP associated with disease. Therefore, we have to correct for multiple testing when we test a large number of SNPs for association.

A number of approaches have been proposed for correcting for multiple testing (Dudbridge 2006). Stranger et al. (2005) compared three approaches—Bonferroni, permutation-based, and the false discovery rate (FDR)—and found substantial overlap of signals detected from all three approaches (Stranger et al. 2005). To apply an FDR approach in a large-scale association study, an initial screening can be based on computing the *positive FDR* (pFDR), which is the expected proportion of false positives among all the positive results, conditional on at least one positive at a given significance level (Efron et al. 2001; Efron and Tibshirani 2002; Storey 2002). A *q value* can be computed for each test, which indicates which pFDR would result from calling that test significant. A *local FDR* can also be calculated for each test—the local FDR is the posterior probability that the null hypothesis is true, given the observed statistic (Efron et al. 2001; Aubert et al. 2004). Both the *q* value and the local FDR are computed for individual tests, the *q* value is preferable if one is going to follow up all positive results, as might happen in a study with moderate power where true and false positives are intermingled. In contrast, if there are a handful of very strong associations, with some moderate associations, then the local FDR is preferable (Dudbridge 2006). These FDR-based approaches still work well even when applied to markers in LD (Sabatti et al. 2003). When hypotheses are stratified, it is possible to control the FDR by stratum, as recommended by Sun (Sun et al. 2006). When choosing the appropriate FDR level, it is preferable to also take into account the nondiscovery rate (Craiu and Sun 2006), so as to minimize the false-negative rate.

As a complement to FDR-based approaches, it is sometimes possible to use more computationally intensive *permutation* procedures that takes the LD of the markers into account and which are considered the "gold standard" in controlling for multiple testing. Many methods have been proposed for fast permutation algorithms (Lin 2005; Seaman and Muller-Myhsok 2005; Dudbridge 2006; Kimmel and Shamir 2006), so applying permutation procedures can be computationally feasible.

When evaluating statistical significance in light of the multiple tests conducted, it is important to remember that these statistical criteria are based simply on the distributions of the observed *p* values and no other prior information. Also, true positives may not be ranked near the top of the list (Zaykin and Zhivotovsky 2005). Replication is an important step of GWA studies for further testing or validating the statistical significance. However, in prioritizing signals of statistical significance for replication, it is important to consider the biological plausibility, the strength of prior evidence and the statistical power of the various associations tested (Whittemore 2005). While some argue that the primary emphasis should be on the statistical evidence, others argue that use of the ever increasing amounts of genomic annotation data is merited (Pharoah et al. 2005; Whittemore 2005; Thomas 2006). Bayesian, weighted FDR, and hierarchical regression models have recently been developed and allow us to incorporate a variety of prior information—for example, location relative to genes, putative function, biological pathways, or previous linkage or association findings—into evaluation of results (Thomas 2006).

Inference from observational studies such as GWA studies of human disease can be impacted by the effects of *confounding*, in particular, due to *population stratification* or *population substructure*, although more traditional epidemiological confounding may also exist. Confounding in the traditional epidemiological sense occurs when a third variable is associated with the predictor and outcome of interest. For example, a researcher interested in the association between coffee drinking and lung cancer designs a case–control study to assess this question. Let us assume that there is a strong positive correlation between coffee drinking and smoking cigarettes, and cigarette smoking is also strongly related to increased lung cancer risk. If the researcher examines the relation between coffee drinking and lung cancer risk without considering the effect of smoking simultaneously, it may appear that coffee drinking increases lung cancer risk even when coffee is not associated with risk for lung cancer at all, because people who drink more coffee are more likely to smoke. In this scenario smoking is a *confounding variable* in the coffee drinking–lung cancer association. To reduce the impact of confounding by smoking, a researcher may design a study to assess the coffee drinking–lung cancer relation in only nonsmoking or smoking individuals or may analyze their data after creating subgroups of never smokers and ever smokers. Another way to handle confounding in this case is to statistically control for it by entering smoking variables into the statistical model while analyzing ever and never smokers together.

GWAs of human disease are not immune to traditional epidemiological confounding, and studies should be designed to reduce the degree of environmental confounding to ensure valid statistical inference. Genetic studies also have their own special type of confounding: population stratification, which occurs when the genomes of cases and controls are not well matched. If we assume there are two subpopulations—1 and 2—and that they differ in both the rates of the disease under study and the frequencies of genetic variants carried, subpopulation membership may confound the relationship between disease status and genetic markers at a particular gene or region of the genome, even though the gene or region is not associated with risk for the disease. For example, if the rate of disease is 20% in subpopulation 1 and the minor allele frequency of a SNP is 0.45 in this subpopulation and the rate of disease in subpopulation 2 is 5% and the minor allele frequency of a SNP in this subpopulation is 0.10, on average cases from subpopulation 1 will be sampled 4 times more often than cases from subpopulation 2 because the rate of disease in subpopulation 1 is 4 times greater than in subpopulation 2. In a sample of 200 chromosomes (50 cases and 50 controls), the frequency of the SNP will be a weighted average of the two sets: 0.38. Likewise, in a sample of controls (which would be more likely to be sampled from subpopulation 2) the frequency of the SNP will be 0.17.

Subpopulation 1 is shown in table 2.2. The OR for the risk allele in subpopulation 1 is 1.0 (0.33, 3.06), $\chi^2_1 = 0$, p value = 1.0. Subpopulation 2 is shown in table 2.3. The OR for the risk allele in subpopulation 2 is 1.0 (0.10, 5.65), $\chi^2_1 = 0$, p value = 1.0. Pooling subpopulations 1 and 2 yields the values shown in table 2.4. The OR for the risk allele in the pooled population is 2.99 (1.48, 6.18), $\chi^2_1 = 11.06$, p value = 0.0009, indicating that the SNP is associated with case status, even though none exists. This example illustrates the main concern regarding the presence of population stratification: it can induce spurious associations.

Two well-established ways to statistically control for population stratification have been developed: *structured association* and *genomic control*. Structured association approaches attempt to estimate the subpopulation membership or percentage of subpopulation membership for each individual, using frequentist methods such as principal components (Price et al. 2006) or Bayesian methods such as STRUCTURE

Table 2.2

Example subpopulation 1: Allele frequencies in cases and controls

	Risk Allele	Nonrisk Allele	Total
Case	36	44	80
Control	9	11	20
Total	45	55	100

Table 2.3

Example subpopulation 2: Allele frequencies in cases and controls

	Risk Allele	Nonrisk Allele	Total
Case	2	18	20
Control	18	72	80
Total	20	80	100

Table 2.4

Example pooled population: Allele frequencies in cases and controls

	Risk Allele	Nonrisk Allele	Total
Case	38	62	100
Control	17	83	100
Total	55	145	200

(Pritchard et al. 2000), and then, as in the traditional epidemiologic confounding example above, the subpopulation information can be used to split the sample into more homogeneous subsamples for analysis, or the information can be used to statistically control for subpopulation membership in the statistical model. Genomic control approaches exploit the fact that when population stratification exists, the chi-square statistic tends to be inflated versus what would be expected under the null hypothesis of no association. Therefore, one can adjust the test statistics for the inflation to empirically remove the effect of population stratification (Devlin et al. 2004).

Epistasis and Gene–Environment Interaction

Epistasis, or *gene–gene interaction*, may indicate a *biological* interaction, a *statistical* interaction, or both. Biological interaction is generally given at the trait level—for example, in the context of one locus masking the effects of a second locus. A classical example of biological epistasis is coat color in mice. At the albino locus there are two variants: the wild-type locus A, which is able to synthesize melanin, which results in coat pigmentation, and the variant a, which, when carried on both chromosomes, results in albinism. At a second locus, agouti, the allele G encodes for melanization of the entire hair producing a black coat; the variant g encodes for black hair to the tip, which is yellow. If a mouse carries two a alleles at the albino locus, it cannot synthesize melanin and thus appears albino, regardless of alleles carried at the agouti locus; thus, the phenotype at the agouti locus is masked by the phenotype at the albino locus. On the other hand, statistical epistasis generally indicates a departure from a linear statistical model of effects at both loci. For example, in the context of a logistic regression model testing for interaction between 2 SNPs, the appropriate test for interaction is a *likelihood ratio test* (LRT) comparing nested models. The *reduced model* is a model including main effects at each SNP and any covariates, for example, if the genetic model for SNP1 was coded as dominant and the genetic model for SNP2 was coded as recessive, the minor (2) allele was the risk allele, and including no covariates:

$$\ln\left(\frac{p}{1-p}\right) = \beta_1(SNP1.dom) + \beta_2(SNP2.rec).$$

The *full model* would include both of the main effect terms plus the interaction term:

$$\ln\left(\frac{p}{1-p}\right) = \beta_1(SNP1.dom) + \beta_2(SNP2.rec) + \beta_3(SNP1.dom * SNP2.rec),$$

which can be thought of as a set of 2-by-2 *contingency tables* comparing frequencies of each type in cases and controls (see tables 2.5 and 2.6). In this example, the full model output gives the following estimates:

Table 2.5

Contingency table showing distributions of genotypes at SNP1 and SNP2 in cases

Cases	SNP2: Genotype 1/1 and 1/2	SNP2: Genotype 2/2
SNP1: Genotype 1/1	153	195
SNP1: Genotype 1/2 and 2/2	248	343

Note. SNP, single nucleotide polymorphism.

Table 2.6

Contingency table showing distributions of genotypes at SNP1 and SNP2 in controls

Controls	SNP2: Genotype 1/1 and 1/2	SNP2: Genotype 2/2
SNP1: Genotype 1/1	332	230
SNP1: Genotype 1/2 and 2/2	242	101

Note. SNP, single nucleotide polymorphism.

	OR	ln(OR)	95% CI	Z score	p value
SNP1	2.22	0.798	(1.71, 2.89)	6.0	<0.000001
SNP2	1.84	0.610	(1.40, 2.41)	4.42	5E-06
Interaction	—	0.588	—	2.94	0.0016

The log likelihood for the model is −1173.1779. The actual *interaction OR* and its *95% confidence interval* (CI) are not usually given in the output of most statistical packages because this statistic is a linear combination of the parameters that comprise it, so what is generally shown is the deviation from log additivity, not the true interaction OR. Therefore, to calculate the OR and 95% CI for the example above, the interaction OR is given as

$$OR_{int} = \exp(\beta_1 + \beta_2 + \beta_3) = \exp(0.798 + 0.610 + 0.588) = 7.36,$$

and to calculate the *standard error* of this linear combination in order to use it in the calculation of the CI, one must first obtain the *variance–covariance matrix* (e.g., using the command **vcov** in R/Splus or **vce** in STATA). The variance–covariance matrix for the example is as follows:

	SNP1	SNP2	Interaction
SNP1	0.018	0.0095	−0.018
SNP2	0.0095	0.019	−0.019
Interaction	−0.018	−0.019	0.040

The variances are given on the diagonal, and the covariances are given in off-diagonal cells. The standard error is calculated as follows:

$$SE_{\beta int} = (\sigma_{\beta 1}^2 + \sigma_{\beta 2}^2 + \sigma_{\beta 3}^2 + (2*\mathrm{cov}(\beta_1, \beta_2)) + (2*\mathrm{cov}(\beta_1, \beta_3)) + (2*\mathrm{cov}(\beta_2, \beta_3)))^{1/2}$$
$$= (0.018 + 0.019 + 0.040 + (2*0.0095) + (2*-0.018) + (2*-0.019))^{1/2}$$
$$= (0.022)^{1/2}$$
$$= 0.015,$$

and a 95% CI may be calculated as

$$\exp(\ln(OR_{int}) \pm 1.96(SE_{\beta int}))$$
$$= \exp((0.798 + 0.610 + 0.588) - (1.96*0.15))$$
$$= \exp(1.99 - 0.294) = 5.45 \text{ for the lower bound of the CI and}$$
$$= \exp((0.798 + 0.610 + 0.588) + (1.96*0.15))$$
$$= \exp(1.99 + 0.294) = 9.82 \text{ for the upper bound of the 95\% CI.}$$

To test for an interaction, we will use a likelihood ratio test. Therefore, we must now compute the log likelihood for the reduced model containing only the main effects for each SNP, which gives a log likelihood of -1177.5338. The LRT tests 2 times the difference in the minus log likelihoods for each model:

$$LRT = 2*(-\ln(LRT\ reduced) - -\ln(LRT\ interaction)) = 2*(1177.5338 - 1173.1779)$$
$$= 8.71,$$

which is distributed as a chi-square with degrees of freedom equal to the difference in the number of parameters estimated in the two models. In the example above, three parameters (one for SNP1, one for SNP2, and one for the interaction) were estimated, whereas in the reduced model, only two paramters were estimated, giving the degrees of freedom for the LRT = 3 − 2 = 1, and the corresponding p value for the test for interaction is 0.0032. A model assessing gene–environment or environment–environment variables may be constructed similarly.

At the GWA level it has been shown that it is computationally tractable to do all possible 2-SNP interactions (e.g., for a 500K SNP chip = 124,999,750,000 interactions; Marchini et al. 2005); however, it is not feasible to do all possible subsets of SNP interactions due to both computational and statistical limitations. Given that for most complex traits it is commonly believed that networks of gene–gene, gene–environment, and environment–environment interactions influence phenotype, how can researchers begin to unravel the complexity? One approach gaining in popularity in related fields such as biomedical text mining, bioinformatics, and gene expression analysis is the use of *data mining algorithms* borrowed from computer science. Although many algorithms have been developed and applied to statistical genetics, we will briefly outline only the most commonly used: *random forest* (Breiman 2000). At initialization, random forest selects a subsample or resampled (bootstrap) sample of observations to create a *training set*; the observations not sampled are set aside as a *test set*. The next step selects a subset of the predictor variables (e.g., SNPs) to test on the training sample; the association between each predictor and outcome is calculated, and the predictor with the strongest association is used to partition the data into two subsets (e.g., individuals carrying 1/1 genotype vs. those carrying 1/2 or 2/2 genotypes at a SNP). In each of the subsets, the remaining predictors are tested for association with the outcome; if a significant association is observed, that predictor is used to further partition the data. The recursive partitioning is continued until the sample size in the subset is below a certain size or until no additional significant association with remaining predictors is observed. This procedure creates one tree; random forest constructs a forest of hundreds to millions of trees. After each tree is created using the training set, the independent or "out-of-bag" test set is run through the tree and the predictive ability of the tree is calculated by comparing correctly classified observations with misclassified observations. This process is then repeated after permuting the predictors to break up any observed association, and the difference in predictive ability for each predictor is calculated by subtracting the rates from the permuted data set from the test set to obtain a measure of *variable importance* for each predictor. To take advantage of all the information in the forest, these variable importance measures are averaged across all of the trees in the forest. Machine learning algorithms such as random forest are attractive for several reasons: they are efficient and computationally tractable for high-dimensional data (such as GWA studies), and they can model both main effects of a single SNP and high-order interactions simultaneously.

Power and Sample Size Calculation

Power and sample size calculations are very important for designing a genetic study. Since both recruiting participants and genotyping may be costly, one may want to obtain more power with smaller sample size. For a linkage study based on LOD scores, Ploughman and Boehnke (1989) proposed estimating power by computer simulation. Providing related parameters such as marker allele frequency, penetrance function, mode of inheritance, and recombination fraction, one can obtain the mean maximum LOD score based on pedigrees for a planned study. Other methods were proposed for calculating power for a linkage study using ASP (Krawczak 2001). Most power calculation methods assume that markers are in linkage equilibrium, and the allele frequency assumption is crucial, particularly for ASP and association studies. Studies have suggested using average power to ensure appropriate power calculation (Ambrosius et al. 2004; Zheng et al. 2004). For association study, PBAT and QUANTO software can be used for power calculation for a variety of study designs including gene–gene interactions (Gauderman 2002; Gauderman 2003; Lange et al. 2004).

Power calculation depends on a number of assumptions. For example, for an association study, one may need to assume effect size for a potential genotype or allele and disease model (e.g., dominant, recessive, or additive). No one calculation will be a best fit for a real study in practice. It is best to perform power calculations using different combinations of the assumptions.

Conclusions

Researchers have a plethora of statistical tools available to determine genetic influence on neuropsychiatric phenotypes. However, the search for genes that control for complex traits is challenging due to issues such as phenotypic and allelic heterogeneity, small effect sizes and statistical power, high dimensionality of data, computational restraints, and undetected population stratification and other forms of confounding. The field of statistical genetics holds great promise for unraveling the complex web of gene–gene, gene–environment, and environment–environment interactions that underlie neuropsychiatric traits, hopefully leading to improved human health.

References

Almasy L, Warren DM (2005). Software for quantitative trait analysis. *Hum Genomics*, 2:191–5.

Ambrosius WT, Lange EM, Langefeld CD (2004). Power for genetic association studies with random allele frequencies and genotype distributions. *Am J Hum Genet*, 74:683–93.

Aubert J, Bar-Hen A, Daudin JJ, Robin S (2004). Determination of the differentially expressed genes in microarray experiments using local FDR. *BMC Bioinformatics*, 5:125.

Begg CB (2005). Reflections on publication criteria for genetic association studies. *Cancer Epidemiol Biomarkers Prev*, 14:1364–5.

Ploughman LM, Boehnke M (1989). Estimating the power of a proposed linkage study for a complex genetic trait. *Am J Hum Genet*, 44:543–51

Bonney GE (1986). Regressive logistic models for familial disease and other binary traits. *Biometrics*, 42:611–25.

Breiman L (2000). Random forests. *Mach Learn*, 45:5–32.

Browne WJ, Subramanian SV, Jones K, Goldstein H (2005). Variance partitioning in multilevel logistic models that exhibit overdispersion. *J Roy Stat Soc A Sta*, 168:599–613.

Craiu R, Sun L (2006). Choosing the lesser evil: trade-off between false discovery rate and non-discovery rate. *Statistica Sinica*, 18:861–80.

Devlin B, Bacanu SA, Roeder K (2004). Genomic control to the extreme. *Nat Genet*, 36:1129–30; author reply 1131.

Devlin B, Risch N (1995). A comparison of linkage disequilibrium measures for fine-scale mapping. *Genomics*, 29:311–22.

Dudbridge F (2006). A note on permutation tests in multistage association scans. *Am J Hum Genet*, 78:1094–5; author reply 1096.

Efron B, Tibshirani R (2002). Empirical Bayes methods and false discovery rates for microarrays. *Genet Epidemiol*, 23:70–86.

Efron B, Tibshirani R, Storey JD, Tusher V (2001). Empirical Bayes analysis of a microarray experiment. *J Amer Statist Assoc*, 96:1151–60.

Fulker DW, Cherny SS, Cardon LR (1995). Multipoint interval mapping of quantitative trait loci, using sib pairs. *Am J Hum Genet*, 56:1224–33.

Gauderman WJ (2002). Sample size requirements for association studies of gene–gene interaction. *Am J Epidemiol*, 155:478–84.

Gauderman WJ (2003). Candidate gene association analysis for a quantitative trait, using parent–offspring trios. *Genet Epidemiol*, 25:327–38.

Haseman JK, Elston RC (1972). The investigation of linkage between a quantitative trait and a marker locus. *Behav Genet*, 2:3–19.

Jorde LB (2000). Linkage disequilibrium and the search for complex disease genes. *Genome Res*, 10:1435–44.

Kimmel G, Shamir R (2006). A fast method for computing high-significance disease association in large population-based studies. *Am J Hum Genet*, 79:481–92.

Krawczak M (2001). ASP—a simulation-based power calculator for genetic linkage studies of qualitative traits, using sib-pairs. *Hum Genet*, 109:675–7.

Laird NM, Horvath S, Xu X (2000). Implementing a unified approach to family-based tests of association. *Genet Epidemiol*, 19(Suppl 1):S36–42.

Laird NM, Lange C (2006). Family-based designs in the age of large-scale gene-association studies. *Nat Rev Genet*, 7:385–94.

Lange C, DeMeo D, Silverman EK, Weiss ST, Laird NM (2004). PBAT: tools for family-based association studies. *Am J Hum Genet*, 74:367–9.

Lin DY (2005). An efficient Monte Carlo approach to assessing statistical significance in genomic studies. *Bioinformatics*, 21:781–7.

Lynch M, Walsh B (1998). Genetics and analysis of quantitative traits. Sunderland, MA: Sinauer.

Marchini J, Donnelly P, Cardon LR (2005). Genome-wide strategies for detecting multiple loci that influence complex diseases. *Nat Genet*, 37:413–7.

Marchini J, Howie B, Myers S, McVean G, Donnelly P (2007). A new multipoint method for genome-wide association studies by imputation of genotypes. *Nat Genet*, 39:906–13.

Mensah FK, Gilthorpe MS, Davies CF, Keen LJ, Adamson PJ, Roman E, et al. (2007). Haplotype uncertainty in association studies. *Genet Epidemiol*, 31:348–57.

Nicodemus KK, Luna A, Shugart YY (2007). An evaluation of power and type I error of single-nucleotide polymorphism transmission/disequilibrium-based statistical methods under different family structures, missing parental data, and population stratification. *Am J Hum Genet*, 80:178–85.

Ozaki K, Ohnishi Y, Iida A, Sekine A, Yamada R, Tsunoda T et al. (2002). Functional SNPs in the lymphotoxin-alpha gene that are associated with susceptibility to myocardial infarction. *Nat Genet*, 32:650–4.

Pharoah PD, Dunning AM, Ponder BA, Easton DF (2005). The reliable identification of disease–gene associations. *Cancer Epidem Biomar*, 14:1362.

Price AL, Patterson NJ, Plenge RM, Weinblatt ME, Shadick NA, Reich D (2006). Principal components analysis corrects for stratification in genome-wide association studies. *Nat Genet*, 38:904–9.

Pritchard JK, Stephens M, Donnelly P (2000). Inference of population structure using multilocus genotype data. *Genetics*, 155:945–59.

Purcell S, Neale B, Todd-Brown K, Thomas L, Ferreira MA, Bender D et al. (2007). PLINK: a tool set for whole-genome association and population-based linkage analyses. *Am J Hum Genet*, 81:559–75.

Sabatti C, Service S, Freimer N (2003). False discovery rate in linkage and association genome screens for complex disorders. *Genetics*, 164:829–33.

Schaid DJ, Rowland CM, Tines DE, Jacobson RM, Poland GA (2002). Score tests for association between traits and haplotypes when linkage phase is ambiguous. *Am J Hum Genet*, 70:425–34.

Schork NJ, Greenwood TA, Braff DL (2007). Statistical genetics concepts and approaches in schizophrenia and related neuropsychiatric research. *Schizophr Bull*, 33:95–104.

Seaman SR, Muller-Myhsok B (2005). Rapid simulation of P values for product methods and multiple-testing adjustment in association studies. *Am J Hum Genet*, 76:399–408.

Snijders T, Bosker R (1999). Multilevel analysis: an introduction to basic and advanced multilevel modeling. London: Sage.

Spielman RS, Ewens WJ (1998). A sibship test for linkage in the presence of association: the sib transmission/disequilibrium test. *Am J Hum Genet*, 62:450–8.

Spielman RS, McGinnis RE, Ewens WJ (1993). Transmission test for linkage disequilibrium: the insulin gene region and insulin-dependent diabetes mellitus (IDDM). *Am J Hum Genet*, 52:506–16.

Storey J (2002). A direct approach to false discovery rates. *J Roy Stat Soc Ser B*, 64:479–98.

Stranger BE, Forrest MS, Clark AG, Minichiello MJ, Deutsch S, Lyle R et al. (2005). Genome-wide associations of gene expression variation in humans. *PLoS Genet*, 1(6):e78.

Sun L, Craiu RV, Paterson AD, Bull SB (2006). Stratified false discovery control for large-scale hypothesis testing with application to genome-wide association studies. *Genet Epidemiol*, 30:519–30.

Thomas DC (2006). High-volume "-omics" technologies and the future of molecular epidemiology. *Epidemiology*, 17:490–1.

Whittemore AS (2005). Genetic association studies: time for a new paradigm? *Cancer Epidemiol Biomarkers Prev*, 14:1359–60.

Zaykin DV, Zhivotovsky LA (2005). Ranks of genuine associations in whole-genome scans. *Genetics*, 171:813–23.

Zheng G, Joo J, Ganesh SK, Nabel EG, Geller NL (2005). On averaging power for genetic association and linkage studies. *Hum Hered*, 59:14–20.

3 Animal Models of Genetic Effects on Cognition

Francesco Papaleo, Daniel R. Weinberger, and Jingshan Chen

The Basic Goal of Genetic Animal Models

Although the application of genetic mouse models to behavioral disorders is at an early stage, rodent genetic manipulation offers advantages over pharmacological models because it is more selective in its molecular targets, is developmental by nature, and can be varied in terms of penetrance, allele dose, and temporal characteristics. We will begin this chapter by considering the different tests available to study cognitive functions in mice and the brain areas principally involved in each of these tasks. We will also describe the different genetic techniques available to modify specific genes potentially involved in cognitive function. We will next present some examples of specific gene modifications being carried out in mice that have been shown to play a role in cognition using the tasks explained in the second section of the chapter. We will conclude with a few words on the usefulness of the different tasks in the assessment of cognitive functions as well as their advantages and disadvantages. Until now, genetic engineering in animals for neuroscience research has been confined almost exclusively to mice. There are several reasons for this. There are a number of readily available strains of inbred mice that are homozygous at virtually all loci, making them a genetically reliable tool. The mouse genome has been extensively sequenced so it can be easily manipulated. Specific inbred strains can be selected to maximize the effect of genetic engineering. It is regrettable that mice have been studied much less completely than rats in terms of cognition, physiology, and pharmacology. It is likely that genetic manipulation of other genomes to enable the study of higher order cognition, including in rats and monkeys, will begin soon.

Methods Employed

Transgenic Mice
Overexpression of a gene of interest in a mouse is a gain-of-function approach to studying the roles of a gene in a systematic manner. It is an important approach for

dissecting a molecular pathway in cognitive function or dysfunction in a mouse model. The first transgenic mouse was successfully developed by microinjection of a cloned gene into pronuclei of fertilized mouse oocytes in 1980 (Gordon et al. 1980). Since then, engineering of the mouse genome has gone from dream to reality, and many eukaryotic genes have been introduced into the mouse genome. Transgenic mouse technology has been widely used in neuroscience research because the functions of most neural genes involved in cognition and other brain functions can be tested at the behavioral level in animal models. Many successful examples of transgenic mouse models evincing cognitive phenotypes have been reported, such as amyloid precursor protein, galanin (GAL), and CaMKII transgenic mice (Hsiao et al. 1995; Mayford et al. 1996; Steiner et al. 2001). A transgene is a simple genetic construct containing the gene of interest, a promoter sequence that will turn the gene on in situ, and a polyadenylation signal for transcription termination of the transgene. The major advantage of transgenic technology is that a genetically altered mouse can be developed in a relatively short time, approximately two to three months. It takes much longer, however, to breed and characterize the transgenic mouse. Unlike homologous-recombination-based genetic alterations, such as stem cell knockouts or knock ins (see below), the transgene randomly inserts into different sites in the mouse genome after microinjection into the oocytes, and the copy number of the transgene at each insertion site varies; different lines of the same transgenic mice show different levels and patterns of the transgene expression. Therefore, more than one line of the transgenic mouse is needed to confirm the function of the transgene. Early transgenic mouse technology used viral promoters such as the SV 40 promoter to drive expression of the transgene. Under these conditions, the transgenes were expressed ubiquitously in the whole mouse body. To express the transgene in a spatial and temporal manner, several modified transgenic mouse technologies have been developed:

Tissue-specific transgenic mouse technology Expression of a transgene in specific neurons or brain regions is important for studying the functions of neural genes. To drive neural specific transgene expression, neuron specific promoters, such as CaMKIIα neuron-specific enolase, and nestin promoters, have been widely used to develop tissues-specific transgenic mice (Forss-Petter et al. 1990; Betz et al. 1996; Chen et al. 1998). The promoters direct transgene expression in cortical, hippocampal, striatal, and cerebellar neurons. However, the promoters of most neural genes are poorly defined, and the regulatory elements for tissue-specific expression might also reside in introns or in other untranslated regions. To achieve more specific expression patterns, bacterial artificial chromosome (BAC) clones containing neural genes, which are about 100 kb long, on average, and are more likely to carry all regulatory elements for the expression of the neural genes, have been used for developing transgenic mice (Gong et al. 2003). However, BAC clones are so large that the efficiency of transgene insertion is much lower. Some BAC clones contain more than one gene, and they have to be modified to delete or disrupt the unintended gene before being introduced into the mouse genome.

Inducible transgenic mouse technology Expression of most neural genes is regulated developmentally or by neurotransmitters and neuromodulators in response to internal or external stimuli. It is important to regulate transgene expression in a temporal manner. In addition, if a transgene is expressed too early during development, compensatory changes or embryonic death might occur. The most widely applied method of inducible transgenic technology involves the tetracycline regulated gene expression system (see figure 3.1; Gossen and Bujard 1992). The tetracycline-regulated gene expression system involves two genes, one encoding the gene of interest under the control of a tetracycline-responsive promoter (TetP) and the other one encoding an artificial transcription factor, tetracycline transactivator (tTA). tTA expression is necessary for activation of the TetP and, thus, expression of the transgene. Activity of tTA is in turn suppressed by tetracycline or doxycycline, an analog of tetracycline with 1,000-fold higher affinity to tTA and higher blood–brain barrier permeability than

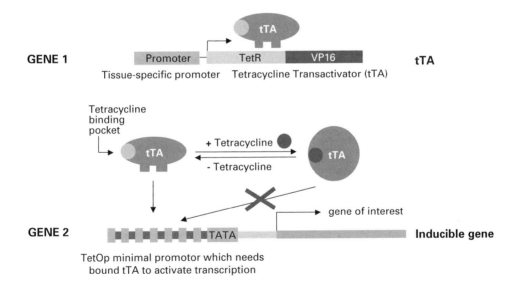

Figure 3.1
Schematic diagram of a tissue-specific tetracycline-regulated gene expression system. Gene 1 encodes tTA under the control of a tissue-specific promoter. Gene 2 encodes the gene of interest under the control of the tetracycline-responsive promoter, TetOp. Mating of mice carrying one or the other of these genes results in offspring with the genes of interest under the control of the tetracycline-regulated promoter.

tetracycline. Thus, adding doxycycline to the drinking water or food suppresses the transgene expression. This technology has been successfully applied to the development of inducible transgenic mice carrying CaMKII, Δ FosB, CREB, and other neural genes (Mayford et al. 1996; Chen et al. 1998; Sakai et al. 2002). A reverse tTA (rtTA) gene regulation system, which is activated by tetracycline, also has been successfully applied to the development of calcineurin transgenic mice (Mansuy et al. 1998). However, leaky expression of the rtTA system and requirement of high doses of doxycycline to activate the rtTA have raised concerns about the rtTA system. Other inducible gene expression systems have also been applied to transgenic animal models, but they are not used as widely as the tetracycline-regulated inducible gene expression system.

"Humanized" transgenic mouse technology   Although humans and mice share about 70% of their DNA sequences, there are major differerences in many genes and there are many human- or primate-specific isoforms of neural genes. It is important to humanize those genes in mice for studying their functions at the behavioral level and for testing drugs specific for human drug targets. To develop animal models for testing human-specific genes or human-specific isoforms, human genes are introduced into the mouse using transgenic technology. Thus, transgenic mice will express the human gene and serve as an important tool for research and drug development (Akassoglou et al. 2003; Miksys et al. 2005). Introduction of the human transgene into a mouse with targeted disruption of the endogenous mouse homologue will generate a genetically modified mouse with exclusively the humanized gene.

Targeted Gene Knockout Mice

Loss of function is another approach to study the role of neural genes in cognition and other brain functions. Genetic manipulation of mouse embryonic stem (ES) cells by homologous recombination in cell culture and inhibition of ES cell differentiation by leukemia inhibitory factor to keep the ES cells at a pluripotent stage are important steps toward the development of targeted gene knockout mice. ES cells with a disrupted target gene by homologous recombination are selected by drug resistance and screening with long polymerase chain reaction or Southern blotting. The selected ES cells are introduced into a foster mom by blastocyst injection to generate chimeric mice, which are then bred with wild-type mice to generate knockout mice. The first targeted gene knockout mouse was developed in 1987 (Thomas and Capecchi 1987). There are several targeted gene knockout technologies that can be used to knock out a gene completely, partially, tissue-specifically, or randomly or to replace a wild-type gene with a small mutation:

Traditional knockout technology   To knock out a specific gene completely, genomic DNA of the gene is first cloned and a major component of the gene such as start codon in the cloned genomic DNA fragment is mutated usually by a deletion mutation to abolish translation (see figure 3.2). A drug selection gene such as neomycin resistance gene (neo) is also introduced so that ES cells carrying the knockout mutant construct will survive in cell culture containing neomycin while other cells will not. The knockout mutant construct consists of two fragments of the cloned genomic DNA flanking at both ends of the selection gene, and one of the fragments contains the mutation. When homologous recombination occurs in the ES cells during mitosis, the wild-type DNA of the targeted gene is replaced with the mutant DNA. Many neural genes including neurotrophic factors, neurotransmitter receptors, and other genes important for neuronal functions have been knocked out with this technology (Forrest et al. 1994; Li et al. 1994; Conover et al. 1995; Picciotto et al. 1998).

Conditional knockout technology   The major problem of the traditional knockout technology is that the genes are knocked out at an early developmental stage, which may result in compensational changes or embryonic death if the gene is important for embryo development. A gene recombination system, cre and loxP, derived from bacteriophage was applied to knock out a gene at a specific stage during development (Gu et al. 1994). Cre is a recombinase, which can recognize a specific DNA sequence, named the LoxP element, and catalyze the recombination of two LoxP elements to

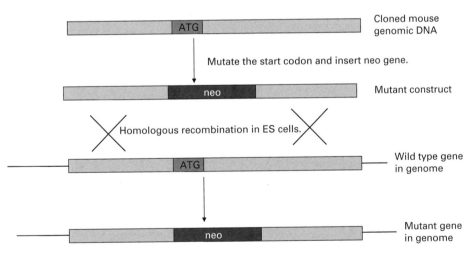

Figure 3.2
Schematic diagram of targeted gene knockout by homologous recombination. Cloned mouse genomic DNA, usually containing the start codon ATG of a specific gene, is mutated by introduction of the drug selection gene, neo (neomycin), to replace a genomic DNA fragment containing the translation start codon, ATG. The mutant construct is introduced into mouse embryonic stem (ES) cells by stable transfection. Homologous recombination within the ES cells results in the mutant ES cells carrying the mutant gene in its genome.

remove the DNA sequence between them. To knock out a specific portion of a gene, two loxP sites are introduced into the genetic construct to flank the portion of the gene, now named a floxed gene. The two loxP sites are usually placed in introns so that they do not alter coding sequences. Mice carrying the floxed targeted gene are generated using traditional knockout technology, and the wild-type gene product is produced in the mouse because the two loxP sites are placed in introns. This mouse is then mated with another mouse line created to express the cre gene driven by a tissue-specific promoter. Thus, recombination between the two loxP sites occurs and the portion of the targeted gene is excised, but only in tissues that express the cre gene, which is named a conditional knockout (see figure 3.3). Conditional knockout of the N-methyl-D-aspartate receptor 1 (NMDAR1) gene is an example of application of the cre/loxP system in a mouse model that has been used to study cognition (Li et al. 1994). Another recombination system, called flp/frt, which is similar to the cre/loxP system, is also used to develop conditional knockout mouse (Meyers et al. 1998).
Gene trapped knockout mouse technology To knock out genes on a large scale, gene trapped knockout technology was developed. This approach utilizes random insertion of a drug resistance gene such as the neo gene lacking a promoter or polyadenylation signal into the mouse genome to trap the native promoter or polyadenylation signal of a gene disrupted due to the insertion of the drug resistance gene (see figure 3.4). The drug selection gene utilizes the promoter or poly(A) signal of the disrupted gene

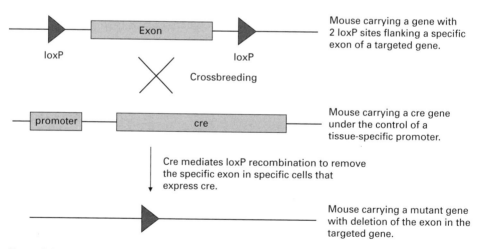

Figure 3.3
Schematic diagram of conditional gene knockout using the cre/loxP recombination system. A mouse carrying the floxed targeted gene and a mouse carrying a cre gene under the control of a tissue-specific promoter are crossbred to bring the two genes together. Recombination between the two loxP sites occurs in the cells expressing cre and the targeted gene is disrupted.

A. Promoter trap:

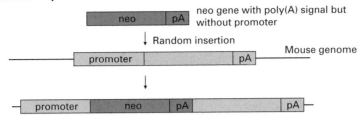

B. Polyadenylation signal trap:

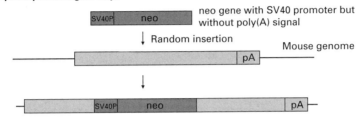

Figure 3.4
Schematic diagram of gene knockout using gene trap technology. (A) A neo gene with a polyadenylation signal (pA) but without a promoter is introduced into a mouse embryonic stem (ES) cell by transfection, and the neo gene construct randomly inserts into the mouse genome in the ES cells. The neo gene utilizes the promoter of the disrupted gene to express and gives the ES cell clone neomycin resistance. (B) A neo gene with an SV40 promoter but without polyadenylation signal is introduced into mouse ES cells by transfection, and the neo gene construct randomly inserts into the mouse genome in the ES cells. The neo gene utilizes the pA signal of the disrupted gene for expression and gives the ES cell clone neomycin resistance.

in stable transfected mouse ES cells, so that the ES cell clone with the trapped disrupted gene can survive in a neomycin selection medium (von Melchner et al. 1992; Niwa et al. 1993). The reason to use the poly(A) signal to trap the disrupted gene is that many promoters are not active in ES cells. Theoretically, all genes can be knocked out randomly using this strategy. However, only about 50% of the genes in the mouse genome have been knocked out so far using gene trapped technology.

Knock-in mouse technology   Most genetic mutations associated with common diseases do not involve a complete knockout of a gene. To more precisely mimic a genetic mutation for a disease or for susceptibility to it, less deleterious mutations have to be introduced into the mouse genome using knock-in technology, which is similar to knockout technology using homologous recombination to introduce mutations into the specific targeted gene (Geng et al. 1999). The major difference is that most of the coding sequence is intact except the small mutation, and the drug selection gene is usually placed in an intron.

National Institutes of Health (NIH) knockout mouse initiatives   Developing a knockout mouse is usually very time-consuming and expensive. It would take even more effort if more than one gene will be brought together by crossbreeding for studying gene–gene interactions. To meet the expanding needs of the research community, the NIH started new animal model initiatives as parts of the NIH Blueprint for Neuroscience Research in an effort to knock out all mouse genes including psychiatric disorder susceptibility genes and to make all knockout mice available to the research community (http://neuroscienceblueprint.nih.gov/neuroscience_resources/animal_models.htm#rodents). Although most of the new initiatives are at their infant stages, some knockout mice or ES cell clones are already available to the research community, distributed by animal centers established by or contracted with NIH.

Behavioral Tests
We describe below the standard approaches to testing cognition in mice. We will not discuss tests of other psychological functions, such as emotion and sensory processing, but it should be noted that genetic manipulation of these functions may also impact on cognition.

Declarative Memory
Morris Water Maze   Currently, the most frequently used paradigm to evaluate learning and memory abilities in rodents is the Morris water maze task. This task is based on the principle that rodents are highly motivated to escape from a water environment by the quickest, most direct route. In this task, the mice are expected to learn the location of a hidden platform submerged in opaque water based on spatial extramaze cues. A step-by-step description of the procedures can be found elsewhere (Crawley 2007). After a period of habituation, mice are trained to locate a visible platform, to test their visual and motor ability, and then they are trained to locate a hidden platform. Over the course of training, mice will swim to the hidden platform with an increasingly direct swim pathway and a diminishing latency to reach the platform. Training sessions are conducted on consecutive days until the established acquisition criteria are reached by the mice (e.g., the latencies to reach the hidden platform must be shorter than a prefixed timing). After the training days, each mouse is tested in a probe trial, in which the platform is removed from the pool and each mouse is tested as in the training. Search time spent in the trained quadrant must be significantly greater than search time spent in the other quadrants of the pool in order to conclude that environmental spatial cues were learned and remembered as the specific strategy for locating the hidden platform. Swim speed and swim pathway provide measures of the procedural abilities of the mouse to perform the task. Probe trials without additional training can be conducted at chosen time points after the end of training, to

evaluate retention (forgetting).The Morris task cannot be used to measure learning and memory in mice with impaired swimming abilities. Moreover, it is among the most stressful cognitive tests for mice. Lesion studies revealed that spatial learning in the water maze task is dependent on hippocampus (Morris et al. 1982) and nucleus accumbens (Annett et al. 1989).

Cued and Contextual Fear Conditioning   This task measures the ability of the mouse to learn and remember an association between an aversive experience and environmental cues (Fanselow 1980; LeDoux 1995). Cued and contextual conditioning requires a different set of sensory and motor abilities compared to the Morris water maze. The parameter measured in this task is freezing behavior, a common response to fearful situations in mice as well as many other species, defined as no movement other than respiration. In the first stage, or the conditioning training, the mouse is placed in a chamber and exposed to a mild footshock paired with an auditory cue. Time spent freezing in this phase is considered the measure of unconditioned fear. Twenty-four hours after the conditioning session, the mouse is returned to the same chamber and the freezing behavior is scored. The time spent freezing in this stage is considered to be the measure of contextually conditioned fear. An hour later, the mouse is placed in a new chamber differing from the first for shape, visual cues, lighting, olfactory cues, and floor surface texture. Freezing behavior in this chamber is scored before and during the presentation of the auditory cue previously associated with the footshock. Freezing is expected to be minimal in the new altered context and to increase suddenly when the mouse is presented with the conditioned sound, demonstrating a cued conditioning. In order to properly evaluate memory performance in mutant mice, a careful examination of sensory and motor abilities, such as pain threshold, hearing, vision, smell, neuromuscular dysfunctions, subthreshold seizures, or sedation, is required (Crawley 2007). An advantage of this task is that specific impairment or improvement of the contextual and/or the cued fear conditioning can yield information about neuroanatomy, neurotransmitters, and gene regulating emotional components of memory. This test also enables the dissection of different phases of memory formation, including acquisition, consolidation, and extinction. The area of the brain that seems to be mainly involved in cued and contextual fear conditioning in rodents is the amygdala (LeDoux 1995; LeDoux 1996; Fanselow and Poulos 2005), but the involvement of the hippocampus is also important as indicated by the disruption of recent but not remote contextual fear memories by posttraining lesions of the hippocampus (Kim and Fanselow 1992; Anagnostaras et al. 1999). The subiculum, cingulated cortex, prefrontal cortex, perirhinal cortex, and sensory cortex, as well as the medial temporal lobe, also appear to mediate components of contextual fear conditioning (Eichenbaum et al. 1996; Squire and Zola 1996; Logue et al. 1997).

Passive and Active Avoidance   Avoidance learning requires that a subject learn that a certain response will result in the termination or prevention of an aversive stimulus. The stimulus typically used in this task is a mild footshock; the response is the avoidance of the location in which the footshock was received. Passive avoidance tasks require the mouse to refrain from entering the chamber in which the aversive stimulus was previously delivered. Active avoidance tasks require the mouse to exit from the chamber in which the aversive stimulus was delivered. General deficits in vision, altered pain threshold, sedation, and motor impairments could interfere with the procedural components of this task.

Y-Maze   The Y-maze recognition task is believed to be a specific and sensitive test of memory that is useful when it is necessary to minimize the confounding influences of nonspecific factors such as those generated in tasks involving deprivation, electric footshock, motoric demands, and so on. Constant proximal and distal visual cues may be placed around the apparatus. The experiment consists of two trials that are separated by a designated intertrial time interval (thirty minutes up to six hours). During the acquisition phase, trial 1, one arm is blocked and referred to as the *novel arm* in trial 2. The position of the closed arm is chosen randomly among the three arms. Mice are allowed to explore the two open arms of the maze for five to fifteen minutes. During the retrieval phase, trial 2, the door that previously blocked one of the arms is removed. The percentage of visits and time spent in the novel arm are compared to random exploration (33%) of the three arms of the maze. The dependent variables measured in trial 2 are (1) first arm entered (between the novel and other arm), (2) the percentage of time spent in each arm for each minute, and (3) the percentage of entries made into each arm for each minute. The Y-maze has been proven to be a hippocampal-dependent spatial memory task.

Barnes Maze   This test takes advantage of the superior abilities of mice to find and escape through small holes. Mice are motivated to escape from a brightly lit, open platform into a small, dark, enclosed box. In the open platform several holes are present. One of those holes opens into a hidden dark box. The mouse learns the spatial location of this exit hole. In contrast to other maze tasks, dietary restriction is not necessary and the dry-land environment is less stressful than that of the Morris swim task (Mayford et al. 1996). As in the Morris water maze, a cued version of the task is used to test general sensorimotor activity of each subject. Apart from the time and distance that the mice need to solve the task, the strategies used by the animal to perform the task can reflect different cognitive processes (for the different strategies, see Barnes 1979).

Social Transmission of Food Preference (STFP) Task   Rodents have a very highly developed olfactory sense. Olfactory discrimination tasks are excellent measures of learning and memory in rats and mice (Eichenbaum et al. 1988; Staubli et al. 1989; Zhang et al. 1998). The STFP is based on the ability of rats to use olfactory cues to transmit food preferences to each other (Ross and Eichenbaum 2006). In this test, animals are required to remember the scent of food smelled on the muzzle of a "demonstrator" mouse earlier. Retention time between the observation session and the choice session is either zero (immediately thereafter) or twenty-four hours later, providing a procedural control and a delay condition. When offered a choice of the flavored food eaten by the demonstrator mouse (cued food) or another novel-flavored food, mice with normal olfactory memory will eat a greater proportion of the familiar cued food than of the novel food. Hippocampal lesions severely impair choice accuracy in this task in rats (Bunsey and Eichenbaum 1995).

Working Memory

T-Maze   In maze learning tasks mice are trained to choose specific arm(s) of the maze to receive reinforcement (food or water) or to avoid footshock. One of the most common tests used to assess prefrontal cortex (PFC)-sensitive working memory in rodents is the T-maze. The T-shaped apparatus is composed of a "starting" alley and two side alleys at the end, in one of which reinforcement (food or sweet solution) is hidden. To motivate the animals to work for these tasks, they are maintained on either a food-restricted or water-restricted diet. Mice are first habituated to the maze so they get used to running to the ends of the alleys to obtain the reinforcer. Different paradigms have been developed to address different kinds of cognitive functions. In the continuous delayed alternation T-maze task, mice are trained to enter and retrieve the reinforcement in the arm opposite to the one they successfully entered on the previous trial. Due to its repetitive nature, this is not the best paradigm to study working memory (Green and Stanton 1989). Moreover, it is sensitive to both frontal cortex and hippocampus lesions (Thompson 1981; Brito and Brito 1990).

The T-maze discrete paired-trial variable-delay alternation task has been established to most closely model important elements of working memory tasks used in studies of human and nonhuman primates. This task requires constant updating of information and response on a trial-by-trial basis (Aultman and Moghaddam 2001). Animals are presented with a sequence of discrete trial pairs in which a randomly chosen forced run is followed by a choice run. In the forced run, the animals are given access to only one arm of the maze and rewarded after entering that arm. After an *intratrial delay*, they are presented with the choice run, during which they have access to both arms and are rewarded (having made the "correct" choice) after entering the arm not entered on the previous forced run. After this choice run and an *intertrial delay*, animals are exposed to the next forced run, and so on. The same intratrial and intertrial delays are used during the training phase. After reaching a prefixed criterion (e.g., more than or equal to 80% correct choices in three consecutive days) mice are tested at different intratrial delays presented randomly. This task has been used to test working memory in rats, as well. As in rats, lesion of the medial PFC in mice significantly increases the number of days required to reach criterion (Kellendonk et al. 2006).

Radial Maze   The radial maze is composed of eight arms radiating from a central platform. As in T-maze paradigms, dietary restriction is used to help motivate learning. As usual, at first the animals are habituated to the maze and to the presence of food at the ends of each of the arms of the apparatus. Correct arm choices are those that are visited once to obtain the reinforcement. Visiting a specific arm more than once, where food has already been obtained and the arm is now empty, is considered an incorrect response. Alternatively, only some of the arms are baited with food, requiring the animal to learn the location of the baited versus unbaited arms and also to learn not to return to an arm already visited. Time to complete the task is recorded and considered as another measure of acquisition.

A different version, called "eight-arm radial maze delayed nonmatch to sample," or "win-shift," has been used to specifically address working memory performances (Seamans and Phillips 1994; Seamans et al. 1995). In each trial there are two phases: the training and testing separated by a delay. During the training phase, four out of the eight arms are open, and four closed, and the rodent has to retrieve the food reward from the open alleys. A new set of four arms is baited each day. After a delay period in the home cage, the mouse is put into the maze where all arms are open, but only the previously blocked arms contain food reinforcement (test phase). In this phase, any reentry into an arm that was entered earlier during the training phase is indicated as an *across-phase* error, and any reentry into an arm that has been entered earlier during the test phase is defined as *within-phase* error. The time taken to retrieve the first reinforcement and the time to complete the two phases of the task are recorded along with the errors. Days to reach prefixed criteria and percentage of mice able to learn the task together constitute an index of the cognitive performance of the animals in this paradigm.

In the "random foraging task" the mice are not provided with any previous information about the location of food in the maze, permitting researchers to assess the mice's ability to acquire or use within-trial information (Seamans et al. 1995). In each trial, four different arms of the eight-arm maze are baited randomly. During every trial, the number and order of arm choices are recorded. Animals are trained until they reach a criterion of one revisit error or fewer for three consecutive days. Errors and times are recorded as in the win-shift version. Transient lesions of the nucleus accumbens and prelimbic area of the PFC impair performance in different versions of the win-shift radial-arm maze task (Seamans and Phillips 1994). However, similar lesions to the prelimbic cortex do not affect animals' performance in a random foraging task. This evidence suggests that the prelimbic cortex is responsible for utilizing previously acquired information to generate a prospective sequence of responses. In contrast, fornix, hippocampus (McDonald and White 1993), and ventral CA1/subiculum are involved in the performance of both the delayed spatial win-shift and random foraging procedures (Floresco et al. 1997).

Morris Water Maze   Different variations of the Morris water maze task have also been developed to address working memory functions in rats and mice (Varvel et al. 2001). In one variation, the platform is randomly located in a different location on each day, and the test is based on a series of two paired trials. In these two trials, separated by a defined delay, the platform is located in the same position and the mouse is released into the water from the same point. If shorter latency to swim to the platform and smaller path length traveled is observed in the second trial as compared to the first, it may be concluded that the rodent had learned the location of the hidden platform, which can be used as an index of the rodent's working memory abilities. Although this version of the Morris water maze task has been used to assess working memory, it is unclear whether the task is primarily dependent on prefrontal or hippocampal function.

Another working memory version of the water maze has been developed by Buresova and colleagues (Buresova et al. 1985). In this experiment, the researchers constructed an eight-arm radial maze within a water maze, and the rat's task consisted of swimming to the end of each arm to a submerged bench. This bench would provide the mice with refuge from the water for twenty seconds, and then it would collapse, forcing the rat to swim to a different maze arm. In this study memory for the visited arms was tested by introducing a delay (forty to 1,280 minutes) between the fourth and fifth arm choices. Again, whether this task is primarily dependent on prefrontal or hippocampal processing has not been established.

Odor Span Task   This task assesses the ability of rodents to remember an increasing number of odors and has been used in both rats and mice (Dudchenko et al. 2000; Young et al. 2007a). In successive discrete trials, food-restricted mice are presented with an increasing number of bowls containing sand scented with different odors. The positive reinforcement is always hidden in the cup scented with the new odor.

Recognition Memory
Object Recognition   In an open field arena, an object (A) or pair of identical objects is presented for a brief period to the mouse. After a delay (ranging from one minute to twenty-four hours), the mouse is brought back to the arena, which contains a duplicate of object A and a novel object (object B). The mouse's natural tendency is to explore the novel object, B, more than the (presumably) familiar object, A. A preference index, a ratio of the amount of time spent exploring the novel object over the

total time spent exploring both objects, is used to measure recognition memory. In this test, cognitive performance does not depend on the retention of a rule, nor on positive or negative reinforcers, and exploits the natural tendency of rodents to explore the environment; cognitive performance in this test primarily involves prefrontal and perirhinal cortex regions and is relatively hippocampal independent (Morrow et al. 2000; Mumby 2001).

Social Recognition   Social recognition tests use the animals' natural tendency towards olfactory investigation of novel conspecifics (Crawley 2007). Social cognition/social discrimination is a specific type of memory that differs from other types of learning and memory. The parameter used to quantify social recognition behaviors is the time spent by the tested subject investigating another animal (stimulus). Anogenital and head sniffing, as well as close following, are considered olfactory investigations. Social recognition tasks use two paradigms:

Habituation–dishabituation paradigm   When one stimulus animal is presented repeatedly to the tested animal, the time spent in investigation gradually decreases, but when a novel animal is presented, the time spent in investigation by the test animal returns to its original level.

Social discrimination paradigm   The test animal is exposed to the stimulus animal and then, after a certain interval, simultaneously presented with the now-familiar conspecific and a novel stranger. Normally, the test animal will spend significantly more time investigating the novel stranger mouse as compared to the habituated original animal.

Instrumental Learning   An operant conditioning chamber (or Skinner box) is an automated laboratory apparatus that presents one or more operanda. This apparatus can automatically detect the occurrence of a behavioral response or action. Typical operanda for mice are nose pokes into holes, and correct action is followed by the delivery of food pellets or liquid diet reinforcers in a trough. Food or water restriction is usually employed. These tasks present several advantages over other learning paradigms, such as strict experimental control and high levels of precision. Moreover, complete automation reduces the labor-intensive nature of the other memory tasks and reduces the manipulation and stress of the subjects tested. Furthermore, operant behavioral tasks are ductile and allow studying several cognitive functions that include working memory, visuospatial attention/sustained attention, reversal flexibility, motivational state, decision making, and impulsivity–compulsivity.

Working Memory Paradigms   Delayed matching to sample (DMTS) and delayed non-matching to sample (DNMTS) position tasks have been developed (Dunnett 1993). A trial begins with the illumination of one of two holes inside the operant chamber (sample phase). After the mouse pokes into the illuminated hole, a delay ensues. During the delay, the mouse is required to make a nose poke into a trough, which results in the illumination of the two holes (choice phase). Under matching conditions, the mouse is reinforced for a poke in the hole that had been illuminated as the sample. In the nonmatching version of the task, the mouse is reinforced for pokes into the hole that had not been presented before. The use of a nose poke response into the trough is designed to reduce postural mediation responses during the delay period, which can weaken any interpretation of performance as pure memory (Chudasama and Muir 1997). The disruption of the septo-hippocampal system has been found to induce delay-dependent accuracy deficits. Nucleus basalis magnocellularis lesions, on the other hand, induce either delay-independent deficits, transient effects, or no accuracy deficits, suggesting a role in nonmnemonic cognitive processes. Finally, lesions of the pedunculopontine tegmental nucleus affected neither working memory nor nonmnemonic cognitive functions on this task but altered responsivity.

Delayed Comparison Procedures   A different paradigm which is not affected by postural mediation responses is the delayed comparison task in which the tested subjects cannot determine the correct response until after the retention interval. For example, in a typical DMTS experimental procedure, a sample stimulus consisting of the red light is presented (e.g., a red light, center location), followed by a retention interval (delay), and, subsequently, by the presentation of choice stimuli (e.g., red, yellow, and green lights in the left, center, and right locations, respectively). The subject exhibits memory for the sample stimulus by successfully identifying the choice stimulus that matches the sample and selectively responding at the location of that stimulus (in the present example, red, left location). Since the location of the correct comparison stimulus is not known to the subject until after the delay, the subject cannot "bridge" this delay by orienting itself towards the correct location. A new intriguing variant of this task is the visual touchscreen procedure recently validated in mice (Izquierdo et al. 2006).

Attention   The five-choice serial reaction time task (5-CSRT) is used to assess sustained attention in rodents (Muir et al. 1996; Baunez and Robbins 1999; Young et al. 2007b) and is analogous to continuous performance used in human studies of attentional processes (Jones and Higgins 1995). Attentional task requires the mouse to simultaneously monitor the light signals over or inside five holes positioned on a wall of an operant chamber. During the task, one of the lights is illuminated briefly, and mice are trained to respond with a nose poke in the hole corresponding to the light. Following a correct response, liquid or food reinforcement is delivered in a dispenser situated in the opposite wall. Different parameters are measured in this task:

Accuracy (percentage of correct responses) $100 \times$ correct responses/(correct + incorrect responses).

Percentage of omission errors (omissions) $100 \times$ omission errors/stimuli presented.

Latency of correct responses   The mean time between stimulus onset and a nose poke in the correct hole.

Anticipatory response rate   The total number of responses in all intertrial intervals (ITIs) of a session/number of trials/ITI length(s). Premature responses occur inappropriately, before the visual targets have displayed, and are considered as an index of impulsive behavior (Evenden 1999).

Perseverative behavior   Animals continue to respond either at the aperture where responding has just happened or at other locations; this is usually used as an index of "compulsive" behavior.

Thus, the 5-CSRT is capable of measuring several different types of performance that include aspects of attention and impulse control. Several lesion studies have supported the previously assumed notion that the anterior cortex (especially medial PFC) plays a principal role in the completion of the 5-CSRT. Furthermore, the hippocampus seems to have relative little impact on different parameters of this task (for review, see Robbins 2002).

Extinction   This is the phenomenon in which a reinforcer (e.g., food or shock) associated with learning a particular task or response is omitted or withdrawn and the response is diminished. In particular, extinction of the conditioned freezing behavior can be studied in the "cued and contextual conditioning" paradigm by repeatedly placing the mouse into the altered new context and presenting it with the conditioned cue. The progressively decreased manifestation of conditioned freezing behavior constitutes an index of extinction.

Reversal and Change in Habits   Reversal learning involves the adaptation of behavior according to new stimulus–reward contingencies. This is a form of cognitive flexibility that focuses on the ability of the subject to disengage a previously learned rule and follow new, opposite rules to solve a specific cognitive task. Reversal learning can be applied to most of the tasks described in this chapter after a particular exercise has been learned. The number of trials and the duration of time necessary to relearn the new reinforcement contingencies as well as the reaction time and/or latency in understanding the new rule of the task serve as indices of reversal learning. Reversal learning is disrupted by lesions of the orbitofrontal cortex in rodents and nonhuman primates (Iversen and Mishkin 1970; Jones and Mishkin 1972; Dias et al. 1996). Lesions to the ventral striatum also disrupt reversal learning, leading to a perseverative response tendency (Taghzouti et al. 1985; Annett et al. 1989; Stern and Passingham 1995).

Shifting and Flexibility

Attentional Set Shifting Task (Digging Version)   Recently, researchers have been focusing on tests which can assess the ability to shift a cognitive set in rodents as analogous to the Wisconsin Card Sorting Test in humans. In rats, an extremely successful test was validated by Birrel and Brown (2000). In this test, rats are trained to dig in bowls to retrieve a food reward. The bowls are presented in pairs, only one of which is baited. The rodent has to select the bowl in which to dig by a sensory dimension such as its odor, the medium that fills the bowl, or the texture of the surface of its cover. In a single session, rats perform a series of discriminations, including reversals, and an intra- and extradimensional shift. Lesions of medial frontal cortex result in the selective impairment of the extradimensional shifting, in which the animals have to understand that the previously relevant dimension is now irrelevant. Orbital prefrontal cortex lesions produce a selective impairment in reversal learning without affecting acquisition, maintenance, and shift of the attentional set. Despite several attempts, only one study so far has demonstrated internal construct and predictive validity of this task also in mice (Garner et al. 2006).

Maze-Based Set-Shifting Task   The apparatus used in this task is a four-arm cross maze that is convertible into a T-maze. The cross shape of the maze allows the experimenter to randomly change the arms used, avoiding mediation of the behavior by external cues. Rats are first trained to retrieve reinforcement at the end of one arm following a response rule (turning left or right). Visual cues are also randomly placed in one of the arms on each trial but do not reliably predict the correct choice (only a confounding irrelevant factor). Between trials, rats are placed back in the holding cage with the possibility of varying the intertrial delay, affecting the memory load. The day after the animals learn the response rule, they are tested in a set-shift paradigm in which they are required to use the visual-cue discrimination strategy instead of the left or right turn to retrieve the food reinforcement. Thus, the rat must shift from the old strategy and attend to the previously irrelevant cue in order to obtain reinforcement. The opposite scheme, training under a visual-cue discrimination strategy and testing set shifting to the turning right–left rule, is also possible. Measurements recorded to evaluate the cognitive function of each rat tested are trials to criterion, time taken to complete the training phase, and incorrect arms entries, which are broken down into perseverative, regressive, and "never-reinforced" errors (Floresco and Magyar 2006). The combination of regressive and never reinforced errors has been used as an index of the animals' ability to engage in and maintain a new strategy. Inactivation of the PFC causes a selective increase in perseverative errors (Ragozzino et al. 1999), whereas inactivation of the dorsomedial striatum yields an increase in regressive errors (Ragozzino et al. 2002). Furthermore, it has been shown that both the nucleus accumbens core and mediodorsal thalamus play a role in this task, inducing different patterns of errors (Floresco and Magyar 2006).

Decision Making, Reaction Time   Decision making is a high-level cognitive process that relates to everyday choices according to long-term and short-term outcomes inter-relationships. It depends on systems responsible for memory as well as those for emotion and affect. With some limitations, different components of human decision-making tasks can be modeled using tasks designed for rodents.

"Delay discounting" tasks are used as a measure of impulsive decision making where "response costs" are varied by imposing a delay before delivery of larger reward versus obtaining an immediate, smaller reward (Evenden and Ryan 1996). Lesions of the core region of the nucleus accumbens increase delay discounting and cause a preference for a smaller immediate reward (Cardinal et al. 2001; van Gaalen et al. 2006), while orbital PFC lesions may both decrease or increase impulsive choice, depending on whether training occurred pre- or postoperatively (Mobini et al. 2002; Winstanley et al. 2004). Lesions to either the prelimbic or anteriorcingulate regions of the medial PFC, however, do not alter this form of decision making (Cardinal et al. 2001).

In "effort-based decision-making" tasks, rats have to choose between a small reward in one arm of a T-maze and a larger reward placed behind a barrier in the other arm. Over the course of training, rats exhibit a preference to exert a greater effort and climb the barrier to obtain a larger reward. Lesions of the anterior cingulate region of the rat medial PFC impair effort-based decision making in a manner similar to that observed after dopamine depletion of the nucleus accumbens, whereas lesions of the prelimbic cortex have no effect (Walton et al. 2002; Walton et al. 2003; Schweimer and Hauber 2005).

A "conditioned punishment" paradigm for rodents modeling the human Iowa Gambling Task has also been developed (Killcross et al. 1997). In this operant task, rats learn to not press one lever that was previously associated with a conditioned aversive tone–shock pairing. During the extinction phase of the test, rats press for food as normal, but pressing one lever now results in the presentation of the negative secondary reinforcement—the conditional stimulus (CS) associated with shock. Intact animals again choose to direct their responding away from the lever producing the aversive CS in the absence of primary aversive stimulus. Lesions of the basolateral amygdala, lesions of the infralimbic region of the medial PFC, or disconnections between these two regions disrupt the ability of the aversive CS to bias the direction of instrumental responding, causing rats to respond on both levers equally (Killcross et al. 1997; Coutureau et al. 2000).

Examples of Mice with Genetic Alterations That Impact Cognition

Calcium/Calmodulin-Dependent Protein Kinase II

The calcium/calmodulin-dependent protein kinase II α (αCaMKII) is expressed in the neurons of the forebrain, and it has been implicated in the neurobiology of memory.

Several αCaMKII mutants have been generated and studied primarily in hippocampus-dependent learning and memory tasks. αCaMKII null mutant mice are impaired in spatial learning as shown in the Morris water maze and fear conditioning tasks (Silva et al. 1992; Silva et al. 1996; Elgersma et al. 2002). However, some learning in these animals is still present after intensive training, and interestingly, αCaMKII heterozygous mice show specific memory loss at long retention delays (Frankland et al. 2001). Using knock-in technology, different lines of mice carrying mutations of the endogenous αCaMKII gene have also been generated (Giese et al. 1998; Elgersma et al. 2002; Miller et al. 2002; Need and Giese 2003). Severe impairment in spatial Morris water maze learning that cannot be ameliorated by overtraining or by environmental enrichment has been found. Moreover, specific molecular characteristics (e.g., phosphorylation of Thr305) seem to be crucial for the reversal learning and contextual discrimination (Elgersma et al. 2002).

The overexpression of αCaMKII also severely affects learning in hippocampus-dependent tasks, such as the Morris water maze, the Barnes maze and contextual conditioning (Bach et al. 1995; Mayford et al. 1996; Bejar et al. 2002; Wang et al. 2003). The αCaMKII transgene activation during the first period after learning specifically impairs recall (Mayford et al. 1996; Wang et al. 2003), which further supports a role of αCaMKII in memory consolidation and/or retrieval. Despite the evidence of severe deficits in hippocampus-dependent learning tasks, no deficit was shown in visible platform water maze, plus maze, cued Barnes maze, olfactory discrimination, the acquisition of instrumental conditioning, and the accelerating rotarod (Silva et al. 1992; Bach et al. 1995; Giese et al. 1998; Wiedenmayer et al. 2000; Elgersma et al. 2002; Elgersma et al. 2004).

Corticotropin-Releasing Factor System

The corticotropin-releasing factor (CRF) system is a major coordinator of endocrine, autonomic, and behavioral responses to stress. Altered CRF levels in cerebrospinal fluid and cerebral cortex tissues have been linked with cognitive impairment in Alzheimer's disease patients. Moreover, decreased amygdala CRF-binding protein messenger RNA was found in postmortem tissue from male bipolar and schizophrenic subjects (Herringa et al. 2006). Mice overexpressing CRF (CRF-tg) are slower than their wild type in solving the Morris water maze task and do not display any improvement over subsequent experimental days. It has been hypothesized that the hyperemotional phenotype of the CRF-tg mice is the principal cause of their poor cognitive performance, because after treatment with the benzodiazepine chlordiazepoxide, retention memory improves (Heinrichs et al. 1996). It has also recently been shown that CRF-tg mice manifest attentional impairments when tested on a 5-CSRT. However, these deficits are independent of alterations in anxiety-like behavior (van Gaalen et al. 2003). Further support for an important role for CRF pathways in cognitive function was provided by the findings of disrupted spatial memory processes in null mutant mice for the receptor 1 of the CRF (CRF$_1$-/-). In particular, the CRF$_1$-/- mice showed no increase in exploration of the novel arm during the retrieval trial of a Y-maze task (Contarino et al. 1999).

Dopamine System

Several components of the dopamine system are thought to play a crucial role in the modulation of various aspects of learning and memory processes. Moreover, dopaminergic dysfunctions, possibly coming from genetic factors, have been associated with cognitive abnormalities in schizophrenia (Winterer and Weinberger 2004), attention-deficit/hyperactivity disorder (DiMaio et al. 2003), Alzheimer's disease (Holmes et al. 2001), Parkinson's disease (Benmoyal-Segal and Soreq 2006), and addiction (Haile et al. 2007).

Dopamine mediates its neural effects via actions at either presynaptic and postsynaptic dopamine D1-like receptors (D1 and D5) or D2-like receptors (D2, D3, or D4). Mice lacking a functional D1 receptor (D1-/-) needed a longer time to find and climb onto the hidden platform in the Morris water maze compared to their D1+/+ and D1+/- littermates. This same deficit was also present in the cued trials, which use a visible platform. D1-/- mice also have ambulatory and visual problems in addition to being smaller and having a lower body weight. (Smith et al. 1998; El-Ghundi et al. 1999). Thus, the effect of D1 genetic manipulation on spatial learning and memory is still uncertain, and future works must take into account these phenotypic abnormalities when selecting behavioral tasks. Despite this, D1 knockout mice showed normal performance in contextual fear conditioning and passive avoidance, and normal reactions to footshocks (El-Ghundi et al. 1999; El-Ghundi et al. 2001). However, both D1-/- and +/- mice exhibit clear extinction deficits, as demonstrated by the delayed ability to reduce both the conditioned avoidance and freezing behavior associated with an environment previously paired with a footshock and now a "footshock-free" environment, and by the deficits in extinguishing an already learned operant behavior for sucrose pellets (El-Ghundi et al. 2001; El-Ghundi et al. 2003).

D2 and D3 receptor null mutant mice show significant deficits in a T-maze spatial delayed alternation task (Glickstein et al. 2002). In particular, the performance of D3 mutants gradually deteriorates with increasing memory load, while D2 mutants showed impaired performance at all the retention intervals used. It could be argued that motivational abnormalities might explain these cognitive deficits; moreover, D2 mutant mice show impaired locomotor activity (Jung et al. 1999). As opposed to D3 null mutant mice, the impaired performance on the working memory task is reversed in the D2-/- mice by treatment with methamphetamine.

A new interesting genetically modified mouse, overexpressing D2 receptors selectively in the striatum (D2tg), has been generated (Kellendonk et al. 2006). The D2tg mice demonstrate deficits in the acquisition of a "win-shift" eight-arm radial maze DNMTS task and a DNMTS T-maze task. These deficits persist even after the transgene is switched off, indicating that the deficit in working memory performance results from developmental, not concurrent, functioning of the upregulated D2 receptors. D2tg mice do not suffer from general cognitive deficits based on normal acquisition of a simple spatial rule in a T-maze apparatus and performance in both the visible and invisible platform versions of the Morris water maze task. This study also demonstrated that specific cognitive deficits produced by the overexpression of striatal D2 receptors are probably correlated with dopamine metabolism and D1 receptor activation in the prefrontal cortex.

Cognitive studies in mice lacking the dopamine D4 are limited. One study found that disruption of D4 receptors induces reduced exploration of a novel object (Dulawa et al. 1999) but has no effect on learned fear responses evaluated by contextual, cued, and instrumental fear-conditioning tests as shown by comparison of wild-type and D4–/– mice (Falzone et al. 2002). However, D4–/– mice have significant increases of D1 and NMDA receptors in different brain regions (Gan et al. 2004) that encourage cautious interpretation of results in this knockout line of mice.

The dopamine transporter (DAT) which transports released neurotransmitter into presynaptic terminals is a major determinant of the intensity and duration of the dopaminergic signal, especially at the level of substantia nigra, ventral tegmental area, and projection areas of the basal ganglia. Mice lacking the DAT(–/–) are characterized by high extracellular dopamine levels and spontaneous hyperlocomotion. Tested in an operant behavioral task for food reinforcement, DAT–/– mice showed a longer extinction process, exerting significantly more responses than heterozygous and wild-type mice when food was no longer delivered by nose poking. On the other hand, no deficit was found in the number of sessions required for acquisition, the number of responses under the FR5 schedule, or the number of responses under the progressive ratio schedule. These findings suggest a greater resistance of DAT–/– mice to the elimination of the response and support roles of dopaminergic systems in habit memory (Hironaka et al. 2004). Future experiments on cognitive function in DAT–/– mice should consider that these mice present a specific deficit in olfactory discrimination similar to that seen in D2–/– mice (Tillerson et al. 2006).

Catechol-O-methyltransferase (COMT) is a major enzyme responsible for catecholamine catabolism, especially for dopamine in the prefrontal cortex. In humans, COMT has a val158met polymorphism that affects enzyme activity and has shown associations with various cognitive functions (Egan et al. 2001; Bilder et al. 2002; Joober et al. 2002; Malhotra et al. 2002; Goldberg et al. 2003; Tsai et al. 2003; Diamond et al. 2004; Nolan et al. 2004). Despite this work in humans, the cognitive phenotype of COMT–/– (Gogos et al. 1998) and COMT overexpressing mice has yet to be characterized.

The membrane-bound enzymes monoamine oxidase (MAO) A and B catalyze the oxidation of monoamines. MAO A-deficient mice but not MAO B–/– mice manifest aggressive behavior (Cases et al. 1995). MAO A null mutant mice also present a prolonged retention of a conditioned passive avoidance compared to their progenitor strain used as control mice (Dubrovina et al. 2006).

Dopamine- and cyclic AMP-regulated phosphoprotein of 32 kDa (DARPP-32) is critically involved in mediating the postsynaptic biological effects of dopamine and is most abundantly expressed in striatal neurons. In accord with the role of the striatal dopamine system in cognitive processes, DARPP-32–/– mice manifest normal performance during the acquisition and increased fixed response (FR) exercise in an operant task for food reinforcer. However, they show a marked deficiency in changing acquired habits during the reacquisition of the discriminated operant task following reversal (Heyser et al. 2000).

Opioid System

The endogenous opioid system is composed of several peptides (β-endorphin, enkephalins, dynorphins, etc.), whose effects are mediated by three distinct receptor pathways, known as the μ-opioid receptor (MOR), the δ-opioid receptor (DOR), and the κ-opioid receptor (KOR).

MOR–/– mice present impaired learning and memory processes in the visuospatial Morris water maze and eight-arm radial maze tasks (Jamot et al. 2003; Jang et al. 2003), as well as in a Pavlovian context fear conditioning task (Sanders et al. 2005). However, in a simple schedule-controlled operant task, no deficits have been found in the learning processes of the MOR–/– mice (Papaleo et al. 2007). These results could reflect a specific rule of MOR pathways in hippocampal- and amygdala-dependent memory tasks.

In contrast, KOR–/– mice show no learning impairment in the eight-arm radial maze and the Morris water maze (Jamot et al. 2003). However, due to the controversial involvement of KOR in learning and/or memory processes in pharmacological studies, more specific evaluation of KOR null mutant mice performance in cognitive tests is required.

Endocannabinoid System

Currently, two different G-protein coupled receptors are known to mediate the biological actions of the endogenous cannabinoids, termed cannabinoid receptor 1 (CB1) and 2 (CB2). Only CB1 receptors are abundant in the central nervous system. Three transgenic mouse lines that lack the CB1 receptor have been used to examine the role of endocannabinoids in cognition (Ledent et al. 1999; Zimmer et al. 1999; Marsicano et al. 2002). CB1–/– mice demonstrated enhanced novel object recognition memory (Reibaud et al. 1999). It has also been shown that the endogenous cannabinoid system plays a critical role in the extinction of aversive memories. Compared to their wild-type littermates, CB1–/– mice show strong and specific impairments of short- and long-term extinction in the auditory fear-conditioning test. Immediately after the training as well as six days later, on repeated tone presentations in the altered context, wild-type mice gradually extinguished freezing behavior, while CB1–/– mice did not show this adaptive behavior. Similar results were found treating the wild type with the CB1 antagonist SR141716A, excluding possible compensatory effects due to the lifelong absence of CB1 in the CB1–/– mice.

Recently, further investigations have clarified that the crucial role played by the cannabinoid CB1 receptor in fear extinction is driven primarily via habituation-like processes and not via the relearning of the association between a stimulus and the nonappearance of a punishment (Kamprath et al. 2006). Varvel and Lichtman (2002) tested another line of CB1 receptor null mutant mice in Morris water maze tasks. CB1–/– mice and their wild-type littermates exhibited identical acquisition rates in a fixed platform procedure; however, the CB1–/– mice demonstrated significant deficits in a reversal task in which the location of the hidden platform was moved to the opposite side of the tank. This phenotype difference was most likely due to an increased perseverance of the CB1–/– mice in that they continued to return to the original platform location. This hypothesis is further supported by the findings that genetic and pharmacological disruption of CB1 receptor pathways impairs the extinction process in the Morris water maze (Varvel et al. 2005). That is, while the learned spatial bias of the control mice decreased across subsequent probe trials, CB1–/– mice and mice repeatedly treated with the CB1 receptor antagonist SR 141716 continued to return to the target location across all trials in the spaced extinction procedure. These various results suggest that endocannabinoids have only a negligible function in memory acquisition, consolidation, and recall but selectively play an integral role in the suppression of nonreinforced learned behaviors. Finally, CB1 does not seem to be important for memory extinction of the stimulus–response association in operant conditioning tasks involving positive reinforcement (Holter et al. 2005).

Fragile X Knockout Mice
A mutation of the gene FMR1 on the X chromosome leads to the transcriptional silencing of the fragile X mental retardation protein, FMRP in humans. This mutation is associated with the fragile X syndrome, one of the most common forms of inherited mental retardation. Interrupting the murine Fmr1 gene generated the first mouse model for the fragile X syndrome ("Fmr1 Knockout Mice" 1994). In Fmr1 null mutant mice, a mild learning deficit was observed in the reversal stage of the Morris water maze test ("Fmr1 Knockout Mice" 1994; Kooy et al. 1996). Similar observations were made in the radial arm maze (Mineur et al. 2002), indicating that fragile X mice have mild learning deficits in tests that are dependent on spatial learning. Fear conditioning

memory results obtained in these mice are still controversial because the knockout animals displayed significantly less freezing behavior following both contextual and conditional fear stimuli (Paradee et al. 1999) while in other two studies no effect of the mutation was reported (Dobkin et al. 2000; Peier et al. 2000).

Two homologues of FMRP have been identified, FXR1P and FXR2P, and a new line of mice specifically lacking the FXR2 has been produced (Bontekoe et al. 2002). These animals show no evidence of pathological abnormalities in the brain or the testes. However, when tested for cognitive and behavioral characteristics, FXR2−/− mice show impaired Morris water maze learning and increased locomotor activity comparable to that of the fragile X knockout mouse. In addition, mice of this genotype have decreased rotarod performance, a delayed hind-limb response in the hotplate test, and less contextual fear.

The Galanin System

GAL inhibits the release of acetylcholine, norepinephrine, serotonin, and glutamate in brain regions important for learning and memory (Laplante et al. 2004). GAL-overexpressing transgenic mice (GAL-tg) have been developed to model the GAL overexpression found in Alzheimer's disease (Steiner et al. 2001). After good acquisition of the visible and hidden platform stages in a Morris water maze task, GAL-tg mice failed to display a selective search for the platform on the probe test (Steiner et al. 2001; Wrenn et al. 2002), suggesting that GAL overexpression leads to specific deficits in spatial memory. Olfactory memory, tested using the STFP task, was also impaired in GAL-tg mice (Wrenn et al. 2003). Moreover, in a fear conditioning paradigm, GAL-tg mice showed significantly less freezing than wild-type controls when presented with the conditioned tone in the novel context but not in the contextual conditioning test (Kinney et al. 2002; Wrenn et al. 2002). However, GAL-tg mice present no deficits in sustained attention as recently reported using a 5-CSRT (Wrenn et al. 2006).

GAL has three identified receptor subtypes termed GAL-R1, GAL-R2, and GAL-R3. All three subtypes are found in brain regions critical for learning and memory including the cortex, hippocampus, cholinergic basal forebrain, and amygdala (Branchek et al. 2000). GAL-R1 null mutant mice (Jacoby et al. 2002) have normal acquisition curves on visible and hidden platform training as compared to their wild-type littermates and normal target quadrant search in the probe trial in the Morris water maze (Wrenn et al. 2004). Similarly, in the STFP task, wild-type and GAL-R1−/− mice show similar preference for the cued food over the novel-flavored food. These results suggest that the GAL-R1 is not necessary for the formation of spatial memory or for olfactory memory. In trace fear conditioning, GAL-R1−/− mice showed significantly less freezing than their wild-type mice when presented with the auditory cue in the novel context; however, no differences were seen in the standard delay conditioning paradigm. These results suggest that functional GAL-R1 receptors are necessary for the formation of specific types of hippocampus-dependent memory. Future studies using mice deficient in GAL-R2 or GAL-R3 will help to elucidate the specific roles for each of these subtypes in learning and memory processes.

Brain-Derived Neurotrophic Factor

Most studies of homozygous mutant mice lacking the brain-derived neurotrophic factor (BDNF) and cognitive consequences of this mutation are inconclusive and/or controversial, probably due to the premature death of these mutants. The classic heterozygous BDNF+/– mouse, in which one allele of the BDNF gene is disrupted in all tissues and at all developmental stages, shows locomotor hyperactivity and deficits in long-term spatial memory but not in prepulse inhibition or social interactions or other emotional behaviors (Lyons et al. 1999; Kernie et al. 2000). Heterozygous BDNF mutant mice also showed a moderate but significant impairment of water maze learning in one study (Linnarsson et al. 1997), while no reduction in performance using the same test was detected in another (Montkowski and Holsboer 1997). Confounding the cognitive results in BDNF+/– mice is the fact that they exhibit abnormalities of eating behavior and locomotor activity (Kernie et al. 2000). Another line of BDNF mutated mice, in which the deletion of BDNF is forebrain restricted, fails to learn to perform the Morris water maze task and presents enhanced freezing behavior during all phases of cued-contextual fear conditioning. Again, the interpretation of these data becomes difficult because these mutant mice manifest low locomotor activity in an open-field arena, display longer escape latencies during the visible platform testing of the Morris water maze, and show enhanced freezing in the altered context of the fear conditioning apparatus prior to presentation of the conditioned stimulus (Gorski et al. 2003). In inducible BDNF knockout mice, the BDNF gene is disrupted in specific brain regions and at certain developmental stages, and, when induced by the tetracycline transactivator, these knockout mice show hyperactivity and profound deficits in context-dependent fear memory (Monteggia et al. 2004). Early inducible knockout of BDNF starting from the late embryonic stage results in more severe context-dependent memory deficits than late knockout of BDNF starting at the age of 3 months. This supports the important role played by BDNF in early neurodevelopment. Finally new transgenic mice carrying the human $BDNF_{Met}$ allele demonstrate less context-dependent memory than wild-type mice but no deficit in cue-dependent fear conditioning (Chen et al. 2006).

   The neurotrophin BDNF is the physiological ligand of the tyrosine kinase receptor, TrkB. Mice with conditional and forebrain-specific knockout for the *TrkB* gene (TrkB-CRE mice) present a normal life span, lack of significant developmental abnormalities, and no changes in simple passive avoidance learning, but they are not able to learn the spatial memory Morris water maze test and are impaired in the eight-arm radial maze test (Minichiello et al. 1999). However, TrkB-CRE mice tested in all the phases of the Morris water maze showed a strong thigmotaxis behavioral strategy. Thinking that this behavior was primarily an expression of a behavioral flexibility deficit, rather than a learning and memory deficit, Vyssotski and colleagues (2002) tested these mice in naturalistic outdoor settings and found that TrkB receptor inactivation primarily affects behavioral flexibility, sparing simple spatial learning and task-specific memories.

NMDA

Genetic disruption of the NMDA receptor subunit 1 (NR1) by traditional and conditional knockout approaches in mice results in hyperlocomotion, stereotypy, abnormal social behavior, and cognitive dysfunction (Mohn et al. 1999; Duncan et al. 2004; Fradley et al. 2005). In particular, it has been shown that NR1 deletion in the hippocampal CA1 region causes severe deficits in both spatial and nonspatial learning in mice (Tsien et al. 1996; Rampon et al. 2000; Shimizu et al. 2000; Rondi-Reig et al. 2001), suggesting that NR1 in the CA1 is important for relational memory. On the other hand, genetic enhancement of NMDA receptor function results in enhanced synaptic coincidence detection and superior learning and memory (Tsien 2000).

Disrupted in Schizophrenia 1

Disrupted in schizophrenia 1 (DISC1) is a leading candidate schizophrenia susceptibility gene. It was recently found that all 129 mouse inbred substrains have a deletion of this gene, which is predicted to abolish production of the full-length protein. This same deletion inserted into a C57BL/6J background produces an impairment of working memory performance during delayed nonmatch to place task discrete trials (Koike et al. 2006).

Proline Dehydrogenase

Human variants of the gene for proline dehydrogenase (*PRODH*) have also been associated with increased susceptibility to schizophrenia. Mutant mice with reduced PRODH enzymatic activity show decreased locomotor activity and deficits in contextual and cued auditory fear conditioning but normal performance in the continuous alternation T-maze task. Interestingly, PRODH mice have a compensatory upregulation of the COMT gene, and pharmacological inhibition of COMT in the PRODH mutant mice produces impaired performance on the T-maze task (Paterlini et al. 2005).

Neuregulin 1

Neuregulin 1 (NRG1) is another gene that has been associated with increased risk for schizophrenia. The neuregulins compose a family of growth and differentiation factors whose effects are mediated via four neuregulin (NRG1–4) genes that bind to the ErbB family of tyrosine kinase transmembrane receptors (ErbB1–4). Centrally, NRG1 is expressed in many regions such as the prefrontal cortex, hippocampus, cerebellum, and substantia nigra in both humans and rodents. Targeted deletion of NRG1 or its ErbB receptors results in midembryonic lethality, with homozygotes dying due to heart defects at embryonic day 10.5–11.5, while heterozygous mice are viable and fertile (Gerlai et al. 2000; Stefansson et al. 2002). NRG1 heterozygote mutant mice exhibit abnormalities in distinct elements of exploratory behavior and their habituation. Furthermore, spatial learning and memory performance, as assessed in the Morris water maze, are disrupted in heterozygous male mutants only.

Oxytocin and Vasopressin

Oxytocin (OT) and Vasopressin (AVP) are closely related nonapeptides that are involved in the neural processing of olfactory cues and social memory. The AVP endogenous system is composed of two central brain receptors, namely V1a receptor (V1aR) and V1b receptor (V1bR). A line of mice lacking a functional V1aR in the brain shows a complete disruption in social recognition. These mice perform normally in the detection and/or processing of general–nonsocial odors, and other nonsocial learning and memory tasks, such as the Morris water maze. Male V1bR–/– mice have also been shown to have minor deficits in social recognition in both the habituation paradigm and the discrimination test for social memory (Bielsky and Young 2004).

OT is critical for normal social recognition in both male and female rodents. Different studies suggest that the effects of OT on social recognition follow an inverted U-shaped dose response curve where moderate doses facilitate, and high doses attenuate social recognition. Mice lacking OT reveal specific deficits in social recognition, with intact olfactory abilities and no nonsocial learning and memory deficit (Bielsky and Young 2004).

Nicotinic Receptors

Acetylcholine acts on central nicotinic acetylcholine receptors (nAChRs) and is involved in attentional processes, learning, memory, and even brain development and degeneration. Among the sixteen genes encoding nAChR subunits that have been identified and cloned in mammals, nine (α2–α7 and β2–β4) are expressed in the CNS. Knockout mice lacking specific nAChR subunits (α3, α4, α5[1], α6, α7, α9, β2, β3[2], β4) and mutant knock-in mice for α4 and α7 subunits have been generated, and their phenotypic characterization is clarifying the specific role of each receptor (Champtiaux and Changeux 2002). In a passive avoidance test, β2–/– animals exhibited longer latencies than their wild type in entering a dark (preferred) compartment previously paired with an aversive stimulus. On the other hand, young adult β2–/– animals performed normally in spatial learning (Morris water maze) and both contextual and auditory-cue condition fear tasks. The performance of aged β2–/– animals, however, was found to be significantly impaired as compared with age-matched wild-type animals in the same Morris water maze and Pavlovian conditioned fear tests. This line of mice, however, was later shown to have visual deficits that could affect the interpretation of these results.

A similar pattern of age-dependent performance deterioration has been observed with the α7-nAChR gene, a potential susceptibility gene for schizophrenia. Young α7-nAChR–/– mice showed no deficits in prepulse inhibition (PPI), spatial learning, or fear-conditioning. α7-nAChR–/– mice, however, exhibited significantly higher omission levels compared to their wild-type littermates in a 5-CSRT task, with worse performance found in older animals (Young et al. 2007b). Furthermore, α7-nAChR–/– mice are significantly impaired in the odor span task in a pattern consistent with impaired attention. These results are further supported by the study of Keller et al. (2005), in which the performance of α5, α7, β2, β3, and β4-nAChRs null mutant mice was tested in a signaled nose poke task. In this study, only mutants lacking α7-nAChR showed impairments during the final and the more difficult phase of this task, again pointing out the crucial role played by the α7AChR subunits on attentional cognitive processes.

Complications and Confounders; Limitations of the Method

Mice and Cognition

The study of cognition in mice is clearly of widespread interest, but it might present some limitations. Although scientists have developed elegant ways to probe and understand cognitive functions in mice, the degree to which these can be seen as models of higher order cognitive processes in humans is uncertain, and the same genes in mice might be "used" for a different purpose. Moreover, many of the tasks described above and used in the various studies of genetically altered mice attempt to parse memory processes, but it is unclear if, for example, working memory can be differentiated from other types of short-term memory processes in these animals, or if we can legitimately isolate frontal cortical functions in a species in which this part of the brain is relatively less developed.

Species Differences Matter

To date, most of the tests used to study "higher cognitive" functions have been designed and validated with pharmacological and lesion studies prevalently in rats. However, due to practical and historical reasons, targeted gene mutations are essentially developed in mice (Crawley 2007). Species–specific differences between rats and mice may represent serious confounders when adapting for mice tests previously validated in rats (Whishaw 1995; Whishaw and Tomie 1996; Frick et al. 2000). For one, rats have a better predisposition to experimental paradigms involving swimming

(Whishaw 1995). Spatial learning abilities of the two species, however, are similar when compared on a dry-land maze, such as in a radial-arm maze (Whishaw and Tomie 1996) or in the spatial open field with objects. This supports the notion that the learning abilities of the two species are similar, though highly dependent on the eco-ethological relevance of the stimuli and settings employed (Kamil and Mauldin 1988; Martin and Bateson 1993).

Using genetically modified mice also critically depends on the genetic background and breeding scheme used. Several behavioral differences between different strains of mice have been reported, especially in tasks of learning and memory (Crawley 2007). Moreover, different kinds of specific strain-related gene deletions that can influence behavioral phenotypes are only beginning to be highlighted (e.g., the DISC1 gene). Genetic modification can also change maternal behavior and, in turn, influence, by virtue of this important developmental environmental aberration, all the cognitive functions of the pups through their entire life. For this reason a homozygote breeding scheme should be avoided and maternal behavior carefully monitored.

Technical Related Problems

Although maze-based tests have the advantages of being inexpensive, being generally readily acquired in rodents, and requiring minimal technological sophistication, these procedures also have important limitations. Mazes are usually space consuming and very labor-intensive. Moreover, subjects might develop strategies which can lead to correct responses for reasons that do not reflect memory abilities. Other potential drawbacks of maze tasks include an increasing inaccuracy in measurement with decreasing delay (very short delays, for example, zero- or two-second delays are impossible to schedule) and the practical restriction in the number of trials per session. Furthermore, most of these tasks are stressful for the animals due to required food restriction, long and intensive manipulations, and the requirement of single housing conditions and the presence of the experimenter in the testing room. All of these factors are crucial concerns when studying genetically modified mice because they raise doubts about how much of the cognitive phenotype is related to the gene and how much results from the complex stress–gene interactions.

An ideal approach should therefore try to minimize nongenetic factors that may influence cognitive performance such as aberrant motivational or emotional states generated by commonly used procedures, for instance, alimentary deprivation or electric footshock. Some of these problems are minimized in different exploration tasks which are based on an innate tendency and therefore do not require the use of food deprivation, aversive reinforcement, or the learning of a rule. Automatic operant behavioral boxes allow accurate and relatively less stressful conditions, and can be adapted to study several different cognitive functions. However, the disadvantages of the operant tasks include long training time, requirement for food restrictions, high cost of the apparatus, and problems linked with the animal's attitude about adopting mediating–orienting strategies to solve these tests. In particular, development of valid memory tasks requires the exclusion of postural mediation of the to-be-made response. This problem has been extensively studied and discussed (Chudasama and Muir 1997), and different strategies to solve it have been employed. To date, the best solution seems to be the delayed comparison tasks (Pontecorvo et al. 1996), where postural mediation is not possible, and tasks such as the visual touchscreen procedure (Aggleton et al. 1997) may also provide useful for valid assessment of working memory. These complex tests, however, have not been commonly used in mice and are still unfamiliar in this context. Finally, a critically important general aspect of cognitive tests in genetically modified mice is the necessity for scrupulous attention to the handling of the mice and the environmental conditions of the experimental area (such as reduced noise, soundproof chamber, dim lights, and extra- and intramaze cues).

Behavioral Data Interpretation

The interpretation of data obtained from mutant mice implicating a role of a particular gene in a particular cognitive test requires a rigorous analysis of all possible factors that may modulate that particular behavioral response. Indeed, a battery of tests assessing the general health of the mutant mouse and other correlated tests investigating the general physical and emotional consequences of the genetic modification must be performed to rule out secondary effects before the complex effect of the gene mutation in equally complex behaviors such as cognitive functions can be inferred.

Limitations of Genetically Modified Mice

The process of creating genetic alterations in mice is problematic in a number of respects. It is important to remember that the mouse is not a smaller version of a human and major differences in DNA sequences define the two genomes. Based on evolutional theory and evidence, the differences in genes important for cognitive function between human and mouse are likely greater than the genes for most other functions. The human genome contains more intronic and other untranslated and regulatory sequences, which show less homology to mouse sequences in analogous genomic regions. These sequences might be very important for gene regulation and for generating more isoforms from each single gene. Many risk alleles associated with diseases are located in these noncoding sequences. Human genes generate more isoforms, and some isoforms are human specific. Even though we can develop transgenic mice carrying a human isoform of a specific gene, it is uncertain whether the human isoform can work properly with its partners in a mouse signaling pathway or network.

It is also extremely difficult to express a transgene at just the right time, in just the right pattern, and at just the right level in a transgenic mouse. It is also much more difficult to introduce small mutations into the mouse genome than to simply disrupt a gene. It is very often the case that a transgenic or knockout mouse does not exhibit the phenotype that we expect to see. Failure to capture the full genetic defect is usually the given explanation.

Transgenes insert into the mouse genome often in multiple copies. After several generations, the transgenes can be methylated and functionally silenced, and thus several copies may be lost and the expression level of the transgene reduced. Morover, transgenes insert into the mouse genome randomly. They may disrupt any gene in their path, or they may affect the expression of unknown genes.

Finally, it is very time-consuming to develop and characterize a transgenic or knock-out mouse. Focusing on a specific gene is almost a must for investigators in the genetic mouse model field due to the time and space limitations. It is theoretically possible to bring many mutations into a mouse by crossbreeding among several mutant mice. However, breeding takes a lot of animal space, and space is a limiting factor for many investigators.

Ways Forward and Novel Approaches

Although the complete knockout of a gene in mice is a reliable approach to test or validate the functions of the gene in vivo, it is very different from establishing the functional implications of allelic variations that impart risk for complex behavioral disorders and for abnormal cognition in humans. Partial and tissue-specific knockout of a gene by conditional knockout, inducible knockout, or knock-in with a single nucleotide substitution mutation will be required to resemble the variable risk alleles more closely. Psychiatric disorders are polygenic conditions likely related to complex gene–gene and gene–environment interactions. Genetic mouse models with single gene mutations do not address this complexity or the interactions between susceptibility genes. New models with mutations in regulatory elements of genes are necessary to model these more complex molecular processes implicated in psychiatric genetics. Also, multiple susceptibility gene defects within the same animal are needed to study gene–gene interactions in exploring the molecular mechanisms underlying the pathophysiology of these polygenic disorders.

References

Aggleton JP, Keen S, Warburton EC, Bussey TJ (1997). Extensive cytotoxic lesions involving both the rhinal cortices and area TE impair recognition but spare spatial alternation in the rat. *Brain Res Bull*, 43:279–87.

Akassoglou K, Douni E, Bauer J, Lassmann H, Kollias G, Probert L (2003). Exclusive tumor necrosis factor (TNF) signaling by the p75TNF receptor triggers inflammatory ischemia in the CNS of transgenic mice. *Proc Natl Acad Sci USA*, 100:709–14.

Anagnostaras SG, Maren S, Fanselow MS (1999). Temporally graded retrograde amnesia of contextual fear after hippocampal damage in rats: within-subjects examination. *J Neurosci*, 19:1106–14.

Annett LE, McGregor A, Robbins TW (1989). The effects of ibotenic acid lesions of the nucleus accumbens on spatial learning and extinction in the rat. *Behav Brain Res*, 31:231–42.

Aultman JM, Moghaddam B (2001). Distinct contributions of glutamate and dopamine receptors to temporal aspects of rodent working memory using a clinically relevant task. *Psychopharmacology (Berl)*, 153:353–64.

Bach ME, Hawkins RD, Osman M, Kandel ER, Mayford M (1995). Impairment of spatial but not contextual memory in CaMKII mutant mice with a selective loss of hippocampal LTP in the range of the theta frequency. *Cell*, 81:905–15.

Barnes CA (1979). Memory deficits associated with senescence: a neurophysiological and behavioral study in the rat. *J Comp Physiol Psychol*, 93:74–104.

Fmr1 knockout mice: a model to study fragile X mental retardation (1994). The Dutch–Belgian Fragile X Consortium. *Cell*, 78:23–33.

Baunez C, Robbins TW (1999). Effects of transient inactivation of the subthalamic nucleus by local muscimol and APV infusions on performance on the five-choice serial reaction time task in rats. *Psychopharmacology (Berl)*, 141:57–65.

Bejar R, Yasuda R, Krugers H, Hood K, Mayford M (2002). Transgenic calmodulin-dependent protein kinase II activation: dose-dependent effects on synaptic plasticity, learning, and memory. *J Neurosci*, 22:5719–26.

Benmoyal-Segal L, Soreq H (2006). Gene–environment interactions in sporadic Parkinson's disease. *J Neurochem*, 97:1740–55.

Betz UA, Vosshenrich CA, Rajewsky K, Muller W (1996). Bypass of lethality with mosaic mice generated by Cre-loxP-mediated recombination. *Curr Biol*, 6:1307–16.

Bielsky IF, Young LJ (2004). Oxytocin, vasopressin, and social recognition in mammals. *Peptides*, 25:1565–74.

Bilder RM, Volavka J, Czobor P, Malhotra AK, Kennedy JL, Ni X, et al. (2002). Neurocognitive correlates of the COMT Val(158)Met polymorphism in chronic schizophrenia. *Biol Psychiatry*, 52:701–7.

Birrell JM, Brown VJ (2000). Medial frontal cortex mediates perceptual attentional set shifting in the rat. *J Neurosci*, 20:4320–4.

Bontekoe CJ, McIlwain KL, Nieuwenhuizen IM, Yuva-Paylor LA, Nellis A, Willemsen R, et al. (2002). Knockout mouse model for Fxr2: a model for mental retardation. *Hum Mol Genet*, 11:487–98.

Branchek TA, Smith KE, Gerald C, Walker MW (2000). Galanin receptor subtypes. *Trends Pharmacol Sci*, 21:109–17.

Brito GN, Brito LS (1990). Septohippocampal system and the prelimbic sector of frontal cortex: a neuropsychological battery analysis in the rat. *Behav Brain Res*, 36:127–46.

Bunsey M, Eichenbaum H (1995). Selective damage to the hippocampal region blocks long-term retention of a natural and nonspatial stimulus–stimulus association. *Hippocampus*, 5:546–56.

Buresova O, Bures J, Oitzl MS, Zahalka A (1985). Radial maze in the water tank: an aversively motivated spatial working memory task. *Physiol Behav*, 34:1003–5.

Cardinal RN, Pennicott DR, Sugathapala CL, Robbins TW, Everitt BJ (2001). Impulsive choice induced in rats by lesions of the nucleus accumbens core. *Science*, 292:2499–501.

Cases O, Seif I, Grimsby J, Gaspar P, Chen K, Pournin S, et al. (1995). Aggressive behavior and altered amounts of brain serotonin and norepinephrine in mice lacking MAOA. *Science*, 268:1763–6.

Champtiaux N, Changeux JP (2002). Knock-out and knock-in mice to investigate the role of nicotinic receptors in the central nervous system. *Curr Drug Targets CNS Neurol Disord*, 1:319–30.

Chen J, Kelz MB, Zeng G, Sakai N, Steffen C, Shockett PE, et al. (1998). Transgenic animals with inducible, targeted gene expression in brain. *Mol Pharmacol*, 54:495–503.

Chen ZY, Jing D, Bath KG, Ieraci A, Khan T, Siao CJ, et al. (2006). Genetic variant BDNF (Val66Met) polymorphism alters anxiety-related behavior. *Science*, 314:140–3.

Chudasama Y, Muir JL (1997). A behavioural analysis of the delayed non-matching to position task: the effects of scopolamine, lesions of the fornix and of the prelimbic region on mediating behaviours by rats. *Psychopharmacology (Berl)*, 134:73–82.

Conover JC, Erickson JT, Katz DM, Bianchi LM, Poueymirou WT, McClain J, et al. (1995). Neuronal deficits, not involving motor neurons, in mice lacking BDNF and/or NT4. *Nature*, 375:235–8.

Contarino A, Dellu F, Koob GF, Smith GW, Lee KF, Vale W, Gold LH (1999). Reduced anxiety-like and cognitive performance in mice lacking the corticotropin-releasing factor receptor 1. *Brain Res*, 835:1–9.

Coutureau E, Gosselin O, Di Scala G (2000). Restoration of latent inhibition by olanzapine but not haloperidol in entorhinal cortex-lesioned rats. *Psychopharmacology (Berl)*, 150:226–32.

Crawley JN, ed. (2007). What's wrong with my mouse? Behavioral phenotyping of transgenic and knockout mice, second edition. Hoboken, NJ: John Wiley & Sons.

Diamond A, Briand L, Fossella J, Gehlbach L (2004). Genetic and neurochemical modulation of prefrontal cognitive functions in children. *Am J Psychiatry*, 161:125–32.

Dias R, Robbins TW, Roberts AC (1996). Primate analogue of the Wisconsin Card Sorting Test: effects of excitotoxic lesions of the prefrontal cortex in the marmoset. *Behav Neurosci*, 110:872–86.

DiMaio S, Grizenko N, Joober R (2003). Dopamine genes and attention-deficit hyperactivity disorder: a review. *J Psychiatry Neurosci*, 28:27–38.

Dobkin C, Rabe A, Dumas R, El Idrissi A, Haubenstock H, Brown WT (2000). Fmr1 knockout mouse has a distinctive strain-specific learning impairment. *Neuroscience*, 100:423–9.

Dubrovina NI, Popova NK, Gilinskii MA, Tomilenko RA, Seif I (2006). Acquisition and extinction of a conditioned passive avoidance reflex in mice with genetic knockout of monoamine oxidase A. *Neurosci Behav Physiol*, 36:335–9.

Dudchenko PA, Wood ER, Eichenbaum H (2000). Neurotoxic hippocampal lesions have no effect on odor span and little effect on odor recognition memory but produce significant impairments on spatial span, recognition, and alternation. *J Neurosci*, 20:2964–77.

Dulawa SC, Grandy DK, Low MJ, Paulus MP, Geyer MA (1999). Dopamine D4 receptor-knock-out mice exhibit reduced exploration of novel stimuli. *J Neurosci*, 19:9550–6.

Duncan GE, Moy SS, Perez A, Eddy DM, Zinzow WM, Lieberman JA, et al. (2004). Deficits in sensorimotor gating and tests of social behavior in a genetic model of reduced NMDA receptor function. *Behav Brain Res*, 153:507–19.

Dunnett SB, ed. (1993). Operant delayed matching and non-matching to position in rats, Sahgal, A edition. Oxford: IRL Press.

Egan MF, Goldberg TE, Kolachana BS, Callicott JH, Mazzanti CM, Straub RE, et al. (2001). Effect of COMT Val108/158 Met genotype on frontal lobe function and risk for schizophrenia. *Proc Natl Acad Sci USA*, 98:6917–22.

Eichenbaum H, Fagan A, Mathews P, Cohen NJ (1988). Hippocampal system dysfunction and odor discrimination learning in rats: impairment or facilitation depending on representational demands. *Behav Neurosci*, 102:331–9.

Eichenbaum H, Schoenbaum G, Young B, Bunsey M (1996). Functional organization of the hippocampal memory system. *Proc Natl Acad Sci USA*, 93:13500–7.

El-Ghundi M, Fletcher PJ, Drago J, Sibley DR, O'Dowd BF, George SR (1999). Spatial learning deficit in dopamine D(1) receptor knockout mice. *Eur J Pharmacol*, 383:95–106.

El-Ghundi M, O'Dowd BF, Erclik M, George SR (2003). Attenuation of sucrose reinforcement in dopamine D1 receptor deficient mice. *Eur J Neurosci*, 17:851–62.

El-Ghundi M, O'Dowd BF, George SR (2001). Prolonged fear responses in mice lacking dopamine D1 receptor. *Brain Res*, 892:86–93.

Elgersma Y, Fedorov NB, Ikonen S, Choi ES, Elgersma M, Carvalho OM, et al. (2002). Inhibitory autophosphorylation of CaMKII controls PSD association, plasticity, and learning. *Neuron*, 36:493–505.

Elgersma Y, Sweatt JD, Giese KP (2004). Mouse genetic approaches to investigating calcium/calmodulin-dependent protein kinase II function in plasticity and cognition. *J Neurosci*, 24:8410–5.

Evenden JL (1999). Varieties of impulsivity. *Psychopharmacology (Berl)*, 146:348–61.

Evenden JL, Ryan CN (1996). The pharmacology of impulsive behaviour in rats: the effects of drugs on response choice with varying delays of reinforcement. *Psychopharmacology (Berl)*, 128:161–70.

Falzone TL, Gelman DM, Young JI, Grandy DK, Low MJ, Rubinstein M (2002). Absence of dopamine D4 receptors results in enhanced reactivity to unconditioned, but not conditioned, fear. *Eur J Neurosci*, 15:158–64.

Fanselow MS (1980). Conditioned and unconditional components of post-shock freezing. *Pavlov J Biol Sci*, 15:177–82.

Fanselow MS, Poulos AM (2005). The neuroscience of mammalian associative learning. *Annu Rev Psychol*, 56:207–34.

Floresco SB, Magyar O (2006). Mesocortical dopamine modulation of executive functions: beyond working memory. *Psychopharmacology (Berl)*, 188:567–85.

Floresco SB, Seamans JK, Phillips AG (1997). Selective roles for hippocampal, prefrontal cortical, and ventral striatal circuits in radial-arm maze tasks with or without a delay. *J Neurosci*, 17:1880–90.

Forrest D, Yuzaki M, Soares HD, Ng L, Luk DC, Sheng M, et al. (1994). Targeted disruption of NMDA receptor 1 gene abolishes NMDA response and results in neonatal death. *Neuron*, 13:325–38.

Forss-Petter S, Danielson PE, Catsicas S, Battenberg E, Price J, Nerenberg M, Sutcliffe JG (1990). Transgenic mice expressing beta-galactosidase in mature neurons under neuron-specific enolase promoter control. *Neuron*, 5:187–97.

Fradley RL, O'Meara GF, Newman RJ, Andrieux A, Job D, Reynolds DS (2005). STOP knockout and NMDA NR1 hypomorphic mice exhibit deficits in sensorimotor gating. *Behav Brain Res*, 163:257–64.

Frankland PW, O'Brien C, Ohno M, Kirkwood A, Silva AJ (2001). Alpha-CaMKII-dependent plasticity in the cortex is required for permanent memory. *Nature*, 411:309–13.

Frick KM, Stillner ET, Berger-Sweeney J (2000). Mice are not little rats: species differences in a one-day water maze task. *Neuroreport*, 11:3461–5.

Gan L, Falzone TL, Zhang K, Rubinstein M, Baldessarini RJ, Tarazi FI (2004). Enhanced expression of dopamine D(1) and glutamate NMDA receptors in dopamine D(4) receptor knockout mice. *J Mol Neurosci*, 22:167–78.

Garner JP, Thogerson CM, Wurbel H, Murray JD, Mench JA (2006). Animal neuropsychology: validation of the Intra-Dimensional Extra-Dimensional set shifting task for mice. *Behav Brain Res*, 173:53–61.

Geng Y, Whoriskey W, Park MY, Bronson RT, Medema RH, Li T, et al. (1999). Rescue of cyclin D1 deficiency by knockin cyclin E. *Cell*, 97:767–77.

Gerlai R, Pisacane P, Erickson S (2000). Heregulin, but not ErbB2 or ErbB3, heterozygous mutant mice exhibit hyperactivity in multiple behavioral tasks. *Behav Brain Res*, 109:219–27.

Giese KP, Fedorov NB, Filipkowski RK, Silva AJ (1998). Autophosphorylation at Thr286 of the alpha calcium-calmodulin kinase II in LTP and learning. *Science*, 279:870–3.

Glickstein SB, Hof PR, Schmauss C (2002). Mice lacking dopamine D2 and D3 receptors have spatial working memory deficits. *J Neurosci*, 22:5619–29.

Gogos JA, Morgan M, Luine V, Santha M, Ogawa S, Pfaff D, Karayiorgou M (1998). Catechol-O-methyltransferase-deficient mice exhibit sexually dimorphic changes in catecholamine levels and behavior. *Proc Natl Acad Sci USA*, 95:9991–6.

Goldberg TE, Egan MF, Gscheidle T, Coppola R, Weickert T, Kolachana BS, et al. (2003). Executive subprocesses in working memory: relationship to catechol-O-methyltransferase Val158Met genotype and schizophrenia. *Arch Gen Psychiatry*, 60:889–96.

Gong S, Zheng C, Doughty ML, Losos K, Didkovsky N, Schambra UB, et al. (2003). A gene expression atlas of the central nervous system based on bacterial artificial chromosomes. *Nature*, 425:917–25.

Gordon JW, Scangos GA, Plotkin DJ, Barbosa JA, Ruddle FH (1980). Genetic transformation of mouse embryos by microinjection of purified DNA. *Proc Natl Acad Sci USA*, 77:7380–4.

Gorski JA, Balogh SA, Wehner JM, Jones KR (2003). Learning deficits in forebrain-restricted brain-derived neurotrophic factor mutant mice. *Neuroscience*, 121:341–54.

Gossen M, Bujard H (1992). Tight control of gene expression in mammalian cells by tetracycline-responsive promoters. *Proc Natl Acad Sci USA*, 89:5547–51.

Green RJ, Stanton ME (1989). Differential ontogeny of working memory and reference memory in the rat. *Behav Neurosci*, 103:98–105.

Gu H, Marth JD, Orban PC, Mossmann H, Rajewsky K (1994). Deletion of a DNA polymerase beta gene segment in T cells using cell type-specific gene targeting. *Science*, 265:103–6.

Haile CN, Kosten TR, Kosten TA (2007). Genetics of dopamine and its contribution to cocaine addiction. *Behav Genet*, 37:119–45.

Heinrichs SC, Stenzel-Poore MP, Gold LH, Battenberg E, Bloom FE, Koob GF, et al. (1996). Learning impairment in transgenic mice with central overexpression of corticotropin-releasing factor. *Neuroscience*, 74:303–11.

Herringa RJ, Roseboom PH, Kalin NH (2006). Decreased amygdala CRF-binding protein mRNA in post-mortem tissue from male but not female bipolar and schizophrenic subjects. *Neuropsychopharmacology*, 31:1822–31.

Heyser CJ, Fienberg AA, Greengard P, Gold LH (2000). DARPP-32 knockout mice exhibit impaired reversal learning in a discriminated operant task. *Brain Res*, 867:122–30.

Hironaka N, Ikeda K, Sora I, Uhl GR, Niki H (2004). Food-reinforced operant behavior in dopamine transporter knockout mice: enhanced resistance to extinction. *Ann NY Acad Sci*, 1025:140–5.

Holmes C, Smith H, Ganderton R, Arranz M, Collier D, Powell J, Lovestone S (2001). Psychosis and aggression in Alzheimer's disease: the effect of dopamine receptor gene variation. *J Neurol Neurosurg Psychiatry*, 71:777–9.

Holter SM, Kallnik M, Wurst W, Marsicano G, Lutz B, Wotjak CT (2005). Cannabinoid CB1 receptor is dispensable for memory extinction in an appetitively-motivated learning task. *Eur J Pharmacol*, 510:69–74.

Hsiao KK, Borchelt DR, Olson K, Johannsdottir R, Kitt C, Yunis W, et al. (1995). Age-related CNS disorder and early death in transgenic FVB/N mice overexpressing Alzheimer amyloid precursor proteins. *Neuron*, 15:1203–18.

Iversen SD, Mishkin M (1970). Perseverative interference in monkeys following selective lesions of the inferior prefrontal convexity. *Exp Brain Res*, 11:376–86.

Izquierdo A, Wiedholz LM, Millstein RA, Yang RJ, Bussey TJ, Saksida LM, Holmes A (2006). Genetic and dopaminergic modulation of reversal learning in a touchscreen-based operant procedure for mice. *Behav Brain Res*, 171:181–8.

Jacoby AS, Hort YJ, Constantinescu G, Shine J, Iismaa TP (2002). Critical role for GALR1 galanin receptor in galanin regulation of neuroendocrine function and seizure activity. *Brain Res Mol Brain Res*, 107:195–200.

Jamot L, Matthes HW, Simonin F, Kieffer BL, Roder JC (2003). Differential involvement of the mu and kappa opioid receptors in spatial learning. *Genes Brain Behav*, 2:80–92.

Jang CG, Lee SY, Yoo JH, Yan JJ, Song DK, Loh HH, Ho IK (2003). Impaired water maze learning performance in mu-opioid receptor knockout mice. *Brain Res Mol Brain Res*, 117:68–72.

Jones B, Mishkin M (1972). Limbic lesions and the problem of stimulus–reinforcement associations. *Exp Neurol*, 36:362–77.

Jones DN, Higgins GA (1995). Effect of scopolamine on visual attention in rats. *Psychopharmacology (Berl)*, 120:142–9.

Joober R, Gauthier J, Lal S, Bloom D, Lalonde P, Rouleau G, et al. (2002). Catechol-O-methyltransferase Val-108/158-Met gene variants associated with performance on the Wisconsin Card Sorting Test. *Arch Gen Psychiatry*, 59:662–3.

Jung MY, Skryabin BV, Arai M, Abbondanzo S, Fu D, Brosius J, et al. (1999). Potentiation of the D2 mutant motor phenotype in mice lacking dopamine D2 and D3 receptors. *Neuroscience*, 91:911–24.

Kamil AC, Mauldin JE (1988). A comparative–ecological approach to the study of learning. In Bolles RC, Beecher MD, eds. Evolution and learning. Hillsdale, NJ: Lawrence Erlbaum Associates.

Kamprath K, Marsicano G, Tang J, Monory K, Bisogno T, Di Marzo V, et al. (2006). Cannabinoid CB1 receptor mediates fear extinction via habituation-like processes. *J Neurosci*, 26:6677–86.

Kellendonk C, Simpson EH, Polan HJ, Malleret G, Vronskaya S, Winiger V, et al. (2006). Transient and selective overexpression of dopamine D2 receptors in the striatum causes persistent abnormalities in prefrontal cortex functioning. *Neuron*, 49:603–15.

Keller JJ, Keller AB, Bowers BJ, Wehner JM (2005). Performance of alpha7 nicotinic receptor null mutants is impaired in appetitive learning measured in a signaled nose poke task. *Behav Brain Res*, 162:143–52.

Kernie SG, Liebl DJ, Parada LF (2000). BDNF regulates eating behavior and locomotor activity in mice. *Embo J*, 19:1290–300.

Killcross AS, Everitt BJ, Robins TW (1997). Symmetrical effects of amphetamine and alpha-flupenthixol on conditioned punishment and conditioned reinforcement: contrasts with midazolam. *Psychopharmacology (Berl)*, 129:141–52.

Kim JJ, Fanselow MS (1992). Modality-specific retrograde amnesia of fear. *Science*, 256:675–7.

Kinney JW, Starosta G, Holmes A, Wrenn CC, Yang RJ, Harris AP, et al. (2002). Deficits in trace cued fear conditioning in galanin-treated rats and galanin-overexpressing transgenic mice. *Learn Mem*, 9:178–90.

Koike H, Arguello PA, Kvajo M, Karayiorgou M, Gogos JA (2006). Disc1 is mutated in the 129S6/SvEv strain and modulates working memory in mice. *Proc Natl Acad Sci USA*, 103:3693–7.

Kooy RF, D'Hooge R, Reyniers E, Bakker CE, Nagels G, De Boulle K, et al. (1996). Transgenic mouse model for the fragile X syndrome. *Am J Med Genet*, 64:241–5.

Laplante F, Crawley JN, Quirion R (2004). Selective reduction in ventral hippocampal acetylcholine release in awake galanin-treated rats and galanin-overexpressing transgenic mice. *Regul Pept*, 122:91–8.

Ledent C, Valverde O, Cossu G, Petitet F, Aubert JF, Beslot F, et al. (1999). Unresponsiveness to cannabinoids and reduced addictive effects of opiates in CB1 receptor knockout mice. *Science*, 283:401–4.

LeDoux J (1996). Emotional networks and motor control: a fearful view. *Prog Brain Res*, 107:437–46.

LeDoux JE (1995). Emotion: clues from the brain. *Annu Rev Psychol*, 46:209–35.

Li Y, Erzurumlu RS, Chen C, Jhaveri S, Tonegawa S (1994). Whisker-related neuronal patterns fail to develop in the trigeminal brainstem nuclei of NMDAR1 knockout mice. *Cell*, 76:427–37.

Linnarsson S, Bjorklund A, Ernfors P (1997). Learning deficit in BDNF mutant mice. *Eur J Neurosci*, 9:2581–7.

Logue SF, Paylor R, Wehner JM (1997). Hippocampal lesions cause learning deficits in inbred mice in the Morris water maze and conditioned-fear task. *Behav Neurosci*, 111:104–13.

Lyons WE, Mamounas LA, Ricaurte GA, Coppola V, Reid SW, Bora SH, et al. (1999). Brain-derived neurotrophic factor-deficient mice develop aggressiveness and hyperphagia in conjunction with brain serotonergic abnormalities. *Proc Natl Acad Sci USA*, 96:15239–44.

Malhotra AK, Kestler LJ, Mazzanti C, Bates JA, Goldberg T, Goldman D (2002). A functional polymorphism in the COMT gene and performance on a test of prefrontal cognition. *Am J Psychiatry*, 159:652–4.

Mansuy IM, Mayford M, Jacob B, Kandel ER, Bach ME (1998). Restricted and regulated overexpression reveals calcineurin as a key component in the transition from short-term to long-term memory. *Cell*, 92:39–49.

Marsicano G, Wotjak CT, Azad SC, Bisogno T, Rammes G, Cascio MG, et al. (2002). The endogenous cannabinoid system controls extinction of aversive memories. *Nature*, 418:530–4.

Martin P, Bateson P (1993). Measuring behaviour—an introductory guide, second edition. Cambridge: Cambridge University Press.

Mayford M, Bach ME, Huang YY, Wang L, Hawkins RD, Kandel ER (1996). Control of memory formation through regulated expression of a CaMKII transgene. *Science*, 274:1678–83.

McDonald RJ, White NM (1993). A triple dissociation of memory systems: hippocampus, amygdala, and dorsal striatum. *Behav Neurosci*, 107:3–22.

Meyers EN, Lewandoski M, Martin GR (1998). An Fgf8 mutant allelic series generated by Cre- and Flp-mediated recombination. *Nat Genet*, 18:136–41.

Miksys SL, Cheung C, Gonzalez FJ, Tyndale RF (2005). Human CYP2D6 and mouse CYP2Ds: organ distribution in a humanized mouse model. *Drug Metab Dispos*, 33:1495–502.

Miller S, Yasuda M, Coats JK, Jones Y, Martone ME, Mayford M (2002). Disruption of dendritic translation of CaMKIIalpha impairs stabilization of synaptic plasticity and memory consolidation. *Neuron*, 36:507–19.

Mineur YS, Sluyter F, de Wit S, Oostra BA, Crusio WE (2002). Behavioral and neuroanatomical characterization of the Fmr1 knockout mouse. *Hippocampus*, 12:39–46.

Minichiello L, Korte M, Wolfer D, Kuhn R, Unsicker K, Cestari V, et al. (1999). Essential role for TrkB receptors in hippocampus-mediated learning. *Neuron*, 24:401–14.

Mobini S, Body S, Ho MY, Bradshaw CM, Szabadi E, Deakin JF, Anderson IM (2002). Effects of lesions of the orbitofrontal cortex on sensitivity to delayed and probabilistic reinforcement. *Psychopharmacology (Berl)*, 160:290–8.

Mohn AR, Gainetdinov RR, Caron MG, Koller BH (1999). Mice with reduced NMDA receptor expression display behaviors related to schizophrenia. *Cell*, 98:427–36.

Monteggia LM, Barrot M, Powell CM, Berton O, Galanis V, Gemelli T, et al. (2004). Essential role of brain-derived neurotrophic factor in adult hippocampal function. *Proc Natl Acad Sci USA*, 101:10827–32.

Montkowski A, Holsboer F (1997). Intact spatial learning and memory in transgenic mice with reduced BDNF. *Neuroreport*, 8:779–82.

Morris RG, Garrud P, Rawlins JN, O'Keefe J (1982). Place navigation impaired in rats with hippocampal lesions. *Nature*, 297:681–3.

Morrow BA, Roth RH, Elsworth JD (2000). TMT, a predator odor, elevates mesoprefrontal dopamine metabolic activity and disrupts short-term working memory in the rat. *Brain Res Bull*, 52:519–23.

Muir JL, Bussey TJ, Everitt BJ, Robbins TW (1996). Dissociable effects of AMPA-induced lesions of the vertical limb diagonal band of Broca on performance of the 5-choice serial reaction time task and on acquisition of a conditional visual discrimination. *Behav Brain Res*, 82:31–44.

Mumby DG (2001). Perspectives on object-recognition memory following hippocampal damage: lessons from studies in rats. *Behav Brain Res*, 127:159–81.

Need AC, Giese KP (2003). Handling and environmental enrichment do not rescue learning and memory impairments in alphaCaMKII(T286A) mutant mice. *Genes Brain Behav*, 2:132–9.

Niwa H, Araki K, Kimura S, Taniguchi S, Wakasugi S, Yamamura K (1993). An efficient gene-trap method using poly A trap vectors and characterization of gene-trap events. *J Biochem*, 113:343–9.

Nolan KA, Bilder RM, Lachman HM, Volavka J (2004). Catechol O-methyltransferase Val158Met polymorphism in schizophrenia: differential effects of Val and Met alleles on cognitive stability and flexibility. *Am J Psychiatry*, 161:359–61.

Papaleo F, Kieffer BL, Tabarin A, Contarino A (2007). Decreased motivation to eat in μ-opioid receptor-deficient mice. *Eur J Neurosci*, 25(11):3398–3405.

Paradee W, Melikian HE, Rasmussen DL, Kenneson A, Conn PJ, Warren ST (1999). Fragile X mouse: strain effects of knockout phenotype and evidence suggesting deficient amygdala function. *Neuroscience*, 94:185–92.

Paterlini M, Zakharenko SS, Lai WS, Qin J, Zhang H, Mukai J, et al. (2005). Transcriptional and behavioral interaction between 22q11.2 orthologs modulates schizophrenia-related phenotypes in mice. *Nat Neurosci*, 8:1586–94.

Peier AM, McIlwain KL, Kenneson A, Warren ST, Paylor R, Nelson DL (2000). (Over)correction of FMR1 deficiency with YAC transgenics: behavioral and physical features. *Hum Mol Genet*, 9:1145–59.

Picciotto MR, Zoli M, Rimondini R, Lena C, Marubio LM, Pich EM, et al. (1998). Acetylcholine receptors containing the beta2 subunit are involved in the reinforcing properties of nicotine. *Nature*, 391:173–7.

Pontecorvo MJ, Sahgal A, Steckler T (1996). Further developments in the measurement of working memory in rodents. *Brain Res Cogn Brain Res*, 3:205–13.

Ragozzino ME, Detrick S, Kesner RP (1999). Involvement of the prelimbic–infralimbic areas of the rodent prefrontal cortex in behavioral flexibility for place and response learning. *J Neurosci*, 19:4585–94.

Ragozzino ME, Ragozzino KE, Mizumori SJ, Kesner RP (2002). Role of the dorsomedial striatum in behavioral flexibility for response and visual cue discrimination learning. *Behav Neurosci*, 116:105–15.

Rampon C, Tang YP, Goodhouse J, Shimizu E, Kyin M, Tsien JZ (2000). Enrichment induces structural changes and recovery from nonspatial memory deficits in CA1 NMDAR1-knockout mice. *Nat Neurosci*, 3:238–44.

Reibaud M, Obinu MC, Ledent C, Parmentier M, Bohme GA, Imperato A (1999). Enhancement of memory in cannabinoid CB1 receptor knock-out mice. *Eur J Pharmacol*, 379:R1–2.

Robbins TW (2002). The 5-choice serial reaction time task: behavioural pharmacology and functional neurochemistry. *Psychopharmacology (Berl)*, 163:362–80.

Rondi-Reig L, Libbey M, Eichenbaum H, Tonegawa S (2001). CA1-specific N-methyl-D-aspartate receptor knockout mice are deficient in solving a nonspatial transverse patterning task. *Proc Natl Acad Sci USA*, 98:3543–8.

Ross RS, Eichenbaum H (2006). Dynamics of hippocampal and cortical activation during consolidation of a nonspatial memory. *J Neurosci*, 26:4852–9.

Sakai N, Thome J, Newton SS, Chen J, Kelz MB, Steffen C, et al. (2002). Inducible and brain region-specific CREB transgenic mice. *Mol Pharmacol*, 61:1453–64.

Sanders MJ, Kieffer BL, Fanselow MS (2005). Deletion of the mu opioid receptor results in impaired acquisition of Pavlovian context fear. *Neurobiol Learn Mem*, 84:33–41.

Schweimer J, Hauber W (2005). Involvement of the rat anterior cingulate cortex in control of instrumental responses guided by reward expectancy. *Learn Mem*, 12:334–42.

Seamans JK, Floresco SB, Phillips AG (1995). Functional differences between the prelimbic and anterior cingulate regions of the rat prefrontal cortex. *Behav Neurosci*, 109:1063–73.

Seamans JK, Phillips AG (1994). Selective memory impairments produced by transient lidocaine-induced lesions of the nucleus accumbens in rats. *Behav Neurosci*, 108:456–68.

Shimizu E, Tang YP, Rampon C, Tsien JZ (2000). NMDA receptor-dependent synaptic reinforcement as a crucial process for memory consolidation. *Science*, 290:1170–4.

Silva AJ, Paylor R, Wehner JM, Tonegawa S (1992). Impaired spatial learning in alpha-calcium-calmodulin kinase II mutant mice. *Science*, 257:206–11.

Silva AJ, Rosahl TW, Chapman PF, Marowitz Z, Friedman E, Frankland PW, et al. (1996). Impaired learning in mice with abnormal short-lived plasticity. *Curr Biol*, 6:1509–18.

Smith DR, Striplin CD, Geller AM, Mailman RB, Drago J, Lawler CP, Gallagher M (1998). Behavioural assessment of mice lacking D1A dopamine receptors. *Neuroscience*, 86:135–46.

Squire LR, Zola SM (1996). Structure and function of declarative and nondeclarative memory systems. *Proc Natl Acad Sci USA*, 93:13515–22.

Staubli U, Thibault O, DiLorenzo M, Lynch G (1989). Antagonism of NMDA receptors impairs acquisition but not retention of olfactory memory. *Behav Neurosci*, 103:54–60.

Stefansson H, Sigurdsson E, Steinthorsdottir V, Bjornsdottir S, Sigmundsson T, Ghosh S, et al. (2002). Neuregulin 1 and susceptibility to schizophrenia. *Am J Hum Genet*, 71:877–92.

Steiner RA, Hohmann JG, Holmes A, Wrenn CC, Cadd G, Jureus A, et al. (2001). Galanin transgenic mice display cognitive and neurochemical deficits characteristic of Alzheimer's disease. *Proc Natl Acad Sci USA*, 98:4184–9.

Stern CE, Passingham RE (1995). The nucleus accumbens in monkeys (*Macaca fascicularis*): III. Reversal learning. *Exp Brain Res*, 106:239–47.

Taghzouti K, Louilot A, Herman JP, Le Moal M, Simon H (1985). Alternation behavior, spatial discrimination, and reversal disturbances following 6-hydroxydopamine lesions in the nucleus accumbens of the rat. *Behav Neural Biol*, 44:354–63.

Thomas KR, Capecchi MR (1987). Site-directed mutagenesis by gene targeting in mouse embryo-derived stem cells. *Cell*, 51:503–12.

Thompson R (1981). Rapid forgetting of a spatial habit in rats with hippocampal lesions. *Science*, 212:959–60.

Tillerson JL, Caudle WM, Parent JM, Gong C, Schallert T, Miller GW (2006). Olfactory discrimination deficits in mice lacking the dopamine transporter or the D2 dopamine receptor. *Behav Brain Res*, 172:97–105.

Tsai SJ, Yu YW, Chen TJ, Chen JY, Liou YJ, Chen MC, Hong CJ (2003). Association study of a functional catechol-O-methyltransferase-gene polymorphism and cognitive function in healthy females. *Neurosci Lett*, 338:123–6.

Tsien JZ (2000). Linking Hebb's coincidence-detection to memory formation. *Curr Opin Neurobiol*, 10:266–73.

Tsien JZ, Huerta PT, Tonegawa S (1996). The essential role of hippocampal CA1 NMDA receptor-dependent synaptic plasticity in spatial memory. *Cell*, 87:1327–38.

van Gaalen MM, Stenzel-Poore M, Holsboer F, Steckler T (2003). Reduced attention in mice overproducing corticotropin-releasing hormone. *Behav Brain Res*, 142:69–79.

van Gaalen MM, van Koten R, Schoffelmeer AN, Vanderschuren LJ (2006). Critical involvement of dopaminergic neurotransmission in impulsive decision making. *Biol Psychiatry*, 60:66–73.

Varvel SA, Anum EA, Lichtman AH (2005). Disruption of CB(1) receptor signaling impairs extinction of spatial memory in mice. *Psychopharmacology (Berl)*, 179:863–72.

Varvel SA, Hamm RJ, Martin BR, Lichtman AH (2001). Differential effects of delta 9-THC on spatial reference and working memory in mice. *Psychopharmacology (Berl)*, 157:142–50.

Varvel SA, Lichtman AH (2002). Evaluation of CB1 receptor knockout mice in the Morris water maze. *J Pharmacol Exp Ther*, 301:915–24.

von Melchner H, DeGregori JV, Rayburn H, Reddy S, Friedel C, Ruley HE (1992). Selective disruption of genes expressed in totipotent embryonal stem cells. *Genes Dev*, 6:919–27.

Vyssotski AL, Dell'Omo G, Poletaeva II, Vyssotsk DL, Minichiello L, Klein R, et al. (2002). Long-term monitoring of hippocampus-dependent behavior in naturalistic settings: mutant mice lacking neurotrophin receptor TrkB in the forebrain show spatial learning but impaired behavioral flexibility. *Hippocampus*, 12:27–38.

Walton ME, Bannerman DM, Rushworth MF (2002). The role of rat medial frontal cortex in effort-based decision making. *J Neurosci*, 22:10996–11003.

Walton ME, Bannerman DM, Alterescu K, Rushworth MF (2003). Functional specialization within medial frontal cortex of the anterior cingulate for evaluating effort-related decisions. *J Neurosci*, 23:6475–9.

Wang H, Shimizu E, Tang YP, Cho M, Kyin M, Zuo W, et al. (2003). Inducible protein knockout reveals temporal requirement of CaMKII reactivation for memory consolidation in the brain. *Proc Natl Acad Sci USA*, 100:4287–92.

Whishaw IQ (1995). A comparison of rats and mice in a swimming pool place task and matching to place task: some surprising differences. *Physiol Behav*, 58:687–93.

Whishaw IQ, Tomie JA (1996). Of mice and mazes: similarities between mice and rats on dry land but not water mazes. *Physiol Behav*, 60:1191–7.

Wiedenmayer CP, Myers MM, Mayford M, Barr GA (2000). Olfactory based spatial learning in neonatal mice and its dependence on CaMKII. *Neuroreport*, 11:1051–5.

Winstanley CA, Theobald DE, Cardinal RN, Robbins TW (2004). Contrasting roles of basolateral amygdala and orbitofrontal cortex in impulsive choice. *J Neurosci*, 24:4718–22.

Winterer G, Weinberger DR (2004). Genes, dopamine and cortical signal-to-noise ratio in schizo-phrenia. *Trends Neurosci*, 27:683–90.

Wrenn CC, Harris AP, Saavedra MC, Crawley JN (2003). Social transmission of food preference in mice: methodology and application to galanin-overexpressing transgenic mice. *Behav Neurosci*, 117:21–31.

Wrenn CC, Kinney JW, Marriott LK, Holmes A, Harris AP, Saavedra MC, et al. (2004). Learning and memory performance in mice lacking the GAL-R1 subtype of galanin receptor. *Eur J Neurosci*, 19:1384–96.

Wrenn CC, Marriott LK, Kinney JW, Holmes A, Wenk GL, Crawley JN (2002). Galanin peptide levels in hippocampus and cortex of galanin-overexpressing transgenic mice evaluated for cogni-tive performance. *Neuropeptides*, 36:413–26.

Wrenn CC, Turchi JN, Schlosser S, Dreiling JL, Stephenson DA, Crawley JN (2006). Performance of galanin transgenic mice in the 5-choice serial reaction time attentional task. *Pharmacol Biochem Behav*, 83:428–40.

Young JW, Crawford N, Kelly JS, Kerr LE, Marston HM, Spratt C, et al. (2007b). Impaired atten-tion is central to the cognitive deficits observed in alpha 7 deficient mice. *Eur Neuropsychophar-macol*, 17:145–55.

Young JW, Kerr LE, Kelly JS, Marston HM, Spratt C, Finlayson K, Sharkey J (2007a). The odour span task: a novel paradigm for assessing working memory in mice. *Neuropharmacology*, 52:634–45.

Zhang Y, Burk JA, Glode BM, Mair RG (1998). Effects of thalamic and olfactory cortical lesions on continuous olfactory delayed nonmatching-to-sample and olfactory discrimination in rats (*Rattus norvegicus*). *Behav Neurosci*, 112:39–53.

Zimmer A, Zimmer AM, Hohmann AG, Herkenham M, Bonner TI (1999). Increased mortality, hypoactivity, and hypoalgesia in cannabinoid CB1 receptor knockout mice. *Proc Natl Acad Sci USA*, 96:5780–5.

II Genetic Approaches to Individual Differences in Cognition and Affective Regulation

4   The Genetics of Intelligence

Danielle Posthuma, Eco J. C. de Geus, and Ian J. Deary

Intelligence

In this chapter we provide an overview of the current state of knowledge on the genetic contribution to individual differences in intelligence. This includes a brief overview of the heritability of intelligence across the life span and of some behavioral and neurophysiological correlates of intelligence, as well as a discussion of molecular genetic studies on intelligence.

Although having been the topic of empirical research for more than a century, the definition of intelligence changes across time and across studies (Sternberg and Detterman 1986). Intelligence was described by fifty-two researchers in the field as follows (Gottfredson 1997):

Intelligence is a very general mental capability that, among other things, involves the ability to reason, plan, solve problems, think abstractly, comprehend complex ideas, learn quickly and learn from experience. It is not merely book learning, a narrow academic skill, or test-taking smarts. Rather, it reflects a broader and deeper capability for comprehending our surroundings—"catching on," "making sense" of things, or "figuring out" what to do.

In practice, intelligence is usually assessed using psychometric (IQ-type) tests, of which there are now hundreds. Scores on these different tests tend to have positive correlations, despite a huge variety in the mental demands of the tests. Principal components or factor analysis of a battery of mental tests applied to a large sample reveals a large first unrotated component or factor, on which all tests have substantial loadings. Scores on this unrotated component are measures of the general factor in intelligence. This general cognitive factor is sometimes referred to as just g. It was discovered by Charles Spearman (1904) and is one of the most replicated findings in psychology, as demonstrated in a reanalysis of over 400 data sets collected during the twentieth century (Carroll 1993). g is a trait with considerable lifelong stability and important predictive validity. A sixty-eight-year follow-up of almost 500 people who took part in the Scottish Mental Survey of 1932 found a raw correlation (stability coefficient) of

0.66 between IQ scores on the same IQ-type test taken at age 11 years and 79 years (Deary et al. 2004). IQ test scores are strongly associated with academic success (Neisser et al. 1996; Deary et al. 2007). They are about the single best predictor of job success (Schmidt and Hunter 1998). Finally, childhood IQ is a significant predictor of how long people live (Batty et al. 2007).

Heritability of Intelligence

A summary of all research on the genetic contributions to intelligence differences in humans reads as follows: "When data across all studies are collapsed, genetic influences account for around 50% of the variance" (Plomin and Spinath 2004). Bouchard and McGue (1981) reviewed the world literature on IQ correlations between relatives with different degrees of genetic and family rearing overlap. They found 111 adequate studies, yielding 526 correlations based on 113,942 pairings. The results were compatible with the prediction that the correlations were higher among people who were genetically more similar. The greater correlations between siblings reared together further suggests an influence of the rearing environment on general intelligence. Many of these studies were based on young children in whom rearing environment effects are especially strong.

From Infancy to Old Age: Twin and Adoption Studies

In children ages 2 to 4, the heritability of mental ability tends to be relatively low (25% to 30%), whereas shared environmental estimates explain 61% to 65% of the variance (Spinath and Plomin 2003). Parental socioeconomic status (SES) and disorganization in the home mediate some of the shared environmental effect, but most of the shared environmental effects on infant IQ are still unexplained (Petrill et al. 2004). The importance of genetic effects increases from infancy to childhood as demonstrated in longitudinal analyses of twin data from different research groups (e.g., Boomsma and van Baal 1998; Spinath and Plomin 2003). At the age of 7, about 47% of the variance in intelligence is due to genetic variance (Spinath and Plomin 2003), whereas at the ages of 11 to 12, 60% to 70% of the variance is due to genetic variance (Bartels et al. 2002; Benyamin et al. 2005; Polderman et al. 2006b). It has been shown that, although the *impact* of genetic factors increases with increasing age, the genetic factors remain the same across ages. In other words, the increasing heritability is not explained by emerging effects of a new set of genes coming into play at different ages in childhood (Plomin and DeFries 1985; Bartels et al. 2002; Polderman et al. 2006b). Instead, the effects of the same set of genes become larger with increasing age ("genetic amplification"). Shared environmental influences show a related decrease in importance and explain around 20% of the variance in intelligence at the age of 11 to 12 (Bartels et al. 2002; Benyamin et al. 2005; Polderman et al. 2006b). Heritability estimates based on adoption studies show a pattern similar to those based on twin studies: the heritability increases from early to late childhood with heritability estimates of 9% at age 1 year, 14% at age 2 years, 10% at age 3 years, 20% at age 4 years, and 36% at age 7 years (Fulker et al. 1988).

In adolescence, the importance of shared environmental influences has completely disappeared, whereas the importance of genetic variance continues to increase; at the age of 17, the heritability of intelligence is estimated to be between 70% and 80% (Luciano et al. 2001a,b; 2006; Rijsdijk et al. 2002). The estimated heritability of intelligence in late adolescence based on adoption studies is 78% (Loehlin et al. 1997). In adulthood, intelligence remains highly heritable (70%–80%), with no significant increases between the ages of 20 and 60 years (Posthuma et al. 2001; 2003). As in young children, adult heritability estimates based on twin studies show a pattern similar to those based on adoption studies. A particularly strong adoption design is the "twins reared apart design," in which twins are separated at a very early age and are adopted by different families. Bouchard (1997) summarized the world literature on monozygotic (MZ) twins reared apart. There are five studies on MZ twins reared apart, with Ns of 12, 19, 38, 45, and 48. The weighted average intraclass correlation is 0.75, which is also an estimate of the heritability, given assumptions about lack of contact and no bias in placement. Bouchard et al. (1990) had shown earlier, in the Minnesota Study of Twins Reared Apart, that the amount of contact between separated twins was not correlated with their similarity on general intelligence.

Much of the information on genetic and environmental contributions to intelligence in old age has come from various analyses within the Swedish Twin Registry, which also has twins reared apart. The Swedish Adoption Twin Study of Ageing is a subset of 25,000 registered same-sex twins born in Sweden between 1886 and 1958. It involves around 300 pairs of MZ and dizygotic (DZ) twins reared apart (MZA, DZA) and together (MZT, DZT; Pedersen et al. 1992). At a mean age of 65.6 years, broad heritability of general intelligence was estimated at about 80%, with evidence of nonadditive genetic effects (Finkel et al. 1996; Pedersen et al. 1992). This corresponds to what is found in old age by others (around 76%; Petrill et al. 1998). Later an even higher heritability of 91% was reported when they corrected for unreliability of measurement at the age of 65 (Reynolds et al. 2005). Shared environment effects were very small, with unique environment accounting for most of the nongenetic variance.

A subsample of the Swedish Twin Registry, the OctoTwin project, includes twins 80 years or older and alive in 1991–1993. The heritability of intelligence was 62%, uncorrected for error of measurement, at a median age of 82 years (range = 80 to >95); 89% lived independently (McClearn et al. 1997). All of the significant environmental contribution was nonshared.

In summary, the heritability of intelligence changes across the life span from about 30% around the age of 3 with, perhaps, a peak of as much as 91% around the age of

65, and some decline in heritability afterwards. Figure 4.1 provides an overview of heritability estimates based on twin samples across the life span (ages 3 to 82 years).

Twin–Singleton Comparisons

Heritability estimates for intelligence are mostly based on twin samples. Twin samples, however, have been criticized for their alleged nongeneralizability. Twin–singleton differences in intrauterine and family environments may lead to different mean levels on phenotypes such as intelligence. It is, therefore, important to investigate whether findings from twin populations can be generalized to singletons.

Twin deliveries are often characterized by prematurity, low birth weight, and lower weight for gestational age (Powers and Kiely 1994). Negative effects of very low birth weight on intellectual development and later IQ are well documented (Shenkin et al. 2004). When growing up, twins may suffer from twin-related stresses in the family environment in which they are reared. A multiple birth puts stress on a family, which may have a negative effect on the (cognitive) development of the twins (Hay and O'Brien 1983).

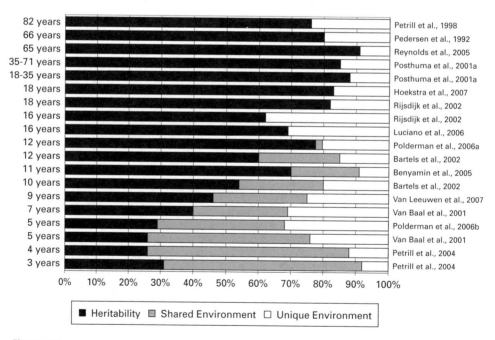

Figure 4.1

Proportion of the variance in IQ explained by genetic factors, shared environmental factors, or unique environmental factors across the life span, based on estimates from twin samples.

A relatively small number of studies have been devoted to detecting twin–singleton differences in cognition (e.g., Nathan and Guttman 1984; Posthuma et al. 2000; Record et al. 1970; Deary et al. 2005; Ronalds et al. 2005; Christensen et al. 2006). Generally, studies that involve children under the age of 12 report significant differences in IQ (up to 5 IQ points) between twins and singletons, favoring singletons (Nathan and Guttman 1984; Record et al. 1970; Deary et al. 2005c; Ronalds et al. 2005). However, after the age of 12 this difference has completely disappeared (Webbink et al. 2008; Posthuma et al. 2000), suggesting there is no lasting cognitive cost of being a twin. The latter was confirmed by Christensen et al. (2006), who found no difference between academic performance of 7,796 singletons compared to 3,411 twins who took the Danish national test of academic achievement in ninth grade (age 15).

It should be noted, however, that even if twins and singletons show mean differences in IQ before the age of 12, this does not necessarily imply that heritability estimates based on samples in this age range are not representative. In fact, the most important issue in generalizability of heritability estimates from twin samples to the general populations is equality of variances. After all, heritability is a ratio of the genetic variance to the total variance of IQ. Thus, the correct question would be "Do twins and singletons show differences in variances on IQ?" This test is usually not carried out. The only exception is in Posthuma et al. (2000). In their adult populations, no differences in either means or variances in IQ were found. Ronalds et al. (2005), who report a large twin–singleton difference in mean IQ score at ages 7 and 9, provide the standard deviations (SD) as well, although they do not formally test for equality of variances. From their table 1 it can be seen that at age 7 the SD for IQ is 15.7 for singletons and 15.8 for twins, and at age 9 it is 16.8 for singletons and 17.6 for twins. These numbers suggest that the variance is not significantly different between twins and singletons and that heritability estimates based on twin samples can thus be generalized to the general population.

Multivariate Studies of IQ and Its Correlates

In this section, we shall address two areas of research in which multivariate modeling approaches have been used to decompose the covariance between IQ and (1) *brain volume* and (2) *brain functioning*.

IQ and Brain Volume

An obvious source of individual differences in intelligence is the size of the brain, which in itself is highly heritable (Baare et al. 2002; Hulshoff Pol et al. 2006; Pennington et al. 2000; Thompson et al. 2001). Since the second half of the nineteenth century, positive relations between head size and intelligence have been observed.

Correlations generally have been around 0.20 (Jensen 1994; Posthuma et al. 2002, 2003) but can be as high as 0.44 (van Valen 1974). Head size is easily measured with a measuring tape as circumference of the head. A more accurate measure of the size of the brain can be obtained through magnetic resonance imaging (MRI). Willerman et al. (1991) correlated brain size as measured with MRI with IQ (measured by the Wechsler Adult Intelligence Scale—Revised; WAIS–R) in a sample of 40 unrelated subjects. They found a correlation of 0.51, which was higher in men (0.65) than in women (0.35). In a follow-up study, Willerman et al. (1992) suggested that, in men, a relatively larger left hemisphere better predicted verbal IQ than it predicted performance IQ, whereas in women the opposite was true. Since then, several studies have provided confirmative evidence that brain volume and IQ correlate around 0.40 (e.g., Egan et al. 1994; Andreasen et al. 1993; Raz et al. 1993; Storfer 1999; Wickett et al. 2000; Posthuma et al. 2002). MacLullich et al. (2002) applied structural equation modeling to one of the largest studies to date ($N = 97$ healthy older men) and found a correlation of 0.42 between a latent general cognitive ability factor from eight mental tests and a latent brain volume factor from six brain areas. McDaniel's (2005) meta-analysis of studies into the relation between brain volume and intelligence found thirty-seven studies with a total N of 1,530. Corrected for range restriction in some samples, the estimated population correlation between brain volume and intelligence was 0.33. Thus, because individual differences in both intelligence and brain volume are partly heritable, and because the two phenotypes are correlated, researchers have examined whether shared genetic effects account for some part of the correlation.

A number of such studies suggest that the correlation between brain volume and IQ derives from the same set of genes' influencing both traits (Hulshoff Pol et al. 2006; Pennington et al. 2000; Posthuma et al. 2002; Wickett et al. 1997). Using a sample of MZ and DZ twins for whom data on both brain volume and IQ was available, Posthuma et al. (2002) calculated correlations between brain volume of a twin and the IQ score of his or her cotwin. They found that this so-called "cross-trait cross-twin" correlation was larger in MZ twins than in DZ twins, which indicates that genes must mediate the correlation between brain volume and IQ. In support of this, they also found that the MZ cross-trait cross-twin correlation was the same as the correlation between brain volume and IQ *in the same person*. This means that the prediction of one's IQ score can be made with similar reliability from one's own brain volume as from the brain volume of one's genetically identical cotwin. A follow-up study that examined genetic correlations between the WAIS–III dimensions of verbal comprehension, perceptual organization, and processing speed and gray and white matter volumes, as well as cerebellar volume, yielded a more complex pattern of results; for example, all three brain volumes were related to working memory capacity, yet verbal comprehension was not related to any of the three (Posthuma et al. 2003). A recent paper by Hulshoff Pol et al. (2006) based on the same sample as Posthuma et al. (2002)

explored the genetic influence on focal gray and white matter densities using voxel-based MRI maps of the brain. Intelligence shared a common genetic origin with superior occipitofrontal, callosal, and left optical radiation white matter and frontal, occipital and parahippocampal gray matter. Phenotypic correlations with IQ were around 0.35 and were completely due to genetic overlap.

IQ and Brain Functioning

Brain volumes, an aspect of structure, provide an important point of entry to the genetic sources of individual differences in IQ but may also be associated with functional aspects of the brain, such as speed of information processing and reaction times. Below we summarize some multivariate genetic studies on IQ and selected measures of brain functioning.

IQ and Speed of Information Processing   Galton (1883) was the first to propose that reaction time is correlated with general intelligence and may be used as a measure of it. His observations and the results of empirical studies afterwards led to the general belief in the speed-of-processing theory of intelligence: the faster the accomplishment of basic cognitive operations, the more intelligent a person will be (Eysenck 1986; Vernon 1987). Since then, reaction times have consistently been negatively related to intelligence (e.g., Vernon 1987; Deary et al. 2001)—that is, a shorter reaction time corresponds to a higher IQ. Correlations with IQ generally range between –0.20 and –0.40 but can be as high as almost –0.50 (Deary et al. 2001) or even –0.60 (Fry and Hale 1996).

Results from twin studies suggest heritabilities for reaction time that are of the same magnitude as those for IQ as reviewed in Spinath and Borkenau (2000). Vernon (1989) found a heritability of 49% in 50 MZ and 52 DZ twins. In the same study it was also found that reaction time tests requiring more complex mental operations show higher heritabilities. A bivariate analysis of the same data set with IQ in 50 MZ and 32 same-sex DZ pairs (15 to 57 years) was reported by Baker et al. (1991). Phenotypic correlations of Verbal and Performance IQ with general speed were both –0.59 and were entirely mediated by genetic factors. This is in line with results from an earlier study in which phenotypic correlations between reaction time (measured as the total number of correct responses on a timed task) and IQ ranged between 0.37 and 0.42, from which 70% to 100% was attributed to genetic factors influencing both reaction time and IQ (Ho et al. 1988).

More recently, Rijsdijk et al. (1998) conducted a multivariate genetic analysis on reaction time data and IQ data, using 213 twin pairs measured at ages 16 and 18. Heritabilities were reported for age 16 of 58%, 57%, and 58% for simple reaction time, choice reaction time, and IQ (measured by Raven's Matrices), respectively. Phenotypic correlations of simple reaction time and choice reaction time with IQ were –0.21 and

−0.22, respectively, and were completely mediated by common genetic factors. Virtually the same picture was shown at age 18, where the same reaction time battery was correlated with IQ as measured with the WAIS.

Neubauer et al. (2000) reported heritability estimates of reaction time data and IQ (measured using Raven) ranging from 11% to 61% and 39% to 81%, respectively. Phenotypic correlations between reaction time data and IQ data were between −0.08 and −0.50, where higher correlations with IQ were found for more complex reaction time tasks. Again, these correlations were mainly (65%) mediated by a common genetic factor.

Evidence for a genetic mediation between reaction time and IQ also emerges from a large twin study by Luciano et al. (2001b). Using reaction time data and IQ data from 166 MZ pairs and 190 DZ pairs, Luciano et al. (2001b) report high heritabilities for both reaction time (79%–90%) and IQ (89%) with phenotypic correlations between −0.31 to −0.56. At least 70% of each of these correlations was due to a common genetic factor.

Another measure of processing speed is inspection time; this is a measure of central nervous system processing and is defined as the minimum display time a subject needs for making an accurate perceptual discrimination on an obvious stimulus (Deary 2001). It is distinct from reaction time; since there is no need to make the discrimination quickly, all that is required is an accurate response. Visual inspection time can easily be measured in a computerized version of the paradigm in which subjects are asked to decide which leg of a vertically asymmetrical Π-shaped figure is longest. Visual inspection time is generally thought to reflect speed of apprehension or perceptual speed. The less time a person needs to make an accurate decision on an obvious stimulus, the higher the IQ. The overall consensus on the relation between inspection time and IQ is given by Deary and Stough (1996): "inspection time accounts for approximately 20% of intelligence-test variance."

Two twin studies have investigated whether the relation between inspection time and IQ is mediated by shared genetic factors or by shared environmental factors (Luciano et al. 2001a; Posthuma et al. 2001a). These two studies were also the first to report on the heritability of inspection time per se. Using 184 MZ pairs and 206 DZ pairs age 16, Luciano et al. (2001a) reported a heritability estimate for inspection time of 36%. Using 102 MZ pairs and 525 DZ/sib pairs belonging to two age cohorts (mean ages = 26 and 50), Posthuma et al. (2001a) reported a slightly higher heritability estimate of inspection time (46%) at both ages.

Luciano et al. (2001a) reported a correlation between inspection time and performance IQ of −0.35 and between inspection time and verbal IQ of −0.26. Posthuma et al. (2001a) reported slightly lower correlations; −0.27 and −0.19, respectively. Both studies unanimously found that the phenotypic correlations between inspection time and performance IQ/verbal IQ were completely mediated by common genetic factors.

In summary, reaction time explains between 10% and 30% of IQ test variance, and this covariance is nearly completely (between 65% and 100%) due to a common genetic origin. Inspection time explains between 10% and 42% of IQ test variance, and this covariance is completely due to a common genetic origin.

Gene–Environment Interaction and Correlation

In the above we have shown the increasing heritability of IQ across the life span and have summarized some of the possible underlying biological pathways that may lead to individual differences in IQ. However, the established high heritability of intelligence of around 60% to 80% in late adulthood is based on the observation that MZ twins correlate about 0.60 to 0.80 on tests of intelligence, whereas DZ twins score around half of that. The results described above are obtained under the assumption that such a pattern of twin correlations is explained by simply adding the separate effects of genes and environmental factors. However, the same pattern of twin correlations may also be the result of *interactions* between genetic and (shared) environmental effects (G × E), or by *correlations* (rGE) between the presence of genes and environmental factors. Below we shall describe the concepts of G × E and rGE and the impact of ignoring these influences in statistical methods.

G × E refers to the situation where the effect of environmental influences is dependent on genotype, or vice versa, when the expression of genes depends on the presence of certain environmental influences. In the context of intelligence, this may, for example, be reflected in a differential impact of an intellectually stimulating family environment on individuals with different genotypes. The hypothesis that there is a nonlinear association between heritability and shared environment and family background was tested in 114 MZ and 205 DZ pairs of 7-year-olds (54% black, 43% white) from the National Collaborative Perinatal Project (Turkheimer et al. 2003). This sample has a high proportion of impoverished families. One useful summary is an analysis in which families were dichotomized into high and low SES. For high-SES families, heritability was 71% and shared environmental contribution was 15%. For low-SES families, heritability was 10% and shared environmental contribution was 58%. This suggests that the causes of individual differences in intelligence are mainly due to environmental differences in low-SES families, whereas in high-SES families differences in intelligence are mainly genetic in origin. Environmental mediation of genetic effects for intelligence has also been shown by Rowe et al. (1999), who found that for low parental education the heritability of intelligence in the offspring was lower (26%) than in the high parental education group (74%). Gene by shared environment (such as parental SES or parental education) interaction will mimic purely additive genetic effects in statistical models that ignore G × E, whereas gene by nonshared environment interaction will mimic nonshared environmental influences.

Whereas G × E refers to genes moderating sensitivity to the environment (or vice versa), rGE refers to genes controlling the exposure to environmental factors, or environmental factors controlling gene frequencies. Generally three types of rGE can be described (Plomin et al. 2001):

Passive This type of rGE occurs when parents transmit both genotypes and relevant environmental factors, a mechanism known as "cultural transmission." For example, intellectually gifted parents may transmit genes influencing intellectual capabilities and also provide an intellectually stimulating environment for their children. This type of rGE necessitates the interaction between related subjects.

Evocative (also known as reactive) This type of rGE occurs when the treatment of individuals by others is based on their genetic predispositions. For example, bright children may be offered additional study materials by their teachers and be selectively admitted to higher type education.

Active This type of rGE occurs when individuals seek out environments based on a genetic predisposition. For instance, intellectually less advantaged children may avoid the library and educational opportunities on the Internet.

Such gene–environment correlation tends to increase the DZ correlation, while the MZ correlation remains the same. Even more complex models allow reciprocal causation between intelligence and environmental factors, resulting in strong correlations between genetic endowment and favorable environmental conditions (Dickens and Flynn 2001).

A final well-known form of actively induced gene–environment correlation is assortative mating, which not only affects the presence of environmental factors in a person himself or herself but also affects resemblance in the offspring. Assortative mating is reflected in a spousal correlation greater than zero, and it is known to indeed exist for intelligence, where spousal correlations are around 0.30. When high-IQ mothers more often elect high-IQ fathers as mates (and vice versa), this will increase the resemblance between parents and offspring as well as among siblings and dizygotic twins. In twin studies, this may conceal the presence of nonadditive genetic effects (gene–gene interactions or genetic dominance) and overestimate the influence of additive genetic factors.

How can we show that complex mechanisms such as gene–gene interaction, gene–environment interaction, and gene–environment correlation are indeed important for intelligence? Finding the actual genes may be a crucial step forward. When genetic variation is no longer a "latent factor" in our model but can actually be measured, investigating genetic effects while allowing for the interplay between genes and environmental factors becomes a realistic goal. Measuring actual genetic variation would further allow testing the effects of genes under different naturally occurring "experimental" environmental conditions, using simple designs—for example, comparing the effect of variation in the gene in groups of children with high- or low-educated parents.

In the past decade genotyping large samples has become feasible, and many clues have emerged as to the genetic basis of intelligence. Below we shall review the progress made.

Molecular Genetics and Intelligence

Whole Genome Approach

A fail-safe approach to identify genes influencing intelligence is to type a large group of subjects at each DNA base pair. However, genotyping thousands of individuals at each of 3 billion loci is currently beyond our means. Researchers therefore adopt strategies of whole genome linkage and association analysis to identify quantitative trait loci (QTLs; Carlson et al. 2004).

Association analysis is similar in design to a classic case–control study in epidemiology. DNA is collected from all participants, and the cognitive trait is compared across the various allelic variants of the DNA marker. Vice versa, frequencies of the various allelic variants may be compared in subjects with a particular deviation in cognition (e.g., schizophrenia) to detect an association between a particular allele and the occurrence of the cognitive deviation. DNA markers can be mutations in a single base pair (single nucleotide polymorphisms; SNPs) or a variable number of repeats of two or more base pairs (microsatellites). Recently, copy number variations—that is, variations in the number of deleted or duplicated versions of segments of the genome—were suggested as additional markers for genetic association studies (Redon et al. 2006). Genetic markers used for association studies need not be part of a functional gene— they are just landmarks in the genome. In a genome-wide association (GWA) study, tens or hundreds of thousands of markers (mostly SNPs) are tested simultaneously. Although only a subset of all possible markers are tested, the ones selected are chosen to represent the untested markers as well as possible, that is, their variation is expected to correlate highly with the variation in unassayed markers. This allows associations to be detected on a genome-wide basis.

The costs of doing GWA studies have been prohibitive until very recently. The existing genome-wide direct association studies for IQ, therefore, used a more cost-effective approach called allelic or "pooled" association. In pooled allelic association, pools of DNA are formed by combining samples from individuals differing in mean score on the trait. The two or more pools are then typed, and a comparison is made of the frequency of alleles for each marker between the comparison groups. False positives are controlled by generating candidates from one sample and then examining these in additional samples to ensure that they replicate. Over the last decade, this method has been championed by Plomin and coworkers, beginning with an association analysis of 100 markers close to candidate genes in high and low IQ groups. Extensions of this approach have led to the report of the association of a functional polymorphism in ALDH5A1 (MIM 271980) with cognitive ability (Plomin et al. 2004). Recently, this group reported the first genome-wide level allelic association study for cognition (Butcher et al. 2005). They found significant association for a composite of cognitive measures (a *g* factor) taken at age 7 years in a sample of 7,000 twins. Five of the 10,000 SNPs showed replicable association. These lay on chromosomes 2, 6, 7, 11, and 18 and together accounted for less than 1% of the variance in cognition. The genes or functions associated within these SNPs are unknown.

In genome-wide linkage analysis, evidence for genetic linkage is obtained through statistical procedures that trace how often the trait and the DNA marker are jointly passed along in familial lineages. If such a cosegregation of DNA marker and trait can be established with sufficient statistical confidence, then one or more genes in those regions are possibly involved in trait similarity among individuals. Linkage analysis thus serves to detect the regions (QTLs) of the genome where genetic variants with a quantitative effect on the trait must be located.

The first whole genome linkage scan for intelligence was published in 2005 (Posthuma et al. 2005). The sample used in this study consisted of a Dutch sample (159 sibling pairs) and an Australian sample (475 sibling pairs). Results indicated two significant areas of linkage to general intelligence (on the long arm of chromosome 2 and the short arm of chromosome 6), and several areas of suggestive linkage (4p, 7q, 20p, 21p). The chromosome 2 area has been implicated in linkage scans for autism and dyslexia, while the chromosome 6 area is the main linkage area for reading ability and dyslexia. The chromosome 6 linkage lies close to, but a bit further downstream to the association that was reported in the genome-wide allelic association study by Butcher et al. (2005).

Four linkage studies for IQ have been published since (Buyske et al. 2006; Dick et al. 2006; Luciano et al. 2006; Wainwright et al. 2006). Two studies with a partly overlapping sample confirmed the importance of the areas on chromosomes 2 and 6 for specific aspects of intelligence (Luciano et al. 2006) as well as academic achievement, which is highly correlated with IQ scores (Wainwright et al. 2006). The Luciano et al. (2006) study additionally showed that both word recognition and IQ were linked to chromosome 2, confirming the notion of the same genes' influencing different aspects of cognitive ability (Plomin and Kovas 2005).

A completely independent study by Dick et al. (2006) using data collected as part of the Collaborative Study on the Genetics of Alcoholism (COGA) also confirmed linkage of intelligence to the chromosome 6 area. A second scan based on that data set (Buyske et al. 2006) found strong evidence for linkage of specific cognitive abilities on chromosome 14, an area that showed suggestive evidence for linkage in three of the five linkage studies. Although the COGA data set has been selected for alcohol dependence and may thus not be representative of the general population, Dick et al. (2006) showed that alcohol dependence explained less than 1% of the variance in IQ scores. Moreover, a correction for ascertainment did not change the results significantly.

These first genome-wide linkages of normal ability in unselected samples show convergence with linkage in clinical disorder. For instance, 2q21–33 holds a gene related to autism (Buxbaum et al. 2001) and has been linked to cognitive deficits in childhood-onset schizophrenia (Addington et al. 2004), while the 6p region has been associated with dyslexia, especially speeded reading measures. It might be more generally the case that small mutations or slightly inefficient variants of genes detected in linkage analyses affect normal ability, while more severe mutants which greatly alter gene function or expression result in disorders such as autism, attention-deficit/hyperactivity disorder, and Williams syndrome.

Candidate Gene Approach

In candidate gene association analysis, known "candidate" genes are selected based on existing neuroscientific evidence. Allelic variation in these genes is measured and tested for association with intelligence. The measured allelic variants can either be (1) the functional variant that is responsible for the gene's effect on intelligence or (2) variants that do not alter the gene effect but are closely correlated with the true (but unmeasured) functional variant, that is, in linkage disequilibrium (LD) with it. Case–control association studies in which, for example, a sample of subjects with high IQ scores (cases) is compared with a sample of subjects with lower IQ (controls) have the highest statistical power but may provide spurious associations as a result of the use of stratified samples. Any trait that has a different distribution across cases and controls (e.g., due to cultural differences between ethnic strata or assortative mating within strata) will show a statistical association with any allele that shows a different frequency across cases and controls. Family-based association studies are statistically less powerful but control for these effects of population stratification, as allelic association is tested exclusively within members of the same family.

In association analysis, the choice of candidate genes is crucial. It is usually based on prior knowledge of the gene's involvement in biological functions relevant to intelligence, such as neurophysiological systems known to influence human memory and cognition. Candidate genes can also be selected based on results from animal studies, in which they have been shown to influence test performance of animal learning and memory. Another source of candidates is genes associated with mental retardation (Inlow and Restifo 2004; Ramakers 2002). Alternatively, allelic variants that show continuous adaptive evolution in modern humans may pose good candidate genes for intelligence (Zhang 2003; Evans et al. 2005; Gilbert et al. 2005). Recently, several studies using a variety of methods have appeared that provide lists of such genes (Dorus et al. 2004; Pollard et al. 2006; Sabeti et al. 2006; Voight et al. 2006).

It is unwise, however, to rely on biological plausibility only. Poor replication of an initially promising association result is a common concern in the molecular genetic study of complex brain functioning. This is illustrated by studies with two allelic variants that have been reported to show continuous adaptive evolution in modern humans, the abnormal spindle-like microcephaly associated (ASPM; Mekel-Bobrov et al. 2005) and microcephalin (MCPH1; Evans et al. 2005) genes. These genes are known to be under positive selection and to be involved in human brain volume, and they therefore pose good candidate genes for IQ (see, e.g., Thompson et al. 2001; Posthuma et al. 2002). Recently, Mekel-Bobrov et al. (2007) used three family-based samples (one Australian and two Dutch) as well as the population-based Scottish Aberdeen (ABC1936) and Lothian (LBC1921) birth cohorts, totaling 2,393 subjects. For the ASPM gene, a significant association was found in four of the five samples, with the nonsignificant result in the youngest (12-year-olds) sample. However, in two samples (Dutch adults and LBC1921) the beneficial allele was the allelic variant under selective pressure (the derived allele), whereas in the other two samples it was the ancestral allele. For MCPH1, a significant positive association was seen for the derived allele in the Dutch 12-year-olds, but this was not replicated in any of the other samples. These results thus remain inconclusive and can probably not be explained by differences in LD patterns across populations (as in that case the specific polymorphism would not have been under selective pressure). Woods and colleagues (2006) further showed that, although it is known that other genetic variants in both ASPM and MCPH1 are involved in the determination of brain volume, selective pressure on these genes cannot be explained by selective pressure on brain volume.

Although the example above encourages caution, association analysis can be very effective. Below we review three cognition–genotype associations that are plausible and have held up in independent replication (see also Posthuma and de Geus 2006). A meta-analysis of thirty-eight studies (more than 20,000 subjects) found that possession of the E4 allele of apolipoprotein E was associated in older people with poorer performance on tests of global cognitive function, episodic memory, and executive function (Small et al. 2004). The E2 allele appeared to be protective. The effect size was small, at about one-tenth of a standard deviation unit. This is an interesting case of variation in a gene that is related to cognition in old age but not in youth (Deary et al. 2002). The mechanisms whereby the variations are detrimental and protective to cognition are not understood, although there are various suggestions (Smith 2002). The follow-up studies of the Scottish Mental Survey of 1932 reported that variation in the genes for Klotho (Deary et al. 2005b) and nicastrin (Deary et al. 2005a) might be associated with general intelligence at both ages 11 and 79 years, but these are, as yet, unreplicated.

The catechol-O-methyltransferase (COMT) gene has been one of the most extensively studied candidate genes in relation to cognitive ability. Decreased COMT activity might be beneficial from a functional perspective, because it increases frontal dopamine signaling. In line with this, Savitz et al. (2006) found that in twenty of the twenty-six studies on the association between the *COMT* val[108/158]met polymorphism and cognitive function, a significant association was reported. All but two of these studies suggested that the low-activity *Met* allele allows for better performance on cognitive tasks that have a working memory component. The association with intelligence may be more complex. Gosso et al. (2008) showed that the link between *COMT* and cognitive functioning follows a complex pattern in which the COMT gene interacts with the dopamine receptor D2 (DRD2) gene. They found an association between the *COMT* gene and intelligence reflecting positive heterosis such that the Met/Met and Val/Val homozygotes performed less well than the Met/Val heterozygotes on working memory tasks. Gosso and colleagues also found a significant interactive effect of the *DRD2* and *COMT* genes, such that heterosis was present only in the *DRD2* genotype that has been linked to lower receptor density. These results support previous findings (Reuter et al. 2005) that suggest that working memory performance requires an optimal level of dopamine signaling within the prefrontal cortex. This optimum level depends on enzymatic activity controlling dopamine level as well as dopamine receptor sensitivity, both of which may differ as a function of genotype. As a consequence, the effects of a single polymorphism in a dopaminergic gene on a well-defined cognitive trait may easily remain hidden if the interaction with other genes in the pathway is not taken into account.

One of the strongest associations in the current literature is the association between intelligence and the cholinergic muscarinic receptor 2 (CHRM2) gene. In 2003, Comings et al. reported that this gene explained 1% of the variance in full-scale IQ. Two years later, suggestive linkage for intelligence was found on 7q, right above the CHRM2 gene (Posthuma et al. 2005). Subsequently, Gosso et al. (2006b) replicated the association between the *CHRM2* gene and intelligence in a combined sample of Dutch 12-year-olds and Dutch young adults. Here the gene explained 2% of the total variance in full scale IQ. Recently Dick et al. (2007) confirmed the same area to be positively associated with intelligence. Although Comings et al. (2003), Gosso et al. (2006b), and Dick et al. (2007) did not include functional variants of the *CHRM2* gene, the variants that showed positive association were all in the same region of this gene, suggesting that functional variants within that region are of importance to intelligence.

Other genes with variations related to intelligence are the SNAP-25 gene (Gosso et al. 2006), the dysbindin 1 (DTNBP1) gene (Burdick et al. 2006), and the cathepsin D gene (Payton et al. 2003). Although it was originally associated specifically with memory, the gene for brain-derived neurotrophic factor has been associated with intelligence (Tsai et al. 2004) and reasoning skills (Harris et al. 2006). All of these have small effects, consistent with a polygenic view of the heritability of intelligence. Most of these genes are also related to other domains of cognitive functioning.

To understand the underlying mechanisms linking individual differences in specific cognitive abilities to intelligence or to brain pathology, we should adopt a multivariate approach in which we allow the same genes to influence these multiple traits. This multivariate approach has the added advantage of increasing the power of gene-finding studies as has been shown, for example, by Zhang et al. (2005), who used multivariate electrophysiological measures from the COGA study that had been linked previously to alcoholism. They found evidence for genetic linkage on two new chromosomes that were not detected in univariate analyses.

Conclusion

The last decade has just started to dissect the now well-established heritability of cognitive ability into its molecular genetic elements. Most researchers ascribe to a polygenic view of the genetic contributions to intelligence differences but are as yet in the dark as to how many genetic variants are involved or how big their effects are. Genome-wide studies to date strongly suggest that there will be no genes with a large or moderate effect, and, therefore, studies aimed at securely identifying genetic contributions to cognitive differences will probably require very large samples, especially when a genome-wide approach is adapted. Statistically more powerful candidate gene studies have so far identified a handful of genes, but only a few of these have as yet shown replicated associations with intelligence. All of the identified genes have small effects, consistent with a polygenic view of the heritability of intelligence. Most of these genes are also related to other domains of cognitive functioning, supporting the recently introduced "generalist genes" theory, which states that the same genes affect multiple cognitive abilities (Plomin and Kovas 2005; Kovas and Plomin 2006; Butcher et al. 2006), as opposed to the classic "specialist genes" view, which states that each gene affects one trait. The "generalist genes" hypothesis also implies that some cognitive disabilities are the extremes of normally distributed dimensions of cognitive abilities. Therefore, some of the same genes that have been associated with normal cognitive abilities could provide important clues to underlying mechanisms of milder but more prevalent forms of impaired cognitive functioning, like reading disorder, dyslexia, and attention-deficit/hyperactivity disorder or even the severe cognitive deficits seen in autism and schizophrenia.

Figure 4.2 summarizes the genetic association and linkage studies for intelligence reviewed above. The figure clearly shows that identifying genes with an influence on cognition is feasible but that we have still a long way to go. Also, identifying these polygenes is only a first step; we still face the daunting task of charting the exact route from genetic variation to variation in brain function and on to individual differences in intelligence. Fortunately, as many chapters in this book show, using state-of-the-art brain imaging in subjects carefully selected for genotype is proving to be a powerful

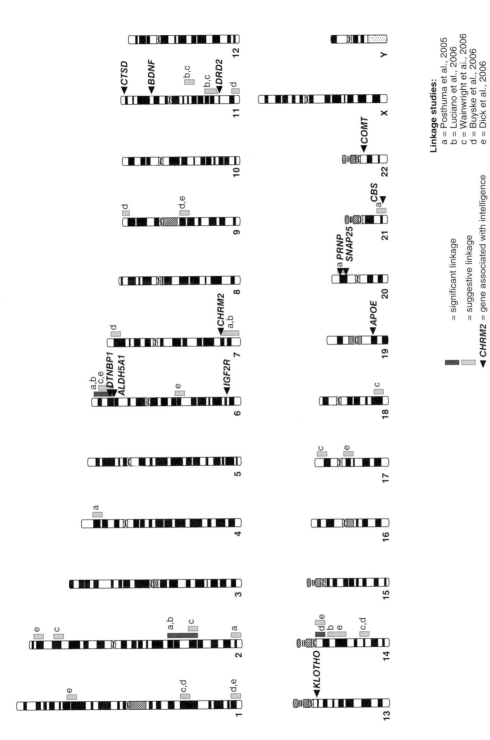

Figure 4.2

Ideogram of the human genome indicating which regions in the genome are likely to contain genes for intelligence, as based on the five linkage studies for intelligence that have been conducted to date. It also shows the chromosomal regions of all the genes that have been associated with intelligence so far (Reprinted with permission from Posthuma and De Geus, 2006).

way to do just that. Nonetheless, understanding how genetic variation affects brain functioning related to cognition remains one of the greatest scientific challenges of the twenty-first century.

References

Addington AM, Gornick M, Sporn AL, Gogtay N, Greenstein D, Lenane M, et al. (2004). Polymorphisms in the 13q33.2 gene G72/G30 are associated with childhood-onset schizophrenia and psychosis not otherwise specified. *Biol Psychiatry*, 55(10):976–80.

Andreasen NC, Flaum M, Swayze V 2nd, O'Leary DS, Alliger R, Cohen G, et al. (1993). Intelligence and brain structure in normal individuals. *Am J Psychiatry*, 150:130–4.

Baare WF, Hulshoff Pol HE, Boomsma DI, Posthuma D, de Geus EJ (2002). Quantitative genetic modeling of variation in human brain morphology. *Cereb Cortex*, 11:816–24.

Baker LA, Vernon PA, Ho HZ (1991). The genetic correlation between intelligence and speed of information processing. *Behav Genet*, 21:351–67.

Bartels M, Rietveld MJH, Van Baal GCM, Boomsma DI (2002). Genetic and environmental influences on the development of intelligence. *Behav Genet*, 32:237–49.

Batty GD, Deary IJ, Gottfredson LS (2007). Premorbid (early life) IQ and later mortality risk: systematic review. *Ann Epidemiol*, 17:278–88.

Benyamin B, Wilson V, Whalley LJ, Visscher, PM, Deary IJ (2005). Large, consistent estimates of the heritability of cognitive ability in two entire populations of 11-year-old twins from Scottish Mental Surveys of 1932 and 1947. *Behav Genet*, 35:525–34.

Boomsma DI, van Baal GCM (1998). Genetic influences on childhood IQ in 5- and 7-year-old Dutch twins. *Dev Neuropsychol*, 14:115–26.

Bouchard TJ (1997). IQ similarity in twins reared apart: findings and responses to critics. In Intelligence, heredity, and environment (pp. 126–60). Cambridge: Cambridge University Press.

Bouchard TJ, Lykken DT, McGue M, Segal NL, Tellegen A (1990). Sources of human psychological differences: the Minnesota Study of Twins Reared Apart. *Science*, 250:223–8.

Bouchard TJ, McGue M (1981). Familial studies of intelligence: a review. *Science*, 212:1055–9.

Burdick KE, Lencz T, Funke B, Finn CT, Szeszko PR, Kane JM, et al. (2006). Genetic variation in DTNBP1 influences general cognitive ability. *Hum Mol Genet*, 15:1563–8.

Butcher LM, Kennedy JK, Plomin R (2006). Generalist genes and cognitive neuroscience. *Curr Opin Neurobiol*, 16:145–51.

Butcher LM, Meaburn E, Knight J, Sham PC, Schalkwyk LC, Craig IW, Plomin R (2005). SNPs, microarrays and pooled DNA: identification of four loci associated with mild mental impairment in a sample of 6000 children. *Hum Mol Genet*, 14:1315–25.

Buxbaum JD, Silverman JM, Smith CJ, Kilifarski M, Reichert J, Hollander E, Lawlor BA, Fitzgerald M, Greenberg DA, Davis KL (2001). Evidence for a susceptibility gene for autism on chromosome 2 and for genetic heterogeneity. *Am J Hum Genet*, 68(6):1514–20.

Buyske S, Bates ME, Gharani N, Matise TC, Tischfield JA, Manowitz P (2006). Cognitive traits link to human chromosomal regions. *Behav Genet*, 36:65–76.

Carlson CS, Eberle MA, Kruglyak L, Nickerson DA (2004). Mapping complex disease loci in whole-genome association studies. *Nature*, 429:446–52.

Carroll JB (1993). Human cognitive abilities: a survey of factor analytic studies. Cambridge: Cambridge University Press.

Christensen K, Petersen I, Skytthe A, Herskind AM, McGue M, Bingley P (2006). Comparison of academic performance of twins and singletons in adolescence: follow-up study. *BMJ*, 333:1095.

Comings DE, Wu S, Rostamkhani M, McGue M, Lacono WG, Cheng LS, MacMurray JP (2003). Role of the cholinergic muscarinic 2 receptor (CHRM2) gene in cognition. *Mol Psychiatry*, 8:10–3.

Deary IJ (2001). Human intelligence differences: towards a combined experimental–differential approach. *Trends Cogn Sci*, 5:164–70.

Deary IJ, Der G, Ford G (2001). Reaction times and intelligence differences: a population-based cohort study. *Intelligence*, 29:389–99.

Deary IJ, Hamilton G, Hayward C, Whalley LJ, Powell J, Starr JM, Lovestone S (2005a). Nicastrin gene polymorphisms, cognitive ability level and cognitive ageing. *Neurosci Lett*, 373:110–4.

Deary IJ, Harris SE, Fox HC, Hayward C, Wright AF, Starr JM, Whalley LJ (2005b). KLOTHO genotype and cognitive ability in childhood and old age in the same individuals. *Neurosci Lett*, 378:22–7.

Deary IJ, Pattie A, Wilson V, Whalley L (2005c). The cognitive cost of being a twin: two whole-population surveys. *Twin Research and Human Genetics*, 8:376–83.

Deary IJ, Stough C (1996). Intelligence and inspection time: achievements, prospects, and problems. *Am Psychologist*, 51:599–608.

Deary IJ, Strand S, Smith P, Fernandes C (2007). Intelligence and educational achievement. *Intelligence*, 35:13–21.

Deary IJ, Whiteman MC, Pattie A, Starr JM, Hayward C, Wright AF, et al. (2002). Cognitive change and the APOE e4 allele. *Nature*, 418:932.

Deary IJ, Whiteman MC, Starr JM, Whalley LJ, Fox HC (2004). The impact of childhood intelligence on later life: following up the Scottish Mental Surveys of 1932 and 1947. *J Pers Soc Psychol*, 86:130–47.

Dick DM, Aliev F, Bierut L, Goate A, Rice J, Hinrichs A, et al. (2006). Linkage analyses of IQ in the Collaborative Study on the Genetics of Alcoholism (COGA) sample. *Behav Genet*, 36:77–86.

Dick DM, Aliev F, Kramer J, Wang JC, Hinrichs A (2007). CHRM2 association of CHRM2 with IQ: converging evidence for a gene influencing intelligence. *Behav Genet*, 37:265–72.

Dickens WT, Flynn JR (2001). Heritability estimates versus large environmental effects: the IQ paradox resolved. *Psychological Review*, 108:346–69.

Dorus S, Vallender EJ, Evans PD, Anderson JR, Gilbert SL, Mahowald M, et al. (2004). Accelerated evolution of nervous system genes in the origin of *Homo sapiens*. *Cell*, 119:1027–40.

Egan V, Chiswick A, Santosh C, Naidu K, Rimmington JE, Best JJK (1994). Size isn't everything—a study of brain volume, intelligence and auditory-evoked potentials. *Pers Indiv Diff*, 17:357–67.

Evans PD, Gilbert SL, Mekel-Bobrov N, Vallender EJ, Anderson JR, Vaez-Azizi LM, et al. (2005). Microcephalin, a gene regulating brain size, continues to evolve adaptively in humans. *Science*, 309:1717–20.

Eysenck HJ (1986). Toward a new model of intelligence. *Pers Indiv Diff*, 7:731–6.

Finkel D, Pedersen NL, McLearn GE, Plomin R, Berg S (1996). Crosssequential analysis of genetic influences on cognitive ability in the Swedish adoption/twin study of ageing. *Aging Neuropsychol Cogn*, 3:84–99.

Fry AF, Hale S (1996). Processing speed, working memory, and fluid intelligence: evidence for a developmental cascade. *Psychol Sci*, 7:237–41.

Fulker DW, DeFries JC, Plomin R (1988). Genetic influence on general mental ability increases between infancy and middle childhood. *Nature*, 336:767–9.

Galton F (1883). *Inquiries into human faculty and its development*. London: Macmillian, Everyman's Library.

Gilbert SL, Dobyns WB, Lahn BT (2005). Genetic links between brain development and brain evolution. *Nat Rev Genet*, 6:581–90.

Gosso MF, de Geus EJC, Polderman TJC, Boomsma DI, Heutink P, Posthuma D (2008). Catechol O-methyl transferase and dopamine D2 receptor gene polymorphisms: evidence of positive heterosis and gene–gene interaction on working memory functioning. *Eur J Hum Gene*, 16: 1075–82.

Gosso MF, de Geus EJC, van Belzen MJ, Polderman TJC, Heutink P, Boomsma DI, Posthuma D (2006a). The SNAP-25 gene is associated with cognitive ability: evidence from a family based study in two independent Dutch cohorts. *Mol Psychiatry*, 11:878–86.

Gosso MF, van Belzen M, de Geus EJC, Polderman JC, Heutink P, Boomsma DI, Posthuma D (2006b). Family based association testing provides further evidence for a role of the CHRM2 gene in cognition. *Genes Brain Behav*, 5:577–84.

Gottfredson LS (1997). Mainstream science on intelligence: an editorial with 52 signatories, history, and bibliography. *Intelligence*, 24:13–23.

Harris SE, Fox H, Wright AF, Hayward C, Starr JM, Whalley LJ, Deary IJ (2006). The brain derived neurotrophic factor polymorphism is associated with age-related change in reasoning skills. *Mol Psychiatry*, 11:505–13.

Hay DA, O'Brien PJ (1983). The La Trobe Twin Study: a genetic approach to the structure and development of cognition in twin children. *Child Dev*, 54:317–30.

Ho HZ, Baker LA, Decker SN (1988). Covariation between intelligence and speed of cognitive processing: genetic and environmental influences. *Behav Genet*, 8:247.

Hoekstra RA, Bartels M, Boomsma DI (2007). Longitudinal genetic study of verbal and nonverbal IQ from early childhood to young adulthood. *Learning and Individual Differences*, 17:97–114.

Hulshoff Pol HE, Schnack HG, Posthuma D, Mandl RCW, Baaré WF, van Oel C, et al. (2006). A genetic neural network involved in human intelligence. *J Neurosci*, 26:10235–42.

Inlow JK, Restifo LL (2004). Molecular and comparative genetics of mental retardation. *Genetics*, 166:835–81.

Jensen AR (1994). Psychometric g related to differences in head size. *Pers Indiv Diff*, 17:597–606.

Kovas Y, Plomin R (2006). Generalist genes: implications for the cognitive sciences. *Trends Cogn Sci*, 10:198–203.

Loehlin JC, Horn JM, Willerman L (1997). Heredity, environment, and IQ in the Texas Adoption Project. In Intelligence, heredity, and environment (pp. 105–125). Cambridge: Cambridge University Press.

Luciano M, Smith GA, Wright MJ, Geffen GM, Geffen LB, Martin NM (2001a). On the heritability of inspection time and its covariance with IQ: a twin study. *Intelligence*, 29:443–57.

Luciano M, Wright MJ, Duffy MA, Wainwright MA, Zhu G, Evans DM, Geffen GM, Montgomery GW, Martin NG (2006). Genome-wide scan of IQ finds significant linkage to a quantitative trait locus on 2q. *Behav Genet*, 36:45–55.

Luciano M, Wright MJ, Smith GA, Geffen GM, Geffen LB, Martin NG (2001b). Genetic covariance among measures of information processing speed, working memory and IQ. *Behav Genet*, 31:581–92.

MacLullich, AMJ, Ferguson, KJ, Deary IJ, Seckl JR, Starr JM, Wardlaw JM (2002). Intracranial capacity and brain volumes are associated with cognition in healthy elderly men. *Neurology*, 59:169–74.

McClearn GE, Johansson B, Berg S, Pedersen NL, Ahern F, Petrill SA, Plomin R (1997). Substantial genetic influence on cognitive abilities in twins 80 or more years old. *Science*, 276:1560–3.

McDaniel MA (2005). Big-brained people are smarter: a meta-analysis of the relationship between in vivo brain volume and intelligence. *Intelligence*, 33:337–46.

Mekel-Bobrov N, Gilbert SL, Evans PD, Vallender EJ, Anderson JR, Hudson RR, et al. (2005). Ongoing adaptive evolution of ASPM, a brain size determinant in *Homo sapiens*. *Science*, 309:1720–2.

Mekel-Bobrov N, Posthuma D, Gilbert SL, Lind P, Gosso MF, Luciano M, et al. (2007). The ongoing adaptive evolution of *ASPM* and *Microcephalin* is not explained by increased intelligence. *Hum Mol Genet*, 16:600–8.

Nathan M, Guttman R (1984). Similarities in test scores and profiles of kibbutz twins and singletons. *Acta Geneticae Medicae et Gemellologiae: Twin Res*, 33:213–8.

Neisser U, Boodoo G, Bouchard TJ Jr, Boykin AW, Brody N, Ceci SJ, Halpern DF, Loehlin JC, Perloff R, Sternberg RJ, Urbina S (1996). Intelligence: knowns and unknowns. Am Psychol 51:77–101.

Neubauer AC, Spinath FM, Riemann R, Angleitner A, Borkenau P (2000). Genetic and environmental influences on two measures of speed of information processing and their relation to psychometric intelligence: evidence from the German Observational Study of Adult Twins. *Intelligence*, 28:267–89.

Payton A, Holland F, Diggle P, et al. (2003). Cathepsin D exon 2 polymorphism associated with general intelligence in a healthy older population. *Mol Psychiatry*, 8:1–5.

Pedersen NL, Plomin R, Nesselroade JR, McClearn GE (1992). A quantitative genetic analysis of cognitive abilities during the second half of the lifespan. *Psychol Sci*, 3:346–53.

Pennington BF, Filipek PA, Lefly D, Chhabildas N, Kennedy DN, Simon JH, et al. (2000). A twin MRI study of size variations in human brain. *J Cogn Neurosci*, 12:223–32.

Petrill SA, Pike A, Price T, Plomin R (2004). Chaos in the home and socioeconomic status are associated with cognitive development in early childhood: environmental mediators identified in a genetic design. *Intelligence*, 32:445–60.

Petrill SA, Plomin R, Berg S, Rabbitt P, Horan M, Davidson Y, Gibbons L, Worthington J, Ollier WE, Pendleton N (1998). The genetic and environmental relationship between general and specific cognitive abilities in twins age 80 and older. *Psychol Sci*, 9:183–9.

Plomin R, DeFries JC (1985). Origins of individual differences in infancy: the Colorado Adoption Project. Orlando: Academic Press.

Plomin R, DeFries JC, McClearn GE, McGuffin P (2001). Behavioral genetics, fourth edition. New York: W. H. Freeman.

Plomin R, Kovas Y (2005). Generalist genes and learning disabilities. *Psychol Bull*, 131:592–617.

Plomin R, Spinath FM (2004). Intelligence: genetics, genes, and genomics. *J Pers Soc Psychol*, 86:112–29.

Plomin R, Turic DM, Hill L, Turic DE, Stephens M, Williams J, Owen MJ, O'Donovan MC (2004). A functional polymorphism in the succinate-semialdehyde dehydrogenase (aldehyde dehydrogenase 5 family, member a1) gene is associated with cognitive ability. *Mol Psychiatry*, 9:582–6.

Polderman TJ, Gosso MF, Posthuma D, Van Beijsterveldt TC, Heutink P, Verhulst FC, Boomsma DI (2006a). A longitudinal twin study on IQ, executive functioning, and attention problems during childhood and early adolescence. *Acta Neurol Belg*, 106(4):191–207.

Polderman TJC, Stins JF, Posthuma D, Gosso MF, Verhulst FC, Boomsma DI (2006b). The phenotypic and genotypic relation between working memory speed and capacity. *Intelligence*, 34: 549–60.

Pollard KS, Salama SR, Lambert N, Lambot MA, Coppens S, Pedersen JS, et al. (2006). An RNA gene expressed during cortical development evolved rapidly in humans. *Nature*, 443:167–72.

Posthuma D, Baare WF, Hulshoff Pol HE, Kahn RS, Boomsma DI, de Geus EJC (2003). Genetic correlations between brain volumes and the WAIS–III dimensions of verbal comprehension, working memory, perceptual organization, and processing speed. *Twin Res*, 6:131–9.

Posthuma D, de Geus EJC (2006). Progress in the molecular genetic study of intelligence. *Cur Dir Psych*, 15(4):151–5.

Posthuma D, de Geus EJ, Baare WF, Hulshoff Pol HE, Kahn RS, Boomsma DI (2002). The association between brain volume and intelligence is of genetic origin. *Nat Neurosci*, 5:83–4.

Posthuma D, de Geus EJC, Bleichrodt N, Boomsma DI (2000). Twin–singleton differences in intelligence? *Twin Res*, 3:83–7.

Posthuma D, de Geus EJC, Boomsma DI (2001a). Perceptual speed and IQ are associated through common genetic factors. *Behav Genet*, 31:593–602.

Posthuma D, Luciano M, de Geus EJ, Wright MJ, Slagboom PE, Montgomery GW, Boomsma DI, Martin NG (2005). A genomewide scan for intelligence identifies quantitative trait loci on 2q and 6p. *Am J Hum Genet*, 77:318–26.

Posthuma D, Neale MC, Boomsma DI, de Geus EJC (2001b). Are smarter brains running faster? Heritability of alpha peak frequency and IQ and their interrelation. *Behav Genet*, 31:567–79.

Powers WF, Kiely JL (1994). The risks confronting twins: a national perspective. *Am J Obstet Gynecol*, 170:456–61.

Ramakers GJ (2002). Rho proteins, mental retardation and the cellular basis of cognition. *Trends Neurosci*, 25:191–9.

Raz N, Torres IJ, Spencer WD, Millman D, Baertschi JC, Sarpel G (1993). Neuroanatomical correlates of age-sensitive and age-invariant cognitive abilities: an in-vivo MRI investigation. *Intelligence*, 17:407–22.

Record RG, McKeown T, Edwards JH (1970). An investigation of the difference in measured intelligence between twins and single births. *Ann Hum Genet*, 34:11–20.

Redon R, Ishikawa S, Fitch KR, Feuk L, Perry GH, Andrews TD, et al. (2006). Global variation in copy number in the human genome. *Nature*, 444:444–54.

Reuter M, Peters K, Schroeter K, Koebke W, Lenardon D, Bloch B, Hennig J (2005). The influence of the dopaminergic system on cognitive functioning: a molecular genetic approach. *Behav Brain Res*, 164:93–9.

Reynolds CA, Finkel D, McArdle JJ, Gatz M, Berg S, Pedersen NL (2005). Quantitative genetic analysis of latent growth curve models of cognitive abilities in adulthood. *Dev Psychol*, 41:3–16.

Rijsdijk FV, Vernon PA, Boomsma DI (1998). The genetic basis of the relation between speed-of-information-processing and IQ. *Behav Brain Res*, 95:77–84.

Rijsdijk FV, Vernon PA, Boomsma DI (2002). Application of hierarchical genetic models to Raven and WAIS subtests: a Dutch twin study. *Behav Genet*, 32:199–210.

Ronalds GA, De Stavola BL, Leon DA (2005). The cognitive cost of being a twin: evidence from comparisons within families in the Aberdeen children of the 1950s cohort study. *BMJ*, 331:1306.

Rowe DC, Jacobson KC, Van den Oord EJ (1999). Genetic and environmental influences on vocabulary IQ: parental education level as moderator. *Child Dev*, 70:1151–62.

Sabeti PC, Schaffner SF, Fry B, Lohmueller J, Varilly P, Shamovsky O, et al. (2006). Positive natural selection in the human lineage. *Science*, 312:1614–20.

Savitz J, Solms M, Ramesar R (2006). The molecular genetics of cognition: dopamine, COMT and BDNF. *Genes Brain Behav*, 5:311–28.

Schmidt FL, Hunter JE (1998). The validity and utility of selection methods in personnel psychology: practical and theoretical implications of 85 years of research findings. *Psychol Bull*, 124:262–74.

Shenkin SD, Starr JM, Deary IJ (2004). Birth weight and cognitive ability in childhood: a systematic review. *Psychol Bull*, 130:989–1013.

Small B, Rosnick CB, Fratiglioni L, Backman L (2004). Apolipoprotien E and cognitive performance: a meta-analysis. *Psychol Aging*, 19:592–600.

Smith JD (2002). Apolipoprotiens and aging: emerging mechanisms. *Ageing Res Rev*, 1:345–65.

Spearman C (1904). "General intelligence" objectively determined and measured. *Am J Psychol*, 15:201–93.

Spinath FM, Borkenau P (2000). Genetic and environmental influences on reaction times: evidence from behaviour–genetic research. *Psychol Beitr*, 42:201–12.

Spinath FM, Plomin R (2003). Amplification of genetic influence on g from early childhood to the early school years. Paper presented at the IVth Meeting of the International Society for Intelligence Research (ISIR), Irvine, CA, 4–6 December.

Sternberg RJ, Detterman DK (1986). What is intelligence? Norwood, NJ: Ablex.

Storfer M (1999). Myopia, intelligence, and the expanding human neocortex: behavioral influences and evolutionary implications. *Int J Neurosci*, 98:153–276.

Thompson PM, Cannon TD, Narr KL, et al. (2001). Genetic influences on brain structure. *Nat Neurosci*, 4:1253–8.

Tsai SJ, Hong CJ, Yu YW, Chen TJ (2004). Association study of a brain derived neurotrophic factor (BDNF) val66met polymorphism and personality trait and intelligence in healthy young females. *Neuropsychobiology*, 49:13–6.

Turkheimer E, Haley A, Waldron M, D'Onofrio B, Gottesman II (2003). Socioeconomic status modifies heritability of IQ in young children. *Psychol Sci*, 14:623–8.

van Leeuwen M, van den Berg SM, Hoekstra RA, Boomsma DI (2007). Endophenotypes for intelligence in children and adolescents. *Intelligence*, 35(4):369–80.

van Valen L (1974). Brain size and intelligence in man. *Am J Phys Anthropol*, 40:417–23.

Vernon PA ed. (1987). *Speed of information-processing and intelligence*. Norwood, NJ: Ablex.

Vernon PA (1989). The heritability of measures of speed of information processing. *Pers Indiv Diff*, 10:573–6.

Voight BF, Kudaravalli S, Wen X, Pritchard JK (2006). A map of recent positive selection in the human genome. *PLoS Biol*, 4(3):e72.

Wainwright MA, Wright MJ, Luciano M, Montgomery GW, Geffen GM, Martin NG (2006). A linkage study of academic skills defined by the Queensland Core Skills Test. *Behav Genet*, 36:56–64.

Webbink D, Posthuma D, Boomsma DI, de Geus EJC, Visscher PM (2008). Do twins have lower cognitive ability than singletons? *Intelligence*, 36:539–47.

Wickett JC, Vernon PA, Lee DH (1997). Within family correlations between general intelligence and MRI-measured brain volume in head size in male adult siblings. *Behav Genet*, 27:611.

Wickett JC, Vernon PA, Lee DH (2000). Relationships between factors of intelligence and brain volume. *Pers Indiv Diff*, 29:1095–1122.

Willerman L, Schultz R, Rutledge JN, Bigler ED (1991). In vivo brain size and intelligence. *Intelligence*, 15:223–8.

Willerman L, Schultz R, Rutledge JN, et al. (1992). Hemisphere size asymmetry predicts relative verbal and nonverbal intelligence differently in the sexes—an MRI study of structure–function relations. *Intelligence*, 16:315–28.

Woods RP, Freimer NB, De Young JA, Fears SC, Sicotte NL, Service SK, et al. (2006). Normal variants of microcephalin and ASPM do not account for brain size variability. *Hum Mol Genet*, 15:2025–9.

Zhang H, Zhong X, Ye Y (2005). Multivariate linkage analysis using the electrophysiological phenotypes in the COGA alcoholism data. *BMC Genet*, 6(Suppl 1):S118.

Zhang J (2003). Evolution of the human ASPM gene, a major determinant of brain size. *Genetics*, 165:2063–70.

5 Candidate Genes Associated with Attention and Cognitive Control

John Fossella, Jin Fan, and Michael I. Posner

Neuroimaging and human genomics both have helped to illuminate important issues of normal and abnormal development. During the last decade, neuroimaging has revealed separate neural networks related to several aspects of human attention (Fan et al. 2005). Use of appropriate imaging methods has made it possible to work out the time course and connectivity of these networks and examine their function in terms of anatomy and circuitry (Posner and Fan 2008). Genetic findings document the correlation of individual differences in performance with specific chromosomal locations. Recent technological advances in genome sequencing and genome manipulation serve as potent drivers of experimentation aimed at linking gene function to normal and abnormal brain development (Goldberg and Weinberger 2004).

For the most part, the study of general features of cognitive processes and of individual differences have been separate domains. However, since genes are important both in developing common networks and in accounting for individual differences there is a new opportunity to relate general features with individual variation. Much of the recent work along this line involves developmental pathologies such as addiction (Goldman et al. 2005; Xu et al. 2006), attention-deficit/hyperactivity disorder (ADHD; Durston et al. 2005), and anxiety (Canli et al. 2005), where genetic and phenotypic variations are likely to be continuous with normal function, and pathologies such as schizophrenia (Harrison and Weinberger 2005) and Williams syndrome (Karmiloff-Smith et al. 2002), where variation in behavior and brain activity often falls outside the normal range. These studies have been remarkable in their ability to link genetic risk factors with variation in the activity of specific anatomical structures. The promise of a continued convergence bodes well for the design of treatments that target specific brain regions. Such progress is timely for the field of psychiatry, since many other medical disciplines have already adopted "genomic and biomarker guided" treatment strategies (Hyman and Fenton 2003).

As the efforts to develop convergence between genetic and imaging methods proceeds, appropriate cautions are worth noting. Statistical limitations abound when experiments are aimed at linking a small number of voxels in a magnetic resonance imaging (MRI) analysis with a single genetic variant. Exploratory analyses that seek to rely purely on statistical power may be impractical in scale, since there are well over 1 million voxels in the MRI scan of the human brain and more than 1 million polymorphic sites in the human genome. An emphasis on strategies that exploit avenues of converging evidence and rely on hypothesis-driven designs may be a more promising way of separating biologically valid results from false-positive and false-negative results. Additional concerns should also be kept in mind even as well-validated findings emerge from the experimental literature. It will be increasingly important to recognize that the genetic material is not determinative but rather exerts mild effects on the development of neural networks that are formed through complex interactions with the environment (Caspi et al. 2002; Jaffee et al. 2005). Lastly, the current rise of pre- and postnatal genetic testing presents a myriad of broader societal dilemmas. Investigators and clinicians who utilize genetic information should recognize the ethical and privacy issues revolving around the new genetic research (Dinwiddie et al. 2004; Rosen 2004).

Genetic Dissection of Attention Networks: Current Strategies

Anatomy of Neural Networks That Carry Out Attention
Our efforts have been to explore the biological origins of normal variation in attention as measured in behavior and in the activation of the neural networks that carry out attention. Our goal for this chapter is to review the current strategy aimed at how genes work in development to shape individual variation in the neural networks that underlie attentional processes. Since deficits in attention are common across psychopathology, the findings obtained using this strategy may eventually be of relevance to studies of psychopathology. A review of the initial concerns involved in the design of our strategy and refinements that have emerged in due course is provided.

Functional neuroimaging has allowed many cognitive tasks to be analyzed in terms of the brain areas they activate. Studies of attention have been among the most frequently examined. Imaging data have supported the presence of three networks related to different aspects of attention. These networks carry out the functions of alerting, orienting, and executive control (Mesulam 1981; Posner and Petersen 1990; Witte and Marrocco 1997). Alerting is defined as achieving and maintaining a state of high sensitivity to incoming stimuli; orienting is the selection of information from sensory input; and executive control is defined as involving the mechanisms for resolving conflict among thoughts, feelings, and responses. The alerting system has been associated with frontal, parietal, and thalamic regions and can be assayed by the use of warning signals prior to targets in a functional magnetic resonance imaging (fMRI) setting (Fan et al. 2005). The influence of warning signals on the level of alertness is thought to be due to modulation of neural activity by the norepinepherine system (Witte and Marrocco 1997).

Orienting involves aligning attention with a source of sensory signals. This may be overt as in eye movements or may occur covertly without any movement. The orienting system for visual events has been associated with posterior brain areas including the superior parietal lobule and temporal parietal junction and, in addition, the frontal eye fields. Orienting can be manipulated by presenting a cue indicating where in space a person should attend, thereby directing attention to the cued location (Posner et al. 1980). Event-related fMRI studies have suggested that the superior parietal lobe is associated with orienting following the presentation of a cue (Corbetta et al. 2000; Fan et al. 2005). The superior parietal lobule in humans is closely related to the lateral intraparietal area in monkeys, which is known to produce eye movements (Andersen et al. 1997). When a target occurs at an uncued location and attention has to be disengaged and moved to a new location, there is activity in the temporal parietal junction (Corbetta et al. 2000). Lesions of the parietal lobule and superior temporal lobe have been consistently related to difficulties in orienting (Friedrich et al. 1998).

Executive control of attention is often studied using tasks that involve conflict, such as various versions of the Stroop task. In the Stroop task subjects must respond to the color of ink (e.g., red) while ignoring the color word name (e.g., b-l-u-e). Resolving conflict in the Stroop task activates midline frontal areas such as the anterior cingulate cortex (ACC) and lateral prefrontal cortex (PFC; Bush et al. 2000; MacDonald et al. 2000). There is evidence for the activation of this network in tasks involving conflict between a central target and surrounding flankers that may be congruent or incongruent with the target. Experimental tasks may provide a means of fractionating the functional contributions of different areas within the executive attention network (Casey et al. 2000).

Reliability and Heritability of Measures of Attention

The dissociable components of attention and the well-established anatomical and pharmacological correlates related to each network present an attractive candidate system for genetic analysis. To begin to study individual differences in these networks, we have developed an attention network test (ANT) that examines the efficiency of the three brain networks we have discussed above (Fan et al. 2002). For genetic studies, where large samples are typically required, the ANT is ideal, as it is easily administered via laptop computer. Differences in reaction times are derived from the task, providing three numbers that represent the skill of each individual in the alerting, orienting, and executive networks. In a sample of 40 normal volunteers, we found these numbers to be reliable over two successive presentations. The correlations between two test sessions were .52, .61, and .77 for alerting, orienting, and conflict, respectively. In addition, we found no significant correlation among the three network numbers in this sample, indicating these three attentional networks are separable.

One common method for demonstrating a genetic influence on individual differences in cognitive processes compares the performance of monozygotic twins, having identical genomes, with dizygotic twins, who share only as much genetic similarity as siblings do. A heritability index can be computed from the differences between these two correlations. A genetic influence on cognitive performance, particularly related to attention, has been explored in this manner in several ways. Studies using the Continuous Performance Task (CPT) have shown that the d' signal detection component of CPT performance has a heritability among normal subjects of 0.49 (Cornblatt et al. 1988). The Span of Apprehension task, a visual search task, has been shown to have a heritability among normal subjects of 0.65 (Bartfai et al. 1991), and the P/N ratio of the Spontaneous Selective Attention Task was shown to have a heritability among normal subjects of 0.41 (Myles-Worsley and Coon 1997). Twin studies using normal control twins show that spatial working memory, divided attention, choice reaction time and selective attention (Cannon et al. 2000), attentional set shifting (Pardo et al. 2000), sensorimotor gating (Geyer and Braff 1987), and smooth pursuit eye tracking (Katsanis et al. 2000) are heritable. The heritability observed at the behavioral level is supported by evidence that brain structures associated with attention can show genetic bases. Anatomical studies in rodents, nonhuman primates, and humans have established that genes are major determinants of overall brain size (Cheverud et al. 1990; Thompson et al. 2001) and structural aspects of specific brain regions such as the frontal cortex (Tramo et al. 1998) and corpus callosum (Oppenheim et al. 1989).

Using the ANT, some evidence of heritability was found for the executive attention component (Fan et al. 2001). Twenty-six pairs of adult monozygotic twins showed strong correlations for both the alerting (r = .46) and executive (r = .73) networks. For another group of twenty-six dizygotic same sex adult twins, we found a similar although somewhat smaller correlation for the alerting network (r = .38), but smaller correlation (.28) for the executive network. The executive control network yielded a high heritability score of 0.89. The genetic origins of executive attention that are supported by this data may relate to certain developmental processes. Our studies of normal children suggest that the conflict network continues to develop until about age 8 with late 10-year-old children not being significantly different in resolving conflict than adults with the same version of the ANT (Rueda et al. 2004). Although the sample size is small and the estimates of heritabiltiy are not very precise, these data provide preliminary support for a genetic accounting of variation in the efficiency in the executive attention network.

Candidate Gene Association Studies

With an anatomically characterized (Fan et al. 2005), reliable (Fan et al. 2002), and heritable (Fan et al. 2001) assay in hand, our strategy progressed to an exploration of

individual genetic factors that might account for individual differences in performance. Given the vast size of the human genome—some 30,000 genes with more than
1 million common genetic variants—a great many design and implementation issues
abound. In practice, two main phenomena tend to limit the success of such "candidate
gene" explorations. Firstly, the effects of a single genetic variant are expected to be
small, historically accounting for less than 5% of variance. Genetic modeling studies
suggest that when many genes underlie a complex trait, such as attention, or a disorder
such as ADHD, great difficulty is expected in detecting significant associations of single
candidate genes (Lohmueller et al. 2003).

The second limitation relates to wide disparities in the frequency of genetic variants
across ethnic groups. In the course of human evolution, errors in the replication of
chromosomal DNA are rare, occurring at a rate of 2.5×10^{-8} (Nachman and Crowell
2000), but occur often enough in our genome of 3 billion nucleotides such that dozens
of base-pair changes can accumulate per generation per genome (Reich et al. 2002).
While many of these minor base pair changes have been lost over time as local mating
populations decline, some changes have persisted and even, perhaps due to natural
selection, increased in frequency. Such ancestral errors in DNA replication, which
arose spontaneously many generations ago, are now distributed across the globe in an
uneven and fragmented way due to the varied migratory patterns of human populations as far back as 10,000 and even 60,000 years ago. In the course of our studies, we
have recognized that the complexities of genetic structure within human populations
are especially troublesome experimental design issues for genetic studies. This is particularly true in North America and Europe, where extensive ethnic admixture has
occurred over the past 100 years. In an effort to minimize the limitations introduced
by populations with a mixture of ethnicities, we favor the selection of genetic variants
that are common and found at high frequency across many different ethnic groups.

With these limitations in mind, we have attempted to select the most promising
candidate genes by considering existing knowledge of neural networks, pharmacology,
gene expression patterns, animal models, and human genetic anomalies. Once candidates are proposed, individuals with specific alleles can be tested with the appropriate
measures to determine whether certain alleles are correlated with performance. Examples of this approach are discussed in great detail in this volume. One of the most
widely cited examples is that of Egan and colleagues (2001) in the study of working
and episodic memory. Based on a dopaminergic hypothesis of schizophrenia, Egan
et al. examined genes related to schizophrenia that might involve the dopamine
pathway. Because schizophrenia is highly heritable, studies of families of patients had
led to genetic linkage to several chromosomal areas. One of these areas is on chromosome 22, in the 22Q11 region that contains the catechol-O-methyltransferase (COMT)
gene that produces an enzyme important in the metabolism of dopamine. Egan et al.
have found that a variant of the COMT gene was related to performance in cognitive

tasks involving working memory. This gene accounted for about 4% of the variance in perseveration errors during the Wisconsin Card Sorting Task. The COMT gene is likely to be important in many aspects of executive function.

We have pursued this approach to evaluate candidate genes for attention with a particular focus on dopaminergic genes and their role in executive attention. The cingulate is particularly rich in dopamine innervation (Descarries et al. 1987), implicating dopamine as the dominant neuromodulator for the executive network. Some data suggest that dopamine concentrations are higher in the dorsolateral prefrontal cortex (DLPFC) than in other cortical regions (Brown et al. 1979). Depleting DLPFC of dopamine produces deficits in performance on executive function tasks such as the delayed response task. These deficits can be as severe as DLPFC lesions (Brozoski et al. 1979). Destruction of the dopaminergic neurons in the ventral tegmental area that project to PFC also impairs performance on executive function tasks (Simon et al. 1980). Local injection of selective DA (D1) antagonists into DLPFC impairs performance on the delayed response task (Sawaguchi and Goldman-Rakic 1991; 1994) while leaving performance on sensory-guided control tasks unimpaired (Seamans et al. 1998). Disruption of the prefrontal–striatal–dopamine system by injections of MPTP (1-methyl-4-phenyl-1,2,3,6-tetrahydropyridine) also impairs performance on the delayed response task (Schneider and Kovelowski 1990), and halting L-dopa treatment to Parkinson's patients produces deficits on frontal cortex dependent cognitive tasks (Lange et al. 1992). Lastly, Watanabe et al. (1997) found that the concentration of extracellular DA in DLPFC increased significantly while monkeys were performing the delayed alternation task (another classic measure of PFC function) but not during a sensory-guided control task, nor in other frontal regions (Area 8 [arcuate] or orbitofrontal) during the delayed alternation task.

We carried out a standard gene association study using a population of 200 adult subjects who performed the ANT on a laboratory computer (Fossella et al. 2002). Although this strategy lacked the needed statistical power to meet the standards set for the reporting of true associations (Lohmueller et al. 2003), no associations or statistical trends were observed for global measures of performance such as overall reaction time. This suggests that there may be some specificity in the role of genetic factors in contributing to specific neural functions. Cheek swabs were obtained from each volunteer, and genomic DNA was extracted and used for genotyping. An analysis of genotype versus performance was conducted for several dopaminergic genes including the *dopamine receptor D4* (DRD4), *monoamine oxidase a* (MAOA), *dopamine transporter* (DAT), and *COMT* genes. The DRD4 and MAOA genes revealed modest associations with behavior. For the DRD4 exon III variable number tandem repeat polymorphism, a comparison of 4-repeat versus non-4-repeat carriers showed some relation to executive attention, but not to orienting, alerting, or overall reaction time. The promoter repeat polymorphism in MAOA (Sabol et al. 1998), an enzyme that is responsible for both dopamine and serotonin breakdown, also showed associations with executive attention. This polymorphism has also been identified as a genetic risk factor in studies of aggression in boys where the 3-repeat allele, which is associated with less efficient conflict resolution in our adult studies, was found to confer some additional risk of aggression in boys who experienced some degree of maltreatment during childhood (Caspi et al. 2002).

Other cognitive studies using somewhat different tasks have also confirmed and extended our initial findings. In two studies involving tasks that require attentional control, alleles of the COMT gene were related to the ability to resolve conflict (Blasi et al. 2005; Diamond et al. 2004). The COMT gene has also been shown to be related to a measure of the ability to solve novel problems (fluid intelligence; Bishop et al. 2007). Additionally, the orienting network has been shown to be influenced by cholinergic drugs in monkeys (Davidson and Marrocco 2000). Different alleles of a cholinergic gene, the alpha 4 subunit of the *neural nicotinic cholinergic receptor* (CHRNA4), was related to performance differences in the ability to orient attention during tasks involving visual search (Greenwood et al. 2005), confirming the link between orienting and the cholinergic system.

Imaging Genetic Analyses on Selected Dopaminergic Candidate Genes

In advancing our strategic plan beyond the genetic and behavioral levels of analysis, we and others have begun to explore whether fMRI can be used to confirm and extend the association between genes and particular underlying networks. As a well-known example, Egan and colleagues (2001) showed that subjects with the Valine allele at the Met158Val polymorphism in COMT showed worse performance and higher levels of brain activation in the PFC. In our studies of the attentional networks, subjects who performed the ANT in the scanner showed that the DRD4 and MAOA alleles which were associated with more efficient handling of conflict in the earlier behavioral studies also differed in amount of activation in the anterior cingulate while performing the ANT (Fan et al. 2003). Because we ran 16 genotypically unselected subjects, we did not have sufficient data to equally subdivide groups based on genotype at the several genes we found to be related to conflict in our behavioral study. However, we did find significant differences in activation for alleles which, we expect, have considerable influence on dopamine activity within the network being studied. Moreover, our scanning data showed significant differences with about 8 subjects per cell, while the same alleles only approach significance in a behavioral study with nearly 100 subjects in each cell. These data support the speculation by Egan and colleagues that a combination of behavioral and fMRI work can provide statistical confirmation even though the influence of any individual gene is rather small. Recent work has replicated the MAOA finding where the low expression (3-repeat) allele was found to be associated with changes in orbitofrontal volume, amygdala and hippocampus hyperreactivity during aversive recall, and impaired cingulate activation during cognitive inhibition (Meyer-Lindenberg et al. 2006). Further structural MRI investigations showed that the DRD4 gene was associated with cortical structure while the DAT1 gene influenced subcortical structure (Durston et al. 2005). This result seems in harmony with the known cortical expression of the DRD4 gene and high subcortical expression of the DAT1 gene (Sesack et al. 1998; 2003). A recent report shows that when executive tasks are conducted in the presence of emotional distraction, COMT is associated with activity in neural structures associated with cognitive control and task-related processing (Bishop et al. 2006).

Gene Expression, Developmental and Environmental Constraints on the Validity of Gene-Associated Brain Activity Findings

Gene Expression Constraints

Our fMRI-based imaging genetic associations with activation in the anterior cingulate gyrus seem, at face level, generally consistent with the known role of DRD4 and MAOA in brain function. This is mainly because these genes have known roles in dopamine signaling and because the ACC is known as a region rich in dopamine receptors and afferent inputs (Descarries et al. 1987). The selection of these two dopaminergic candidate genes was initially based upon (1) associations with disorders where attention is disrupted, (2) pharmacological relationship to the executive attention network, and (3) each allele's having been biochemically characterized with respect to biochemical activity or expression level. One criterion we did *not* include in our design was the *pattern of gene expression* exhibited by our candidate genes. Indeed, DRD4 and MAOA have broad domains of gene expression. A consideration of this criterion naturally prompts a closer look at the structural and functional imaging genetic data and raises new questions concerning interpretations of the data. Why, for example, might gene-associated activity in relatively specific brain regions occur when the task is known to activate multiple nodes in a widely distributed neural network? Also, why might areas such as the insula or cerebellum, which do *not* show enriched expression of the MAOA or DRD4 genes, show gene-associated brain activity?

Relationships between where a gene is expressed and where it exerts an effect during an imaging genetic study are complex. Firstly, it should be noted that many of the genes used in imaging genetic studies are widely expressed. Recent imaging genetic studies on the *serotonin transporter* (5-HTT) and COMT illustrate this point. A query of gene expression data in UniGene, a public access repository of genomic data (NCBI-UniGene 2005), shows wide-ranging expression patterns of 5-HTT (bone, colon, muscle, lung, placenta, pancreas). Within the brain, 5-HTT is expressed in a very restricted anatomical manner, namely, in serotonergic cells projecting from the median and dorsal raphe nuclei, the supralemniscal cell group, and the oral pontine nucleus (Austin et al. 1994). Patterns of brain activity associated with a 5-HTT promoter length polymorphism include the ACC, basolateral amygdala, and PFC (reviewed in Hariri et al. 2006). Although these brain regions do not express large quantities of the 5-HTT, these broad anatomical areas are likely candidates for gene-associated effects on brain activity, given that serotonin modulates synaptic activity of prefrontal–amygdala connections (Stutzmann et al. 1998). Similarly COMT shows a broad pattern of expression (bladder, bone, cervix, heart, kidney, liver, lung, ovary, prostate, skin, stomach, and other areas) and cortical and subcortical neurons in the human brain. Imaging genetic studies show that functional activity within areas of the DLPFC is associated with structural variants of COMT when subjects perform tasks involving working memory (Egan et al. 2001). Despite the high levels of expression of COMT in the striatum, gene-associated brain activation is mainly found in the DLPFC. This is consistent, however, with findings showing that COMT activity accounts for less-than15% of total dopamine turnover in the striatum but greater than 60% in the PFC (Sesack et al. 1998).

In our efforts to explore the basis for the specificity of gene-associated brain activity, we investigated a well-studied genetic polymorphism, TaqIA, which lies downstream of the dopamine receptor D2 (DRD2) gene, in the protein encoding region of a neighboring gene, *ankyrin repeat and kinase domain containing 1* (ANKK1), which is *not* expressed in the brain. A simple starting hypothesis for ANKK1, a negative control of sorts, was that no gene-associated brain activity would be found, since the TaqIA polymorphism was located in a gene that is not expressed in the brain. However, imaging genetic studies on the ANT showed that carriers of the A1 allele have gene-associated functional activation in an anatomically specific, dopamine-rich region of the brain comprising the anterior cingulate gyrus (Fossella et al. 2006). This finding, while inconsistent with the starting hypothesis, was, in fact, consistent with other imaging genetic data. In the case of the TaqIA polymorphism, a closer look at the genomic region where it resides shows that the polymorphism is located downstream from the neighboring DRD2 gene. There is much evidence documenting a role for DRD2 in the frontal lobe. Hence, it is possible that although the TaqIA polymorphism lies inside the ANKK1 gene, it may be correlated in some way with variation in the DRD2 gene. A view of patterns of linkage disequilibrium (LD) provided an explanation for the discrepancy of gene expression and gene-associated brain activity. To query this, we accessed the International HapMap Project (2003), sponsored by the International HapMap Consortium, which is a free and open online tool (found online at www.hapmap.org). Extensive single nucleotide polymorphism (SNP) analyses from populations consisting of Yoruba in Ibadan, Nigeria; Japanese in Tokyo, Japan; Han Chinese in Beijing, China; and Utah residents with ancestry from northern and western Europe permits pairwise analyses of LD between variable sites in the genome. A quick view of public haplotype data revealed that the C/T transition TaqIA sites (dbSNP rs1800497) sit inside a well-delineated haplotype block. Evidence for LD extending between the TaqIA site and DRD2 was found. A view of phased haplotypes using the hierarchical clustering methodology tools available at the HapMap Web browser shows evidence for haplotypes that encompass the TaqIA site and the DRD2 gene.

The discrepancy between gene expression and gene-associated brain activity posed by the TaqIA polymorphism highlights the need to more carefully investigate candidate polymorphisms in the course of study design and also places additional cautions in the interpretation of gene-associated brain activity. In the course of updating our strategy, we propose to include information concerning the expression pattern of the candidate gene in the developing and adult human brain. If the hypothesized areas of gene-associated functional activation are not overlapping with the known expression pattern, then an investigator may have difficulty interpreting the findings from a cellular or synaptic perspective. Additionally, it may be useful to query the public genome resources such as HapMap for information on the extent of LD within and outside of the candidate gene of interest. The addition of tagged SNPs within candidate genes would also support the meta-analysis of imaging genetic data across studies using different populations.

Developmental Constraints

Another issue that arises upon inspection of gene-associated brain activity findings relates to the timing of gene action. In the case of COMT, for example, the evidence suggests that COMT performs an ongoing physiological function, and that variation in the structure of the enzyme leads to individual differences that can be measured and that arise from the real-time function of the enzyme. Alternately, current differences observed in brain activity for separate genetic groups may be consequences of a genetic polymorphism that acted early in the development of a specific brain structure or altered the function of an early developmental process upon which other more mature processes depend. For example, COMT and several other genes are deleted in a disorder called 22Q11 deletion syndrome. These children have only a single functioning copy of the chromosomal region containing COMT and show a number of signs of mental retardation as well as physical abnormalities; they are also at greatly increased risk of developing schizophrenia (Karayiorgou and Gogos 2004). Two experiments have examined a version of the ANT task suitable for children, and both found greatly reduced ability to resolve conflict (Bearden et al. 2005; Sobin et al. 2005a). One effort to determine the pathway by which the deletion might work combines the ANT with studies using prepulse inhibition, which is a behavioral technique that specifies a known anatomical pathway. The results suggest that striatal–cingulate pathways are very important to the combined deficits in executive attention of prepulse inhibition (Sobin et al. 2005b).

The effects of variation in the promoter region of the *serotonin transporter* (5-HTT) also can be viewed from a developmental perspective. Variation within 5-HTT is often associated with the amygdala or negative affect (Hariri et al. 2002; Sen et al. 2004); however, two reports have also suggested the involvement of serotonin systems in tasks related to executive attention. Canli et al. (2005) suggest that the short allele of the 5-HTT is related to neural control systems that influence cognitive and affective control systems. Their findings relate the 5-HTT gene to areas that are parts of the executive attention network, and studies with young children (Auerbach et al. 2001) suggest that 5-HTT may interact with dopamine to influence critical aspects of negative affect. A finding using the ANT suggests that a promotor polymorphism in a gene, TPH, related to serotonin synthesis is related to executive attention as measured by the ANT (Reuter et al., 2007). Interestingly, a mouse model shows that inhibition of 5-HTT exerts a paradoxical negative inluence on social and emotional responsivity when inhibition occurs during a brief time period of early postnatal development (Ansorge et al. 2004). This developmental effect is the opposite of that observed when 5-HTT blocking agents are administered to adults. Finally, research on developmental disorders such as Williams syndrome and fragile-X mental retardation that arise from minute chromosomal lesions and have been studied suggests that even when the genetic lesion is well defined, the developmental outcome can affect many neural systems and show variation in severity (Churchill et al. 2002). Simple genotype–phenotype mappings do not sufficiently explain this variability, and emphasis should be placed not on these mappings but rather on the role of genes in developmental processes (Scerif and Karmiloff-Smith 2005; Meyer-Lindenberg and Weinberger 2006).

A small-scale study using the child version of the ANT showed a significant relation between a repeat polymorphism in the 3′-untranslated region of the *dopamine transporter* (DAT1) and executive attention as measured by the reaction time differences between incongruent and congruent trials (Rueda et al. 2005). In that study the DAT1 was also related to parent reports of their child's effortful control, and EEG suggested differences in the underlying executive attention network. Currently, we are working to replicate and extend this finding by genotyping children who are involved in a longitudinal study from 7 months to 4 years. This study will examine various tasks involving executive attention in infants and young children in relation to a number of candidate dopamine- and serotonin-related genes. Since attention measures will be made at three ages on the same children, this research will provide an opportunity to see if the genes play the same role at all of these ages.

Environmental Constraints

As noted above, the anatomical limits of gene expression as well as the timing of gene expression are important constraints to consider when interpreting gene-associated brain activity data. It is important to note also, then, that the environment is an especially potent driver of gene expression throughout brain development. For example, anoxia (Mehmet et al. 1994), maternal separation (Avishai-Eliner et al. 1999), amyloid protein expression (Dodart et al. 1999), and drug abuse (Ladenheim et al. 2000) all induce hypometabolism, gliosis, and programmed cell death in the ACC, a central node in the executive attention network. Exposure to environmental and social stress can induce the expression of *glucocorticoid receptor* (GR), a transcription factor which mediates the cellular response to stress (McEwen 2000) and influences functional coupling in the amygdala (Stutzmann et al. 1998). Our group has reported that other genes as well can be influenced by environmental forces. We found that the expression of *tgf-alpha*, a factor in the postnatal maturation of dopamine neurons, was found to be downregulated by neonatal separation stress in male pups (Romeo et al. 2004). Additional evidence that stress may influence dopaminergic function can be found in the work of Benes and colleagues, who showed that dopaminergic innervation of interneurons in layers II and V of the ACC are elevated in postmortem analyses of schizophrenia. The hyperinnervation of interneuronal DRD2 contacts is suspected to disable local inhibition of pyramidal cells and lead to excess glutamatergic signaling and waves of excitotoxicity in downstream brain areas (Benes 2000).

Current genetic and imaging genetic work has begun to explore the way that the genome and the environment may interact to influence cognition. Epidemiological findings by Caspi and colleagues show that interactions of genotype together with certain aspects of stress or neglect can influence the onset of depression and aggression (Caspi et al. 2002; 2003). Imaging genetic studies on the genetic loci involved in these Gene × Environment phenomena reveal gene-associated brain activity in regions of affective and cognitive control, in particular, the ACC (Heinz et al. 2005; Meyer-Lindenberg et al. 2006; Pezawas et al. 2005). Such environmental interactions pose an experimental challenge to imaging genetic research, since it is often difficult to ascertain an experimental volunteer's past experience with stress and or neglect. Similarly, it is difficult to determine the current state of stress for a subject who may or may not experience anxiety in the local laboratory or scanner environment. Canli and colleagues have evaluated this issue in more detail via the introduction of baseline brain activity conditions to begin to explore 5-HTTLPR-related individual differences in the response of subjects to the scanner environment (Canli et al. 2005).

Current Focus on the Genetic Dissection of ACC Function

With some experience gained from the preliminary work described above, and an increased awareness of several inherent constraints, our strategy continues to evolve and is now poised to examine more deeply a recurrent finding, that of gene-associated activity in the ACC. This brain region, situated bilaterally on the medial surface of the frontal lobes around the rostrum of the corpus callosum and bounded by the callosal sulcus and the cingulate sulcus, has numerous projections into the motor cortex and thus advantageously sits where it may make a significant contribution in the control of sensory, cognitive, and emotionally guided actions. Indeed, it may not be surprising to repeatedly find dopaminergic-gene-associated brain activity in the ACC, since it receives afferents from more thalamic nuclei than any other cortical region and also receives diffuse monoaminergic innervation from all major neuromodulatory nuclei (Bush et al. 2000; Vogt et al. 1995).

Several lines of converging evidence suggest that variation in the structure and function of the ACC may be a suitable region for intense genetic study. Firstly, several tasks that activate the ACC such as spatial working memory, divided attention, and attentional set shifting have been examined in identical and fraternal twin populations and have been found to have high heritabilities (Cannon et al. 2000; Pardo et al. 2000). The structure of the ACC was recently examined in healthy relatives of schizophrenic patients. These healthy relatives, who presumably carry some of the genetic risk for schizophrenia, showed 11.4% less right cingulate gray matter volume, 8% reduction in surface area, and bilateral reductions in thickness of up to 2.5% (Goghari et al. 2006). Twin studies reveal that about 60% of the variance in N2 and P3 amplitudes can be attributed to genetic factors (Anokhin et al. 2004). Prior investigations on these event-related-potential components have implicated the ACC as the most likely neural generator of the N2 potential (van Veen and Carter 2002). Pezawas and colleagues showed that carriers of the short allele showed volume reductions of 25% in gray matter in the perigenual ACC and that this same short allele genetic group also showed decreased positive feedback between the rostral ACC and the amygdala as well as decreased negative coupling between caudal regions of the ACC and amygdala (Pezawas et al. 2005).

Gene Expression Profiling Candidates

To follow up on our own findings of gene-associated ACC activity, we are beginning to exploit several bioinformatic tools to locate converging evidence for genetic studies on the ACC. For example, cell types in the mammalian cortex, which are traditionally categorized by anatomical location, axonal morphology, and spiking properties, can now be defined using gene expression profiling. An example of this was recently implemented in the mouse cingulate cortex, where DNA microarrays were employed to obtain gene expression profiles for three types of interneurons and two types of projection neurons (layer 5 and layer 6) in the cingulate cortex as well as a number of other cortical and subcortical regions (Sugino et al. 2006). A collection of genes whose expression is unique to these cells is now available for further study. Some of the genes reported include *secreted frizzled-related protein 2* (sFRP2), *natriuretic peptide precursor C* (NPPC), *endothelin converting enzyme-like 1* (ECEL1), *tachykinin, precursor 1* (TAC1), and *neurexophilin 3* (NXPH3). In a mouse model of neuronal migration in the frontal midline, the presence of sFRP2 protein impaired the anterior turning of commissural axons after midline crossing (Lyuksyutova et al. 2003). ECEL1 is a member of the M13 family of zinc-containing endopeptidases known to be important regulators of neuropeptide and peptide hormone activity. The TAC1 gene encodes the neuropeptides substance P and neurokinin A. Mice without TAC1 function showed decreased depression- and anxiety-related behaviors (Bilkei-Gorzo et al. 2002). TAC1 also emerged as a top candidate gene for depressive illness in a unique multistage analysis of animal model gene expression and human genetic linkage termed "Convergent Functional Genomics" (Ogden et al. 2004). Finally, NXPH3 is a tightly bound extracellular ligand of α-neurexins, a family of presynaptic α-latrotoxin receptors. NXPH3 expression is restricted mostly to layer 6b of the cerebral cortex, where it occurs in subplate-derived excitatory neurons as well as granule cells in the vestibulocerebellum, and knockout mice display impaired sensory information processing and motor coordination (Beglopoulos et al. 2005).

Similar approaches have been carried out using human samples. In their report entitled "A Gene Atlas of the Mouse and Human Protein-Encoding Transcriptomes," Su and colleagues provide gene expression data on more than 33,000 unique genes in more than seventy human tissues (Su et al. 2004). These data have been deposited in the Gene Expression Omnibus (GEO), a public repository sponsored by the National Library of Medicine that archives and freely distributes high-throughput gene expression data submitted by the scientific community. GEO currently stores approximately a billion individual gene expression measurements, derived from over 100 organisms, addressing a wide range of biological issues. These huge volumes of data may be effectively explored, queried, and visualized using user-friendly Web-based tools (accessible at www.ncbi.nlm.nih.gov/geo). Among the brain regions assayed by Su et al. were frontal cortex, parietal cortex, cingulate cortex, hippocampus, amygdala, cerebellum, and whole brain. Our own query into the GEO data for cingulate cortex messenger RNA (mRNA) versus frontal cortex mRNA versus whole brain revealed a number of candidates that are expected to show enriched expression in the ACC. Among some of the most statistically significant candidates we found are *membrane metallo-endopeptidase* (MME), zinc transporter (SLC39A5), *Sin3A-associated protein* (SAP18), *tubby homologue* (TUB), and *sidekick 1* (SDK1). MME belongs to a collection of zinc metaloproteinases. As the essential role of zinc in brain development and synaptic transmission is well studied (Sandstead et al. 2000), the function of the zinc-containing endopeptidases MME and ECEL1 may function in zinc-rich synaptic boutons found in the limbic system, in particular, in the cingulate region (Takeda et al. 2000). SAP18 has been implicated in developmental pathways that regulate the structure of the frontal midline and is a downstream target of HOXA1, a retinoic acid-dependent candidate gene. Homozygous truncating mutations in HOXA1 give rise to a mental retardation and autism spectrum disorder among other developmental disruptions

(Tischfield et al. 2005). Lastly, SDK1 has a putative role as a neuronal targeting molecules, guiding developing neurons to specific synapses (Hayashi et al. 2005).

In addition to these molecular candidates, there exists an extensive literature on genes that regulate the patterning and morphogenesis of the mammalian forebrain (Sur and Rubenstein 2005). In our ongoing efforts, we are focused on these and other well-studied biochemical pathways likely to influence the structure and function of the ACC. One such pathway, the *hedgehog* signaling pathway, consists of a network of proteins that function in a number of tissues and developmental stages (reviewed in Cohen 2003). Implication of the hedgehog pathway in the development of the mammalian forebrain comes from genetic and imaging research on holoprosencephaly, a disorder where the embryonic forebrain does not sufficiently divide into the double lobes of the cerebral hemispheres and instead the lobes are conjoined across the midline, resulting in an absence of interhemispheric cleft. In our ongoing and future studies, we will examine weak hypomorphic and hypermorphic alleles for subtle effects on structure and activity in the ACC.

References

Andersen RA, Snyder LH, Bradley DC, Xing J (1997). Multimodal representation of space in the posterior parietal cortex and its use in planning movements. *Annu Rev Neurosci*, 20:303–30.

Anokhin AP, Heath AC, Myers E (2004). Genetics, prefrontal cortex, and cognitive control: a twin study of event-related brain potentials in a response inhibition task. *Neurosci Lett*, 368:314–8.

Ansorge MS, Zhou M, Lira A, Hen R, Gingrich JA (2004). Early-life blockade of the 5-HT transporter alters emotional behavior in adult mice. *Science*, 306:879–81.

Auerbach JG, Faroy M, Ebstein R, Kahana M, Levine J (2001). The association of the dopamine D4 receptor gene (DRD4) and the serotonin transporter promoter gene (5-HTTLPR) with temperament in 12-month-old infants. *J Child Psychol Psychiatry*, 42:777–83.

Austin MC, Bradley CC, Mann JJ, Blakely RD (1994). Expression of serotonin transporter messenger RNA in the human brain. *J Neurochem*, 62:2362–7.

Avishai-Eliner S, Hatalski CG, Tabachnik E, Eghbal-Ahmadi M, Baram TZ (1999). Differential regulation of glucocorticoid receptor messenger RNA (GR-mRNA) by maternal deprivation in immature rat hypothalamus and limbic regions. *Brain Res Dev Brain Res*, 114:265–8.

Bartfai A, Pedersen NL, Asarnow RF, Schalling D (1991). Genetic factors for the span of apprehension test: a study of normal twins. *Psychiatry Res*, 38:115–24.

Bearden CE, Jawad AF, Lynch DR, Monterossso JR, Sokol S, McDonald-McGinn DM, et al. (2005). Effects of COMT genotype on behavioral symptomatology in the 22q11.2 deletion syndrome. *Child Neuropsychol*, 11(1):109–17.

Beglopoulos V, Montag-Sallaz M, Rohlmann A, Piechotta K, Ahmad M, Montag D, et al. (2005). Neurexophilin 3 is highly localized in cortical and cerebellar regions and is functionally important for sensorimotor gating and motor coordination. *Mol Cell Biol*, 25:7278–88.

Benes FM (2000). Emerging principles of altered neural circuitry in schizophrenia. *Brain Res Brain Res Rev*, 31:251–69.

Bilkei-Gorzo A, Racz I, Michel K, Zimmer A (2002). Diminished anxiety- and depression-related behaviors in mice with selective deletion of the Tac1 gene. *J Neurosci*, 22:10046–52.

Bishop SJ, Cohen JD, Fossella J, Casey BJ, Farah MJ (2006). COMT genotype influences prefrontal response to emotional distraction. *Cogn Affect Behav Neurosci*, 6(1):62–70.

Bishop SJ, Fossella J, Croucher CJ, Duncan J (2008). COMT val158met genotype affects recruitment of neural mechanisms supporting fluid intelligence. *Cereb Cortex*, 18(9):2132–40.

Blasi G, Mattay VS, Bertolino A, Elvevag B, Callicott JH, Das S, et al. (2005). Effect of catechol-O-methyltransferase val158met genotype on attentional control. *J Neurosci*, 25:5038–45.

Brown RM, Crane AM, Goldman PS (1979). Regional distribution of monoamines in the cerebral cortex and subcortical structures of the rhesus monkey: concentrations and in vivo synthesis rates. *Brain Res*, 168(1):133–50.

Brozoski TJ, Brown RM, Rosvold HE, Goldman PS (1979). Cognitive deficit caused by regional depletion of dopamine in prefrontal cortex of rhesus monkey. *Science*, 205:929–32.

Bush G, Luu P, Posner MI (2000). Cognitive and emotional influences in anterior cingulate cortex. *Trends Cogn Sci*, 4(6):215–22.

Canli T, Omura K, Haas BW, Fallgatter A, Constable RT, Lesch KP (2005). Beyond affect: a role for genetic variation of the serotonin transporter in neural activation during a cognitive attention task. *Proc Natl Acad Sci USA*, 102:12224–9.

Cannon TD, Huttunen MO, Lonnqvist J, Tuulio-Henriksson A, Pirkola T, Glahn D, et al. (2000). The inheritance of neuropsychological dysfunction in twins discordant for schizophrenia. *Am J Hum Genet*, 67:369–82.

Casey BJ, Thomas KM, Welsh TF, Badgaiyan RD, Eccard CH, Jennings JR, et al. (2000). Dissociation of response conflict, attentional selection, and expectancy with functional magnetic resonance imaging. *Proc Natl Acad Sci USA*, 97:8728–33.

Caspi A, McClay J, Moffitt TE, Mill J, Martin J, Craig IW, et al. (2002). Role of genotype in the cycle of violence in maltreated children. *Science*, 297:851–4.

Caspi A, Sugden K, Moffitt TE, Taylor A, Craig IW, Harrington H, et al. (2003). Influence of life stress on depression: moderation by a polymorphism in the 5-HTT gene. *Science*, 301:386–9.

Cheverud JMK, Falk D, Vannier M, Konigsber L, Helmkamp RC, Hildebolt C (1990). Heritability of brain size and surface features in rhesus macaques (*Macaca mulatta*). *J Hered*, 81:51–7.

Churchill JD, Grossman AW, Irwin SA, Galvez R, Klintsova AY, Weiler IJ, et al. (2002). A converging-methods approach to fragile X syndrome. *Dev Psychobiol*, 40:323–38.

Cohen MM Jr. (2003). The hedgehog signaling network. *Am J Med Genet A*, 123(1):5–28.

Cornblatt BA, Risch NJ, Faris G, Friedman D, Erlenmeyer-Kimling L (1988). The Continuous Performance Test, identical pairs version (CPT-IP): I. New findings about sustained attention in normal families. *Psychiatry Res*, 26:223–38.

Corbetta M, Kincade JM, Ollinger JM, McAvoy MP, Shulman GL (2000). Voluntary orienting is dissociated from target detection in human posterior parietal cortex. *Nat Neurosci*, 3:292–7.

Davidson MC, Marrocco RT (2000). Local infusion of scopolamine into intraparietal cortex slows covert orienting in rhesus monkeys. *J Neurophysiol*, 83:1536–49.

Descarries L, Lemay B, Doucet G, Berger B (1987). Regional and laminar density of the dopamine innervation in adult rat cerebral cortex. *Neuroscience*, 21:807–24.

Diamond A, Briand L, Fossella J, Gehlbach L (2004). Genetic and neurochemical modulation of prefrontal cognitive functions in children. *Am J Psychiatry*, 161:125–32.

Dinwiddie SH, Hoop J, Gershon ES (2004). Ethical issues in the use of genetic information. *Int Rev Psychiatry*, 16:320–8.

Dodart JC, Mathis C, Bales KR, Paul SM, Ungerer A (1999). Early regional cerebral glucose hypometabolism in transgenic mice overexpressing the V717F beta-amyloid precursor protein. *Neurosci Lett*, 277:49–52.

Durston S, Fossella JA, Casey BJ, Hulshoff Pol HE, Galvan A, Schnack HG, et al. (2005). Differential effects of DRD4 and DAT1 genotype on fronto-striatal gray matter volumes in a sample of subjects with attention deficit hyperactivity disorder, their unaffected siblings, and controls. *Mol Psychiatry*, 10:678–85.

Egan MF, Goldberg TE, Kolachana BS, Callicott JH, Mazzanti CM, Straub RE, et al. (2001). Effect of COMT Val108/158 Met genotype on frontal lobe function and risk for schizophrenia. *Proc Natl Acad Sci USA*, 98:6917–22.

Fan J, Fossella J, Sommer T, Wu Y, Posner MI (2003). Mapping the genetic variation of executive attention onto brain activity. *Proc Natl Acad Sci USA*, 100:7406–11.

Fan J, McCandliss BD, Fossella J, Flombaum JI, Posner MI (2005). The activation of attentional networks. *Neuroimage*, 26:471–9.

Fan J, McCandliss BD, Sommer T, Raz A, Posner MI (2002). Testing the efficiency and independence of attentional networks. *J Cogn Neurosci*, 14:340–7.

Fan J, Wu Y, Fossella JA, Posner MI (2001). Assessing the heritability of attentional networks. *BMC Neurosci*, 2:14.

Fossella J, Green AE, Fan J (2006). Evaluation of a structural polymorphism in the ankyrin repeat and kinase domain containing 1(ANKK1) gene and the activation of executive attention networks. *Cogn Affect Behav Neurosci*, 6(1):71–8.

Fossella J, Sommer T, Fan J, Wu Y, Swanson JM, Pfaff DW, et al. (2002). Assessing the molecular genetics of attention networks. *BMC Neurosci*, 3:14.

Friedrich FJ, Egly R, Rafal RD, Beck D (1998). Spatial attention deficits in humans: a comparison of superior parietal and temporal–parietal junction lesions. *Neuropsychology*, 12:193–207.

Geyer MA, Braff DL (1987). Startle habituation and sensorimotor gating in schizophrenia and related animal models. *Schizophr Bull*, 13:643–68.

Goghari VM, Rehm K, Carter CS, Macdonald AW 3rd (2006). [Epub ahead of print.] Regionally specific cortical thinning and gray matter abnormalities in the healthy relatives of schizophrenia patients. *Cereb Cortex*.

Goldberg TE, Weinberger DR (2004). Genes and the parsing of cognitive processes. *Trends Cogn Sci*, 8(7):325–35.

Goldman D, Oroszi G, Ducci F (2005). The genetics of addictions: uncovering the genes. *Nat Rev Genet*, 6:521–32.

Greenwood PM, Fossella JA, Parasuraman R (2005). Specificity of the effect of a nicotinic receptor polymorphism on individual differences in visuospatial attention. *J Cogn Neurosci*, 17:1611–20.

Hariri AR, Drabant EM, Weinberger DR (2006). Imaging genetics: perspectives from studies of genetically driven variation in serotonin function and corticolimbic affective processing. *Biol Psychiatry*, 59:888–97.

Hariri AR, Mattay VS, Tessitore A, Kolachana B, Fera F, Goldman D, et al. (2002). Serotonin transporter genetic variation and the response of the human amygdala. *Science*, 297:400–3.

Harrison PJ, Weinberger DR (2005). Schizophrenia genes, gene expression, and neuropathology: on the matter of their convergence. *Mol Psychiatry*, 10:804.

Hayashi K, Kaufman L, Ross MD, Klotman PE (2005). Definition of the critical domains required for homophilic targeting of mouse sidekick molecules. *Faseb J*, 19:614–6.

Heinz A, Braus DF, Smolka MN, Wrase J, Puls I, Hermann D, et al. (2005). Amygdala–prefrontal coupling depends on a genetic variation of the serotonin transporter. *Nat Neurosci*, 8:20–1.

Hyman SE, Fenton WS (2003). Medicine. What are the right targets for psychopharmacology? *Science*, 299:350–1.

Jaffee SR, Caspi A, Moffitt TE, Dodge KA, Rutter M, Taylor A, et al. (2005). Nature × Nurture: genetic vulnerabilities interact with physical maltreatment to promote conduct problems. *Dev Psychopathol*, 17(1):67–84.

Karayiorgou M, Gogos JA (2004). The molecular genetics of the 22q11-associated schizophrenia. *Brain Res Mol Brain Res*, 132:95–104.

Karmiloff-Smith A, Scerif G, Thomas M (2002). Different approaches to relating genotype to phenotype in developmental disorders. *Dev Psychobiol*, 40:311–22.

Katsanis J, Taylor J, Iacono WG, Hammer MA (2000). Heritability of different measures of smooth pursuit eye tracking dysfunction: a study of normal twins. *Psychophysiology*, 37:724–30.

Kinsman SL (2004). White matter imaging in holoprosencephaly in children. *Curr Opin Neurol*, 17(2):115–9.

Ladenheim B, Krasnova IN, Deng X, Oyler JM, Polettini A, Moran TH, et al. (2000). Methamphetamine-induced neurotoxicity is attenuated in transgenic mice with a null mutation for interleukin-6. *Mol Pharmacol*, 58:1247–56.

Lange KW, Robbins TW, Marsden CD, James M, Owen AM, Paul GM (1992). L-dopa withdrawal in Parkinson's disease selectively impairs cognitive performance in tests sensitive to frontal lobe dysfunction. *Psychopharmacology (Berl)*, 107:394–404.

Lohmueller KE, Pearce CL, Pike M, Lander ES, Hirschhorn JN (2003). Meta-analysis of genetic association studies supports a contribution of common variants to susceptibility to common disease. *Nat Genet*, 33:177–82.

Lyuksyutova AI, Lu CC, Milanesio N, King LA, Guo N, Wang Y, et al. (2003). Anterior–posterior guidance of commissural axons by Wnt-frizzled signaling. *Science*, 302:1984–8.

MacDonald AW, Cohen JD, Stenger VA, Carter CS (2000). Dissociating the role of the dorsolateral prefrontal and anterior cingulate cortex in cognitive control. *Science*, 288:1835–8.

McEwen BS (2000). The neurobiology of stress: from serendipity to clinical relevance. *Brain Res*, 886:172–89.

Mehmet H, Yue X, Squier MV, Lorek A, Cady E, Penrice J, et al. (1994). Increased apoptosis in the cingulate sulcus of newborn piglets following transient hypoxia-ischaemia is related to the degree of high energy phosphate depletion during the insult. *Neurosci Lett*, 181:121–5.

Mesulam MM (1981). A cortical network for directed attention and unilateral neglect. *Ann Neurol*, 10:309–25.

Meyer-Lindenberg A, Buckholtz JW, Kolachana B, R Hariri A, Pezawas L, Blasi G, et al. (2006). Neural mechanisms of genetic risk for impulsivity and violence in humans. *Proc Natl Acad Sci USA*, 103:6269–74.

Meyer-Lindenberg A, Weinberger DR (2006) Intermediate phenotypes and genetic mechanisms of psychiatric disorders. *Nat Rev Neurosci*, 7:818–27.

Mueller C, Patel S, Irons M, Antshel K, Salen G, Tint GS, et al. (2003). Normal cognition and behavior in a Smith–Lemli–Opitz syndrome patient who presented with Hirschsprung disease. *Am J Med Genet A*, 123(1):100–6.

Myles-Worsley M, Coon H (1997). Genetic and developmental factors in spontaneous selective attention: a study of normal twins. *Psychiatry Res*, 71:163–74.

Nachman MW, Crowell SL (2000). Estimate of the mutation rate per nucleotide in humans. *Genetics*, 156:297–304.

Ogden CA, Rich ME, Schork NJ, Paulus MP, Geyer MA, Lohr JB, et al. (2004). Candidate genes, pathways and mechanisms for bipolar (manic–depressive) and related disorders: an expanded convergent functional genomics approach. *Mol Psychiatry*, 9:1007–29.

Oppenheim JS, Skerry JE, Tramo MJ, Gazzaniga MS (1989). Magnetic resonance imaging morphology of the corpus callosum in monozygotic twins. *Ann Neurol*, 26:100–4.

Pardo PJ, Knesevich MA, Vogler GP, Pardo JV, Towne B, Cloninger CR, et al. (2000). Genetic and state variables of neurocognitive dysfunction in schizophrenia: a twin study [In Process Citation]. *Schizophr Bull*, 26:459–77.

Pezawas L, Meyer-Lindenberg A, Drabant EM, Verchinski BA, Munoz KE, Kolachana, B. S., et al. (2005). 5-HTTLPR polymorphism impacts human cingulate–amygdala interactions: a genetic susceptibility mechanism for depression. *Nat Neurosci*, 8:828–34.

Posner MI, Fan J (2008). Attention as an organ system. In Pomerantz JR, ed. Topics in integrative neuroscience: from cells to cognition. Cambridge: Cambridge University Press.

Posner MI, Petersen SE (1990). The attention system of the human brain. *Annu Rev Neurosci*, 13:25–42.

Posner MI, Snyder CR, Davidson BJ (1980). Attention and the detection of signals. *J Exp Psychol*, 109:160–74.

Reich DE, Schaffner SF, Daly MJ, McVean G, Mullikin JC, Higgins JM, et al. (2002). Human genome sequence variation and the influence of gene history, mutation and recombination. *Nat Genet*, 32:135–42.

Reuter M, Ott U, Vaitl D, Hennig J (2007). Impaired executive control is associated with a variation in the promoter region of the tryptophan hydroxylase 2 gene. *J Cogn Neurosci*, 19(3): 401–8.

Romeo RD, Fossella JA, Bateup HS, Sisti HM, Brake WG, McEwen BS (2004). Maternal separation suppresses TGF alpha mRNA expression in the prefrontal cortex of male and female neonatal C57BL/6 mice. *Brain Res Dev Brain Res*, 152(1):73–7.

Rosen C (2004). Preaching eugenics. Oxford: Oxford University Press.

Rueda MR, Fan J, McCandliss BD, Halparin JD, Gruber DB, Lercari LP, et al. (2004). Development of attentional networks in childhood. *Neuropsychologia*, 42:1029–40.

Rueda MR, Rothbart MK, McCandliss BD, Saccomanno L, Posner MI (2005). Training, maturation, and genetic influences on the development of executive attention. *Proc Natl Acad Sci USA*, 102:14931–6.

Sabol SZ, Hu S, Hamer D (1998). A functional polymorphism in the monoamine oxidase A gene promoter. *Hum Genet*, 103:273–9.

Sandstead HH, Frederickson CJ, Penland JG (2000). History of zinc as related to brain function. *J Nutr*, 130(2S Suppl):496–502S.

Sawaguchi T, Goldman-Rakic PS (1991). D1 dopamine receptors in prefrontal cortex: involvement in working memory. *Science*, 251:947–50.

Sawaguchi T, Goldman-Rakic PS (1994). The role of D1-dopamine receptor in working memory: local injections of dopamine antagonists into the prefrontal cortex of rhesus monkeys performing an oculomotor delayed-response task. *J Neurophysiol*, 71:515–28.

Scerif G, Karmiloff-Smith A (2005). The dawn of cognitive genetics? Crucial developmental caveats. *Trends Cogn Sci*, 9(3):126–35.

Schneider JS, Kovelowski CJ 2nd (1990). Chronic exposure to low doses of MPTP: I. Cognitive deficits in motor asymptomatic monkeys. *Brain Res*, 519:122–8.

Seamans JK, Floresco SB, Phillips AG (1998). D1 receptor modulation of hippocampal–prefrontal cortical circuits integrating spatial memory with executive functions in the rat. *J Neurosci*, 18:1613–21.

Sen S, Burmeister M, Ghosh D (2004). Meta-analysis of the association between a serotonin transporter promoter polymorphism (5-HTTLPR) and anxiety-related personality traits. *Am J Med Genet B Neuropsychiatr Genet*, 127(1):85–9.

Sesack SR, Carr DB, Omelchenko N, Pinto A (2003). Anatomical substrates for glutamate–dopamine interactions: evidence for specificity of connections and extrasynaptic actions. *Ann NY Acad Sci*, 1003:36–52.

Sesack SR, Hawrylak VA, Guido MA, Levey AI (1998). Cellular and subcellular localization of the dopamine transporter in rat cortex. *Adv Pharmacol*, 42:171–4.

Simon H, Scatton B, Moal ML (1980). Dopaminergic A10 neurones are involved in cognitive functions. *Nature*, 286:150–1.

Sobin C, Kiley-Brabeck K, Karayiorgou M (2005a). Associations between prepulse inhibition and executive visual attention in children with the 22q11 deletion syndrome. *Mol Psychiatry*, 10:553–62.

Sobin C, Kiley-Brabeck K, Karayiorgou M (2005b). Lower prepulse inhibition in children with the 22q11 deletion syndrome. *Am J Psychiatry*, 162:1090–9.

Stutzmann GE, McEwen BS, LeDoux JE (1998). Serotonin modulation of sensory inputs to the lateral amygdala: dependency on corticosterone. *J Neurosci*, 18:9529–38.

Su AI, Wiltshire T, Batalov S, Lapp H, Ching KA, Block D, et al. (2004). A gene atlas of the mouse and human protein-encoding transcriptomes. *Proc Natl Acad Sci USA*, 101:6062–7.

Sugino K, Hempel CM, Miller MN, Hattox AM, Shapiro P, Wu C, et al. (2006). Molecular taxonomy of major neuronal classes in the adult mouse forebrain. *Nat Neurosci*, 9:99–107.

Sur M, Rubenstein JL (2005). Patterning and plasticity of the cerebral cortex. *Science*, 310:805–10.

Takeda A, Takefuta S, Okada S, Oku N (2000). Relationship between brain zinc and transient learning impairment of adult rats fed zinc-deficient diet. *Brain Res*, 859:352–7.

Thompson PM, Cannon TD, Narr KL, van Erp T, Poutanen VP, Huttunen M, et al. (2001). Genetic influences on brain structure. *Nat Neurosci*, 4:1253–8.

Tischfield MA, Bosley TM, Salih MA, Alorainy IA, Sener EC, Nester MJ, et al. (2005). Homozygous HOXA1 mutations disrupt human brainstem, inner ear, cardiovascular and cognitive development. *Nat Genet*, 37:1035–7.

Tramo MJ, Loftus WC, Stukel TA, Green RL, Weaver JB, Gazzaniga MS (1998). Brain size, head size, and intelligence quotient in monozygotic twins. *Neurology*, 50:1246–52.

van Veen V, Carter CS (2002). The anterior cingulate as a conflict monitor: fMRI and ERP studies. *Physiol Behav*, 77:477–82.

Vogt BA, Nimchinsky EA, Vogt LJ, Hof PR (1995). Human cingulate cortex: surface features, flat maps, and cytoarchitecture. *J Comp Neurol*, 359:490–506.

Watanabe M, Kodama T, Hikosaka K (1997). Increase of extracellular dopamine in primate prefrontal cortex during a working memory task. *J Neurophysiol*, 78:2795–8.

Witte EA, Marrocco RT (1997). Alteration of brain noradrenergic activity in rhesus monkeys affects the alerting component of covert orienting. *Psychopharmacology (Berl)*, 132:315–23.

Xu K, Ernst M, Goldman D (2006). Imaging genomics applied to anxiety, stress response, and resiliency. *Neuroinformatics*, 4(1):51–64.

6 Genetics of Corticolimbic Function and Emotional Reactivity

Ahmad R. Hariri, Erika E. Forbes, and Kristin L. Bigos

Neuroimaging technologies, because of their unique ability to capture the structural and functional integrity of distributed neural circuitries within individuals, provide a powerful approach to explore the genetic basis of individual differences in corticolimbic function, emotional reactivity, and vulnerability to mood disorders. Functional magnetic resonance imaging (fMRI) studies especially have established important physiological links between genetic polymorphisms affecting serotonin neurotransmission and robust differences in corticolimbic circuit function that have been linked to temperamental anxiety and increased risk for depression. Importantly, many of these biological relationships have been revealed in relatively small samples of subjects and in the absence of observable differences at the level of behavior, underscoring the power of a direct assay of brain anatomy and physiology in exploring the functional impact of genetic variation. Through the continued integration of genes, brain, and behavior, neuroimaging technologies represent a critical tool in ongoing efforts to understand the neurobiology of normal and pathological emotional behaviors. Multidisciplinary research capitalizing on such neuroimaging-based integration will contribute to the identification of predictive markers and biological pathways for neuropsychiatric disease vulnerability as well as the generation of novel targets for therapeutic intervention.

Conceptual Basis and Overview

Genes have unparalleled potential impact on all levels of biology. In the context of disease states, particularly behavioral disorders, genes represent the cornerstone of mechanisms that either directly or in concert with environmental events ultimately result in disease. Moreover, genes offer the potential to identify at-risk individuals and biological pathways for the development of new treatments. While most human behaviors cannot be explained by genes alone, and certainly much variance in aspects of brain structure and function will not be genetically determined directly, it is anticipated that variations in genetic sequence impacting function will contribute an appreciable amount of variance to these resultant complex biological and behavioral phenomena. This conclusion is implicit in the results of studies of twins that have revealed heritabilities ranging from 40% to 70% for various aspects of cognition, temperament, and personality (Plomin et al. 1994). In the case of psychiatric illness, genes appear to be the only consistent risk factors that have been identified across populations, and the majority of susceptibility for major psychiatric disorders is accounted for by inheritance (Moldin and Gottesman 1997).

Association Studies of Genes Involved in Emotion Regulation

Behavioral and molecular genetics approaches have not been applied to questions of particular emotion regulation responses as defined in studies of behavior or physiology. For instance, it would be a stretch to examine the behavioral, cognitive, or physiological components of the emotion regulation strategy of situation modification in relation to a specific gene variant. Instead, typical research in genetics has addressed the association between genes and proxy variables for emotion regulation. These proxy variables represent broad individual differences in emotional style or tendency and have generally been in the areas of personality or affective disorders. While these variables are related to emotion regulation constructs, they are more broad and heterogeneous.

Behavioral and molecular genetics approaches have been applied to two topics that are relevant to stable emotion regulatory style: personality and affective disorders. Personality refers to stable normal individual differences, many of which pertain to emotional experience and expression. Affective disorders, while more in the realm of abnormal emotional experience, can be considered examples of pathological emotion dysregulation. These disorders—which include intense and long-duration depressed, manic, or anxious emotional states—involve reduced emotional flexibility. Presumably, difficulty with modulating the frequency, intensity, or duration of affective states underlies these disorders. For example, depression is characterized by sustained sadness and unusually low-frequency, low-intensity positive affect. The genes that predispose people to experience the disorders therefore may constitute genetic influences on effective, healthy emotion regulation.

Molecular genetics approaches to emotion regulation often focus on polymorphisms leading to variability in neurotransmitter availability or neurotransmitter receptor function. For example, extraversion's characteristics of dominance, novelty seeking, and reward sensitivity are thought to be driven by variability in function of the dopamine (DA) system. There are many neurotransmitter systems, each of which has a complex function and influence on brain and behavior. In addition, the influence of the various neurotransmitter systems on emotion regulation is presumably complex and interrelated. Research on the association between neurotransmitter genes and emotion-regulation-related characteristics has focused on narrow aspects of specific neurotransmitter systems. Two particular systems appear to be especially relevant to questions of emotion regulation, however: the serotonin (5-hydroxytryptamine; 5-HT) system and the dopamine system. Serotonin has been implicated in the generation and regulation of emotional behavior, and manipulation of serotonin activity has effects on behaviors such as impulsivity and aggression. The dopamine system plays a critical role in reward processing and has been linked to normal individual differences in reward traits as well as to disorders involving enhanced reward-seeking such as addiction.

We address both neurotransmitter systems in our review of association studies below, and we focus specifically on the 5-HT system in our discussion of imaging genetics in the remainder of the chapter. In addition, while we address genetic factors in both normal and abnormal individual differences in the review of association studies, we emphasize normal individual differences in our treatment of imaging genetics. As we explain below, the conceptual foundation for imaging genetics lends itself best to first examining normal variability in neural function.

Personality

Extraversion is likely to involve approach towards goals despite setbacks and assertion that serves to modify a current situation. Such behavioral approach or appetitive component processes of extraversion are, in part, mediated by a mesolimbic neural circuitry, which is tightly regulated by DA. Consequently, studies of the genetic underpinnings of extraversion have focused on polymorphisms related to DA function (Ebstein et al. 2002; Noblett and Coccaro 2005). Specifically, genetic variants of DA receptor subtypes, such as the D2 and D4 receptors, which mediate the myriad neuromodulatory effects of DA, as well as the dopamine transporter, which facilitates the active reuptake of DA from the extracellular space, have been examined in relation to the broad trait of extraversion and to one of its facets, novelty seeking. More recently, studies have begun to examine other genes that influence broader DA and other catecholamine availability, including catechol-O-methyltransferase (COMT) and monoamine oxidase A (MAOA). As recent reviews and meta-analyses have noted, the associations between specific DA polymorphisms and complex measures of personality have been inconsistent across studies, with null findings being relatively common (Schinka et al. 2002; Strobel et al. 2003).

Another significant line of related research from the field of personality genetics is the examination of serotonin (5-HT) subsystem polymorphisms on negative emotional behaviors such as neuroticism, impulsivity, and aggression. A gene of particular interest has been a relatively frequent length variant in the promoter or regulatory region of the 5-HT transporter (5-HTT) gene (see below). Numerous studies have indicated that the short (S) variant of this gene, resulting in relatively increased 5-HT signaling, is associated with higher levels of temperamental anxiety. Other investigators have established links between variation in 5-HT genes controlling biosynthesis, receptor function, and metabolic degradation with additional dimensional measures of negative emotionality such as impulsive aggression (Manuck et al. 1998; 1999; 2000). Despite some replication, these lines of investigation have also been marked by null findings (Glatt and Freimer 2002), with several reports, including meta-analyses, emphasizing that the ability to detect associations depends on the personality instruments used, with "broad bandwidth" personality measures (e.g., extraversion) typically representing constructs that are too heterogeneous to map meaningfully onto biological systems (Munafo et al. 2005).

Affective Disorders

The leap from studies of genetic influences on dimensional indices of normal variability in personality and temperament to studies of genetic influences on affective disorders such as depression and anxiety is understandable given the correlation of these indices with symptoms of these disorders and the genetic influences on such correlations (Carey 1994). For example, depression and the personality trait of neuroticism appear to share genetic influence, and in addition, the correlation between depression and neuroticism appears to be influenced by genetic factors (Kendler et al. 1993a; 1993b). Such attempts to link polymorphisms directly with clinical syndromes have been fueled by the suggestion that genes might have more detectable influence at extreme, pathological ends of the emotional trait distribution. While any specific gene in isolation is unlikely to serve as a predisposition to a complex disorder such as major depressive disorder, the influence of a particular gene is more likely to be detected in a clinical population than in individuals with lower levels of the emotional dysfunction involved in the disorder. If neuroticism and depression share genetic influence (Kendler et al. 1993a; 1993b), and if depression can be seen as an extreme version of high neuroticism, then influences of 5-HT polymorphisms, for instance, may be more clear when depression is the target construct.

Studies of genetic influences on depression and anxiety in humans have emphasized the role of genes related to 5-HT and hypothalamic–pituitary–adrenal (HPA) axis function (for a more thorough review, see Leonardo and Hen 2006). Both the 5-HT and HPA systems play a critical role in emotional reactivity and regulation and are thus prime candidates for studies of these mood disorders. Many candidate polymorphisms in these systems have been linked to increased risk for mood disorders. Moreover, the existence of an association has been demonstrated to be moderated by the environment. In particular, social stress, such as maltreatment during childhood or divorce in adulthood, appears to unmask genetic vulnerability for depression and anxiety.

Limitations of Behavioral Association Studies

All of the findings from traditional behavioral association studies have been inconsistent, with an impressive amount of null findings for each gene studied. In many ways, this underscores the argument that in the context of behavior and psychiatric illness there are only susceptibility genes and not disease genes which clearly and specifically determine affective disorders. Association studies have important limitations, not the least of which is the long chain of events from gene function to personality or psychiatric disorder. Additional limitations include the specificity of findings to particular personality instruments, the reliance on self-report rather than observed behavior, the failure to account for developmental effects, and the difficulties of defining and examining gene-by-environment effects. Since genes are directly involved in the development and function of brain regions subserving specific emotional processes, functional polymorphisms in genes may be strongly related to the function of these specific neural systems and, in turn, mediate–moderate their involvement in behavioral outcomes.

Serotonin and the Neurobiology of Emotional Regulation

Converging evidence from animal and human studies has revealed that serotonin is a critical neuromodulator in the generation and regulation of emotional behavior (Lucki 1998). Serotonergic neurotransmission has also been an efficacious target for the pharmacological treatment of mood disorders including depression, obsessive–compulsive disorder, anxiety, and panic (Blier and de Montigny 1999). Moreover, genetic variation in several key 5-HT subsystems, presumably resulting in altered central serotonergic tone and neurotransmission, has been associated with various aspects of personality and temperament (Munafo et al. 2005; Schinka et al. 2004; Sen et al. 2004) as well as susceptibility to affective illness (Murphy et al. 1998; Reif and Lesch 2003). However, enthusiasm for the potential of such genetic variation to affect behaviors and especially disease liability has been tempered by weak, inconsistent, and failed attempts at replication of specific associations with psychiatric syndromes (Glatt and Freimer 2002).

The inability to substantiate such relationships through consistent replication in independent cohorts may simply reflect methodological issues such as inadequate control for population stratification, insufficient power, and/or inconsistency in the methods applied. Alternatively, and perhaps more importantly, such inconsistency may reflect the underlying biological nature of the relationship between allelic variants in serotonin genes, each of presumably small effect, and observable behaviors in the domain of mood and emotion that typically reflect complex functional interactions and emergent phenomena. Given that the biological impact of variation in a gene traverses an increasingly divergent path from cells to neural systems to behavior, the response of brain regions subserving emotional processes in humans (e.g., amygdala, hippocampus, prefrontal cortex, anterior cingulate gyrus) represents a critical first step in their impact on behavior. Thus, functional polymorphisms in 5-HT genes may be strongly related to the integrity of these underlying neural systems and mediate–moderate their ultimate effect on behavior (Hariri and Weinberger 2003).

Common Polymorphisms Impacting the Amygdala and Temperamental Anxiety

Serotonin Transporter

Individual differences in serotonin (5-HT) function have been repeatedly and consistently associated with variability in affect and temperament in mouse, monkey, and humans (Manuck et al. 1998; Lucki 1998). Moreover, abnormal 5-HT neurotransmission has been implicated in the pathophysiology of mood and anxiety disorders, and 5-HT substrates are a key target of drugs used to treat these disorders. A common polymorphism in the promoter region (5-HTTLPR) of the serotonin transporter (5-HTT) gene is easily the most studied of genetic variants impacting 5-HT neurotransmission. Such interest is in part mediated by the critical role of the 5-HTT in regulating 5-HT signaling at both pre- and postsynaptic receptors (via active clearance of released 5-HT from the synapse) as well as the widespread use of antidepressant drugs which selectively block this reuptake mechanism. In comparison to the 5-HTTLPR long (L) allele, the short (S) allele has been associated with reductions in 5-HTT expression and 5-HT reuptake in vitro (Lesch et al. 1996). While this in vitro effect was initially confirmed using in vivo single photon emission computed tomography (Heinz et al. 2000), recent positron emission tomography (PET) studies offering more specific radiotracers and improved spatial resolution have failed to find altered 5-HTT levels associated with the 5-HTTLPR (Parsey et al. 2006; Shioe et al. 2003). Rather, effects of the 5-HTTLPR have been documented in other 5-HT subsystems, most notably the 5-HT$_{1A}$ receptor (David et al., 2005; Lee et al. 2005), and such downstream effects may be critical in mediating the neural and behavioral effects of the 5-HTTLPR (Fisher et al. 2006; Hariri and Holmes 2006).

At the behavioral level, possession of either one or two copies of the S allele has been associated with increased levels of temperamental anxiety (Munafo et al. 2005; Schinka et al. 2004; Sen et al. 2004), conditioned fear responses (Garpenstrand et al. 2001), and development of depression (Lesch et al. 1996), especially in the context of environmental stress (Caspi et al. 2003; Kendler et al. 2005). Studies using fMRI have provided a unique understanding of how the 5-HTTLPR may impact temperamental anxiety and risk for depression. In a small but influential study, fMRI revealed that the reactivity of the amygdala, a brain region critical in mediating emotional arousal, to threat-related facial expressions was significantly exaggerated in S allele carriers

(Hariri et al. 2002). Since this original report, there have been multiple replications of the association between the S allele and relatively increased amygdala reactivity in both healthy volunteers (Munafò et al. 2008) and patients with mood disorders (Domschke et al. 2006; Furmark et al. 2004). In addition, the 5-HTTLPR S allele has been further linked with reduced gray matter volumes in and functional coupling between the amygdala and medial prefrontal cortex (Pezawas et al. 2005). As the magnitude of amygdala reactivity (as well as its functional coupling with medial prefrontal cortex) is associated with temperamental anxiety, these imaging genetics findings suggest that the 5-HTTLPR S allele may be associated with increased risk for depression upon exposure to environmental stressors because of its mediation of exaggerated corticolimbic reactivity to potential threat.

Monoamine Oxidase A

5-HT neurotransmission is also regulated through intracellular degradation via the metabolic enzyme, MAOA. A common genetic polymorphism in the MAOA gene, resulting in a relatively low-activity enzyme, has been associated with increased risk for violent or antisocial behavior. A recent fMRI study reported that the low-activity MAOA allele is associated with relatively exaggerated amygdala reactivity and diminished prefrontal regulation of the amygdala (Meyer-Lindenberg et al. 2006). The magnitude of functional coupling between these regions predicted levels of temperamental anxiety, suggesting that the genetic association between the MAOA low-activity variant and abnormal behavior may be mediated through this circuit. Interestingly, both the 5-HTTLPR S and MAOA low-activity alleles presumably result in relatively increased 5-HT signaling and exaggerated amygdala reactivity. As the directionality of these effects are consistent with animal studies documenting anxiogenic effects of 5-HT (Maier and Watkins 2005), the imaging genetics data provide important insight regarding the neurobiological and behavioral effects of 5-HT.

Tryptophan Hydroxylase-2

Recent imaging genetics studies examining the impact of variation in 5-HT subsystems highlight the potential reciprocal nature by which functional imaging and molecular genetics approaches can be mutually informative in advancing our understanding of the biological mechanism of behavior. Tryptophan hydroxylase-2 (TPH2) is the rate-limiting enzyme in the synthesis of neuronal 5-HT and thus plays a key role in regulating 5-HT neurotransmission. A recent study found that a single nucleotide polymorphism (SNP) in the regulatory region of the human TPH2 gene affects amygdala function (Brown et al. 2005). Specifically, the T allele of the relatively frequent G(-844)T polymorphism was associated with relatively exaggerated amygdala reactivity. This report provides further insight into the biological significance of TPH2 in the human central nervous system and represents a critical next step in our understanding of the importance of this newly identified second tryptophan hydroxylase isoform for human brain function. Moreover, it marks an important advance in the application of functional neuroimaging to the study of genes, brain, and behavior. In contrast to previous studies of genetic effects on brain function, where the molecular and cellular effects of the candidate variants had been previously demonstrated (e.g., 5-HTTLPR and MAOA), these fMRI data provide the first evidence for potential functionality of a novel candidate polymorphism. In this way, the initial identification of a systems-level effect of a specific polymorphism provides impetus for the subsequent characterization of its functional effects at the molecular and cellular level. Building on this initial imaging genetics finding (and a subsequent replication; Canli et al. 2005), a recent molecular study has demonstrated that the G(-844)T is in strong linkage with another promoter SNP that impacts transcriptional regulation of TPH2 and may affect enzyme availability and 5-HT biosynthesis. Such scientific reciprocity between imaging and molecular genetics illustrates how the contributions of abnormalities in candidate neural systems to complex behaviors and emergent phenomena, possibly including psychiatric illnesses, can be understood from the perspective of their neurobiological origins.

Summary and Future Directions

The results of these studies underscore the power of in vivo neuroimaging technologies and provide compelling evidence that the application of imaging genetics promises a unique opportunity to explore and evaluate the functional impact of brain-relevant genetic polymorphisms. In turn, these efforts will contribute to the identification of biological mechanisms and pathways that mediate individual differences in temperamental anxiety and vulnerability to mood disorders. While current imaging genetics studies highlight a powerful new approach to the study of genes, brain, and behavior, the true potential of this approach will only be realized by aggressively expanding the scope and scale of the experimental protocols.

Although single gene effects on brain function can be readily documented in small samples ($ns < 20$), the contributions of multiple genes acting in response to variable environmental pressures is ultimately necessary for the development of truly predictive markers that account for the majority of variance in any given phenotype, such as stress resiliency. For example, the interactive effect of the brain-derived neurotrophic factor (BDNF) val66met and 5-HTTLPR on corticolimbic circuitry has been examined recently in an imaging genetics sample of over 100 subjects (Pezawas et al. 2008). An epistatic mechanism between these molecules is suggested by pharmacological and animal models linking 5-HTT and BDNF in cell signaling related to stress-mediated neuroplasticity (Luellen et al. 2007; Ren-Patterson et al. 2006). Surprisingly, the BDNF met66 allele, which is associated with abnormal regulated BDNF release and reduced hippocampal activity, appears to block the effects of the 5-HTTLPR S allele on reduced amygdala volume. Presumably the reduced responsivity of the met66 allele protects against the exaggerated 5-HT signaling associated with the 5-HTTLPR S allele. Such studies provide an example of the biological epistasis that likely underlies the pathogenesis of a complex disease in the human brain.

Combining existing neuroimaging modalities is another important future direction for imaging genetics. Implementation of multimodal strategies is critical for identifying intermediate mechanisms mediating the effects of genetic polymorphisms on neural circuit function and related behaviors. The potential of multimodal neuroimaging was recently demonstrated in a study employing both PET and fMRI to identify the impact of 5-HT$_{1A}$ autoreceptor regulation of 5-HT release on amygdala reactivity (Fisher et al. 2006). In the study, adult volunteers underwent [^{11}C] WAY100635 PET, to determine 5-HT$_{1A}$ autoreceptor binding potential, an in vivo index of receptor density. During the same day, all subjects also underwent fMRI to determine the functional reactivity of the amygdala. Remarkably, the density of 5-HT$_{1A}$ autoreceptors accounted for 30% to 44% of the variability in amygdala reactivity. Downstream effects on 5-HT$_{1A}$ autoreceptors, notably reduced receptor density, have been hypothesized to mediate neural and behavioral changes associated with the 5-HTTLPR S allele (David et al. 2005). Thus, these findings suggest that 5-HT$_{1A}$ autoreceptor regulation of corticolimbic circuitry represents a key molecular mechanism mediating the effects of the 5-HTTLPR.

Ultimately, we anticipate that such mechanistic understanding will allow for the early identification of individuals at greater risk for behavioral problems that can have long-term health-related implications. Continued imaging genetics research at the interface of genes, brain, and behavior holds great promise in further explicating the neurobiological mechanisms through which risk for psychiatric disease emerges in the context of environmental adversity (Hariri and Holmes 2006; Caspi and Moffitt 2006). Such knowledge will, in turn, facilitate the development of therapeutic interventions, tailored to individual neurobiologies, which will be more effective in combating the enormous personal and public health burden associated with common psychiatric disorders.

Acknowledgments

Portions of this article have been published in *Biological Psychiatry* (Hariri et al. 2006), *Future Neurology* (Hariri and Fisher 2007), *Neuroimaging Clinics* (Bigos and Hariri 2007), and the *Handbook of Emotion Regulation* (Hariri and Forbes, *Genetics of Emotion Regulation,* 2006, Ed. Gross, J.J.).

This research was supported in part by National Institute of Mental Health grants K01-MH072837 (ARH), K01-MH074769 (EEF), and F31-MH076420 (KLB) as well as the

National Alliance for Research on Schizophrenia and Depression Young Investigator Awards (ARH and EEF).

References

Bigos KL, Hariri AR (2007). Neuroimaging: At the interface of genes, brain and behavior. *Neuroimaging Clin N Am*, 17(4):459–67.

Blier P, de Montigny C (1999). Serotonin and drug-induced therapeutic responses in major depression, obsessive–compulsive and panic disorders. *Neuropsychopharmacology*, 21(2 Suppl): 91–8S.

Brown SM, Peet E, Manuck SB, Williamson DE, Dahl RE, Ferrell RE, et al. (2005). A regulatory variant of the human tryptophan hydroxylase-2 gene biases amygdala reactivity. *Mol Psychiatry*, 10:805.

Canli T, Congdon E, Gutknecht L, Constable RT, Lesch KP (2005). Amygdala responsiveness is modulated by tryptophan hydroxylase-2 gene variation. *J Neural Transm*, 112:1479–85.

Carey G (1994). Genetic association study in psychiatry: analytical evaluation and a recommendation. *Am J Med Genet*, 54:311–7.

Caspi A, Moffitt TE (2006). Gene–environment interactions in psychiatry: joining forces with neuroscience. *Nat Rev Neurosci*, 7:583–90.

Caspi A, Sugden K, Moffitt TE, Taylor A, Craig IW, Harrington H, et al. (2003). Influence of life stress on depression: moderation by a polymorphism in the 5-HTT gene. *Science*, 301:386–9.

David SP, Murthy NV, Rabiner EA, Munafo MR, Johnstone EC, Jacob R, et al. (2005). A functional genetic variation of the serotonin (5-HT) transporter affects 5-HT1A receptor binding in humans. *J Neurosci*, 25:2586–90.

Domschke K, Braun M, Ohrmann P, Suslow T, Kugel H, Bauer J, et al. (2006). Association of the functional -1019C/G 5-HT1A polymorphism with prefrontal cortex and amygdala activation measured with 3 T fMRI in panic disorder. *Int J Neuropsychopharmacol*, 9:349–55.

Ebstein RP, Zohar AH, Benjamin J, Belmaker RH (2002). An update on molecular genetic studies of human personality traits. *Appl Bioinformatics*, 1(2):57–68.

Fisher PM, Meltzer CC, Ziolko SK, Price JC, Hariri AR (2006). Capacity for 5-HT1A-mediated autoregulation predicts amygdala reactivity. *Nat Neurosci*, 9:1362–3.

Furmark T, Tillfors M, Garpenstrand H, Marteinsdottir I, Langstrom B, Oreland L, et al. (2004). Serotonin transporter polymorphism linked to amygdala excitability and symptom severity in patients with social phobia. *Neurosci Lett*, 362:1–4.

Garpenstrand H, Annas P, Ekblom J, Oreland L, Fredrikson M (2001). Human fear conditioning is related to dopaminergic and serotonergic biological markers. *Behav Neurosci*, 115:358–64.

Glatt CE, Freimer NB (2002). Association analysis of candidate genes for neuropsychiatric disease: the perpetual campaign. *Trends Genet*, 18(6):307–12.

Hariri AR, Drabant EM, Weinberger DR (2006). Imaging genetics: perspectives from studies of genetically driven variation in serotonin function and corticolimbic affective processing. *Biol Psychiatry*, 59(10):888–97.

Hariri AR, Fisher PM (2007). The role of the 5-HT1A autoreceptor in amygdala reactivity and depression. *Future Neurol*, 2(2):121–4.

Hariri AR, Forbes E (2007). Genetics of emotion regulation. In Gross JJ, ed, *Handbook of Emotion Regulation*. New York: Guilford Press.

Hariri AR, Holmes A (2006). Genetics of emotional regulation: the role of the serotonin transporter in neural function. *Trends Cogn Sci*, 10(4):182–91.

Hariri AR, Mattay VS, Tessitore A, Kolachana B, Fera F, Goldman D, et al. (2002). Serotonin transporter genetic variation and the response of the human amygdala. *Science*, 297:400–3.

Hariri AR, Weinberger DR (2003). Functional neuroimaging of genetic variation in serotonergic neurotransmission. *Genes Brain Behav*, 2:314–49.

Heinz A, Jones DW, Mazzanti C, Goldman D, Ragan P, Hommer D, et al. (2000). A relationship between serotonin transporter genotype and in vivo protein expression and alcohol neurotoxicity. *Biol Psychiatry*, 47:643–9.

Kendler KS, Kessler RC, Neale MC, Heath AC, Eaves LJ (1993a). The prediction of major depression in women: toward an integrated etiologic model. *Am J Psychiatry*, 150:1139–48.

Kendler KS, Kuhn JW, Vittum J, Prescott CA, Riley B (2005). The interaction of stressful life events and a serotonin transporter polymorphism in the prediction of episodes of major depression: a replication. *Arch Gen Psychiatry*, 62:529–35.

Kendler KS, Neale MC, Kessler RC, Heath AC, Eaves LJ (1993b). A longitudinal twin study of personality and major depression in women. *Arch Gen Psychiatry*, 50:853–62.

Lee M, Bailer UF, Frank GK, Henry SE, Meltzer CC, Price JC, et al. (2005). Relationship of a 5-HT transporter functional polymorphism to 5-HT1A receptor binding in healthy women. *Mol Psychiatry*, 10:715–6.

Leonardo ED, Hen R (2006). Genetics of affective and anxiety disorders. *Annu Rev Psychol*, 57:117–37.

Lesch KP, Bengel D, Heils A, Sabol SZ, Greenberg BD, Petri S, et al. (1996). Association of anxiety-related traits with a polymorphism in the serotonin transporter gene regulatory region. *Science*, 274:1527–31.

Lucki I (1998). The spectrum of behaviors influenced by serotonin. *Biol Psychiatry*, 44:151–62.

Luellen BA, Bianco LE, Schneider LM, Andrews AM (2007). Reduced brain-derived neurotrophic factor is associated with a loss of serotonergic innervation in the hippocampus of aging mice. *Genes Brain Behav*, 6:482–90.

Maier SF, Watkins LR (2005). Stressor controllability and learned helplessness: the roles of the dorsal raphe nucleus, serotonin, and corticotropin-releasing factor. *Neurosci Biobehav Rev*, 29:829–41.

Manuck SB, Flory JD, Ferrell RE, Dent KM, Mann JJ, Muldoon MF (1999). Aggression and anger-related traits associated with a polymorphism of the tryptophan hydroxylase gene. *Biol Psychiatry*, 45:603–14.

Manuck SB, Flory JD, Ferrell RE, Mann JJ, Muldoon MF (2000). A regulatory polymorphism of the monoamine oxidase—A gene may be associated with variability in aggression, impulsivity, and central nervous system serotonergic responsivity. *Psychiatry Res*, 95:9–23.

Manuck SB, Flory JD, McCaffery JM, Matthews KA, Mann JJ, Muldoon MF (1998). Aggression, impulsivity, and central nervous system serotonergic responsivity in a nonpatient sample. *Neuropsychopharmacology*, 19:287–99.

Meyer-Lindenberg A, Buckholtz JW, Kolachana B, Hariri AR, Pezawas L, Blasi G, et al. (2006). Neural mechanisms of genetic risk for impulsivity and violence in humans. *Proc Natl Acad Sci USA*, 103:6269–74.

Moldin SO, Gottesman II (1997). At issue: genes, experience, and chance in schizophrenia—positioning for the 21st century. *Schizophr Bull*, 23:547–61.

Munafò MR, Brown SM, Hariri AR (2008). Serotonin transporter (5-HTTLPR) genotype and amygdala activation: a meta-analysis. *Biol Psychiatry*, 63(9):852–7.

Munafò MR, Clark T, Flint J (2005). Does measurement instrument moderate the association between the serotonin transporter gene and anxiety-related personality traits? A meta-analysis. *Mol Psychiatry*, 10:415–9.

Murphy DL, Andrews AM, Wichems CH, Li Q, Tohda M, Greenberg B (1998). Brain serotonin neurotransmission: an overview and update with an emphasis on serotonin subsystem heterogeneity, multiple receptors, interactions with other neurotransmitter systems, and consequent implications for understanding the actions of serotonergic drugs. *J Clin Psychiatry*, 59(Suppl 15):4–12.

Noblett KL, Coccaro EF (2005). Molecular genetics of personality. *Curr Psychiatry Rep*, 7(1):73–80.

Parsey RV, Hastings RS, Oquendo MA, Hu X, Goldman D, Huang YY, et al. (2006). Effect of a triallelic functional polymorphism of the serotonin-transporter-linked promoter region on expression of serotonin transporter in the human brain. *Am J Psychiatry*, 163:48–51.

Pezawas L, Meyer-Lindenberg A, Drabant EM, Verchinski BA, Munoz KE, Kolachana BS, et al. (2005). 5-HTTLPR polymorphism impacts human cingulate–amygdala interactions: a genetic susceptibility mechanism for depression. *Nat Neurosci*, 8:828–34.

Pezawas L, Meyer-Lindenberg A, Goldman AL, Verchinski BA, Chen G, Kolachana BS, Egan MF, Mattay VS, Hariri AR, Weinberger DR (2008). Evidence of biologic epistasis between BDNF and SLC6A4 and implications for depression. *Mol Psychiatry*, 13(7):709–16.

Plomin R, Owen MJ, McGuffin P (1994). The genetic basis of complex human behaviors. *Science*, 264:1733–9.

Reif A, Lesch KP (2003). Toward a molecular architecture of personality. *Behav Brain Res*, 139:1–20.

Ren-Patterson RF, Cochran LW, Holmes A, Lesch KP, Lu B, Murphy DL (2006). Gender-dependent modulation of brain monoamines and anxiety-like behaviors in mice with genetic serotonin transporter and BDNF deficiencies. *Cell Mol Neurobiol*, 26:753–78.

Schinka JA, Busch RM, Robichaux-Keene N (2004). A meta-analysis of the association between the serotonin transporter gene polymorphism (5-HTTLPR) and trait anxiety. *Mol Psychiatry*, 9:197–202.

Schinka JA, Letsch EA, Crawford FC (2002). DRD4 and novelty seeking: results of meta-analyses. *Am J Med Genet*, 114:643–8.

Sen S, Burmeister M, Ghosh D (2004). Meta-analysis of the association between a serotonin transporter promoter polymorphism (5-HTTLPR) and anxiety-related personality traits. *Am J Med Genet*, 127B(1):85–9.

Shioe K, Ichimiya T, Suhara T, Takano A, Sudo Y, Yasuno F, et al. (2003). No association between genotype of the promoter region of serotonin transporter gene and serotonin transporter binding in human brain measured by PET. *Synapse*, 48(4):184–8.

Strobel A, Spinath FM, Angleitner A, Riemann R, Lesch KP (2003). Lack of association between polymorphisms of the dopamine D4 receptor gene and personality. *Neuropsychobiology*, 47:52–6.

7 Genes Associated with Individual Differences in Cognitive Aging

Terry E. Goldberg and Venkata S. Mattay

Aging is associated with a broad range of psychological and physiological changes, including a decline in cognition, which is thought to contribute to loss of independence and a lower quality of life. This decline is variable across individuals, and understanding the mechanisms underlying cognitive aging may provide a means to identify interventions to prevent or attenuate this process. Most importantly, the individual differences in normal cognitive aging are multifactorial, with 26% to 54% of this variance arising from genetic factors and the balance possibly being secondary to environmental factors including demographic, social, educational, psychological, cognitive, medical, dietary, and biological (e.g., stress, physical exercise) factors. In this chapter, we will focus on a review of genetic polymorphisms that may be associated with changes in the rate of cognitive decline. Much of the literature is related to studies using neuropsychological tests which report a single final behavioral measure that is a product of multiple interactive processes. More recently, investigators have started utilizing imaging genetics, a form of genetic association analysis that is proving to be more sensitive in delineating genetic effects on individual differences in cognition, behavior, and susceptibility to neuropsychiatric disorders. Brain imaging techniques allow for the estimation of genetic effects at the level of neural systems or brain information processing, which represents a more proximate biological link to genes and serves as an obligatory intermediate of cognition and behavior.

Cognitive Aging

There are several overarching conceptualizations of the effects of aging on cognition. Salthouse (2000; 2003), using a variety of structural equation models, has proposed that speed-of-processing declines may account for most of the declines observed in other domains of cognition. Additionally, tests of episodic memory have also demonstrated declines independent of speed. Craik and Bialystok (2006) have suggested that cognitive control or manipulation of representations (which themselves remain intact) accounts for much of the observed decline in cognitive abilities. Unfortunately, these phenotypic aspects of cognition have not been consistently examined in genetic association studies in the context of aging.

Similarly there are several prominent microstructural- and neurophysiological-based approaches to aging. In the rodent, age-related cognitive impairments are probably more closely related to loss of connectivity rather than loss of neurons per se (Gallagher 2003). Burke and Barnes (2006) emphasized several plasticity-related features in the aging brain. There appear to be regionally specific changes in dendritic branching and spine density, notably in prefrontal cortex in rats and in humans. Axospinous synapses may be reduced in subregions of the hippocampus. Long-term potentiation, a cellular marker of memory, may also be disturbed (it may be more difficult to induce or decay faster with age). Neural ensembles in the medial temporal lobe may have different dynamics in young versus aged rats. Spatial representations in old rats do not change when they should (i.e., they are "rigid") in CA3, while in CA1 spatial representations of the environment are less stable or perhaps less separable or distinct from other representations.

At the behavioral level, cross-sectional data indicate rather linear declines in numerous cognitive domains, including speed of processing, episodic memory, and reasoning. However, longitudinal data suggest that only speed demonstrates linear decreases before the age of 50 years (Seattle Longitudinal Study; Schaie 2005). The difference between cross-sectional studies and longitudinal studies has been oft remarked upon but may not be as great as it first appears. Cohort differences (e.g., the so-called Flynn effect on IQ) may work to amplify differences in cross-sectional studies, while practice effects and biased attrition may work to minimize effects in longitudinal studies. Some other domains, including semantic memory, autobiographical memory, and simple working memory may be relatively preserved at least until the age of 70 years (Hedden and Gabrieli 2004). Perhaps more controversially, implicit memory and familiarity based decisions in recognition memory also appeared to be preserved. At a systems level, Rypma and D'Esposito (2000) found that working memory related changes in bood-oxygen-level-dependent (BOLD) activation in aging were restricted to dorsolateral prefrontal cortex, occurred during retrieval, not encoding, and were correlated with performance such that greater activation was associated with greater speed in responding. It is also interesting to note that dorsolateral prefrontal cortical age related volume changes are perhaps larger than all other regions (Raz et al. 1997).

Genes, Longevity, and Cognitive Aging

Several genes are thought to affect aging or, more precisely, longevity. One such highly conserved gene is SIR2. It affects chromatin silencing and can modulate the effects of caloric restriction, a well-known environmental manipulation that impacts life span in yeast. Mutations in other genes that have been shown to have large effects on longevity are in the insulin/insulin-like growth factor-1 pathway (e.g., daf-2) and the clk genes in c. elegans, methuselah in drosophila, and p66 in mice (Guarente and Kenyon 2000). These genes, to a greater or lesser extent, make organisms less vulnerable to oxidative stresses. It is unknown if variants in these genes will affect aging in humans and/or affect cognitive decline in aging, as longevity may not necessarily be coterminal with cognitive preservation. Nevertheless, recently several attempts have been made to link factors associated with longevity (e.g., caloric restriction) and neuroprotective effects against dementia-related neuropathologies, including amyloid plaque burden (Qin et al. 2006). Finally, in humans a mutation in the WRN gene causes Werner's syndrome, a disorder of premature aging (see below).

Parenthetically, it is interesting to note that the heritability of longevity is actually quite low, perhaps under .20 (Christiansen et al. 2004). While several genes associated with diseases (e.g., breast cancer, colon cancer) can truncate the life span, it nevertheless is the case that concordance rates for longevity in monozygotic (MZ) and dizygotic (DZ) twins are rather similar, suggesting a large environmental component.

In principle, genes with potential impact on cognitive aging may be protective or amplify decline. In figure 7.1 we illustrate three possible models of genetic effects on decline in cognition with age. In the first panel genotypic differences may be present from early in development, but because an individual who carries the disadvantageous variant might reach some psychometric threshold earlier than noncarriers, cognitive problems may manifest earlier as the person ages and result in earlier detection (panel 1a). In the next two panels, allelic effects on cognition are amplified over time, either continuously and linearly (as in 1b), resulting in slope difference, or becoming identifiable more abruptly, as in a threshold effect (1c). We will illustrate the former in a section below about the gene for brain-derived neurotrophic factor (BDNF). The latter has sometimes been proposed as a model for the transition from healthy status to dementia due to the influence of the E4 variant of the apolipoprotein E (APOE) gene (see below). As such it may be more relevant to neurological disease than normal aging per se.

There may be several mechanisms by which aging amplifies subtle genotype-based differences in cognition. First, failures in DNA repair or telomere degradation may make compensatory changes that a disadvantageous genotype "causes" less likely over time. Environmentally based insults (e.g., head injuries, environmental toxins, or CNS pathogens) might also reduce compensatory neural responses. Finally, developmentally programmed expression changes might differentially impact one or another genotype (e.g., note the effect of promoter variants in catechol-O-methyltransferase [COMT] val/met genotypic associations with neurophysiology and neurocognition, as in Diaz-Asper et al., 2008 and Meyer-Lindenberg et al. 2006).

In assessing the genetic effects on cognition during aging, two methods have generally been employed. One has involved examination of increasing or decreasing

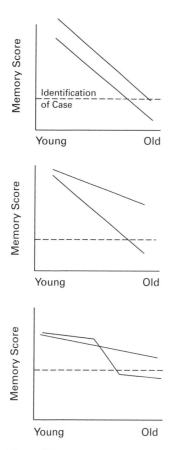

Figure 7.1
Theoretical model of genotype by age interactions on cognition.

heritability of cognitive function with age and has derived from twin studies. The work has been well summarized by Deary et al. (2002) and is presented briefly below. A second approach, as characterized by Deary, is to classify candidate genes based on those associated with dementias–neurodegenerative diseases, those associated with cardiovascular and other systemic diseases, those related to apoptosis and oxidative stress, and those related to individual variability in cognition, intelligence, and behavior (see table 7.1). The study of candidate genes to date in humans has been surprisingly limited, as has been the range of cognitive functions. Much of the work has concentrated on APOE variants and often in the context of research on Alzheimer's disease (AD). Thus, time intervals have generally been short and restricted to older individuals.

Table 7.1

Genes with potential impact on cognitive aging

Gene	Cytogenetic Location	Findings
A. Genes related to dementias		*Some genes, in particular those associated with late-onset dementia, have been implicated in age-related cognitive decline*
APOE (apolipoprotein E)	Chr. 19q13.2	The E4 allele is considered a "frailty gene," predisposing carriers to increased susceptibility to brain injury and poorer recovery from trauma (Smith, *Aging Res Rev* 2002, 345–65). The allele is associated with higher rates of age-related decline, increased incidence and earlier development of the more common late-onset form of AD. See text for details.
APP (amyloid precursor protein), presenelin 1 and 2 (PS1 and PS2)	APP: Chr. 21q21 PS1: Chr.14q24.3 PS2: Chr1q31-q42	While mutations in these three genes have been implicated in the rare familial form of Alzheimer's disease, to date there is no evidence linking these genes to heritability of cognitive aging differences.
SORL1 (sortilin-related receptor)	Chr. 11q23-q24	SORL1 regulates trafficking of APP into recyling pathways. Decreased expression of SORL1 results in channeling of the amyloid precursor protein into B-amyloid generating pathways. The variant form of the gene for SORL1 is associated with decreased expression of SORL1 and increased risk for late-onset Alzheimer's disease (Rogaeva et al., *Nat Genet* 2007, 39[2]:168–77). The impact of this gene on age-related cognitive decline is yet to be examined.
B. Genes related to systemic disease or cardiovascular function		*Since vascular and systemic disease can affect cognition, a search for associations between cardiovascular disease related genes and differences in cognitive aging is justified.*
ACE (gene for angiotensin I converting enzyme)	Chr. 17q23.3	ACE is involved in blood pressure regulation. The polymorphism in the gene for this enzyme is a proposed risk factor for vascular dementia. Polymorphisms in this gene have been associated with increased volume of subcortical white matter lesions (Henskens, *Stroke* 2005; 36:1869–73). White matter hyperintensities have been linked to age-related changes in memory functioning (Nordahl et al., *J Cogn Neurosci* 18:418–29). However, results of studies looking for association between this genetic variant and normal cognitive aging differences have been variable (Bartres-Faz et al., *Neurosci Lett* 2000, 290:177–80; Visshcer et al., *Neurosci Lett* 2003, 347:175–8).

Table 7.1
(continued)

Gene	Cytogenetic Location	Findings
C. Genes related to apoptosis, oxidative stress		*The brain is vulnerable to oxidative damage from free radicals due to its high rate of aerobic metabolism. Therefore, genes that influence this process are potential contributors to cognitive aging.*
Klotho	Chr. 13q12	The gene for Klotho is highly expressed in the brain. Klotho is a protein thought to play a critical role in regulating and suppressing age-related disorders via antioxidant mechanisms (Nagai et al., *FASEB* 2002, 17:50–2; Masuda et al., *Mech Ageing Dev* 2005, 126:1274–83). In mice, a mutant version of this gene has been linked to longevity and premature cognitive aging (Beckman, *Physiol Rev* 1998; 78:547–81).
PRNP (prion protein gene)	Chr. 20pter-p12	The PRNP gene has been implicated in antioxidant activity. A frequent polymorphism in this gene, due to a nucleotide change from A to G at codon 129, results in a valine substitution for methionine and has been linked to human long-term memory (Papassotiropoulos et al., *Hum Mol Genet* 2005, 14:2241–46). Methionine homozygosity has been associated with increased risk of Creutzfeldt–Jakob disease (Knight et al., *J Neurol Neurosurg Psychiatry* 2004, 75[Suppl. 1]:i36–42), susceptibility to cognitive impairment (Berr et al., *Neurology* 1998 51:734–7; Croes et al., *Ann Neurol* 2003, 54:275–6), and early onset Alzheimer's disease (Del Bo et al., *Neurobiol Aging* 2006, 27:5).
Insulin-like growth factor	Chr. 15q26.3	Insulin-like growth factor-a (IGF-1) and type 1 IGF receptor play an important role in neuronal development and function. A genetic variation of this protein has been linked to longevity in humans (Bonafe, *J Clin Endocrinol Metab* 2003, 88:3299–04) and to cognitive function in rats (Sonntag et al., *Neuroscience* 1999, 88:269–79).
DAPK1 (death associated protein kinase 1)	Chr. 9q34.1	DAPK1 is highly expressed in the brain and is a pro-apoptotic mediator in the programmed cell death pathway. DAPK1 inhibition has been shown to enhance learning and memory in mice, and evidence indicates the DAPK1 genetic variants modulate susceptibility to late-onset Alzheimer's disease (Li, *Hum Mol Genet* 2006, 15:2560–8).
D. Genes associated with individual variability in cognition–memory		*In humans, polymorphisms of genes related to neurotrophic factors, neurotransmitters, and receptor proteins have been associated with individual differences in cognition–memory function, as well as with the endophenotypes of functional-imaging-assessed brain responses to cognitive–memory tasks (see below for examples). The effects of these genes on differences in cognitive aging trajectories and susceptibility to neurodegenerative diseases are being explored.*

Gene	Location	Description
Catecholaminergic genes (e.g., gene for catechol-O-methyl transferase [COMT])	Chr. 22q11.21-q11.23	Evidence suggests that monoamines enhance neurophysiological signal to noise and efficiency in information processing. Polymorphisms of monoaminergic genes could potentially play a role in the individual differences in the trajectories of cognitive aging. See text for details on the effects of val158met polymorphism of COMT, a protein thought to regulate dopamine flux in the prefrontal cortex, on cognitve aging.
Serotonergic genes (genes for 5-HT2a receptor, serotonin transporter)	5-HT2a: Chr. 13q14-q21 SLC6A4: Chr. 17q11.1-q12	Serotonin is an important modulator of memory and learning. A functional genetic variation of the 5-HT2a receptor has been shown to modulate memory in healthy individuals (de Quervain, *Nat Neurosci* 2003, 6:1141–2). The effect of variable number tandem repeat (VNTR) polymorphism of the serotonin transporter gene has been investigated for its effects on cognition as well as its decline with aging. Individuals homozygous for the VNTR 12 allele showed a faster rate of decline for all cognitive tests, including tests of fluid intelligence, semantic memory, and general cognitive ability (Payton et al., *Mol Psych* 2005, 10:1133–9).
Trophic genes (BDNF)	Chr. 11p13	Neurotrophins including brain derived neurotrophic factor (BDNF) regulate cortical neuron survival, proliferation, and synaptic growth in the developing CNS. Converging evidence indicates that it is a critical element in modulating synaptic changes such as long-term potentiation in the hippocampus associated with learning and memory formation. A common val66met polymorphism in the BDNF gene has been shown to affect intracellular packaging and regulated secretion of BDNF (Egan et al., *Cell* 2003, 112:257–69). The BDNF met allele was found to be associated with reduced brain volumes, decreased N-acetyl aspartate (Egan et al., *Cell* 2003, 112:257–69), and altered hippocampal engagement during a memory task in healthy volunteers (Hariri et al., *J Neurosci* 2003, 23:6690–4). See text for details.
KIBRA	Chr. 5q35.1	A brain protein thought to be a putative modulator of synaptic plasticity. It is expressed in memory-related structures, and allele-dependent differences have been noted in memory performance as well as in hippocampal activations during memory retrieval (Papassotiropoulos et al., *Science* 2006, 314:475–8). The effect of this gene on cognitive aging is yet to be explored.
GRM3 (glutamate receptor, metabotropic)	Chr. 7q21.1-q21.2	GRM3 is responsible for regulating glutamate in synapses and has been implicated in schizophrenia and cognitive deficits (Egan et al., *PNAS* 2004, 101:12604–9). Carriers of the "A" variant, compared to the "G" variant, have demonstrated lower N-acetyl aspartate levels with Magnetic Resonance spectoscopy. "A" carriers also had poorer performance on cognitive tests of prefrontal and hippocampal function. The "G" variant was associated with more "efficient" processing in the prefrontal cortex as well as higher scores on verbal and cognitive tests. To date, there have been no published reports of the effect of this gene on cognitive aging.

Table 7.1
(continued)

Gene	Cytogenetic Location	Findings
DISC1 (disrupted in schizophrenia)	Chr. 1q42.1	DISC1 has been suggested to play a role in neuronal migration, neurite outgrowth, signal transduction, cyclic adenosine monophosphate (cAMP) signaling, cytoskeleton modulation, and translational regulation. It has been implicated in schizophrenia, schizoaffective disorder, bipolar affective disorder, and major depression and has a causal relationship to working memory, cognitive aging, decreased gray matter volume in the prefrontal cortex, and abnormalities in hippocampal structure and function (Hennah et al., *Schizophr Bull* 2006, 32:409–16; Cannon et al., *Arch Gen Psychiatry* 2005, 62:1205–13; Callicott et al., *Proc Natl Acad Sci USA* 2005, 102:8627–32). Based on results from a behavioral study which revealed lower cognitive ability scores in elderly females homozygous for the Cys allele, Thomson et al. suggest that variation in DISC1 may affect cognitive aging particularly in women (Thomson et al., *Neurosci Lett* 2005, 389:41–5).

Note. Chr., chromosome.

Heritability among many cognitive abilities (including speed of processing, memory, crystallized intelligence, and fluid intelligence) is high in adulthood (i.e., >.50), though it may decline to a limited degree very late in life (Finkel and Pedersen 2000). Several complex models have been proposed to understand the relationships among aging, genetic variance, and cognitive domain. For instance, using a Swedish sample of 292 MZ and DZ twins, Finkel and Pedersen found that .90 of the age-related variance in a general cognitive factor was shared with processing speed and .70 of the genetic variance in the cognitive factor was shared with processing speed. These results indicate that much of the age-related decline in cognition is due to processing speed reduction. However, while processing speed itself is genetically determined, it is as yet unclear if the genes ultimately found to be associated with processing speed will also be genes associated with individual differences in cognitive aging.

Numerous genes in the CNS have been shown to demonstrate expression changes in microarray studies of the aging rodent brain. In a particularly compelling example, Blalock et al. (2003) identified 161 genes whose expression was significantly up or down regulated with aging and correlated with declines in memory performance in rats. These genes fell into several categories including those related to oxidative stress, inflammation, and mitochondrial functions, activity-dependent plasticity (expression down), myelin turnover (up), protein trafficking (down), and calcium signaling (up). It is important to recognize that proteins that show expression differences between younger and older organisms in brain microarray studies might not be due to genetic effects, as they may be compensatory and not reflect genetic individual differences. Also, some genes might have polymorphisms that do not effect expression but nevertheless might impact cognitive aging. Nevertheless, the expression differences certainly can be used to select candidate genes for further analysis.

APOE

APOE polymorphisms are important to consider in cognitive aging because the E4 allele increases risk for AD and has a clear impact on cognitive functions known to be impaired in AD, including episodic memory function. In the context of individuals who convert to AD, E4 predicts signficant declines in episodic memory and increasingly abnormal cortical physiology (Reiman et al. 1996). No other gene has been examined as intensively in this regard. The mechanism by which it could affect cognition outside the context of disease is unclear.

One study examined cognitive integrity on the CERAD cognitive battery in a longitudinal study of a religious order (the so-called Nun Study; Riley et al. 2000). The analysis was restricted to individuals who were 75 to 98 years old ($n = 241$) and who performed within the normal range on all five CERAD cognitive tests. Individuals who carried the E4 allele remained cognitively intact for shorter durations than noncarriers. Lavretsky et al. (2003) found that in individuals aged 51 to 85 years, APOE4 predicted greater decline in verbal memory (over relatively short periods). Similar results have been found by other groups (Bondi et al. 1995; Bretsky et al. 2003; Bennett et al. 2003). However, given the magnitude of the changes over such periods and that many of the studies compare young old to older old subjects, it is possible that declines were occurring in the context of a dementing process. This argument has been made by Savitz et al. (2006), who suggested the findings result from early preclinical impairments associated with the disease process.

The strongest evidence that APOE4 is a gene associated with cognitive aging comes from a longitudinal study of Scottish individuals first tested at age 11 years and retested at 80 years (the study was restricted to 466 subjects without dementia, of whom 121 were E4 carriers). Variations in cognitive change could be predicted by E4 status and appeared at least partially independent of Alzheimer's dementia. Thus at age 11 the differences between carriers and noncarriers was 1.4 points, whereas at age 80 it was 4.1 points (Deary et al. 2002). The findings remained positive even when individuals with possible incipient dementia were excluded. This study is important because it is longitudinal, includes young subjects, and excludes individuals with dementia. In contrast, a recent and very large cross-sectional study of Australian Caucasians ranging in age from 20 years to 64 years found no APOE genotypic associations with cognition (Jorm et al. 2007). This study involved over 6,500 individuals and used a relatively sophisticated set of cognitive phenotypes, including those relating to speed of processing, reaction time, episodic memory, and complex working memory.

Making the picture more complicated are findings from middle-aged groups younger than 60 years that demonstrated various impairments in attentional cueing (Greenwood and Parasuraman 2003), and verbal learning and visual memory (Flory 2000) were predicted by E4 status. These might suggest that genotypic differences were present early and can be identified with more sensitive phenotypic assays.

As an addendum to this section, several individual studies and a recent meta-analysis suggest that E2 carriers have reduced rates of AD, that is, E2 may be neuroprotective. Interestingly, Wilson et al. (2002) found that individuals from a religious order study who carried the E2 allele demonstrated slower rates of decline in memory but not other cognitive domains than non-E2 genotypes.

Catechol-O-Methyltransferease

COMT is a gene that plays a critical role in the degradation of dopamine at the cortical level. The val form of the protein is putatively more efficient at degrading dopamine at the synapse than the met allele, because of differences in thermolability. Val carriers demonstrate worse performance in selected working memory tasks than do met individuals in childhood and adulthood. A study of the so-called val/met polymorphism in young, middle-aged, and older adults (age range 35–85) found greater rates of decline on tests of executive function including the Tower, block design, and fluency over a five-year period in val carriers in the middle-aged group only. The finding is somewhat less than compelling given that the results were not present in the elderly group.

Disrupted in Schizophrenia 1

Disrupted in schizophrenia 1 (DISC1) is a gene implicated in schizophrenia and is expressed in limbic areas. It is thought to play a role in cell migration and neuritic growth. The effect of genotype at a functional exonic single nucleotide polymorphism (SNP) was found on general cognitive ability in a sample of Scottish subjects assessed between the ages of 11 and 79 years. A Genotype × Sex effect was found (the association was stronger in females than males, such that cys/cys females' function was worse than males') at 79 after an adjustment was made to equate childhood cognitive ability (Thomson et al. 2005). Similar findings have been obtained in this same sample for SNPs from PRNP, a gene involved in structural changes at the synapse, and Klotho, a gene involved in oxidative stress (Kachiwala et al. 2005; Deary et al. 2005; see table 7.1 for more details).

WRN

Werner's syndrome is an autosomal recessive disease characterized by premature aging. In a study by Bendixen et al. (2004), WRN SNPs not associated with the disease itself were examined for their impact on a variety of aging parameters, including cognition (based on a composite of the Mini Mental, verbal learning, span, and fluency) in a sample of 213 older DZ twin pairs in Scandinavia. A rare allele in intron 1 (4% frequency) was found to be associated with better cognition. We note that this study is neither cross-sectional nor longitudinal, but because the candidate gene has a priori relevance we include it in the review.

SLC64A

An intronic variation in the serotonin transporter gene (VTNR2 in intron 2) was associated with a faster rate of cognitive decline in a group of approximately 400 individuals followed up to fifteen years in the age range of 50 to 85 years (Payton et al. 2005). The polymorphism is thought to impact expression of the protein. Tests of fluid intelligence, processing speed, semantic memory, and verbal recall were studied. A complex regression model was used that controlled for practice effects and baseline, confounding medical conditions, age, and gender. The largest effect of the polymorphism was found on fluid intelligence, the smallest for memory and processing speed. Subjects homozygous for the twelve base pair repeats showed the largest decline (4.4 points vs. 2.9 points); this is the genotype that putatively is associated with the highest level of expression. Another transporter polymorphism (HTTLPR) was associated neither with cognitive decline nor cognition, though it has previously been shown to be associated with affective reactivity in young and middle aged individuals by several groups of investigators (Hariri et al. 2003).

Brain-Derived Neurotrophic Factor

We have recently undertaken a pilot study on the feasibility of examining the possibility that the effects of the val66met polymorphism on human episodic memory might be amplified with age. This polymorphism has previously been shown to be associated with differences in intracellular trafficking and activity dependent secretion at the molecular level, NAA differences at the neurochemical level, BOLD differences in the medial temporal lobe at the neurophysiological level, and episodic memory differences at the behavioral level (Egan et al. 2003; Hariri et al. 2003). Met carriers were disadvantaged at all levels compared to val homozygotes. These findings have been replicated (Dempster et al. 2005; Ho et al. 2006).

Here we assessed the predictive power of age, BDNF val-val/met carrier genotype, and the interaction of Age × BDNF Genotype on verbal delayed memory for stories in a healthy control group composed of more than 260 individuals aged 18 to 55 years. Only the interaction term entered significantly in a stepwise regression ($F1,262 = 7.74$, $p = .006$) with $R^2 = .03$. By examining figure 7.2, it can be seen that the difference in the genotypes in verbal memory was larger in an older group than in the younger group (for the sake of illustration only, age was dichotomized at 45 years). Met carriers showed increasingly worse performance compared to val homozygotes with advancing age.

In a study of the effects of age on BDNF val66met genotype associations with verbal and visual reasoning in the previously mentioned Scottish birth cohorts (Harris et al. 2006), a genotypic difference was found in the elderly after controlling for childhood

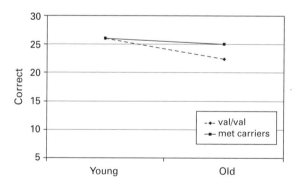

Figure 7.2
The impact of the brain-derived neurotrophic factor (BDNF) val66met genotypes is amplified with age. In younger healthy controls, the effect of genotype is minimal. In controls of later middle age, the genotypic effect is quite striking on verbal memory for stories.

cognitive performance. However, unexpectedly, it was the met homozygote group that performed best in the aged individuals. The reasons for the differences between this and prior studies are unknown.

Summary

The number of candidate genes that have been examined for associations to cognitive aging is small to date. However, with the advent of whole genome scans, it should soon be possible to interrogate 5,000,000 or more SNPs (determined by sequencing or map-based methods) for their effect on age-related cognitive changes. This methodology will present its own problems, including the bioinformatics of data storage and manipulation and statistical genetics issues having to do with corrections for multiple comparisons to reduce spurious findings. Moreover, it is possible that some of the SNPs that will be identified will be related to systemic diseases that impact CNS function or longevity genes that impact general vigor or mental acuity. (Given the rather low heritability of longevity, perhaps the latter is a less likely confound.)

One goal of this research is to elucidate those proteins involved in cognitive aging and target them for treatment. Treatments may range from pharmacological (e.g., procholinergic therapy), cognitive therapy that perhaps increases cognitive reserve through increases in neuronal connectivity, and exercise, now known to produce reliable increases in BDNF levels in the brain (Cotman and Berchtold 2002).

Generally, phenotypic selection has not always been informed by the cognitive aging literature, that is, those tasks that are most sensitive to aging effects on information processing and that include speed and some aspects of episodic memory and, perhaps, monitoring memory processing (e.g., rejection of false memories using what have been termed "distinctiveness heuristics"; Schacter and Stolnick 2004). Furthermore, we have used "aging" in this chapter to refer to a single, unfractionated process. It is probable that aging may be the result of multiple factors, including many that are environmental but can nevertheless be monitored at the molecular level (e.g., telomere wear). Thus, Gene × Environmental Biomarker × Age interactions may, in fact, be necessary to begin the real dissection of cognitive aging.

References

Bendixen MH, Nex<o/> BA, Bohr VA, Frederiksen H, McGue M, Kølvraa S, Christensen K (2004). A polymorphic marker in the first intron of the Werner gene associates with cognitive function in aged Danish twins. *Exp Gerontol*, 39:1101–7.

Bennett DA, Wilson RS, Schneider JA, Evans DA, Aggarwal NT, Arnold SE, et al. (2003). Apolipoprotein E epsilon4 allele, AD pathology, and the clinical expression of Alzheimer's Disease. *Neurology*, 60:246–52.

Bigler ED, Lowry CM, Kerr B, Tate DF, Hessel CD, Earl HD, et al. (2003). Role of white matter lesions, cerebral atrophy, and APOE on cognition in older persons with and without dementia: the Cache County, Utah, study of memory and aging. *Neuropsychology*, 17:339–52.

Blalock EM, Chen KC, Sharrow K, Herman JP, Porter NM, Foster TC, Landfield PW (2003). Gene microarrays in hippocampal aging: statistical profiling identifies novel processes correlated with cognitive impairment. *J Neurosci*, 23:3807–19.

Bondi MW, Salmon DP, Monsch AU, Galasko D, Butters N, Klauber MR, et al. (1995). Episodic memory changes are associated with the APOE-epsilon 4 allele in nondemented older adults. *Neurology*, 45:2203–6.

Bretsky P, Guralnik JM, Launer L, Albert M, Seeman TE (2003). The role of APOE-epsilon4 in longitudinal cognitive decline: MacArthur Studies of Successful Aging. *Neurology*, 60:1077–81.

Burke SN, Barnes CA (2006). Neural plasticity in the aging brain. *Nat Rev Neurosci*, 7:30–40.

Christiansen L, Petersen HC, Bathum L, Frederiksen H, McGue M, Christensen K (2004). The catalase -262C/T promoter polymorphism and aging phenotypes. *J Gerontol A Biol Sci Med Sci*, 59:B886–9.

Cotman CW, Berchtold NC (2002). Excercise: a behavioral intervention to enhance brain health and plasticity. *Trends Neurosci*, 25(6):295–301.

Craik FIM, Bialystok E (2006). Cognition through the lifespan: mechanisms of change. *Trends Cogn Sci*, 10(3):131–8.

Deary IJ, Harris SE, Fox HC, Hayward C, Wright AF, Starr JM, Whalley LJ (2005). KLOTHO neurocognitive ability in childhood and old age in the same individuals. *Neursci Lett*, 378:22–37.

Deary IJ, Whiteman MC, Pattie A, Starr JM, Hayward C, Wright AF, et al. (2002). Cognitive change and the APOE epsilon 4 allele. *Nature*, 418:932.

Dempster E, Toulopoulou T, McDonald C, Bramon E, Walshe M, Filbey F, et al. (2005). Association between BDNF val[66] met genotype and episodic memory. *Am J Med Genet B Neuropsychiatr Genet*, 134:73–5.

Diaz-Asper CM, Goldberg TE, Kolachana BS, Straub RE, Egan MF, Weinberger DR (2008).Genetic variation in catechol-O-methyltransferase: effects on working memory in schizophrenic patients, their siblings, and healthy controls. *Biol Psychiatry*, 63:72–9.

Egan MF, Goldberg TE, Kojima M, Callicott J, Kolachan BS, Bertolino A, et al. (2003). The BDNF val66met polymorphism affects activity dependent secretion of BDNF and human memory and hippocampal function. *Cell*, 112:257–69.

Finkel D, Pedersen NL (2000). Contribution of age, genes, and environment to the relationship between perceptual speed and cognitive ability. *Psychol Aging*, 15:56–64.

Flory JD, Manuck SB, Ferrell RE, Ryan CM, Muldoon MF (2000). Memory performance and the apolipoprotein E polymorphism in a community sample of middle-aged adults. *Am J Med Genet*, 96:707–11.

Gallagher M (2003). Aging and hippocampal/cortical circuits in rodents. *Alzheimer Dis Assoc Disord*, 17(2):S45–7.

George MM, Austad SN, Johnson TE (1996). Genetic analysis of aging: role of oxidative damage and environmental stresses. *Nat Genet*, 13:25–34.

Greenwood PM, Parasuraman R (2003). Normal genetic variation, cognition, and aging. *Behav Cogn Neurosci Rev*, 2:278–306.

Guarente L, Kenyon C (2000). Genetic pathways that regulate aging in model organisms. *Nature*, 408:255–62.

Hariri AR, Goldberg TE, Mattay VS, Kolachana BS, Callicott JH, Egan MF, Weinberger DR (2003). Brain derived neurotrophic factor val66met polymorphism affects human memory-related hippocampal activity and predicts memory performance. *J Neurosci*, 23:6690–4.

Harris SE, Fox H, Wright AF, Hayward C, Starr JM, Whalley LJ, Deary IJ (2006). The brain derived neurotrophic factor Val66Met polymorphism is associated with age-related change in reasoning skills. *Mol Psychiatry*, 11:505–13.

Hedden T, Gabrieli JDE (2004). Insights into the aging mind: a view from cognitive neuroscience. *Nat Rev Neurosci*, 5:87–96.

Ho BC, Milev P, O'Leary DS, Librant A, Andreasen NC, Wassink TH (2006). Cognitive and magnetic resonance imaging brain morphometric correlates of brain-derived neurotrophic factor val[66]met gene polymorphism in patients with schizophrenia and healthy volunteers. *Arch Gen Psychiatry*, 63:731–40.

Jorm A, Mather KA, Butterworth P, Anstey KJ, Christensen H, Esteal S (2007). APOE genotype and cognitive functioning in a large age-stratified population sample. *Neuropsychology*, 21:1–8.

Kachiwala SJ, Harris SE, Wright AF, Hayward C, Starr JM, Whalley LJ, Deary IJ (2005). Genetic influences on oxidative stress and their association with normal cognitive aging. *Neurosci Lett*, 386:116–20.

Lavretsky H, Ercoli L, Siddarth P, Bookheimer S, Miller K, Small G (2003). Apolipoprotein epsilon4 allele status, depressive symptoms, and cognitive decline in middle-aged and elderly persons without dementia. *Am J Geriatr Psychiatry*, 11:667–73.

Meyer-Lindenberg A, Nichols T, Callicott JH, Ding J, Kolachana B, Buckholtz J, Mattay VS, Egan M, Weinberger DR (2006). Impact of complex genetic variation in COMT on human brain function. *Mol Psychiatry*, 11:867–77, 797.

Parasuraman R, Greenwood PM, Sunderland T (2002). The apolipoprotein E gene, attention, and brain function. *Neuropsychology*, 16:254–74.

Payton A, Gibbons L, Davidson Y, Ollier W, Rabbitt P, Worthington J, et al. (2005). Influence of serotonin transporter gene polymorphisms on cognitive decline and cognitive abilities in a non-demented elderly population. *Mol Psychiatry*, 10:1133–9.

Qin W, Tianie Y, Ho L, Zhao Z, Wang J, Chen L, et al. (2006). [Epub ahead of print.] Neuronal SIRT1 activation as a novel mechanism underlying the prevention of Alzheimer's disease amyloid neuropathology by calorie restriction. *J Biol Chem*.

Raz N, Gunning FM, Head D, Dupuis JH, McQuain J, Briggs SD, et al. (1997). Selective aging of the human cerebral cortex observed in vivo: differential vulnerability of the prefrontal gray matter. *Cereb Cortex*, 7:268–82.

Reiman EM, Caselli RJ, Yun LS, Chen K, Bandy D, Minoshima S, et al. (1996). Preclinical evidence of Alzheimer's disease in persons homozygous for the epsilon 4 allele for apolipoprotein E. *N Engl J Med*, 334:752–8.

Riley KP, Snowdon DA, Saunders AM, Roses AD, Mortimer JA, Nanayakkara N (2000). Cognitive function and apolipoprotein E in very old adults: findings from the Nun Study. *J Gerontol B Psychol Sci Soc Sci*, 55(2):S69–75.

Rypma B, D'Esposito M (2000). Isolating the neural mechanisms of age-related changes in human working memory. *Nat Neurosci*, 3:509–15.

Salthouse TA (2000). Aging and measures of processing speed. *Biol Psychol*, 54:35–54.

Salthouse TA (2003). Memory aging from 18 to 80. *Alzheimer Dis Assoc Disord*, 17:162–7.

Savitz J, Solms M, Ramesar R (2006). Apolipoprotein E variants and cognition in healthy individuals: a critical opinion. *Brain Res Rev*, 51:125–35.

Schacter DL, Stolnick SD (2004). The cognitive neuroscience of memory distortion. *Neuron*, 44:149–60.

Schaie KW (2005). What can we learn from longitudinal studies of adult development? *Res Hum Dev*, 2(3):133–58.

Small BJ, Graves AB, McEvoy CL, Crawford FC, Mullan M, Mortimer JA (2000). Is APOE-epsilon4 a risk factor for cognitive impairment in normal aging? *Neurology*, 54:2082–8.

Small BJ, Rosnick CB, Fratiglioni L, Backman L (2004). Apolipoprotein E and cognitive performance: a meta-analysis. *Psychol Aging*, 19:592–600.

Small GW, Ercoli LM, Silverman DH, Huang SC, Komo S, Bookheimer SY, et al. (2000). Cerebral metabolic and cognitive decline in persons at genetic risk for Alzheimer's disease. *Proc Natl Acad Sci USA*, 97:6037–42.

Smith CD, Andersen AH, Kryscio RJ, Schmitt FA, Kindy MS, Blonder LX, Avison MJ (1999). Altered brain activation in cognitively intact individuals at high risk for Alzheimer's disease. *Neurology*, 53:1391–6.

Thomson PA, Harris SE, Starr JM, Whalley LJ, Porteous DJ, Deary IJ (2005). Association between genotype at an exonic SNP in DISC1 and normal cognitive aging. *Neurosci Lett*, 389:41–5.

Wilson RS, Bienias JL, Berry-Kravis E, Evans DA, Bennett DA (2002). The apolipoprotein E epsilon 2 allele and decline in episodic memory. *J Neurol, Neurosurg Psychiatry*, 73:672–7.

III Genetic Studies of Cognition and Treatment Response in Neuropsychiatric Disease

8 Genetics of Dyslexia: Cognitive Analysis, Candidate Genes, Comorbidities, and Etiologic Interactions

Bruce F. Pennington, Lauren M. McGrath, and Shelley D. Smith

Recent work on the genetics of dyslexia lies at the intersection of several fields: cognitive neuroscience, behavioral genetics, molecular genetics, and, increasingly, developmental neurobiology. In this chapter, we will first describe how work on dyslexia has benefited from the "marriage" of cognitive neuroscience and behavioral and molecular genetics, then we will provide an update on recent breakthroughs in identifying candidate genes for dyslexia, then we will describe how we have utilized the genetics of dyslexia to understand its comorbidities, and finally we will end with some recent work examining gene by gene (G × G) and gene by environment (G × E) interactions in dyslexia. Some of what we have learned about dyslexia has broader implications for the genetics of other complex behavioral disorders, which include virtually all psychiatric disorders.

The First Step Is Cognitive Dissection

Among complex behavioral disorders, dyslexia is somewhat unique because it is so well defined at the cognitive level of analysis. We understand both the normal and abnormal development of reading much better than we understand the normal and abnormal development of other domains, like emotion regulation, which are relevant for psychopathologies (Pennington 2002). The cognitive analysis of dyslexia has provided us both with a fairly precise diagnostic phenotype and with cognitive components of that diagnostic phenotype. These cognitive components have proved useful as endophenotypes in genetic and neuroimaging studies of dyslexic and normal reading.

Since the goal of reading is reading comprehension, we begin our cognitive analysis with the components of reading comprehension (see figure 8.1). This figure shows that reading comprehension can be first broken down into cognitive components and then into developmental precursors of these cognitive components. One key component is fluent printed word recognition, which is highly predictive of reading comprehension, especially in the early years of reading instruction (Curtis 1980). The other

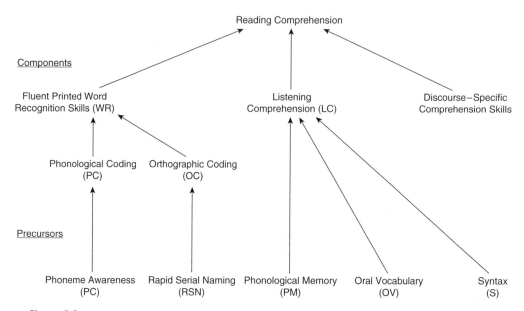

Figure 8.1

A schematic of factors impacting reading comprehension.

key component is listening comprehension, that is, oral language comprehension. Hoover and Gough (1990) proposed a simple model of skill in reading comprehension in which there are only these two components of reading comprehension: word recognition and listening comprehension. Figure 8.1 adds a third component, discourse-specific comprehension skills, to this simple model because understanding a text (or lecture) requires greater use of other comprehension skills (like inferencing, comprehension monitoring, and building a mental representation of the meaning of the text) than does conversational speech or reading single sentences.

Because fluent printed word recognition is necessary (but not sufficient) for reading comprehension, the field of dyslexia research long ago made a key simplifying assumption. That is, they defined dyslexia as problems in printed word recognition rather than as problems in reading comprehension. Consequently, reading comprehension problems without a word recognition problem are not counted as dyslexia. Instead, individuals with such problems are called "poor comprehenders," and the cognitive causes of their reading comprehension problems are distinct from those that interfere with word recognition (Nation 2005).

As we will see later, although this simplifying assumption is valid, dyslexics as a group have oral as well as written language problems. For instance, more recent research (e.g., Keenan et al. 2006) has found that dyslexics, as a group, also have problems with oral language comprehension, not just reading comprehension. Nevertheless, because this assumption greatly simplified the cognitive analysis of dyslexia, it eventually led to the major breakthroughs described below. The analogy in psychiatry would be that instead of taking on the entire syndrome of schizophrenia or major depression, cognitive neuroscientists should tackle one key feature, understand its development thoroughly at a cognitive level, and then use that feature and its cognitive components in genetic studies. Then, as the features are understood, they can be recombined into appropriate syndromes based on a common genetic etiology.

Thus, the diagnostic phenotype in dyslexia is an idiopathic deficit in the speed and accuracy of printed word recognition, where deficit is usually defined relative to age norms, although IQ discrepancy definitions are sometimes still used, and where idiopathic means that the reading deficit cannot be explained by an uncorrected hearing or visual problem, inadequate reading instruction, an acquired neurological insult, or mental retardation.

Printed word recognition can be broken into two component written language skills, phonological and orthographic coding (see figure 8.1). Phonological coding (PC) refers to the ability to use knowledge of rule-like letter–sound correspondences to pronounce words that have never been seen before (usually measured by pseudoword reading), and orthographic coding (OC) refers to the use of word-specific patterns to aid in word recognition and pronunciation (see Harm and Seidenberg 2004 for a neural network model of reading that implements both PC and OC). Words that do not follow typical letter–sound correspondences (e.g., have or yacht) must rely, at least in part, on OC to be recognized, as do homophones (e.g., rows vs. rose). Thus, PC and OC are essentially two endophenotypes of dyslexia. It has been established that dyslexia is characterized by deficits in PC and OC and that such deficits are coheritable with dyslexia (Gayan and Olson 2001) and linked to dyslexia genetic loci (see table 8.1).

But the cognitive analysis of dyslexia doesn't end with PC and OC. Because reading development depends on earlier spoken language development, dyslexia researchers have investigated the oral language precursors of reading skill and disability. These precursors include phonological awareness (PA) and rapid serial naming (RSN), but also broader language skill (see figure 8.1). PA is measured by tasks that require one to manipulate the sound structure of spoken words (e.g., what is cat without the /c/?). Tasks that require the manipulation of individual phonemes, as opposed to syllables, are most highly linked to reading skill. RSN is assessed by presenting the child with a card with rows of color patches or familiar objects and asking him or her to name each item in each row as rapidly as possible. Broader language skill is measured by tests of vocabulary and syntax. Predyslexic children have deficits on these precursors to reading skill (Pennington and Lefly 2001; Scarborough 1990), and these deficits are likewise coheritable with dyslexia (Gayan and Olson 2001) and linked to dyslexia genetic loci (see table 1 in Fisher and DeFries 2002). Thus, these precursors likewise qualify as endophenotypes for dyslexia, although they are not exclusively related to

Table 8.1
Linkage and association studies for replicated linkage peaks

Linkage Regions	Supportive Results	Negative Results
1p36-p34 (DYX8)	Rabin et al. (1993) Grigorenko et al. (2001) Tzenova et al. (2004)	
2p16-p15 (DYX3)	Fagerheim et al. (1999) Fisher et al. (2002) Francks et al. (2002) Petryshen et al. (2002) Kaminen et al. (2003) Peyrard-Janvid et al. (2004)	Chapman et al. (2004)
3p12-q13 (DYX5)	Nopola-Hemmi et al. (2001) Fisher et al. (2002)	
6p22.2 (DYX2)	Smith et al. (1991) Cardon et al. (1994, 1995) Grigorenko et al. (1997) Fisher et al. (1999) Gayán et al. (1999) Grigorenko et al. (2000) Fisher et al. (2002) Kaplan et al. (2002) Turic et al. (2003) Marlow et al. (2003) Grigorenko et al. (2003)	Field and Kaplan (1998) Nöthen et al. (1999) Petryshen et al. (2000) Chapman et al. (2004)
15q21 (DYX1)	Smith et al. (1983) Smith et al. (1991) Fulker et al. (1991) Grigorenko et al. (1997) Nöthen et al. (1999) Nopola-Hemmi et al. (2000) Morris et al. (2000) Chapman et al. (2004)	Rabin et al. (1993) Bisgaard et al. (1987)
18p11.2 (DYX6)	Fisher et al. (2002) Marlow et al. (2003)	Chapman et al. (2004) Schumacher et al. (2006)
Xq27.3 (DYX9)	Fisher et al. (2002) de Kovel et al. (2004)	

Note. Originally published in McGrath et al. (2006).

dyslexia, since children with speech sound disorder also have problems with PA as is discussed later.

We said earlier that individuals with dyslexia as a group have problems with oral language comprehension. This result might be expected given that they have been shown to have problems with broader language skill as preschoolers (Scarborough 1990). Since various components of oral and written language interact in development (e.g., phonological skill facilitates acquisition of new words and thus helps build lexical semantics, but lexical development also promotes phonological development), these various components are correlated. Thus, almost inevitably, a group selected because they are deficient on one component of language development (e.g., printed word recognition) will have deficits in other components of language development. This consideration means that various speech and language disorders will almost inevitably be comorbid and raises the problem of determining which cognitive and etiologic risk factors cause the particular comorbidity in question.

Therefore, even when we begin with a developmental disorder with a very narrow diagnostic phenotype, like dyslexia, because development is interactive, the disorder will almost inevitably have broader correlated cognitive features and comorbidities. This appears to be a generic problem in neurodevelopmental disorders, a category which includes virtually all psychiatric diagnoses. This means that expecting that a specific causal pathway runs from a specific etiologic risk factor to a specific cognitive risk factor to a specific disorder is very unrealistic because more than one pathway influences each disorder and more than one disorder is influenced by a given pathway (Pennington 2006). However, a careful dissection of a single pathway, as has been done with dyslexia, can lead to major advances.

These written and spoken cognitive components of printed word recognition have also guided neuroimaging studies of reading skill and disability. These neuroimaging studies have found that printed word recognition requires visual association areas, perisylvian language areas, and white matter connections between them. Although this work is far from complete, and inconsistent findings are common (Eckert 2004), we have gained a better understanding of the distributed reading network in the brain and which components of this network function differently in dyslexia (for reviews, see Demonet et al. 2004; Price and McCrory 2005).

In sum, by using cognitive methods to dissect this particular complex behavioral disorder, dyslexia, considerable progress has been made in understanding both its genetics and its neural networks. This prior work set the stage for identifying candidate genes for dyslexia and investigating their function.

Candidate Genes for Dyslexia

The cognitive dissection of dyslexia described above proceeded hand in hand with decades of work demonstrating that dyslexia and its cognitive components are familial and heritable (Pennington and Olson 2005) and are linked to several quantitative trait loci (QTLs) across the genome (Fisher and DeFries 2002). Seven replicated QTLs have been identified on chromosomes 1p34-p36 (DYX8), 2p11-16 (DYX3), 3p12-q13 (DYX5), 6p21.3-22 (DYX2), 15q15-21 (DYX1), 18p11 (DYX6), and Xq27.3 (DYX9; see table 8.1). Two additional genetic loci for dyslexia are included on the most recent Human Gene Nomenclature Committee list (www.gene.ucl.ac.uk/nomenclature/). These are on 6q13-q16 (DYX4: Petryshen et al. 2001) and 11p15 (DYX7: Hsiung et al. 2004). Thus, there are currently nine genetic risk loci, but two of these require additional replication to be convincing. This linkage work has now been followed by the initial identification of four candidate genes in three of these linkage regions: 3p12-q13 (ROBO1), 6p21.3-22 (DCDC2 and KIAA0319), and 15q15-21 (DYX1C1, initially labeled as EKN1). These candidate gene studies are reviewed in Francks and Fisher (2006) and McGrath et al. (2006).

The first candidate gene to be identified was DYX1C1 (Taipale et al. 2003), so it has been the target of the most replication attempts, six so far. Five of these failed to find any association between DYX1C1 variants and dyslexia phenotypes (Bellini et al. 2005; Cope et al. 2005; Marino et al. 2005; Meng et al. 2005; Scerri et al. 2004), but one study by Wigg et al. (2004) found an association in the opposite direction, such that the more common, nonrisk alleles of the haplotypes proposed by Taipale et al. (2003) were associated with the phenotype. They also found a significant association with an additional single nucleotide polymorphism that was not tested by Taipale et al. (2003). More work is therefore needed to confirm or reject this candidate gene.

The other three candidate genes, ROBO1 (Hannula-Jouppi et al. 2005), DCDC2 (Meng et al. 2005), and KIAA0319 (Francks et al. 2004), were identified more recently and thus have been tested less for replication. The DCDC2 candidate was replicated by Schumacher et al. (2006) and KIAA0319 by Cope et al. (2005).

One of the most exciting aspects of the work on the three recent candidate genes is that the role of each in brain development has been studied in animal models. Joseph LeTurco (using RNA interference technology) found that shutting down the expression of DCDC2 (Meng et al. 2005) and KIAA0319 (Paracchini et al. 2006) interferes with neuronal migration, consistent with the pioneering work of Galaburda (1985), who discovered ectopias in the brains of deceased dyslexics. ROBO1 was known to be involved in brain development, specifically in axon pathfinding. Andrews et al. (2006) genetically modified mice so that they were lacking ROBO1 completely (a ROBO1 knockout). Although the knockout mice died at birth, they demonstrated prenatal axonal tract defects and neuronal migration defects in the forebrain.

These results from animal models indicate that alterations in DCDC2, KIAA0319, and ROBO1 could disrupt human brain development in a way that is consistent with what little is known about the neuropathology of dyslexia. However, to really prove causation requires several more steps: (1) the functional and/or regulatory mutations in these particular genes have to be identified, (2) it has to be demonstrated that these particular mutations disrupt brain development in animal models, and, most difficult of all, (3) it has to be shown that human dyslexics with these mutations have similar disruptions in brain development. In sum, the identification of candidate genes for dyslexia has taken us all the way from cognitive dissection to developmental neurobiology, so that we are now able to test specific hypotheses about how brain development is disrupted in this prevalent disorder. This work is now developing rapidly, so new insights about brain development in dyslexia are likely.

Using Genetics to Understand Comorbidity

Earlier we commented on how even a very narrow diagnostic phenotype will almost inevitably have associated cognitive problems. For dyslexia, these are in predictable domains, such as speech and language, but also in less predictable ones—namely, attention. Dyslexia has been demonstrated to be comorbid with speech sound disorder (SSD), language impairment (LI), and attention-deficit/hyperactivity disorder (ADHD); evidence for these comorbidities is reviewed in Pennington et al. (2005). We and others have been investigating the reasons for the comorbidities of dyslexia with SSD and ADHD using both cognitive and genetic methods.

It has been found that dyslexia risk loci are also linked to SSD (Smith et al. 2005; Stein et al. 2004). Specifically SSD has been found to be linked to the dyslexia risk loci on chromosomes 3p12-q13 (where ROBO1 is located), 6p21.3-22 (where DCDC2 and KIAA0319 are located), and 15q-21 (where EKN1 is located). There is also suggestive evidence of linkage of SSD to 1p34-p36 (Smith et al. 2005). At the cognitive level, SSD and dyslexia share deficits in PA, phonological memory, and broader language skill. Surprisingly, they do not share a deficit in RSN (Raitano 2004; Tunick et al., submitted), except when SSD is accompanied by dyslexia.

Although dyslexia and LI also share similar cognitive deficits to those shared by dyslexia and SSD, so far the risk loci identified for LI do not overlap with those for dyslexia (Bartlett et al. 2002; Specific Language Impairment (SLI)-Consortium 2002; 2004). Moreover, there is emerging evidence that genetic influences on the two components in Hoover and Gough's (1990) simple model, printed word recognition and listening comprehension, are largely independent (Keenan et al. 2006). Since listening comprehension is related to LI, these behavior genetic results are consistent with the linkage results. Yet these results present a bit of a puzzle because it is not clear how there can be a cognitive overlap but not genetic overlap between dyslexia and LI. Future research needs to address this puzzle.

Risk loci are also shared by dyslexia and ADHD on chromosomes 6p21.3-22 (Willcutt et al. 2002), and there is suggestive evidence of bivariate linkage on 14q32, 13q32, and 20q11 (Gayan et al. 2005). In this latter study, bivariate LOD scores > 1.0 were also found near dyslexia loci, specifically at 2p11-q14 and 6p24-25. In a genome-wide linkage study of reading ability in sibling pairs selected for ADHD, Loo et al. (2004) also found evidence for shared linkage peaks. They identified linkage peaks on chromosomes 16p, 17q, and possibly 10q that influenced both ADHD and the reading ability of children with ADHD (Loo et al. 2004). Other studies have found ADHD linkage to the dyslexia loci on chromosomes 3 and 15 (Bakker et al. 2003). Finally, the linkage of dyslexia to the dopamine receptor D4 (DRD4) region on chromosome 11 might seem to suggest a pleiotropic locus, because it is known that a variant of DRD4 is a risk allele for ADHD, but these authors did not find an association between dyslexia and DRD4 alleles (Hsiung et al. 2004). In sum, of the nine dyslexia loci listed earlier, four show evidence for a possible pleiotropic effect on ADHD (DYX1 on 15, DYX2 on 6, DYX3 on 2, and DYX5 on 3) and five do not (DYX4 on 6q, DYX6 on 18, DYX7 on 11, DYX8 on 1, and DYX9 on X). Thus, there is evidence for both shared and differential linkage for dyslexia and ADHD.

 In terms of cognitive risk factors, dyslexia and ADHD do not share deficits in phoneme awareness or general language skill, but they do share deficits in RSN and in processing speed more generally (Shanahan et al., in preparation, in press). Thus, the cognitive overlap between dyslexia and ADHD is virtually the opposite of its overlap with SSD: while dyslexia and SSD share deficits in phoneme awareness and general language skill but not in RSN, dyslexia and ADHD share deficits in RSN but not in phoneme awareness or general language skill.

Thus, the picture that is emerging from these studies of the comorbidities of dyslexia is consistent with the multiple deficit model (Pennington 2006) in which partial genetic and partial cognitive overlap leads to comorbidity, with each single disorder being determined by its own combination of etiologic (genetic and environmental) and cognitive risk factors. This is a model of comorbidity that is likely applicable to psychopathologies in general.

G × G and G × E Interactions

The discovery of multiple risk loci and candidate genes for dyslexia opens the door for studies of interactions among etiologic risk factors in the development of this disorder and its comorbidities. For instance, researchers have begun to study G × G interactions involving dyslexia candidate genes (Hatakeyama et al. 2004).

In our own studies, we have used linkage information to begin to study the additive and interactive effects of multiple dyslexia risk loci (McGrath and Pennington 2005). In our sib-pair linkage study of children with SSD (Smith et al. 2005), we found that articulation phenotypes showed linkage to both the 6p22 and 15q21 dyslexia linkage regions. We were interested in whether children who possessed risk alleles in both linkage regions would possess worse articulation skills than children with one or no risk alleles. We estimated risk allele status by using information about whether the sib-pair contributed to or detracted from the linkage signal. We grouped children into those who were likely to possess a risk allele and those who were unlikely to possess a risk allele at the 6p22 and 15q21 location. We found a linear additive effect of risk allele status on the articulation phenotype: 2 risk alleles < 1 risk allele < 0 risk alleles (McGrath and Pennington 2005). We consider this analysis preliminary because it was conducted with an inferred risk allele status rather than a directly measured risk allele, but we also consider the results worthy of further study.

We have also been investigating the interaction of the dyslexia risk loci with the home language and literacy environment (McGrath et al., 2007). Currently, there are two models for Gene × Environment interactions in the literature that have received support in various developmental disorders (for a review, see Rutter et al. 2006). These are the diathesis–stress model (e.g., Caspi et al. 2002; 2003) and the bioecological model (e.g., Bronfenbrenner and Ceci 1994; Kremen et al. 2005; Rowe et al. 1999; Turkheimer et al. 2003). These models make opposite predictions about the expected direction of G × E interaction, because environmental risk factors may either strengthen or weaken the effect of genes on phenotypes. In the case of the diathesis–stress model, environmental risk factors compound genetic risk factors to create worse outcomes. In the case of the bioecological model, environmental risk factors mask genetic background differences whereas optimal environments allow genetic differences to be manifested. The common analogy for the bioecological G × E interaction is two fields, one rich in nutrients and one deprived of nutrients. Certainly, in the deprived field, all of the plants will be short because of the environmental adversity. However, in the nutrient-filled field, there will be considerably variability in plant height that is primarily determined by the genetic endowment of the plant. Thus, the environment in which the seed was planted determines how the genetic liability of the plant is expressed, a bioecological G × E interaction (Lewontin 1970, cited in Neisser et al. 1996).

So far, research investigating G × E in cognitive and academic traits has tended to find the bioecological type of G × E (Kremen et al. 2005; Rowe et al. 1999; Turkheimer et al. 2003), whereas research in psychopathologies has tended to find the diathesis–stress type of G × E (Cadoret et al. 1995; Caspi et al. 2002; 2003; Eley et al. 2004; Silberg et al. 2001). We investigated G × E using continuous measures of the home language–literacy environment in a sample of children with SSD and their siblings. We tested for G × E at the two reading disability (RD) linkage peaks with the strongest evidence of linkage to speech phenotypes, 6p22 and 15q21. The interactions were tested using composite speech, language, and preliteracy phenotypes. Results showed four significant and trend-level G × E interactions at both the 6p22 and 15q21 locations across several phenotypes and home environmental measures. All of the interactions were consistent with the bioecological model of G × E (McGrath et al., 2008). Although these linkage-based methods are a step away from the ideal of using identified risk alleles to test for G × E (e.g., Caspi et al. 2002; 2003), until risk alleles are identified for SSD and RD, these linkage-based methods can be used as a first approximation. For instance, they could be used to develop hypotheses about which combinations of genes and environments are likely to show bioecological or diathesis–stress G × E interactions in different disorders. These hypotheses could be tested more rigorously once the risk alleles for SSD and RD are identified.

Summary

By beginning with a narrow diagnostic phenotype and subjecting it to systematic cognitive analysis, dyslexia researchers have found several endophenotypes for dyslexia which have proven very useful in genetic studies. This work has culminated in the identification of four candidate genes for dyslexia and has led to cognitive and genetic studies of the comorbidities of dyslexia and beginning work on multilocus effects and G × E interactions. Once risk alleles of these candidate genes are more clearly identified, it will be very interesting to utilize them in neuroimaging studies, including diffusion tensor imaging studies. The latter studies may help test whether the axonal and neuronal migration defects found in animal models that manipulate these candidate genes are also found in humans with the same risk alleles.

Acknowledgments

This work was supported by research grants HD049027 and HD027802.

References

Andrews W, Liapi A, Plachez C, Camurri L, Zhang J, Mori S, et al. (2006). Robo1 regulates the development of major axon tracts and interneuron migration in the forebrain. *Development*, 133(11):2243–52.

Anthoni H, Zucchelli M, Matsson H, Muller-Myhsok B, Fransson I, Schumacher J, et al. (2007). A locus on 2p12 containing the co-regulated MRPL19 and C2ORF3 genes is associated to dyslexia. *Hum Mol Genet*, 16(6):667–77.

Bakker SC, van der Meulen EM, Buitelaar JK, Sandkuijl LA, Pauls DL, Monsuur AJ, et al. (2003). A whole-genome scan in 164 Dutch sib pairs with attention-deficit/hyperactivity disorder: suggestive evidence for linkage on chromosomes 7p and 15q. *Am J HumGenet*, 72(5):1251–60.

Bartlett CW, Flax JF, Logue MW, Vieland VJ, Bassett AS, Tallal P, et al. (2002). A major susceptibility locus for specific language impairment is located on 13q21. *Am J Hum Genet*, 71(1):45–55.

Bellini G, Bravaccio C, Calamoneri F, Donatella Cocuzza M, Fiorillo P, Gagliano A, et al. (2005). No evidence for association between dyslexia and DYX1C1 functional variants in a group of children and adolescents from Southern Italy. *J Mol Neurosci*, 27(3):311–14.

Brkanac Z, Chapman NH, Matsushita MM, Chun L, Nielsen K, Cochrane E, et al. (2007). Evaluation of candidate genes for DYX1 and DYX2 in families with dyslexia. *Am J Med Genet B Neuropsychiatr Genet*, 144(4):556–60.

Bronfenbrenner U, Ceci SJ (1994). Nature-nurture reconceptualized in developmental perspective: a bioecological model. *Psychol Rev*, 101(4):568–86.

Cadoret RJ, Yates WR, Troughton E, Woodworth G, Stewart MA (1995). Genetic-environmental interaction in the genesis of aggressivity and conduct disorders. *Arch Gen Psychiatry*, 52(11):916–24.

Cardon LR, Smith SD, Fulker DW, Kimberling WJ, Pennington BF, DeFries JC (1994). Quantitative trait locus for reading disability on chromosome 6. *Science*, 266(5183):276–79.

Cardon LR, Smith SD, Fulker DW, Kimberling WJ, Pennington BF, DeFries JC (1995). Quantitative trait locus for reading disability: correction. *Science*, 268(5217):1553.

Caspi A, McClay J, Moffitt TE, Mill J, Martin J, Craig IW, et al. (2002). Role of genotype in the cycle of violence in maltreated children. *Science*, 297(5582):851–54.

Caspi A, Sugden K, Moffitt TE, Taylor A, Craig IW, Harrington H, et al. (2003). Influence of life stress on depression: moderation by a polymorphism in the 5-HTT gene. *Science*, 301(5631):386–89.

Chapman NH, Igo RP, Thomson JB, Matsushita M, Brkanac Z, Holzman T, et al. (2004). Linkage analyses of four regions previously implicated in dyslexia: confirmation of a locus on chromosome 15q. *Am J Med Genet B Neuropsych Genet*, 131(1):67–75.

Cope NA, Harold D, Hill G, Moskvina V, Stevenson J, Holmans P, et al. (2005). Strong evidence that KIAA0319 on chromosome 6p is a susceptibility gene for developmental dyslexia. *Am J Hum Genet*, 76(4):581–91.

Cope NA, Hill G, van den Bree M, Harold D, Moskvina V, Green EK, et al. (2005). No support for association between dyslexia susceptibility 1 candidate 1 and developmental dyslexia. *Mol Psychiatry*, 10(3):237–8.

Curtis ME (1980). Development of components of reading skill. *J Educ Psychol*, 72:656–69.

de Kovel CG, Hol FA, Heister JG, Willemen JJ, Sandkuijl LA, Franke B, et al. (2004). Genomewide scan identifies susceptibility locus for dyslexia on Xq27 in an extended Dutch family. *J Med Genet*, 41(9):652–7.

Deffenbacher KE, Kenyon JB, Hoover DM, Olson RK, Pennington BF, DeFries JC, et al. (2004). Refinement of the 6p21.3 quantitative trait locus influencing dyslexia: linkage and association analyses. *Hum Genet*, 115(2):128–38.

Demonet JF, Taylor MJ, Chaix Y (2004). Developmental dyslexia. *Lancet*, 363(9419):1451–60.

Eckert M (2004). Neuroanatomical markers for dyslexia: A review of dyslexia structural imaging studies. *Neuroscientist*, 10:362–71.

Eley TC, Sugden K, Corsico A, Gregory AM, Sham P, McGuffin P, et al. (2004). Gene-environment interaction analysis of serotonin system markers with adolescent depression. *Mol Psychiatry*, 9(10):908–15.

Fagerheim T, Raeymaekers P, Tonnessen FE, Pedersen M, Tranebjaerg L, Lubs HA (1999). A new gene (DYX3) for dyslexia is located on chromosome 2. *J Med Genet*, 36(9):664–9.

Field LL, Kaplan BJ (1998). Absence of linkage of phonological coding dyslexia to chromosome 6p23-p21.3 in a large family data set. *Am J Hum Genet*, 63(5):1448–56.

Fisher SE, DeFries JC (2002). Developmental dyslexia: genetic dissection of a complex cognitive trait. *Nat RevNeurosci*, 3(10):767–80.

Fisher SE, Francks C (2006). Genes, cognition and dyslexia: learning to read the genome. *Trends Cogn Sci*, 10(6):250–7.

Fisher SE, Francks C, Marlow AJ, MacPhie IL, Newbury DF, Cardon LR, et al. (2002). Independent genome-wide scans identify a chromosome 18 quantitative-trait locus influencing dyslexia. *Nat Genet*, 30(1):86–91.

Fisher SE, Marlow AJ, Lamb J, Maestrini E, Williams DF, Richardson AJ, et al. (1999). A quantitative-trait locus on chromosome 6p influences different aspects of developmental dyslexia. *Am J Hum Genet*, 64(1):146–56.

Francks C, Fisher SE, Olson RK, Pennington BF, Smith SD, DeFries JC, et al. (2002). Fine mapping of the chromosome 2p12–16 dyslexia susceptibility locus: quantitative association analysis and positional candidate genes SEMA4F and OTX1. *Psychiatric Genet*, 12(1):35–41.

Francks C, Paracchini S, Smith SD, Richardson AJ, Scerri TS, Cardon LR, et al. (2004). A 77-kilobase region of chromosome 6p22.2 is associated with dyslexia in families from the United Kingdom and from the United States. *Am J Hum Genet*, 75(6):1046–58.

Fulker DW, Cardon LR, DeFries JC, Kimberling WJ, Pennington BF, Smith SD (1991). Multiple regression analysis of sib-pair data on reading to detect quantitative trait loci. *Reading & Writing*, 3(3):299–313.

Galaburda AM, Sherman GF, Rosen GD, Aboitiz F, Geschwind N (1985). Developmental dyslexia: four consecutive patients with cortical anomalies. *Ann Neurol*, 18(2):222–33.

Gayan J, Olson RK (2001). Genetic and environmental influences on orthographic and phonological skills in children with reading disabilities. *Dev Neuropsychol*, 20(2):483–507.

Gayan J, Smith SD, Cherny SS, Cardon LR, Fulker DW, Brower AM, et al. (1999). Quantitative-trait locus for specific language and reading deficits on chromosome 6p. *Am J Hum Genet*, 64(1):157–64.

Gayan J, Willcutt E, Fisher SE, Francks C, Cardon L, Olson RK, et al. (2005). Bivariate linkage scan for reading disability and attention-deficit/hyperactivity disorder localizes pleiotropic loci. *J Child Psychol Psychiatry*, 46(10):1045–56.

Grigorenko EL, Wood FB, Golovyan L, Meyer M, Romano C, Pauls D (2003). Continuing the search for dyslexia genes on 6p. *Am J Med Genet B Neuropsychiatric Genet*, 118(1):89–98.

Grigorenko EL, Wood FB, Meyer MS, Hart LA, Speed WC, Shuster A, et al. (1997). Susceptibility loci for distinct components of developmental dyslexia on chromosomes 6 and 15. *Am J Hum Genet*, 60(1):27–39.

Grigorenko EL, Wood FB, Meyer MS, Pauls DL (2000). Chromosome 6p influences on different dyslexia-related cognitive processes: further confirmation. *Am J Hum Genet*, 66(2):715–23.

Grigorenko EL, Wood FB, Meyer MS, Pauls JE, Hart LA, Pauls DL (2001). Linkage studies suggest a possible locus for developmental dyslexia on chromosome 1p. *Am J Med Genet*, 105(1):120–9.

Hannula-Jouppi K, Kaminen-Ahola N, Taipale M, Eklund R, Nopola-Hemmi J, Kaariainen H, et al. (2005). The axon guidance receptor gene ROBO1 is a candidate gene for developmental dyslexia. *PLoS Genet*, 1(4):e50.

Harden KP, Turkheimer E, Loehlin JC (2007). Genotype by environment interaction in adolescents' cognitive aptitude. *BehavGenet*, 37(2):273–83.

Harm MW, Seidenberg MS (2004). Computing the meanings of words in reading: cooperative division of labor between visual and phonological processes. *Psychol Rev*, 111(3):662–720.

Harold D, Paracchini S, Scerri T, Dennis M, Cope N, Hill G, et al. (2006). Further evidence that the KIAA0319 gene confers susceptibility to developmental dyslexia. *Mol Psychiatry*, 11(12):1085–91, 1061.

Hatakeyama S, Matsumoto M, Yada M, Nakayama KI (2004). Interaction of U-box-type ubiquitin-protein ligases (E3s) with molecular chaperones. *Genes Cells*, 9(6):533–48.

Hoover WA, Gough PB (1990). The simple view of reading. *Reading and Writing*, 2(2):127–60.

Hsiung GY, Kaplan BJ, Petryshen TL, Lu S, Field,LL (2004). A dyslexia susceptibility locus (DYX7) linked to dopamine D4 receptor (DRD4) region on chromosome 11p15.5. *Am J Med Genet B Neuropsychiatric Genet*, 125(1):112–9.

Igo RP Jr, Chapman NH, Berninger VW, Matsushita M, Brkanac Z, Rothstein JH, et al. (2006). Genomewide scan for real-word reading subphenotypes of dyslexia: novel chromosome 13 locus and genetic complexity. *Am J Med Genet B Neuropsychiatric Genet*, 141(1):15–27.

Kaminen N, Hannula-Jouppi K, Kestila M, Lahermo P, Muller K, Kaaranen M, et al. (2003). A genome scan for developmental dyslexia confirms linkage to chromosome 2p11 and suggests a new locus on 7q32. *J Med Genet*, 40(5):340–5.

Kaplan DE, Gayan J, Ahn J, Won TW, Pauls D, Olson RK, et al. (2002). Evidence for linkage and association with reading disability on 6p21.3–22. *Am J Hum Genet*, 70(5):1287–98.

Keenan JM, Betjemann RS, Wadsworth SJ, DeFries JC, Olson RK (2006). Genetic and environmental influences on reading and listening comprehension. *J Res Reading*, 29:79–91.

Kremen WS, Jacobson KC, Xian H, Eisen SA, Waterman B, Toomey R, et al. (2005). Heritability of word recognition in middle-aged men Varies as a function of parental education. *Behav Genet*, 35(4):417–33.

Lewontin R (1995). *Human Diversity*. New York: Scientific American Library.

Loo SK, Fisher SE, Francks C, Ogdie MN, MacPhie IL, Yang M, et al. (2004). Genome-wide scan of reading ability in affected sibling pairs with attention-deficit/hyperactivity disorder: unique and shared genetic effects. *Mol Psychiatry*, 9(5):485–93.

Marino C, Citterio A, Giorda R, Facoetti A, Menozzi G, Vanzin L, et al. (2007). Association of short-term memory with a variant within DYX1C1 in developmental dyslexia. *Genes Brain Behav*, 6(7):640–6.

Marino C, Giorda R, Luisa Lorusso M, Vanzin L, Salandi N, Nobile M, et al. (2005). A family-based association study does not support DYX1C1 on 15q21.3 as a candidate gene in developmental dyslexia. *Eur J Hum Genet*, 13(4):491–9.

Marlow AJ, Fisher SE, Francks C, MacPhie IL, Cherny SS, Richardson AJ, et al. (2003). Use of multivariate linkage analysis for dissection of a complex cognitive trait. *Am J Hum Genet*, 72(3):561–70.

McGrath LM, Pennington BF (2005). *Speech sounds disorder: Genes, environments, and interactions.* Unpublished master's thesis, University of Denver, Denver, CO.

McGrath LM, Pennington BF, Willcutt EG, Boada R, Shriberg LD, Smith SD (2007). Gene x Environment Interactions in Speech Sound Disorder. *DevPsychopathol*, 19:1047–72.

McGrath LM, Smith SD, Pennington BF (2006). Breakthroughs in the search for dyslexia candidate genes. *Trends Mol Med*, 12(7):333–41.

Meng H, Hager K, Held M, Page GP, Olson RK, Pennington BF, et al. (2005). TDT-association analysis of EKN1 and dyslexia in a Colorado twin cohort. *Hum Genet*, 118(1):87–90.

Meng H, Smith SD, Hager K, Held M, Liu J, Olson RK, et al. (2005). DCDC2 is associated with reading disability and modulates neuronal development in the brain. *Proc Natl Acad Sci USA*, 102(47):17053–8.

Miscimarra L, Stein C, Millard C, Kluge A, Cartier K, Freebairn L, et al. (2007). Further evidence of pleiotropy influencing speech and language: analysis of the DYX8 region. *Hum Hered*, 63(1):47–58.

Monaco A P (2007). Multivariate linkage analysis of specific language impairment (SLI). *Ann Hum Genet*, 71(Pt 5):660–73.

Morris DW, Robinson L, Turic D, Duke M, Webb V, Milham C, et al. (2000). Family-based association mapping provides evidence for a gene for reading disability on chromosome 15q. *Hum Mol Genet*, 9(5):843–8.

Nation K (2005). Children's reading comprehension difficulties. In MJ Snowling and C Hulme (eds), *The Science of Reading* (pp. 248–65). Oxford: Blackwell.

Nopola-Hemmi J, Myllyluoma B, Haltia T, Taipale M, Ollikainen V, Ahonen T, et al. (2001). A dominant gene for developmental dyslexia on chromosome 3. *J Med Genet*, 38(10):658–64.

Nopola-Hemmi J, Taipale M, Haltia T, Lehesjoki AE, Voutilainen A, Kere J (2000). Two translocations of chromosome 15q associated with dyslexia. *J Med Genet*, 37(10):771–5.

Nothen MM, Schulte-Korne G, Grimm T, Cichon S, Vogt IR, Muller-Myhsok B, et al. (1999). Genetic linkage analysis with dyslexia: evidence for linkage of spelling disability to chromosome 15. *Eur Child Adolescent Psychiatry*, 8(Suppl 3):56–9.

Paracchini S, Scerri T, Monaco AP (2007). The genetic lexicon of dyslexia. *Annu Rev Genomics Hum Genet*, 8:57–79.

Paracchini S, Thomas A, Castro S, Lai C, Paramasivam M, Wang Y, et al. (2006). The chromosome 6p22 haplotype associated with dyslexia reduces the expression of KIAA0319, a novel gene involved in neuronal migration. *Hum Mol Genet*, 15(10):1659–66.

Pennington B, Willcutt E, Rhee SH (2005). Analyzing comorbidity. In R. Kail (ed), *Advances in Child Development and Behavior* (vol. 33, pp. 262–304). Oxford: Elsevier.

Pennington BF (2002). *The Development of Psychopathology: Nature and Nurture*. New York: Guilford.

Pennington BF (2006). From single to multiple deficit models of developmental disorders. *Cognition*, 101(2):385–413.

Pennington BF, Lefly DL (2001). Early reading development in children at family risk for dyslexia. *Child Dev*, 72(3):816–33.

Pennington BF, Olson RK (2005). Genetics of dyslexia. In M Snowling, C Hulme (eds.), *The Science of Reading: A Handbook* (pp. 453–72). Oxford: Blackwell Publishing.

Petryshen TL, Kaplan BJ, Fu Liu M, de French NS, Tobias R, Hughes ML, et al. (2001). Evidence for a susceptibility locus on chromosome 6q influencing phonological coding dyslexia. *Am J Med Genet*, 105(6):507–17.

Petryshen TL, Kaplan BJ, Hughes ML, Tzenova J, Field LL (2002). Supportive evidence for the DYX3 dyslexia susceptibility gene in Canadian families. *J Med Genet*, 39(2):125–6.

Petryshen TL, Kaplan BJ, Liu MF, Field LL (2000). Absence of significant linkage between phonological coding dyslexia and chromosome 6p23–21.3, as determined by use of quantitative-trait methods: confirmation of qualitative analyses. *Am J Hum Genet*, 66(2):708–14.

Peyrard-Janvid M, Anthoni H, Onkamo P, Lahermo P, Zucchelli M, Kaminen N, et al. (2004). Fine mapping of the 2p11 dyslexia locus and exclusion of TACR1 as a candidate gene. *Hum Genet*, 114(5):510–6.

Price CJ, McCrory E (2005). Functional brain imaging studies of skilled reading and developmental dyslexia. In MJ Snowling, C Hulme (eds), *The Science of Reading* (pp. 473–96). Oxford: Blackwell.

Rabin M, Wen XL, Hepburn M, Lubs HA, Feldman E, Duara R (1993). Suggestive linkage of developmental dyslexia to chromosome 1p34-p36. *Lancet*, 342(8864):178.

Raitano NA, Pennington BF, Tunick RA, Boada R, Shriberg L (2004). Pre-literacy skills of subgroups of children with speech sound disorders. *J Child Psychol Psychiatry*, 45:821–35.

Rosen GD, Bai J, Wang Y, Fiondella CG, Threlkeld SW, LoTurco JJ, et al. (2007). Disruption of neuronal migration by RNAi of Dyx1c1 results in neocortical and hippocampal malformations. *Cereb Cortex*, 17(11):2562–72.

Rowe DC, Jacobson KC, Van den Oord EJ (1999). Genetic and environmental influences on vocabulary IQ: parental education level as moderator. *Child Dev*, 70(5):1151–62.

Rutter M, Moffitt TE, Caspi A (2006). Gene-environment interplay and psychopathology: multiple varieties but real effects. *J Child Psychol Psychiatry*, 47(3–4):226–61.

Scarborough HS (1990). Very early language deficits in dyslexic children. *Child Dev*, 61(6):1728–43.

Scerri TS, Fisher SE, Francks C, MacPhie IL, Paracchini S, Richardson AJ, et al. (2004). Putative functional alleles of DYX1C1 are not associated with dyslexia susceptibility in a large sample of sibling pairs from the UK. *J Med Genet*, 41(11):853–7.

Schumacher J, Anthoni H, Dahdouh F, Konig IR, Hillmer AM, Kluck N, et al. (2006). Strong genetic evidence of DCDC2 as a susceptibility gene for dyslexia. *Am J Hum Genet*, 78(1):52–62.

Schumacher J, Konig IR, Plume E, Propping P, Warnke A, Manthey M, et al. (2006). Linkage analyses of chromosomal region 18p11-q12 in dyslexia. *J Neural Transmission*, 113(3):417–23.

Shanahan MA, Pennington BF, Yerys BE, Scott A, Boada R, Willcutt EG, et al. (2006). Processing speed deficits in attention deficit/hyperactivity disorder and reading disability. *J Abnorm Child Psychol*, 34(5):585–602.

Silberg J, Rutter M, Neale M, Eaves L (2001). Genetic moderation of environmental risk for depression and anxiety in adolescent girls. *Br J Psychiatry*, 179:116–21.

SLI-Consortium (2002). A genomewide scan identifies two novel loci involved in specific language impairment. *Am J Hum Genet*, 70(2):384–98.

SLI-Consortium (2004). Highly significant linkage to the SLI1 locus in an expanded sample of individuals affected by specific language impairment. *Am J Hum Genet*, 74(6):1225–38.

Smith S, Kimberling W, Pennington BF, Lubs H (1983). Specific reading disability: Identification of an inherited form through linkage analysis. *Science*, 219:1345–7.

Smith SD (2007). Genes, language development, and language disorders. *Ment Retard Dev Disabil Res Rev*, 13(1):96–105.

Smith SD, Kimberling WJ, Pennington BF (1991). Screening for multiple genes influencing dyslexia. *Reading and Writing*, 3:285–98.

Smith SD, Pennington BF, Boada R, Shriberg LD (2005). Linkage of speech sound disorder to reading disability loci. *J Child Psychol Psychiatry*, 46(10):1045–56.

Stein CM, Millard C, Kluge A, Miscimarra LE, Cartier KC, Freebairn LA, et al. (2006). Speech sound disorder influenced by a locus in 15q14 region. *Behav Genet*, 36(6):858–68.

Stein CM, Schick JH, Taylor H, Shriberg LD, Millard C, Kundtz-Kluge A, et al. (2004). Pleiotropic effects of a chromosome 3 locus on speech-sound disorder and reading. *Am J Hum Genet*, 74(2):283–97.

Taipale M, Kaminen N, Nopola-Hemmi J, Haltia T, Myllyluoma B, Lyytinen H, et al. (2003). A candidate gene for developmental dyslexia encodes a nuclear tetratricopeptide repeat domain protein dynamically regulated in brain. *Proc Natl Acad Sci USA*, 100(20):11553–8.

Threlkeld SW, McClure MM, Bai J, Wang Y, LoTurco JJ, Rosen GD, et al. (2007). Developmental disruptions and behavioral impairments in rats following in utero RNAi of Dyx1c1. *Brain Res Bull*, 71(5):508–14.

Tunick RA, Pennington BF, Boada R (submitted). Cofamiliality of speech sound disorder and reading disability.

Turic D, Robinson L, Duke M, Morris DW, Webb V, Hamshere M, et al. (2003). Linkage disequilibrium mapping provides further evidence of a gene for reading disability on chromosome 6p21.3-22. *Mol Psychiatry*, 8(2):176–85.

Turkheimer E, Haley A, Waldron M, D'Onofrio B, Gottesman, II (2003). Socioeconomic status modifies heritability of IQ in young children. *Psychol Sci*, 14(6):623–8.

Tzenova J, Kaplan BJ, Petryshen TL, Field LL (2004). Confirmation of a dyslexia susceptibility locus on chromosome 1p34–p36 in a set of 100 Canadian families. *Am J Med Genet B Neuropsychiatric Genet*, 127(1):117–24.

Wang Y, Paramasivam M, Thomas A, Bai J, Kaminen-Ahola N, Kere J, et al. (2006). DYX1C1 functions in neuronal migration in developing neocortex. *Neuroscience*, 143(2):515–22.

Wigg KG, Couto JM, Feng Y, Anderson B, Cate-Carter TD, Macciardi F, et al. (2004). Support for EKN1 as the susceptibility locus for dyslexia on 15q21. *Mol Psychiatry*, 9(12):1111–21.

Wigg KG, Couto JM, Feng Y, Crosbie J, Anderson B, Gate-Carter T, et al. (2005). Investigation of the Relationship of Attention Deficit Hyperactivity Disorder to the EKN1 Gene on Chromosome 15q21. *Scientific Studies Reading*, 9(3):261–83.

Willcutt EG, Pennington BF, Smith SD, Cardon LR, Gayan J, Knopik VS, et al. (2002). Quantitative trait locus for reading disability on chromosome 6p is pleiotropic for attention-deficit/hyperactivity disorder. *Am J Med Genet*, 114(3):260–8.

9 Cognitive Intermediate Phenotypes in Schizophrenia Genetics

Gary Donohoe, Terry E. Goldberg, and Aiden Corvin

Schizophrenia is a complex brain disorder affecting perception, social function, and cognition. A significant genetic contribution to the disorder is well established, and statistical evidence for the involvement of genes including dysbindin, neuregulin 1 (*NRG1*), disrupted in schizophrenia 1 (*DISC1*), and G72—recently renamed as D-amino acid oxidase activator (DAOA)—has been replicated across independent studies. The identification of susceptibility genes has yet to be translated into an understanding of their function or of the mechanisms by which they contribute to the disorder.

Understanding the function of these genes is a growing priority. The original rationale for parsing complex disorders into intermediate phenotypes or "intermediate phenotypes" (see below for further explanation of this term) was that such intermediate phenotypes may have a less complex genetic architecture, facilitating gene identification. However, where genes have been identified, intermediate phenotypes may be equally valuable in establishing gene function. In this chapter we describe the main cognitive phenotypes used in schizophrenia research, namely, working memory (WM), attention, and episodic memory, along with the measures used to quantify them. We outline the evidence of their utility in genetics research, particularly for understanding the role of candidate genes in frontostriatal and frontotemporal functioning, along with the methodological issues involved. We conclude that several candidate genes associated with schizophrenia risk are implicated in cognitive performance both in patients and in the general population, making this research as important for understanding the genetics of normal cognition as for schizophrenia pathogenesis.

Basic Goals of the Line of Work

A key question in schizophrenia genetics is whether identified candidate genes are contributing to the complex heterogeneous symptoms of "schizophrenia." Data from genetics, functional neuroimaging, and neuropsychology indicate both overlap and discontinuity between schizophrenia and other psychotic disorders (Cardno and Gottesman 2000; Quraishi and Frangou 2002; McDonald et al. 2004). Furthermore, many of the deficits evident in patients are evident in an attenuated form in their unaffected relatives. Finally, some of the genes described as putative schizophrenia susceptibility genes (e.g., NRG1, DISC1, and DAOA) have also been implicated in other psychiatric disorders (Green et al. 2005; Blackwood et al. 2001; Schumacher et al. 2004). Vulnerability to "schizophrenia" may be due to genetic and environmental variation in the development and/or maintenance of specific neural systems. If so, assaying function at, or closer to, the level of these systems would likely improve our understanding of the biology involved (Meyer-Lindenberg and Weinberger 2006).

This rationale has led to interest in identifying particular aspects of the broader schizophrenia phenotype of use to genetics study, an approach termed the "intermediate" phenotypes strategy. This approach was first suggested by Gottesman and Shields (1972) to promote the use of discrete biological traits in investigating the genetic basis of psychiatric disorders. The rationale was that specific phenotypes may represent more straightforward phenomena than phenotypes based on behavioral syndromes, and hence the number of genes required to produce variation in these traits may be fewer than those involved in producing a clinical disorder. This may facilitate identification of genes, but in addition, including family members who express the intermediate phenotype but not the full clinical disorder may increase study power. Where specific susceptibility genes for a disorder have already been identified, intermediate phenotypes may point towards neural pathways by which individual genes contribute liability, using phenotypes that are dimensional rather than categorical.

Neurocognitive deficits have been identified as potential intermediate phenotypes in schizophrenia research. These deficits are present from an early stage of the disorder and often predate the emergence of clinical symptoms (Erlenmeyer-Kimling et al. 2000; Niendam et al. 2003). They are relatively stable over time and closely related to functional outcome (Green et al. 2004). Furthermore, genetic epidemiological research using family and twin studies indicates that some of these deficits may themselves have a substantial genetic component (Goldberg et al. 1990; 1995; Cannon et al. 2000). One issue for cognitive deficits as intermediate phenotypes is their independence from clinical state: performance on attentional measures, for example, has been shown to correlate with negative symptoms (Nieuwenstein 2001). However, the amount of variance shared by these variables appears to be small, and cognitive function often emerges as a separate factor from clinical symptoms in factor analysis (Good et al. 2004; for a review, see Donohoe and Robertson 2003).

Methods Employed for Identifying Potential Cognitive Intermediate Phenotypes

Selecting cognitive intermediate phenotypes for schizophrenia is complicated by the number of deficits involved, different theories about their neurocognitive basis, and differences in assessment. Deficits in lower stages of information processing have been assessed using neurophysiological indices (e.g., mismatch negativity; Javitt et al. 1997). Higher stages of information processing have been variously targeted in terms of general cognitive functioning, prefrontal function (characterized as deficits in attention or WM), and memory function. In establishing suitable intermediate phenotypes in general, the following criteria have been suggested (Gottesman and Gould 2003; Freedman et al. 1999):

1. An association with illness in the population or cosegregation with illness in affected families.
2. Genetic epidemiological research establishing that the deficit is heritable.
3. Independence from clinical state and medication effects.
4. The ability to reliably distinguish case from control populations.
5. Well-established neurochemical and neuroanatomical underpinnings.

For cognitive intermediate phenotypes in particular, the following criteria are also critically important:

1. The brain–behavior relationship of the task is well understood.
2. The psychometric properties of the task are well established.
3. The task can be administered to large numbers of participants relatively easily.
4. The task used allows replication of findings by other research groups.

Based on the above criteria, genetic epidemiological studies (including family and twin studies) have resulted in a particular focus on deficits in WM, attentional control, and episodic memory as suitable intermediate phenotypes for schizophrenia. In the rest of this chapter, we review the evidence for these cognitive functions as intermediate phenotypes, along with the evidence to date for their linkage or association to susceptibility loci or genes.

Findings from the Literature

Working Memory Deficits as an Intermediate Phenotype

WM is involved in a wide range of cognitive operations that require simultaneous storage and processing of information (Baddeley 1990). Conceptualized in terms of storage subsystems coordinating by a central executive, this function represents an active system of maintaining and manipulating information that provides the basis for complex cognitive abilities. Neuroanatomical studies consistently highlight the dorsolateral prefrontal cortex as the primary brain area implicated in WM performance (Weinberger et al. 2001; Braff et al. 2001; Levy and Goldman-Rakic 2000; Carter et al. 1998; Egan et al. 2001; MacDonald and Carter 2003; Callicott et al. 2003). Similarly, the importance of dopamine in regulating WM is consistently reported (Goldman-Rakic 1999; Goldberg et al. 2003; Castner et al. 2004).

Familiality of WM Deficits in Schizophrenia Different classes of relatives share more or less genetic material (e.g., monozygotic [MZ] twins share 100% of genes, dizygotic [DZ] twins–siblings 50%, and half-siblings 25%), making it possible to estimate the proportion of individual differences in risk in a population at a given time that is due to genetic differences, termed heritability (h^2). For example, the estimated heritability for the schizophrenia phenotype is 65% to 80% (Cardno and Gottesman 2000). Because of practical sampling constraints, demonstration of cognitive deficit in relatives of schizophrenic probands, at a higher rate than in controls, is taken as evidence of heritability, and a number of family studies of this type have been performed. The availability of twin data is much more limited, and a literature review failed to identify any relevant adoption studies.

Of nine family studies identified measuring WM in relatives using a well-established task, such as the spatial delayed response task or one of the Wechsler WM tasks, almost all found evidence for impaired WM performance across the range of tests used (Conklin et al. 2000; 2005; Glahn et al. 2003; Goldberg et al. 2003; Tuulio-Henriksson et al. 2003; Myles-Worsley and Park 2002; Keri et al. 2004; Krabbendam et al. 2001; Park et al. 1995). The single twin study, based on the Finnish twin register, included 48 discordant twin pairs (18 MZ and 30 DZ) and 8 pairs concordant for schizophrenia. This study reported significant statistical evidence for a linear decrease in performance on a spatial WM task as genetic risk of schizophrenia increased (Cannon et al. 2000). In general, effect sizes observed were moderate, despite the range of tasks used involving both verbal and spatial modalities. The largest effects were seen for the spatial delayed response paradigm, with Park et al.'s (1995) study showing large effect sizes for both versions of the task used. The study by Tuulio-Henriksson et al. (2003) is interesting in its comparison of singleton relatives versus relatives from multiplex families (families with more than one affected member), where multiplex families showed greater spatial WM deficits than simplex family members but less significant verbal WM differences.

WM in Linkage and Candidate Gene Association Studies Two Finnish studies have reported suggestive evidence of linkage between chromosomal loci and WM function in schizophrenia. The first, following up a region of putative schizophrenia locus at chromosome 1q, identified suggestive evidence of linkage to a marker at 1q42 in twin pairs discordant for schizophrenia (Gasperoni et al. 2003). The second, an analysis of genome-wide data for 168 schizophrenia families using variance components analysis, identified suggestive evidence of linkage to chromosome 2q36 (Paunio et al. 2004). Given that these studies included both Wechsler Memory Scale (WMS) visual span and digit span tasks, but that evidence of linkage was found only for the visual WM task, this may be taken as further evidence for the utility of spatial WM in schizophrenia.

Evidence that WM performance relates to putative schizophrenia candidate genes derives largely from investigation of the catechol-O-methyltransferase (COMT) val158met polymorphism. COMT is an enzyme that metabolizes released dopamine and accounts for ~60% of dopamine degradation in the frontal cortex. A functional valine to methionine polymorphism at codon 158 results in a 75% reduction in its enzymatic activity. That dopamine is known to influence cognitive performance and that lower transmission of dopamine in the prefrontal cortex is associated with impaired WM task performance led to the hypothesis that the contribution of COMT to schizophrenia risk may be due to its impact on cognition (Egan et al. 2001).

There have been mixed reports of association between schizophrenia and markers at the COMT locus (including val158met; for review, see Fan et al. 2005). Evidence for association with prefrontally mediated cognitive performance in schizophrenia has been more consistently replicated, mostly using the Wisconsin Card Sorting Task (WCST; Rosa et al. 2004; Nolan et al. 2004; Goldberg et al. 2003; Tsai et al. 2003; Bilder et al. 2002; Joober et al. 2002; Malhotra et al. 2002; Egan et al. 2001). A key difficulty in interpreting the specificity of these results has been the use of the WCST, which is not cognitively selective but rather was designed to measure more general prefrontal deficits. Differences between studies in variance accounted for by genotype are likely to be partly due to such issues of cognitive measurement (e.g., 4% of variance in WM explained by COMT in Egan et al. 2001 using the WCST vs. 11% in WM accounted for by COMT in Bilder et al. 2002 using Trail Making Test and WMS digit span). Greater consistency between studies investigating WM is likely to occur with the use of more selective measures of WM.

An association between WM deficits and genetic variation has now been reported for a number of leading schizophrenia susceptibility genes including dysbindin (Donohoe et al. 2007), DAOA (Goldberg et al. 2006), DISC1 (Burdick et al. 2005; Callicott et al. 2005), and RGS4 (Buckholtz et al. 2007), as well as for the dopamine transporter gene (DAT1; Rybakowski et al. 2004), the gene encoding for dopamine- and cyclic AMP-regulated phosphoprotein of 32 kDa (DARPP-32; Meyer-Lindenberg et al. 2007) and the gene encoding the Notch receptor Notch4 (Wassink et al. 2003). However, for none of these genes has the association with WM been exclusive. In the case of dysbindin, while Donohoe et al.'s (2007) finding of association was specific to the Cambridge Neuropsychological Test Automated Battery spatial WM performance, Burdick et al. (2006) found an association between risk variants at dysbindin and a more general index of cognitive ability comprised of a single factor solution for a number of Wechsler Adult Intelligence Scale (WAIS) subtests. One reason for such differences between studies may relate to differences in the dysbindin risk variants themselves. Alternatively, as WM and general cognitive ability are highly correlated, these results on apparently different indices may simply be two sides of the same cognitive "coin." This view is supported by a similar dual association (this time in the same sample) in the study by Buckholtz et al. (2007), where variants at RGS4 were associated both with differences in regional activations (but not behavioral performance) during performance of the N-back WM task and with trend level association with WAIS–III IQ performance. A recent study of neuregulin 1 by Hall et al. (2006), reporting an association with both the Hayling sentence completion task (an executive task rather than a WM task) and premorbid IQ, also provides support for this contention. Similarly, a recent study of DARPP-32 reported associations with both WM (N-back) performance and WAIS IQ/reading performance (Meyer-Lindenberg et al. 2007). A second question is whether these associations are specific to patients with schizophrenia: again, there is growing evidence that this is not the case. The association between haplotype variants at dysbindin and cognitive performance has also been demonstrated in normal controls (Burdick et al. 2005; Fallgatter et al. 2006; Stefanis et al. 2007). This again suggests that even "schizophrenia" genes (i.e., genes associated with increased risk for the disorder) are exerting an influence on cognition that is independent of illness risk and may just as properly be described as "cognitive" genes.

Attentional Deficits as an Intermediate Phenotype: Findings from the Literature
Attention involves the controlled or voluntary focusing of awareness. As such, it requires both active maintenance of focus on relevant stimuli and the equally active suppression or ignoring of nonrelevant stimuli. In contemporary neuropsychology, attention is typically fractionated into more specific components—for example, alerting, orienting (or selection), and execution (involving error and conflict monitoring)—each crucial for maintaining coherent behavior in the face of multiple action or response alternatives. Predictably, these attentional processes are subserved by distinct neural systems that include right parietal (alerting), superior parietal (orienting), and anterior cingulate (execution) regions, among others (Raz and Buhle 2006).

Inheritance of attentional deficits in schizophrenia has typically been measured by various Continuous Performance Tasks (CPT; e.g., Cornblatt et al. 1994). While often thought of as one task measuring sustained attention, there are several versions, each involving additional aspects of attention (e.g., perceptual load in the degraded stimulus [DS] versions, selective attention in versions with distractors) or cognition (e.g., WM in the identical pairs version; Cornblatt and Keilp 1994) to a greater or lesser degree. Given the various facets of attention involved in the allocation of cognitive resources, and the distributed network underpinning cognitive control (dorsal and medial prefrontal cortex, cingulate cortex, thalamus, and basal ganglia), it is unsurprising that different tasks are sensitive to different locations in the attentional system.

Familiality of Attentional Deficits in Schizophrenia   Family studies have tended to use the more demanding versions of the CPT (Snitz et al. 2006). All studies reviewed included either increased perceptual load or selective attention elements. Four found that relatives of patients were impaired using the DS version (Chen et al. 2004; Laurent et al. 2000; Saoud et al. 2000; Chen et al. 1998), and three did so using the identical pairs (IP) version (Appels et al. 2003; Laurent et al. 1999; Franke et al. 1994). Among studies failing to find evidence of a genetic contribution to task deficits, one found that CPT performance was not predictive of genetic loading for schizophrenia (Keefe 1997), and one smaller study by Jones et al. (2001) using the CPT–DS found that neither schizophrenia relatives nor patients differed significantly from controls in CPT performance. The single reported twin study of CPT did not support a genetic contribution to CPT function (Cannon et al. 2000). The heterogeneity of effect sizes probably was related to different versions of the task used (e.g., the 1-9 and 3-7 versions showing smaller effect sizes) but possibly also to differences in sample characteristics and sample size. Such evidence has already led to other reviewers' concluding that CPT performance may be of limited utility for molecular studies (Heinrichs 2004; Keri and Janka 2004).

CPT and Molecular Genetics Studies   Despite limited evidence for the heritability of CPT deficits in schizophrenia, several authors have suggested that including familial carriers of CPT deficits in linkage studies may increase study power (Chen and Faraone 2000; Egan et al. 2000). Recently, Hallmayer et al. (2003) found that CPT-IP scores among other variables contributed to the delineation of a subgroup that was useful for linkage analysis because it enabled linkage based quantitatively on grade of membership rather than simply on "caseness." Hallmayer et al. (2005) reported that a cognitive deficit group (based on scores on the DS and IP versions of the CPT, in addition to general cognitive ability scores) showed evidence of linkage to the region on chromosome 6p containing the schizophrenia susceptibility gene dysbindin 1.

There has been somewhat mixed success in demarcating the cognitive effects of schizophrenia risk variants on the basis of CPT performance, despite promising linkage results described above. Egan et al. (2004) reported a functional polymorphism of the type-three metabotropic glutamate receptor gene (GRM3) was associated with both schizophrenia and deficits in verbal fluency and verbal memory but not with CPT performance. Similarly no difference in CPT performance was associated with COMT in studies by either Goldberg et al. (2003) or Bilder et al. (2002), although the latter group did find evidence that the Met/Met allele of COMT was associated with better sustained attention in a small sample of patients. By contrast, studies of DAOA by Goldberg et al. (2006) and of DARP-32 by Meyer Lindenberg et al. (2007) found that the distractibility version of the CPT was one of a number of cognitive tasks (including the N-back task) associated with variants at either gene in their schizophrenia family samples.

Blasi et al. (2005) report that COMT genotype was associated with performance on a measure of flexible switching of attention, the Local Global Task, making it possible that other aspects of attention (e.g., attentional flexibility) may be of greater utility as cognitive endophenotyes. The positive findings reported above with the WCST, a task often conceptualized in terms of cognitive flexibility, support this view. Alternatively, greater success with WM measures may result from the lack of sensitivity of CPT tasks in genetic studies (associated perhaps with much larger confidence intervals surrounding the effect sizes for these tasks than other tasks; see the meta-analysis by Snitz et al. 2006). Yet another possibility is that attentional measures are less strongly associated with the general cognitive decline observed in schizophrenia (Donohoe et al. 2006) than are WM tasks, and it is this more general decline that WM tasks are indexing in genetic studies. More studies of measures of the various aspects of attention will be required before these speculations are confirmed.

Memory Deficits as an Intermediate Phenotype: Findings from the Literature

Impaired memory functioning has been one of the most widely reported cognitive deficits in schizophrenia (Cirillo and Seidman 2003; Aleman et al. 1999). Deficits in episodic memory—mnemonic processes that record, retain, and retrieve autobiographical knowledge about experiences that occurred at a specific time and place (Tulving 1985)—have received particular attention in genetic studies of schizophrenia. Since the earliest investigations of memory impairments (Scoville and Milner 1957), lesion studies have consistently associated impaired episodic memory with bilateral medial temporal lobe function (including the hippocampus, parahippocampus, entorhinal and perirhinal cortices; Squire and Zola 1996; Fernandez et al. 1999). The distinct roles of these brain structures have been parsed on the basis of the information modality being encoded (verbal, visual, and spatial), encoding versus retrieval processes (Squire et al. 2004), and how memory retrieval is elicited (item retrieval vs. associative processing, recollection vs. familiarity).

A number of tasks have been used to study verbal episodic memory in studies investigating the genetic basis of memory deficits in families with schizophrenia. Most have used verbal list learning tasks (especially the California Verbal Learning Test; CVLT) and story recall (using the logical memory subtest from the WMS; Wechsler 2000). Visual tasks that have also been used in genetics studies have mainly included visual reproduction (using the WMS visual reproduction subtest), and facial recognition (using either the WMS or Warrington facial recognition subtest). Each of these tasks is widely used clinically with good validity and reliability.

Epidemiological studies of declarative memory using the tasks listed above have consistently found evidence for impaired episodic memory performance in samples of MZ twins (Goldberg et al. 1990; 1993; 1995; Gourovitch et al. 1999) and first-degree relatives (Staal et al. 2000; Bilder et al. 2002; Egan et al. 2001; Cannon et al. 1994; 2000; Conklin et al. 2002; Toulopoulou et al. 2003a; 2003b). Evidence of significant differences between relatives and controls is found across tasks, despite differences in memory modality (verbal vs. visual) and type of retrieval (recall vs. recognition). Verbal memory deficits tend show a medium effect size for differences between unaffected relatives and matched control samples (for a recent review, see Whyte et al. 2005). Effect sizes for visual memory deficits tend to be smaller, and a number of studies that reported statistical difference between relatives and controls on verbal memory tasks failed to find a similar association on visual memory tasks (Toulopoulou et al. 2003; Egan et al. 2001; Faraone et al. 1999). Additionally, verbal list learning but not visual reproduction contributed to discrimination of degree of genetic loading for unaffected MZ and DZ twins of patients with schizophrenia (Cannon et al. 2000). There is also evidence of a larger effect size for free immediate recall than for delayed recall deficits or recognition deficits; however, simple distinctions between recall and recognition for the purposes of phenotypic utility are probably not warranted (Cannon et al. 1994; Gourovitch et al. 1999; Conklin et al. 2002).

Memory Recall and Molecular Studies   Two linkage studies to date have investigated the genetic underpinnings of episodic memory impairments in schizophrenia (Paunio et al. 2004; Hallmayer et al. 2003). In Hallmayer et al.'s (2003) study, memory was assessed as part of an "integrated" cognitive and personality phenotype in a linkage analysis study exploring candidate regions on chromosome 6, 10, 22. This neurocognitive phenotype yielded suggestive linkage to chromosome 6, but not 10 and 12. A more recent study by the same group (Paunio et al. 2004) found evidence for linkage of verbal episodic memory at chromosome 4q21.

A number of association studies have also been carried out using episodic memory intermediate phenotypes. Bilder et al. (2002) found no evidence of association between the COMT val158met polymorphism and episodic memory, either for verbal or visual stimuli. However, in the gene coding for brain-derived neurotrophic factor (BDNF), a polymorphism (val66met) has been implicated in memory functioning. A study of patients with schizophrenia, their healthy relatives, and normal controls found an association between the Met allele of the BDNF val66met polymorphism and diminished verbal episodic memory performance and lower hippocampal functioning during a recognition memory task (Egan et al. 2003). At the same time, the authors failed to find evidence of association between BDNF allele frequency and risk for schizophrenia, leading them to conclude that the genotype may contribute to the cognitive deficits seen in schizophrenia rather than to illness risk per se. A second study by the same group (Hariri et al. 2003) found that the interaction between this polymorphism and hippocampal activation explained 25% of the variance in memory performance on the visual recognition task. Since then, two further studies have replicated this finding of association with BDNF (Dempster et al. 2005; Tan et al. 2005), both using the WMS logical memory subtest, with a further study finding association with the WMS facial recognition subtest (Donohoe et al. 2007).

Several studies have now reported association between memory function and other candidate schizophrenia genes. DeQuervain et al. (2003) found that in a normal sample, those with the HIS/TYR genotype of the 5-HT2a receptor polymorphism H452Y had a 21% lower performance on a verbal memory task than those with the His/His genotype. Egan et al. (2004) reported that the GRM3, in addition to being associated with increased risk for schizophrenia, was associated with poorer verbal episodic memory performance in terms of both behavioral performance and cortical activation, although this has yet to be replicated. By contrast, probably the most consistent evidence for a susceptibility genes role in memory function is DISC1, a gene putatively interacting with other candidate susceptibility genes, for example, Ndel1. Callicott et al. (2005) report that a three-single-nucleotide-polymorphism (SNP) haplotype was associated with risk for schizophrenia, and the homozygous SER allele carriers showed poorer performance on the WMS logical memory subtest (delayed recall). Cannon et al. (2005) found that performance on the CVLT was also associated with genetic variance in DISC1, although Burdick et al. (2005) failed to find a similar association using the same measure.

DAOA, a gene which, as mentioned above, was formerly known as G72, is another schizophrenia susceptibility gene whose involvement in episodic memory has been replicated. Goldberg et al. (2006) first reported evidence of a trend association between performance on the WMS verbal paired associates and DAOA, supported by a more robust association between DAOA and hippocampal activation, without observing evidence of association with schizophrenia. This association between DAOA and verbal episodic memory performance was recently confirmed by Donohoe et al. (in press) in an investigation of an arginine to lysine substitution at DAOA codon 30 (Arg30Lys). In addition to being associated with increased risk for schizophrenia in their sample, this variant was associated with both immediate and delayed verbal memory, but not with measure of frontostriatal function. The biological evidence of DAOA's role in schizophrenia remains unclear. However, its putative role in biasing N-methyl-D-aspartate (NMDA) signaling, which is linked to memory function via its role in long-term potentiation, makes further study of this gene's involvement in memory function warranted.

The significant body of evidence supporting the utility of memory recall, particularly in the verbal modality, as a phenotype for schizophrenia genetics studies is perhaps unsurprising given that verbal memory deficits are among the largest cognitive deficits associated with the disorder. Again, however, the data do not support the view that these variants are contributing selectively to variance in memory function. For example, in the case of DISC1, several studies found associations with additional aspects of cognition, particularly WM (Callicott et al. 2005; Burdick et al. 2005; Hennah et al. 2005). In the case of DAOA, Goldberg et al. (2006) also found association with CPT performance as already noted. Perhaps, therefore, a more accurate conclusion to draw from these data is that rather than representing a "discrete" phenotype, verbal episodic memory represents a "sensitive" phenotype for detecting the involvement of susceptibility genes at the level of brain function.

Statistical Issues, Complications, and Confounds

In the above review of WM, attentional control, and episodic memory deficits as intermediate phenotypes in the genetic analysis of schizophrenia, many of the complications and confounds, both theoretical and statistical, have already been noted. In this next section the main issues are itemized and described further:

1. Although family and twin data strongly support a genetic contribution to measures of spatial WM, they rarely allow an estimation of *heritability* (h^2), not least because of the *diversity of tasks* employed. Such diversity in the behavioral and cognitive demands of various WM tasks, and hence in the brain regions implicated, is a significant problem for interpreting the resulting genetic associations. An important example here has been the use of the WCST, which is not cognitively selective but rather was designed to measure more general prefrontal deficits.

2. *Multiple testing* is a significant issue for family and association studies in schizophrenia. In candidate studies this derives in large part from the number of SNPs required to adequately characterise the variance at particular gene loci. This difficulty becomes even more problematic with larger genes (e.g., DISC1) and as the associated alleles vary between samples (e.g., dysbindin; for a review, see Muttsuddi et al. 2006). As multiple phenotypes are introduced, this difficulty is compounded exponentially as individual SNPs and haplotype are tested for each additional (cognitive) phenotype, thus raising the likelihood of type I error, or "false positives."

3. Alternatively, *genetic heterogeneity*—such that multiple loci are likely to influence the same phenotype (e.g., episodic memory deficits)—reduces the variance that any one gene can explain, thus increasing the likelihood that the presumably small influence of individual variants will be overlooked (increasing type II error, or "false negatives"). In addition to locus heterogeneity, allelic heterogeneity—where multiple variants at the same locus are associated with a particular phenotype—may also be a confounding factor in cognitive phenotypic studies.

4. *Pleiotropy*, which occurs when one gene influences several traits, has already been demonstrated by several candidate schizophrenia genes (e.g., DAOA; Goldberg et al. 2006; DISC1; Porteous et al. 2006). If schizophrenia genes are generalist "cognition" genes rather than genes with specific cognitive effects, a focus on any one aspect of cognition to the exclusion of others may result in a specificity of findings which is unwarranted.

5. Even adopting the cognitive intermediate phenotype strategy as a means of understanding gene function at a behavioral level, several confounds exist to any data

generated by this approach. In particular, *phenocopies*—nongenetically determined phenotypes with features similar to the genetically determined phenotype (e.g., resulting from drug or alcohol abuse, head injury, systemic illness, birth complications, CNS infections, etc.)—will reduce the power of association studies by introducing random genetic variation.

6. When an individual genetic variant is associated with deficits in one or more aspects of cognition, variants at other gene loci may also be contributing to this association. The effects of *epistasis*, the masking effects of one gene's activity on another's, are occluded by the single gene approach adopted in most cognitive intermediate phenotype studies to date. The interactive effects of genes on cognitive function in schizophrenia were recently illustrated in a study of GRM3 and the COMT val158met polymorphism (Tan et al. 2007). In this study, the influence of the A allele at GRM3 rs64650844 on N-back WM performance was influenced by the COMT val/val or met/met background. It is likely that additional interacting variants will be identified in cognitive phenotype studies, where one gene acts as to modify the influence of another on gene function.

Conclusions—The Future of Cognitive Intermediate Phenotypes in the Genetic Analysis of Schizophrenia

The use of intermediate phenotypes has become increasingly popular, if not de rigueur, in genetic association studies of neuropsychiatric disorders. While originally studied for their potential to aid in the discovery of novel schizophrenia genes, the utility of this approach for gene "discovery" remains unproven (Flint and Munafò 2007). Instead, the evidence to date suggests that success with using cognitive intermediate phenotypes in schizophrenia genetics has primarily been in providing important evidence for convergent validity of genes already statistically associated with disease risk. That is, in many studies it appears that positive associations between individual genetic variants and intermediate cognitive phenotypes have been used to establish construct validity or add to the biological plausibility of illness association findings rather than to provide compelling evidence of the genes' increasing susceptibility per se. In this context, and from the perspective of neuropsychology, it is interesting that the two most replicated findings of association between cognitive dysfunction and candidate schizophrenia genes—COMT and BDNF—are with genes for which the evidence of association with the schizophrenia phenotype is limited. Thus, these studies appear to have a role in elucidating the molecular basis of cognition independent of their role in elucidating the molecular genetics of schizophrenia.

Of the genes that are currently identified as being most likely to contribute to schizophrenia susceptibility (e.g., dysbindin, NRG1, DISC1, DAOA, and RGS4; Owen et al. 2004), all have been associated with cognitive deficits, and several of these findings replicated. In addition to supporting the hypothesis that these genes increase disease risk at least partly via an influence on cognition, several of these genetic variants have also been reported to influence cognition in the normal population (e.g., Hennah et al. 2005; Burdick et al. 2006; Stefanis et al. 2007). Again, this supports the wider role of these "susceptibility" genes for understanding variation in human cognition.

Several issues remain to be addressed by this approach, including whether it is more beneficial to study the effects of candidate genes in patients or in the normal population. Neuropsychological investigations of candidate genes' penetrance for frontostriatal or frontotemporal function in patients are likely to be hampered by nongenetic systematic factors affecting performance and diluting the effects of the gene. The recent meta-analysis by Barnett et al. (2007) showing an effect for the COMT val158met polymorphism on cognition in controls but not patients is consistent with this view. That genetic effects on intermediate phenotypes are more apparent in the normal population is seen in other disorders—for example, the effect of the fat mass and obesity (FTO) gene on body mass index in diabetes sufferers and nonsufferers (Frayling 2007). Similarly, in Alzheimer's disease, downstream cellular changes are observed in the disorder which are compensatory for the disorder but are nonetiologic (Armstrong et al. 2003).

Alternatively, some authors have argued that epistatic interaction in individuals who are genetically enriched for a disorder may result in individual gene effects being more apparent in cases than in controls. For example, Goldberg et al. (2006), in their study of DAOA, found that several SNPs at the 3′ end of the gene impacted multiple intermediate phenotypes associated with schizophrenia (reviewed above), but only in cases, and in the absence of association with disease risk. They argued that DAOA genotypes amplified effect in cases may represent an epistatic risk factor that increases the likelihood of schizophrenia-type cognitive impairments in individuals with other impairments. In other words, the genetic background against which variation in this gene occurs may determine the magnitude of its impact. Nevertheless, this argument can be criticized on the grounds that it reflected not epistasis but cohort effects in which a spurious finding was obtained. For instance, if there were no prior association studies, would the results have been viewed similarly? Such uncertainty again highlights the need for cognitive phenotype studies of schizophrenia to consider the interactive effects of genes which contribute to the function of individual neural pathways. Studies of gene interactions will therefore be an important next step in the cognitive genomics of schizophrenia.

Perhaps the most pressing issue that remains to be resolved in the cognitive genetics of schizophrenia is whether associations with specific cognitive deficits are, in fact, specific—a key assumption of the endophenotype approach. The data reviewed above would not appear to support this assumption, with several genes associated with more than one cognitive deficit (e.g., dysbindin, NRG1, DISC1, DAOA). Some commentators argue that the complex biology of interaction between genes contributing to brain function makes a specific role unlikely (e.g., Kovas and Plomin 2006; Meyer-Lindenberg and Weinberger 2006). Even if this is the case, and the assumption of specificity turns out to be false, we suspect that the cognitive endophenotype approach will nonetheless continue to be crucial to schizophrenia genetics. The behavioral study of individual cognitive functions to date shows evidence of being highly sensitive to the genetic involvement of schizophrenia susceptibility genes. It is this rather than the discreteness of the relationship between individual genes and cognitive functions that is likely to be most important in understanding their role in the pathophysiology of the disorder.

Acknowledgments

This work was supported by Science Foundation Ireland (SFI) and the Higher Education Authority (Ireland). Our thanks to Prof. Michael Gill and Prof. Ian Robertson for their helpful comments on a draft of this chapter.

References

Aggleton JP, Brown MW (1999): Episodic memory, amnesia, and the hippocampal–anterior thalamic axis. *Behav Brain Sci,* 22:425–44.

Aleman A, Hijman R, de Haan EH, Kahn RS (1999). Memory impairment in schizophrenia: a meta-analysis. *Am J Psychiatry,* 156:1358–66.

Appels MC, Sitskoorn MM, Westers P, Lems E, Kahn RS (2003). Cognitive dysfunctions in parents of schizophrenic patients parallel the deficits found in patients. *Schizophr Res,* 63:285–93.

Armstrong DM, Sheffield R, Mishizen-Eberz AJ, Carter TL, Rissman RA, Mizukami K, Ikonomovic MD (2003). Plasticity of glutamate and GABAA receptors in the hippocampus of patients with Alzheimer's disease. *Cell Mol Neurobiol,* 23:491–505.

Baddeley A, Wilson BA (2002). Prose recall and amnesia: implications for the structure of working memory. *Neuropsychologia,* 40:1737–43.

Baddeley AD (1990). Human memory: theory and practice. London: Lawrence Erlbaum Associates.

Baddeley AD (2001). Is working memory still working? *Am Psychol,* 56:851–64.

Barnett JH, Jones PB, Robbins TW, Müller U (2007). Effects of the catechol-O-methyltransferase Val158Met polymorphism on executive function: a meta-analysis of the Wisconsin Card Sort Test in schizophrenia and healthy controls. *Mol Psychiatry,* 12(5):502–9.

Bilder RM, Volavka J, Czobor P, Malhotra AK, Kennedy JL, Ni X, et al. (2002). Neurocognitive correlates of the COMT Val(158)Met polymorphism in chronic schizophrenia. *Biol Psychiatry*, 52:701–7.

Blackwood DH, Fordyce A, Walker MT, St Clair DM, Porteous DJ, MuirWJ (2001). Schizophrenia and affective disorders-cosegregation with a translocation at chromosome 1q42 that directly disrupts brain-expressed genes: clinical and P300 findings in a family. *Am J Hum Genet*, 69:428–33.

Blasi G, Mattay VS, Bertolino A, Elvevag B, Callicott JH, Das S, et al. (2005). Effect of catechol-O-methyltransferase val158met genotype on attentional control. *J Neurosci*, 25:5038–45.

Botvinick M, Nystrom LE, Fissell K, Carter CS, Cohen JD (1999). Conflict monitoring versus selection-for-action in anterior cingulate cortex. *Nature*, 402:179–81.

Braff DL, Geyer MA, Light GA, Sprock J, Perry W, Cadenhead KS, et al. (2001). Impact of prepulse characteristics on the detection of sensorimotor gating deficits in schizophrenia. *Schizophr Res*, 49:171–8.

Buckholtz JW, Meyer-Lindenberg A, Honea RA, Straub RE, Pezawas L, Egan MF,Vakkalanka R, Kolachana B, Verchinski BA, Sust S, Mattay VS, Weinberger DR, Callicott JH (2007). Allelic variation in RGS4 impacts functional and structural connectivity in the human brain. *J Neurosci*, 27(7):1584–93.

Burdick KE, Hodgkinson CA, Szeszko PR, Lencz T, Ekholm JM, Kane JM, et al. (2005). DISC1 and neurocognitive function in schizophrenia. *Neuroreport*, 16:1399–402.

Burdick KE, Lencz T, Funke B, Finn CT, Szeszko PR, Kane JM, Kucherlapati R, Malhotra AK (2006). Genetic variation in DTNBP1 influences general cognitive ability. *Hum Mol Genet*, 15(10):1563–8.

Burgess PW (1998). Theory and methodology in executive function research. In Rabbitt P, ed. Methodology of frontal and executive function (pp. 81–116). East Sussex: Psychology Press.

Callicott JH, Egan MF, Mattay VS, Bertolino A, Bone AD, Verchinksi B, et al. (2003). Abnormal fMRI response of the dorsolateral prefrontal cortex in cognitively intact siblings of patients with schizophrenia. *Am J Psychiatry*, 160:709–19.

Callicott JH, Straub RE, Pezawas L, Egan MF, Mattay VS, Hariri AR, et al. (2005). Variation in DISC1 affects hippocampal structure and function and increases risk for schizophrenia. *Proc Natl Acad Sci USA*, 102:8627–32.

Cannon TD, Hennah W, van Erp TG, Thompson PM, Lonnqvist J, Huttunen M,Gasperoni T, Tuulio-Henriksson A, Pirkola T, Toga AW, Kaprio J, Mazziotta J, Peltonen L (2005). Association of DISC1/TRAX haplotypes with schizophrenia, reduced prefrontal gray matter, and impaired short- and long-term memory. *Arch Gen Psychiatry*, 62(11):1205–13.

Cannon TD, Huttunen MO, Lonnqvist J, Tuulio-Henriksson A, Pirkola T, Glahn D, et al. (2000). The inheritance of neuropsychological dysfunction in twins discordant for schizophrenia. *Am J Hum Genet*, 67:369–82.

Cannon TD, Zorrilla LE, Shtasel D, Gur RE, Gur RC, Marco EJ, et al. (1994). Neuropsychological functioning in siblings discordant for schizophrenia and healthy volunteers. *Arch Gen Psychiatry,* 51:651–61.

Cardno AG, Gottesman II (2000). Twin studies of schizophrenia: from bow-and-arrow concordances to star wars Mx and functional genomics. *Am J Med Genet,* 97(1):12–7.

Carter CS, Perlstein W, Ganguli R, Brar J, Mintun M, Cohen JD (1998). Functional hypofrontality and working memory dysfunction in schizophrenia. *Am J Psychiatry,* 155:1285–7.

Castner SA, Goldman-Rakic PS, Williams GV (2004). Animal models of working memory: insights for targeting cognitive dysfunction in schizophrenia. *Psychopharmacology (Berl),* 174:111–25.

Chen WJ, Chang CH, Liu SK, Hwang TJ, Hwu HG (2004). Sustained attention deficits in nonpsychotic relatives of schizophrenic patients: a recurrence risk ratio analysis. *Biol Psychiatry,* 55:995–1000.

Chen WJ, Faraone SV (2000). Sustained attention deficits as markers of genetic susceptibility to schizophrenia. *Am J Med Genet,* 97(1):52–7.

Chen WJ, Liu SK, Chang CJ, Lien YJ, Chang YH, Hwu HG (1998). Sustained attention deficit and schizotypal personality features in nonpsychotic relatives of schizophrenic patients. *Am J Psychiatry,* 155:1214–20.

Cirillo MA, Seidman LJ (2003). Verbal declarative memory dysfunction in schizophrenia: from clinical assessment to genetics and brain mechanisms. *Neuropsychol Rev,* 13:43–77.

Cohen JD, Servan-Schreiber D (1992). Context, cortex, and dopamine: a connectionist approach to behavior and biology in schizophrenia. *Psychol Rev,* 99:45–77.

Conklin HM, Calkins ME, Anderson CW, Dinzeo TJ, Iacono WG (2002). Recognition memory for faces in schizophrenia patients and their first-degree relatives. *Neuropsychologia,* 40:2314–24.

Conklin HM, Curtis CE, Calkins ME, Iacono WG (2005). Working memory functioning in schizophrenia patients and their first-degree relatives: cognitive functioning shedding light on etiology. *Neuropsychologia,* 43:930–42.

Conklin HM, Curtis CE, Katsanis J, Iacono WG (2000). Verbal working memory impairment in schizophrenia patients and their first-degree relatives: evidence from the digit span task. *Am J Psychiatry,* 157:275–7.

Cornblatt BA, Keilp JG (1994). Impaired attention, genetics, and the pathophysiology of schizophrenia. *Schizophr Bull,* 20:31–46.

Cornblatt BA, Malhotra AK (2001). Impaired attention as an intermediate phenotype for molecular genetic studies of schizophrenia. *Am J Med Genet,* 105:11–15.

Dempster E, Toulopoulou T, McDonald C, Bramon E, Walshe M, Filbey F, Wickham H, Sham PC, Murray RM, Collier DA (2005). Association between BDNF val66 met genotype and episodic memory. *Am J Med Genet B Neuropsychiatr Genet,* 134B(1):73–5.

de Quervain DJ, Henke K, Aerni A, Coluccia D, Wollmer MA, Hock C, et al. (2003). A functional genetic variation of the 5-HT2a receptor affects human memory. *Nat Neurosci*, 6:1141–2.

Donohoe G, Robertson IH (2003). Can specific deficits in executive functioning explain the negative symptoms of schizophrenia? A review. *Neurocase,* 9:97–108.

Donohoe G, Morris DW, Clarke S, McGhee KA, Schwaiger S, Nangle JM, et al. (2007). Variance in neurocognitive performance is associated with dysbindin-1 in schizophrenia: a preliminary study. *Neuropsychologia,* 45(2):454–8.

Donohoe G, Morris DW, Robertson IH, Clarke S, McGhee KA, Schwaiger S, Nangle JM, Gill M, Corvin A (2007). Variance in facial recognition performance associated with BDNF in schizophrenia. *Am J Med Genet B Neuropsychiatr Genet*, 144B(4):578–9.

Egan MF, Goldberg TE, Gscheidle T, Weirich M, Bigelow LB, Weinberger DR (2000). Relative risk of attention deficits in siblings of patients with schizophrenia. *Am J Psychiatry,* 157:1309–16.

Egan MF, Goldberg TE, Gscheidle T, Weirich M, Rawlings R, Hyde TM, et al. (2001). Relative risk for cognitive impairments in siblings of patients with schizophrenia. *Biol Psychiatry,* 50:98–107.

Egan MF, Goldberg TE, Kolachana BS, Callicott JH, Mazzanti CM, Straub RE, et al. (2001). Effect of COMT Val108/158 Met genotype on frontal lobe function and risk for schizophrenia. *Proc Natl Acad Sci USA,* 98:6917–22.

Egan MF, Kojima M, Callicott JH, Goldberg TE, Kolachana BS, Bertolino A, et al. (2003). The BDNF val66met polymorphism affects activity-dependent secretion of BDNF and human memory and hippocampal function. *Cell,* 112:257–69.

Egan MF, Straub RE, Goldberg TE, Yakub I, Callicott JH, Hariri AR, et al. (2004). Variation in GRM3 affects cognition, prefrontal glutamate, and risk for schizophrenia. *Proc Natl Acad Sci USA,* 101:12604–9.

Erlenmeyer-Kimling L, Rock D, Roberts SA, Janal M, Kestenbaum C, Cornblatt B, et al. (2000). Attention, memory, and motor skills as childhood predictors of schizophrenia-related psychoses: the New York High-Risk Project. *Am J Psychiatry,* 157:1416–22.

Fallgatter AJ, Herrmann MJ, Hohoff C, Ehlis AC, Jarczok TA, Freitag CM, and Deckert J (2006). DTNBP1 (dysbindin) gene variants modulate prefrontal brain function in healthy individuals. *Neuropsychopharmacology*, 31(9):2002.

Fan JB, Zhang CS, Gu NF, Li XW, Sun WW, Wang HY, Feng GY, St Clair D, He L (2005). Catechol-O-methyltransferase gene Val/Met functional polymorphism and risk of schizophrenia: a large-scale association study plus meta-analysis. *Biol Psychiatry*, 57(2):139–44.

Fan JB, Sklar P (2005). Meta-analysis reveals association between serotonin transporter gene STin2 VNTR polymorphism and schizophrenia. *Mol Psychiatry,* 10:928–38.

Faraone SV, Seidman LJ, Kremen WS, Pepple JR, Lyons MJ, Tsuang MT (1995). Neuropsychological functioning among the nonpsychotic relatives of schizophrenic patients: a diagnostic efficiency analysis. *J Abnorm Psychol,* 104:286–304.

Faraone SV, Seidman LJ, Kremen WS, Toomey R, Pepple JR, Tsuang MT (1999). Neuropsychological functioning among the nonpsychotic relatives of schizophrenic patients: a 4-year follow-up study. *J Abnorm Psychol*, 108:176–81.

Faraone SV, Seidman LJ, Kremen WS, Toomey R, Pepple JR, Tsuang T (2000). Neuropsychologic functioning among the nonpsychotic relatives of schizophrenic patients: the effect of genetic loading. *Biol Psychiatry*, 48:120–6.

Fernandez G, Effern A, Grunwald T, Pezer N, Lehnertz K, Dumpelmann M, et al. (1999). Real-time tracking of memory formation in the human rhinal cortex and hippocampus. *Science*, 285:1582–5.

Fernandez G, Klaver P, Fell J, Grunwald T, Elger CE (2002). Human declarative memory formation: segregating rhinal and hippocampal contributions. *Hippocampus*, 12:514–9.

Franke P, Maier W, Hardt J, Hain C, Cornblatt BA (1994). Attentional abilities and measures of schizotypy: their variation and covariation in schizophrenic patients, their siblings, and normal control subjects. *Psychiatry Res*, 54:259–72.

Freedman R, Adler LE, Leonard S (1999). Alternative phenotypes for the complex genetics of schizophrenia. *Biol Psychiatry*, 45:51–8.

Freedman R, Olincy A, Ross RG, Waldo MC, Stevens KE, Adler LE, et al. (2003). The genetics of sensory gating deficits in schizophrenia. *Curr Psychiatry Rep*, 5(2):155–61.

Flint J, Munafò MR (2007). The endophenotype concept in psychiatric genetics. *Psychol Med*, 37(2):163–80.

Frayling TM (2007). Genome-wide association studies provide new insights into type 2 diabetes aetiology. *Nat Rev Genet*, 8(9):657–62.

Fuster JM (1999). Synopsis of function and dysfunction of the frontal lobe. *Acta Psychiatrica Scandinavica*, 395:51–7.

Gasperoni TL, Ekelund J, Huttunen M, Palmer CG, Tuulio-Henriksson A, Lonnqvist J, et al. (2003). Genetic linkage and association between chromosome 1q and working memory function in schizophrenia. *Am J Med Genet B Neuropsychiatr Genet*, 116:8–16.

Glahn DC, Therman S, Manninen M, Huttunen M, Kaprio J, Lonnqvist J, et al. (2003). Spatial working memory as an intermediate phenotype for schizophrenia. *Biol Psychiatry*, 53:624–6.

Goldberg TE, Egan MF, Gscheidle T, Coppola R, Weickert T, Kolachana BS, et al. (2003). Executive subprocesses in working memory: relationship to catechol-O-methyltransferase Val158Met genotype and schizophrenia. *Arch Gen Psychiatry*, 60:889–96.

Goldberg TE, Ragland JD, Torrey EF, Gold JM, Bigelow LB, Weinberger DR (1990). Neuropsychological assessment of monozygotic twins discordant for schizophrenia. *Arch Gen Psychiatry*, 47:1066–72.

Goldberg TE, Straub RE, Callicott JH, Hariri A, Mattay VS, Bigelow L, Coppola R, et al. (2006). The G72/G30 gene complex and cognitive abnormalities in schizophrenia. *Neuropsychopharmacology*, 31:2022–32.

Goldberg TE, Torrey EF, Gold JM, Bigelow LB, Ragland RD, Taylor E, et al. (1995). Genetic risk of neuropsychological impairment in schizophrenia: a study of monozygotic twins discordant and concordant for the disorder. *Schizophr Res*, 17:77–84.

Goldberg TE, Torrey EF, Gold JM, Ragland JD, Bigelow LB, Weinberger DR (1993). Learning and memory in monozygotic twins discordant for schizophrenia. *Psychol Med*, 23:71–85.

Goldman-Rakic PS (1999). The physiological approach: functional architecture of working memory and disordered cognition in schizophrenia. *Biol Psychiatry*, 46:650–61.

Good KP, Rabinowitz J, Whitehorn D, Harvey PD, DeSmedt G, Kopala LC (2004). The relationship of neuropsychological test performance with the PANSS in antipsychotic naive, first-episode psychosis patients. *Schizophr Res*, 68:11–19.

Gottesman II, Gould TD (2003). The intermediate phenotype concept in psychiatry: etymology and strategic intentions. *Am J Psychiatry*, 160:636–45.

Gottesman II, Shields J (1972). Schizophrenia and genetics: a twin study vantage point. New York: Academic Press.

Gourovitch ML, Torrey EF, Gold JM, Randolph C, Weinberger DR, Goldberg TE (1999). Neuropsychological performance of monozygotic twins discordant for bipolar disorder. *Biol Psychiatry*, 45:639–46.

Green EK, Raybould R, Macgregor S, Gordon-Smith K, Heron J, Hyde S, et al. (2005). Operation of the schizophrenia susceptibility gene, neuregulin 1, across traditional diagnostic boundaries to increase risk for bipolar disorder. *Arch Gen Psychiatry*, 62:642–8.

Green MF, Kern RS, Braff DL, Mintz J (2000). Neurocognitive deficits and functional outcome in schizophrenia: are we measuring the "right stuff"? *Schizophr Bull*, 26:119–36.

Green MF, Kern RS, Heaton RK (2004). Longitudinal studies of cognition and functional outcome in schizophrenia: implications for MATRICS. *Schizophr Res*, 72:41–51.

Hall J, Whalley HC, Job DE, Baig BJ, McIntosh AM, Evans KL, Thomson PA, Porteous DJ, Cunningham-Owens DG, Johnstone EC, Lawrie SM (2006). A neuregulin 1 variant associated with abnormal cortical function and psychotic symptoms. *Nat Neurosci*, 9(12):1477–8.

Hallmayer JF, Jablensky A, Michie P, Woodbury M, Salmon B, Combrinck J, et al. (2003). Linkage analysis of candidate regions using a composite neurocognitive phenotype correlated with schizophrenia. *Mol Psychiatry*, 8:511–23.

Hallmayer JF, Kalaydjieva L, Badcock J, Dragovic M, Howell S, Michie PT, et al. (2005). Genetic evidence for a distinct subtype of schizophrenia characterized by pervasive cognitive deficit. *Am J Hum Genet*, 77:468–76.

Hariri AR, Goldberg TE, Mattay VS, Kolachana BS, Callicott JH, Egan MF, et al. (2003). Brain-derived neurotrophic factor val66met polymorphism affects human memory-related hippocampal activity and predicts memory performance. *J Neurosci*, 23:6690–4.

Hennah W, Tuulio-Henriksson A, Paunio T, Ekelund J, Varilo T, Partonen T, Cannon TD, Lönnqvist J, Peltonen L (2005). A haplotype within the DISC1 gene is associated with visual memory functions in families with a high density of schizophrenia. *Mol Psychiatry*, 10(12):1097–103.

Heinrichs RW (2004). Meta-analysis and the science of schizophrenia: variant evidence or evidence of variants? *Neurosci Biobehav Rev*, 28:379–94.

Heinrichs RW, Zakzanis KK (1998). Neurocognitive deficit in schizophrenia: a quantitative review of the evidence. *Neuropsychology*, 12:426–45.

Ho BC, Milev P, O'Leary DS, Librant A, Andreasen NC, Wassink TH (2006). Cognitive and magnetic resonance imaging brain morphometric correlates of brain-derived neurotrophic factor Val66Met gene polymorphism in patients with schizophrenia and healthy volunteers. *Arch Gen Psychiatry*, 63:731–40.

Hyman SE, Fenton WS (2003). Medicine. What are the right targets for psychopharmacology? *Science*, 299:350–51.

Javitt DC, Strous RD, Grochowski S, Ritter W, Cowan N (1997). Impaired precision, but normal retention, of auditory sensory ("echoic") memory information in schizophrenia. *J Abnorm Psychol*, 106:315–24.

Jones LA, Cardno AG, Sanders RD, Owen MJ, Williams J (2001). Sustained and selective attention as measures of genetic liability to schizophrenia. *Schizophr Res*, 48:263–72.

Joober R, Gauthier J, Lal S, Bloom D, Lalonde P, Rouleau G, et al. (2002). Catechol-O-methyltransferase Val-108/158-Met gene variants associated with performance on the Wisconsin Card Sorting Test. *Arch Gen Psychiatry*, 59:662–3.

Keefe RS, Lees-Roitman SE, Dupre RL (1997). Performance of patients with schizophrenia on a pen and paper visuospatial working memory task with short delay. *Schizophr Res*, 26:9–14.

Keri S, Janka Z (2004). Critical evaluation of cognitive dysfunctions as intermediate phenotypes of schizophrenia. *Acta Psychiatr Scand*, 110:83–91.

Kohler S, Black SE, Sinden M, Szekely C, Kidron D, Parker JL, et al. (1998). Memory impairments associated with hippocampal versus parahippocampal-gyrus atrophy: an MR volumetry study in Alzheimer's disease. *Neuropsychologia*, 36:901–14.

Kovas Y, Plomin R (2006). Generalist genes: implications for the cognitive sciences. *Trends Cogn Sci*, 10(5):198–203.

Krabbendam L, Marcelis M, Delespaul P, Jolles J, van Os J (2001). Single or multiple familial cognitive risk factors in schizophrenia? *Am J Med Genet* 105:183–8.

Kremen WS, Faraone SV, Seidman LJ, Pepple JR, Tsuang MT (1998). Neuropsychological risk indicators for schizophrenia: a preliminary study of female relatives of schizophrenic and bipolar probands. *Psychiatry Res*, 79:227–40.

Laurent A, Biloa-Tang M, Bougerol T, Duly D, Anchisi AM, Bosson JL, et al. (2000). Executive/attentional performance and measures of schizotypy in patients with schizophrenia and in their nonpsychotic first-degree relatives. *Schizophr Res,* 46:269–83.

Laurent A, Moreaud O, Bosson JL, Naegele B, Boucharlat J, Saoud M, et al. (1999). Neuropsychological functioning among non-psychotic siblings and parents of schizophrenic patients. *Psychiatry Res,* 87:147–57.

Laurent A, Saoud M, Bougerol T, d'Amato T, Anchisi AM, Biloa-Tang M, et al. (1999). Attentional deficits in patients with schizophrenia and in their non-psychotic first-degree relatives. *Psychiatry Res,* 89:147–59.

Lee JC, Everitt BJ, Thomas KL (2004). Independent cellular processes for hippocampal memory consolidation and reconsolidation. *Science,* 304:839–43.

Levy R, Goldman-Rakic PS (2000). Segregation of working memory functions within the dorsolateral prefrontal cortex. *Exp Brain Res,* 133(1):23–32.

Lyons MJ, Toomey R, Seidman LJ, Kremen WS, Faraone SV, Tsuang MT (1995). Verbal learning and memory in relatives of schizophrenics: preliminary findings. *Biol Psychiatry,* 37:750–3.

MacDonald AW 3rd, Carter CS (2003). Event-related FMRI study of context processing in dorsolateral prefrontal cortex of patients with schizophrenia. *J Abnorm Psychol,* 112:689–97.

Malhotra AK, Kestler LJ, Mazzanti C, Bates JA, Goldberg T, Goldman D (2002). A functional polymorphism in the COMT gene and performance on a test of prefrontal cognition. *Am J Psychiatry,* 159:652–4.

Meyer-Lindenberg A, Straub RE, Lipska BK, Verchinski BA, Goldberg T, Callicott JH, Egan MF, Huffaker SS, Mattay VS, Kolachana B, Kleinman JE, Weinberger DR (2007). Genetic evidence implicating DARPP-32 in human frontostriatal structure, function, and cognition. *J Clin Invest,* 117(3):672–82.

Meyer-Lindenberg A, Weinberger DR (2006). Intermediate phenotypes and genetic mechanisms of psychiatric disorders. *Nat Rev Neurosci,* 7:818–27.

McDonald C, Bullmore ET, Sham PC, Chitnis X, Wickham H, Bramon E, et al. (2004). Association of genetic risks for schizophrenia and bipolar disorder with specific and generic brain structural intermediate phenotypes. *Arch Gen Psychiatry,* 61:974–84.

Mutsuddi M, Morris DW, Waggoner SG, Daly MJ, Scolnick EM, Sklar P (2006). Analysis of high-resolution HapMap of DTNBP1 (Dysbindin) suggests no consistency between reported common variant associations and schizophrenia. *Am J Hum Genet,* 79(5):903–9.

Myles-Worsley M, Park S (2002). Spatial working memory deficits in schizophrenia patients and their first degree relatives from Palau, Micronesia. *Am J Med Genet,* 114:609–15.

Niendam TA, Bearden CE, Rosso IM, Sanchez LE, Hadley T, Nuechterlein KH, et al. (2003). A prospective study of childhood neurocognitive functioning in schizophrenic patients and their siblings. *Am J Psychiatry,* 160:2060–2.

Nieuwenstein MR, Aleman A, de Haan EH (2001). Relationship between symptom dimensions and neurocognitive functioning in schizophrenia: a meta-analysis of WCST and CPT studies. Wisconsin Card Sorting Test. Continuous Performance Test. *J Psychiatr Res*, 35:119–25.

Nolan KA, Bilder RM, Lachman HM, Volavka J (2004). Catechol O-methyltransferase Val158Met polymorphism in schizophrenia: differential effects of Val and Met alleles on cognitive stability and flexibility. *Am J Psychiatry*, 161:359–61.

O'Donovan MC, Williams NM, Owen MJ (2003). Recent advances in the genetics of schizophrenia. *Hum Mol Genet*, 12 Spec No 2:R125–33.

O'Driscoll GA, Florencio PS, Gagnon D, Wolff AV, Benkelfat C, Mikula L, et al. (2001). Amygdala–hippocampal volume and verbal memory in first-degree relatives of schizophrenic patients. *Psychiatry Res*, 107:75–85.

Owen MJ, Williams NM, O'Donovan MC (2004). The molecular genetics of schizophrenia: new findings promise new insights. *Mol Psychiatry*, 9:14–27.

Park S, Holzman PS, Goldman-Rakic PS (1995). Spatial working memory deficits in the relatives of schizophrenic patients. *Arch Gen Psychiatry*, 52:821–8.

Passingham R (1998). Attention to action. In Robbins TW, Roberts AC, Weiskratz L, eds. The prefrontal cortex: executive and cognitive functions (pp. 131–43). Oxford: Oxford University Press.

Paunio T, Tuulio-Henriksson A, Hiekkalinna T, Perola M, Varilo T, Partonen T, et al. (2004). Search for cognitive trait components of schizophrenia reveals a locus for verbal learning and memory on 4q and for visual working memory on 2q. *Hum Mol Genet*, 13:1693–702.

Perlstein WM, Dixit NK, Carter CS, Noll DC, Cohen JD (2003). Prefrontal cortex dysfunction mediates deficits in working memory and prepotent responding in schizophrenia. *Biol Psychiatry*, 53:25–38.

Quraishi S, Frangou S (2002). Neuropsychology of bipolar disorder: a review. *J Affect Disord*, 72:209–26.

Reuter B, Kathmann N (2004). Using saccade tasks as a tool to analyze executive dysfunctions in schizophrenia. *Acta Psychol (Amst)*, 115:255–69.

Raz A, Buhle J (2006). Typologies of attentional networks. *Nat Rev Neurosci*, 7(5):367–79.

Rosa A, Peralta V, Cuesta MJ, Zarzuela A, Serrano F, Martinez-Larrea A, et al. (2004). New evidence of association between COMT gene and prefrontal neurocognitive function in healthy individuals from sibling pairs discordant for psychosis. *Am J Psychiatry*, 161:1110–2.

Rybakowski JK, Borkowska A, Czerski PM, Kapelski P, Hauser J (2004). Performance on prefrontal test in schizophrenia and polymorphism of dopamine transporter gene. *Am J Med Genet B Neuropsychiatr Genet*, 130B:59.

Salgado-Pineda P, Baeza I, Perez-Gomez M, Vendrell P, Junque C, Bargallo N, et al. (2003). Sustained attention impairment correlates to gray matter decreases in first episode neuroleptic-naive schizophrenic patients. *Neuroimage*, 19:365–75.

Saoud M, d'Amato T, Gutknecht C, Triboulet P, Bertaud JP, Marie-Cardine M, et al. (2000). Neuropsychological deficit in siblings discordant for schizophrenia. *Schizophr Bull*, 26:893–902.

Schreiber H, Rothmeier J, Becker W, Jurgens R, Born J, Stolz-Born G, et al. (1995). Comparative assessment of saccadic eye movements, psychomotor and cognitive performance in schizophrenics, their first-degree relatives and control subjects. *Acta Psychiatr Scand*, 91:195–201.

Schumacher J, Abon Jamra R, Becker T, Klopp N, Franke P, Jacob C, et al. (2004). Investigation of the DAOA/G30 locus in panic disorder. *Mol Psychiatry*, 10:428–9.

Scoville WB, Milner B (1957). Loss of recent memory after bilateral hippocampal lesions. *J Neurochem*, 20:11–21.

Shallice T (1988). From neuropsychology to mental structure. New York: Cambridge University Press.

Shedlack K, Lee G, Sakuma M, Xie SH, Kushner M, Pepple J, et al. (1997). Language processing and memory in ill and well siblings from multiplex families affected with schizophrenia. *Schizophr Res*, 25:43–52.

Snitz BE, Macdonald AW 3rd, Carter CS (2006). Cognitive deficits in unaffected first-degree relatives of schizophrenia patients: a meta-analytic review of putative endophenotypes. *Schizophr Bull*, 32(1):179–94.

Squire LR, Zola SM (1996). Structure and function of declarative and nondeclarative memory systems. *Proc Natl Acad Sci USA*, 93:13515–22.

Squire LR, Stark CE, Clark RE (2004). The medial temporal lobe. *Annu Rev Neurosci*, 27:279–306.

Staal WG, Hijman R, Hulshoff Pol HE, Kahn RS (2000). Neuropsychological dysfunctions in siblings discordant for schizophrenia. *Psychiatry Res*, 95:227–35.

Stefanis NC, van Os J, Avramopoulos D, Smyrnis N, Evdokimidis I, Hantoumi I, et al. (2004). Variation in catechol-O-methyltransferase val158 met genotype associated with schizotypy but not cognition: a population study in 543 young men. *Biol Psychiatry*, 56:510–5.

Stefanis NC, Trikalinos TA, Avramopoulos D, Smyrnis N, Evdokimidis I, Ntzani EE, Ioannidis JP, Stefanis CN (2007). Impact of schizophrenia candidate genes on schizotypy and cognitive endophenotypes at the population level. *Biol Psychiatry*, 62(7):784–92.

Straub RE, Jiang Y, MacLean CJ, Ma Y, Webb BT, Myakishev MV, et al. (2002). Genetic variation in the 6p22.3 gene DTNBP1, the human ortholog of the mouse dysbindin gene, is associated with schizophrenia. *Am J Hum Genet*, 71:337–48.

Swanson J, Oosterlaan J, Murias M, Schuck S, Flodman P, Spence MA, et al. (2000). Attention deficit/hyperactivity disorder children with a 7-repeat allele of the dopamine receptor D4 gene have extreme behavior but normal performance on critical neuropsychological tests of attention. *Proc Natl Acad Sci USA*, 97:4754–9.

Tan YL, Zhou DF, Cao LY, Zou YZ, Wu GY, Zhang XY (2005). Effect of the BDNF Val66Met genotype on episodic memory in schizophrenia. *Schizophr Res*, 77:355–6.

Tan HY, Chen Q, Sust S, Buckholtz JW, Meyers JD, Egan MF, Mattay VS, Meyer-Lindenberg A, Weinberger DR, Callicott JH (2007). Epistasis between catechol-O-methyltransferase and type II metabotropic glutamate receptor 3 genes on working memory brain function. *Proc Natl Acad Sci USA*, 104(30):12536–41.

Toomey R, Faraone SV, Seidman LJ, Kremen WS, Pepple JR, Tsuang MT (1998). Association of neuropsychological vulnerability markers in relatives of schizophrenic patients. *Schizophr Res*, 31:89–98.

Toulopoulou T, Morris RG, Rabe-Hesketh S, Murray RM (2003). Selectivity of verbal memory deficit in schizophrenic patients and their relatives. *Am J Med Genet B Neuropsychiatr Genet*, 116:1–7.

Toulopoulou T, Rabe-Hesketh S, King H, Murray RM, Morris RG (2003). Episodic memory in schizophrenic patients and their relatives. *Schizophr Res*, 63:261–71.

Tsai SJ, Yu YW, Chen TJ, Chen JY, Liou YJ, Chen MC, et al. (2003). Association study of a functional catechol-O-methyltransferase-gene polymorphism and cognitive function in healthy females. *Neurosci Lett*, 338:123–6.

Tully T (1997). Regulation of gene expression and its role in long-term memory and synaptic plasticity. *Proc Natl Acad Sci USA*, 94:4239–41.

Tulving E (1985). How many memory systems are there? *Am Psychologist* 40:385–98.

Tuulio-Henriksson A, Arajarvi R, Partonen T, Haukka J, Varilo T, Schreck M, et al. (2003). Familial loading associates with impairment in visual span among healthy siblings of schizophrenia patients. *Biol Psychiatry*, 54:623–8.

Tuulio-Henriksson A, Haukka J, Partonen T, Varilo T, Paunio T, Ekelund J, et al. (2002). Heritability and number of quantitative trait loci of neurocognitive functions in families with schizophrenia. *Am J Med Genet*, 114:483–90.

Volz H, Gaser C, Hager F, Rzanny R, Ponisch J, Mentzel H, et al. (1999). Decreased frontal activation in schizophrenics during stimulation with the continuous performance test—a functional magnetic resonance imaging study. *Eur Psychiatry*, 14:17–24.

Wassink TH, Nopoulos P, Pietila J, Crowe RR, Andreasen NC (2003). NOTCH4 and the frontal lobe in schizophrenia. *Am J Med Genet B Neuropsychiatr Genet*, 118:1–7.

Weickert TW, Goldberg TE, Marenco S, Bigelow LB, Egan MF, Weinberger DR (2003). Comparison of cognitive performances during a placebo period and an atypical antipsychotic treatment period in schizophrenia: critical examination of confounds. *Neuropsychopharmacology*, 28: 1491–1500.

Weinberger DR, Egan MF, Bertolino A, Callicott JH, Mattay VS, Lipska BK, et al. (2001). Prefrontal neurons and the genetics of schizophrenia. *Biol Psychiatry*, 50:825–44.

Wechsler D (1998). Wechsler Memory Scale, third edition (WAIS–III). New York: Psychological Corporation.

Wechsler, D. (2000): Weschler Adult Intelligence Scale, Third edition (WAIS-III). Psychological Corporation, New York.

Whyte MC, McIntosh AM, Johnstone EC, Lawrie SM (2005). Declarative memory in unaffected adult relatives of patients with chizophrenia: a systematic review and meta-analysis. *Schizophr Res*, 78(1):13–26.

Wilson RS, Bienias JL, Berry-Kravis E, Evans DA, Bennett DA (2002). The apolipoprotein E epsilon 2 allele and decline in episodic memory. *J Neurol Neurosurg Psychiatry,* 73:672–7.

10 The Genetic Basis for the Cognitive Deterioration of Alzheimer's Disease

John M. Ringman and Jeffrey L. Cummings

The past half-century has brought unprecedented advances in our understanding of the genetic basis of human variation and disease. The genetic origins of phenotypes that are readily attributable solely to genetic factors (e.g., eye color) have been the easiest to define. The genetic bases of more complex phenotypes such as cognitive ability are harder to define because (1) the most appropriate ways to measure them are controversial, (2) they are influenced by many epigenetic and environmental factors, and (3) they are undoubtedly subject to the influence of many genes with diverse functions. The genetic bases for adult-onset dementing illnesses have been even more challenging to characterize because of the additional complication of uncertain disease penetrance due to their onset late in life. Nonetheless, significant progress has been made in delineating the genes involved in many neurological diseases with onset in adulthood (see table 10.1). Among these, Alzheimer's disease (AD) has emerged as a model for polygenetic illnesses in which the condition is subject to influence by genes with both deterministic and probabilistic effects. The purpose of this chapter is to review the genetic basis of cognitive decline in AD.

The chain of events leading from DNA sequence to cognitive phenotype is complex, and not surprisingly many sequence variants have been purported to contribute to cognitive decline or behavioral phenotypes within the context of neurodegenerative diseases. In order to define a specific role of a gene variant on cognition, one must consider multiple levels of explanation. For instance, if it is demonstrated that allele X exerts its effect on disease Y by causing a relative increase in the production of protein Z, one is still left wondering how the neuroanatomical and neurophysiological substrates that ultimately mediate the cognitive effect have been altered. For this reason, we have chosen to focus our review on AD, a condition in which the roles of specific genes are relatively well established. This will hopefully allow us to understand the connections between DNA and cognition in more depth.

Many protein products of genes implicated in neurodegenerative disorders are pleiotropic, that is, have diverse chemical and structural intra- and extracellular roles. As the biochemical function of genes involved in neurodegenerative diseases are

Table 10.1

Partial list of genetically inherited conditions in which intellectual decline in adulthood is a prominent feature

Disease Entity	Product of Causative Genes
Alzheimer's disease	Amyloid precursor protein Presenilin 1 Presenilin 2 Apolipoprotein E (susceptibility gene)
Frontotemporal lobar degenerations	Microtubule-associated protein tau Progranulin Chromatin modifying protein 2B Valosin-containing protein
Huntington's disease	Huntingtin
Spinocerebellar ataxias	Various
Wilson's disease	ATP7B
Parkinson's disease	Alpha-synuclein Dardarin Parkin DJ-1 Pink-1 LRRK2

Prion diseases
    Familial Creutzfeldt–Jakob disease
    Gerstmann–Sträussler–Scheinker
    Fatal familial insomnia
	Prion protein (PRNP)

Mitochondrial disorders
    Mitochondrial encephalomyopathy lactic acidosis
    and stroke-like episodes (MELAS)
	tRNALeu(UUR)

Cerebral autosomal dominant arteriopathy with subcortical infarcts and leukoencephalopathy	Notch3

elucidated in vitro and in animal models, an emerging theme is that many appear to play roles in development and cellular repair. It therefore appears that late-life neuro-degenerative diseases may, at least in some cases, be conceived of as being due to developmental abnormalities. An illustrative example in which the distinction between a developmental and degenerative disorder is blurred is that of Rett syndrome (RS). RS is a rare disorder in which children (predominantly girls) develop normally during the first few months but between 6 and 18 months of life begin to lose motor and speech skills. Growth retardation occurs and neurological function worsens with many affected persons developing seizures and autistic behaviors. Persons with RS typically regress to the point of an essentially vegetative state by age 8 (Hagberg et al. 1983). In 1999 mutations in the gene coding for methyl-CpG-binding protein (MeCP2) located on the X chromosome were found to be responsible (Amir et al. 1999). MeCP2 is found early in mature neurons; it binds to methylated DNA and represses the transcription of many genes (Caballero and Hendrich 2005), including the gene coding for brain-derived neurotrophic factor (BDNF; Martinowich et al. 2003). Though the specific genes, overexpression of which is critical in causing RS, have yet to be unequivocally identified, BDNF is required for maintenance and growth of neurons during development, and misregulation of its expression provides a testable model for the etiology of RS. RS therefore provides an example in which a degenerative disorder appears after a period of normal development, albeit in childhood. Other examples of illnesses in which the distinction between developmental and degenerative disorders is blurred are childhood-onset Huntington's disease (Gonzalez-Alegre and Afifi 2006) and the changes of AD occurring in Down's syndrome (DS) that will be discussed in more depth below.

Part of the definition of dementia of the Alzheimer's type as per the *Diagnostic and Statistical Manual of Mental Disorders*, fourth edition, is that the "course is characterized by gradual onset and continuing cognitive decline." Dementia is generally conceived of as being composed of acquired cognitive deficits. It is also the case that the genetically determined dementias, in which the responsible genetic alterations have been present since conception, have their principal manifestations after some delay in adulthood. However, it is possible that some genetic variations that are known to cause progressive dementia (a state) might also have more subtle, lifelong influences on cognition and behavior (a trait) through their roles in development. There is some evidence for this that will be discussed below.

Alzheimer's Disease

AD is a clinicopathologic entity defined by the presence of a dementing syndrome associated with distinctive pathological changes. The cognitive presentation typically begins with loss of recent episodic memory followed over months to years by deficits in executive function, visuospatial function, language, and praxis. There are, however, many exceptions to this pattern (Galton et al. 2000) in that visuopatial deficits (posterior cortical atrophy; Renner et al. 2004), language deficits (primary progressive aphasia; Li et al. 2000), or even asymmetrical motor deficits (akin to those of corticobasal degeneration; Doran et al. 2003) can initially dominate the clinical picture.

The pathology diagnostic of AD consists of diffuse and neuritic senile plaques (SPs) as well as neurofibrillary tangles (NFTs) with a characteristic distribution. SPs consist of extracellular depositions of proteins including various isoforms of beta-amyloid protein (Aβ), alpha-antichymotrypsin, and apolipoprotein E (APOE). There are also cellular elements including dystrophic processes of neurons and glia as well as microglial cells. In mature neuritic SPs, the neuronal processes contain paired helical filaments (PHFs) that are, in turn, composed in part of abnormally phosphorylated tau protein. These PHFs consist of other cytoskeletal elements as well and are also found as NFTs within the cell bodies of dying neurons and as extracellular "ghost tangles" spatially distinct from SPs. Intraneuronal protein aggregates termed Lewy bodies that consist, in part, of the protein alpha-synuclein are found in the brain in approximately 60% of AD cases (Hamilton 2000). Lewy bodies are classically associated with a phenotype consisting of, in addition to progressive dementia, Parkinsonism, delirium-like fluctuations in mental status, and visual hallucinations (McKeith et al. 1996). They are most frequently found in the amygdala but are also found in the cortex and are equally prevalent in sporadic AD, familial AD (FAD), and DS (Hamilton 2000).

Though many specifics regarding the etiology of AD remain to be worked out, extensive genetic, pathological, and animal studies have suggested the following (simplified) chain of events in the cause of AD. Aberrant posttranslational processing of amyloid precursor protein (APP) leads to a relative overproduction of the forty-two-amino-acid-length version of Aβ (Aβ_{42}; Scheuner et al. 1996). Aβ_{42} monomer or oligomeric aggregates of Aβ_{42} are neurotoxic and trigger neuronal dysfunction and death (Gong et al. 2003). This also ultimately leads to the deposition of Aβ in plaques, but the relative importance of soluble and plaque-associated Aβ in causing the symptoms of the illness is an area of active investigation. The extent and location of NFT formation tend to correlate better with clinical status than do that of SPs (Gomez-Isla et al. 1997). NFT formation occurs in a number of diverse neurological conditions and may therefore represent a nonspecific response to toxic influences (Wisniewski et al. 1979). As a marker of a final common pathway for neuronal death, NFT formation might therefore be expected to correlate better with patients' status. Studies of a triple transgenic mouse model (featuring the betaAPPSwe, the M146V PS1, and the P301L tau mutations) that duplicate the pathological aspects of human AD with some fidelity appear to confirm this chain of events (Oddo et al. 2006).

The hierarchical distribution of AD, particularly NFT, pathology explains the progression of symptoms observed in the condition. Studies of persons dying with dementia have demonstrated that the highest concentration of NFTs are found in the periallocortex and allocortex of the medial temporal lobe followed by portions of the amygdala and the nucleus basalis of Meynert, followed by the proisocortex and heteromodal association cortex (Arnold et al. 1991). Primary motor and sensory cortex are relatively spared. SPs are more evenly distributed throughout cortex and are less evident in the medial temporal lobe. In persons dying with a progressive but isolated memory impairment (amnestic mild cognitive impairment), NFTs were found in the medial temporal lobe (Petersen et al. 2006). Spread of these NFTs to the neocortex was associated with more global cognitive impairment. The cause of the memory deficits occurring early in AD therefore may be attributed to NFT formation and related neuronal loss (Gomez-Isla et al. 1996) occurring in structures critical for memory formation.

Despite this association, it has been known that the brains of some persons dying without any known cognitive decline feature varying degrees of AD pathology (Arriagada et al. 1992), including, in some cases, an advanced stage of disease (Snowdon 2003). These imperfect correlations between neuropathological changes and clinical status are likely due, at least in part, to variable "cognitive reserve" between persons. That is, there are individual differences in people's ability to compensate for the effects of brain damage (e.g., due to the neuronal loss of AD) before showing symptoms (Stern 2006). These may be related to genetic predisposition and environmental influences (e.g., nutritional and educational) as well as things as mundane as one's premorbid test-taking abilities.

AD is classically defined as a unitary entity in which the typical clinical picture occurs in association with the pathological changes described above. However, as our understanding of the genetic origins of the common "sporadic" late-onset form, the young-onset familial forms, and AD associated with DS has advanced, AD has now been established to be a model of genetic heterogeneity. That is, diverse genetic influences give rise to a common phenotype, and therefore it may be more appropriate to refer to the condition as the "Alzheimer's diseases." In the following sections, we will discuss genetic factors known to contribute to this clinical–pathological phenotype.

Amyloid Precursor Protein (Chromosome 21)

Families with a young-onset form of FAD in which the inheritance appeared to be autosomal dominant in nature have been known to exist for nearly as long as AD has been defined (Lowenberg and Waggoner 1934). This form of AD is rare, estimated to account for between 2% and 5% of AD cases, though an accurate number is lacking because of difficulty in determining the appropriate denominator. It had also been recognized for some time that all persons with DS who survive into their sixth decade have the pathological features of AD in their brain (Mann 2004). As DS is due to triplication of chromosome 21 in 95% of cases and the gene for APP, metabolites of which are major constituents of the SPs that characterize the disorder, is found on chromosome 21, the search for a genetic cause of AD focused on this region. Linkage of a single family with young-onset AD to a missense mutation in the APP gene was achieved in 1991 (Goate et al. 1991). To date, at least twenty-three different missense mutations in the APP gene have been associated with FAD (www.molgen.ua.ac.be/ADMutations, accessed February 6, 2009), and more recently five families in which complete duplication of the APP gene is responsible for the disease have been identified (Rovelet-Lecrux et al. 2006). Collectively, however, APP alterations account for a small percentage (estimated at 15%; Campion et al. 1999) of FAD cases.

Biochemical studies suggest that these genetic alterations cause AD by causing aberrant metabolism of APP (Scheuner et al. 1996; Hori et al. 2007), and there is recent preliminary evidence that variability in the promoter region of APP might contribute to AD risk (Brouwers et al. 2006). The neuropathological manifestations of APP mutations (and FAD in general) are generally typical of those of sporadic AD of later onset. However, at least two APP mutations have been associated with deposition of amyloid primarily in the blood vessels and present clinically with recurrent cerebral hemorrhages (Levy et al. 1990).

Persons with pathogenic APP alterations tend to demonstrate unequivocal symptoms of disease at a mean age in the 50s (Lippa et al. 2000; Mullan et al. 1993a). The cognitive phenotype is similar to that seen with "sporadic" AD of later onset. Two reports of independent pedigrees with different substitutions at the same codon (717) in APP both found deficits in recent memory, cognitive processing speed, and attention to complex cognitive sets with sparing of language and visuospatial function early in the course of the disorder (Karlinsky et al. 1992; Farlow et al. 1994). Affected members of two families with a V717I substitution from the United Kingdom presented with memory impairment and dyscalculia (Rossor et al. 1993). Lack of insight into the illness was a significant feature in members of a family with a V717G mutation in APP(35). Memory deficits were again the predominant presenting symptom in two members of a Japanese family with a D678N substitution in APP (Wakutani et al. 2004).

In addition to cognitive deterioration, nearly 90% of persons with late-onset AD develop clinically significant behavioral abnormalities over the course of the disease (Mega et al. 1996). Apathy is common, followed by agitation, anxiety, and depression. In FAD due to APP mutations, antisocial behavior has been observed in at least two affected members of one family with a T714I mutation (Edwards-Lee et al. 2005). Persons in the preclinical stage of the condition offer the opportunity to characterize behavioral changes during the preclinical phase of the disease. In a description of multiple pedigrees with the V717I mutation in APP, Mullan et al. (1993b) reported that relatives noted personality changes including apathy and withdrawal in subsequently affected persons years prior to cognitive symptoms. As such psychiatric and behavioral abnormalities are common in the population overall, blinded and objective studies in preclinical FAD mutation carriers with appropriate controls are necessary to establish whether or not such behavioral changes precede cognitive deterioration in FAD.

Though the cognitive deterioration in APP-related FAD is similar to that seen in late-onset AD, other noncognitive features are less typical. The age of onset is, of course, younger, and myoclonus and seizures, which frequently occur late in the course of late-onset AD, can occur early in FAD associated with APP alterations (Rossor et al. 1993). Also, the course of FAD is generally more aggressive with average life span being shorter (Swearer et al. 1996).

Down's Syndrome

Essentially all patients with typical DS who live beyond age 50 have AD pathology in their brain (Mann 2004). In addition to the 95% of cases of DS that are due to triplication of all of chromosome 21, approximately 4% of DS cases are due to partial trisomy in which translocations of the distal portion of the long arm of this chromosome are duplicated on chromosome 14 or 22. This region, triplication of which is critical for development of the DS phenotype, is near the locus for the APP gene. A case of such a translocation in which no pathological changes of AD were seen in the brain of a woman dying at age 78 was found by fluorescent in situ hybridization not to have triplication of the APP gene despite having the rest of the DS phenotype (Prasher et al. 1998). Higher levels of the $A\beta_{40}$ and $A\beta_{42}$ metabolic products of APP have been observed in the plasma of persons with DS (Tokuda et al. 1997), providing convincing evidence that it is indeed triplication of the APP gene that underlies the formation of SPs and NFTs in the brains of DS patients.

There are differences between the brains of young persons with DS and the population at large that are no doubt related to the baseline intellectual deficits and potentially to the ultimate manifestations of progressive cognitive decline. The brain is shortened in the anterior–posterior direction with the frontal lobes, cerebellum, and hippocampi being smaller (Crome and Stern 1972). Neuronal count is low in temporal cortex, hippocampus, and brain stem (Ross et al. 1984). Abnormal dendritic spines and synaptogenesis as well as delayed myelination have all been found, and it is hypothesized that the abnormal wiring seen in DS results from difficulties coordinating the growth and transcription factors normally involved in brain development (Mann 2004).

SPs begin to appear in the brains of some persons with DS in the second decade of life, and their prevalence increases rapidly over the following decades until the 40s and 50s at which time they are present in nearly 100% of DS brains (Mann 2004). The essentially inevitable development of AD pathology in DS has allowed extensive study of the sequence of events leading to full-blown AD through the postmortem examination of the brains of persons with DS dying at different ages (Mann 2004). These studies have revealed that diffuse SPs (containing mostly $A\beta_{42}$) initially form in the cortex (especially, the parahippocampal and middle and inferior temporal gyri). Neuritic SPs which contain microglial cells, $A\beta_{40}$, and numerous other proteins and proteoglycans as well as dystrophic cell processes and PHFs form later in these areas as well as in the hippocampus and in more widespread areas of cortex. NFTs are initially found in the entorhinal cortex, hippocampus, and amygdala and later in the cortex. This chain of events appears to be similar to that of sporadic AD, and the ultimate pathological pictures of AD and DS are essentially indistinguishable.

The cognitive manifestations of these pathological changes are somewhat difficult to define because of the challenge of applying standard diagnostic criteria for dementia to individuals with a mental retardation syndrome. Normative measures for neuropsychological tests do not apply to this population, and, therefore, ideally one should demonstrate a decline in intellectual function through sequential testing. Also, to demonstrate functional decline, one must have reliable information on persons' baseline level of self-care. Because of these issues and differences in the way dementia is diagnosed in persons with DS, studies of the prevalence of clinical dementia in persons with DS have had variable results. Using one set of criteria (the Cambridge Examination for Mental Disorders of the Elderly criteria), one group of investigators found the prevalence of dementia to be 3.4% in the 30- to 39-year-old age group, increasing to 40% in the 50- to 59-year-old age group (Holland et al. 1998). This finding is in agreement with others in that it suggests that the cognitive impairment occurring in DS lags behind the pathological changes of AD by years or decades. In order to reconcile this finding with the cognitive reserve hypothesis discussed above, one must speculate that even persons with DS have some ability to compensate for brain injury. In addition, one must consider other influences besides AD pathology on cognition in DS such as hypothyroidism and menopausal state (Schupf et al. 2003). In a prospective four-year study in which persons with DS underwent sequential neuropsychological testing, deficits in memory and orientation preceded aphasia, agnosia, and apraxia in a manner similar to that seen in sporadic AD(47). Other investigators have emphasized premorbid impairment of abilities attributable to the frontal lobe in DS (Rowe et al. 2006) that are exacerbated early in DS dementia (Holland et al. 2000; Nelson et al. 2001). This is consistent with a low reserve capacity for these functions that consequently manifest early in disease progression.

Presenilins

Alterations of the genes coding for presenilin 1 (PS1) on chromosome 14 (Sherrington et al. 1995; Schellenberg et al. 1992) and presenilin 2 (PS2) on chromosome 1 (Rogaev et al. 1995) were identified as causes of familial AD in the mid-1990s. To date, 168 alterations in the PS1 gene thought to be pathogenic have been identified, and alterations of PS1 (www.molgen.ua.ac.be/ADMutations, accessed February 6, 2009) are thought to account for around 56% of autosomal dominant FAD cases (Campion et al. 1999). PS2 mutations, however, are much less frequent (Sherrington et al. 1996) with only fourteen pathogenic mutations having been identified.

Molecular biology studies have identified many roles the presenilin proteins appear to play in cells. Multiple studies have confirmed that presenilin is part of the enzyme complex responsible for the gamma-secretase activity that is part of the pathway by which APP is cleaved into $A\beta_{40}$ and $A\beta_{42}$ fragments (Brunkan and Goate 2005). Pathogenic mutations of PS1 are widely thought to cause FAD by favoring the gamma-secretase cleavage of APP into the $A\beta_{42}$ isoform (Scheuner et al. 1996), though this enzyme complex also cleaves a number of other proteins (Brunkan and Goate 2005). Also, many other functions of PS1 have been identified, including roles in oxidative stress (Cecchi et al. 2002), immune function (Tournoy et al. 2004), and that of a calcium channel (Leissring et al. 2001). Whether through its gamma-secretase activity or other pathways, PS1 also seems to play a role in neural development. Embryos of transgenic mice in which both copies of the PS1 gene have been knocked out have abnormalities of neuronal migration and differentiation characterized by disorganization of the cerebral cortex (Handler et al. 2000). Also, a patient with a PS1 mutation who developed young-onset AD and came to autopsy was noted to have ectopic neurons in the white matter (Takao et al. 2001). Furthermore, mice in which PS1 is conditionally knocked out develop a neurodegenerative disease that appears to be independent of $A\beta_{42}$ generation (Saura et al. 2004; Marjaux et al. 2004). These observations indicate that a comprehensive explanation of PS1 function is still forthcoming but that it may contribute to clinical FAD through effects both in development and senescence.

FAD due to mutations of the PS1 gene typically has the youngest age of onset (44–46 years of age) followed by APP (49) with PS2 mutation causing the oldest (58–59) and most variable age of onset (Lippa et al. 2000). The cognitive changes that occur in preclinical and clinically affected persons with PS1 mutations have been described. In 1995 Kennedy et al. described the results of neuropsychological testing in three members of a family whose disease was linked to chromosome 14 (Kennedy et al. 1995). These investigators reported initial deficits in verbal and global memory with subsequent decline in arithmetic and spatial skills. They also felt that language was less fluent in these subjects compared to those with late-onset AD. This group described similar findings in affected members of two other families with PS1 mutations in a later paper (Fox et al. 1997). When they compared deficits between persons with familial AD due to mutations in PS1 and APP to those of persons with sporadic AD, they found that persons with familial AD had relatively spared object naming and perception though they scored lower on a verbal intelligence test. They also made the observation that the age of disease onset within a family with a PS1 mutations tended to be fairly consistent. Lopera et al. reported deficits on nearly every measure in the administered battery in affected members of a large Columbian family with a PS1 mutation (Lopera et al. 1997). They performed repeated testing on 12 patients and found further decline in verbal memory, language, and on tests of construction and abstraction over the following eighteen months (Rosselli et al. 2000).

An early description of cognitive changes in preclinical familial AD was reported in 1994 (Newman et al. 1994). In this report, a person at risk for familial AD had a relatively selective verbal memory deficit twenty-six months prior to presenting for

assessment for a subjective cognitive problem. This deficit was followed by other recognition deficits and problems performing the Wisconsin Card Sort Test. This same
group later reported their findings of serial neuropsychological testing in 63 subjects
at risk for familial AD assessed over six years (Fox et al. 1998). The 10 patients that
worsened to the point of being diagnosed with AD over this period again showed
the pattern of initial verbal memory deficits but also lower performance IQ scores
before more global cognitive dysfunction occurred. Neuropsychological testing was
performed at baseline and one year later in 14 Mexican persons at risk for familial
AD who had not yet been diagnosed with dementia (Diaz-Olavarrieta et al. 1997). At
baseline, 6 subjects had significant memory deficits relative to controls of which 4 also
had visuospatial deficits and 3 of these had language deficits as well. These deficits
persisted after one year. In a follow-up study of the Mexican population, Ringman
et al. performed cognitive testing on 51 nondemented persons (30 mutation carriers
and 21 noncarriers) at risk for PS1 mutations (Ringman et al. 2005). They found that
mutation carriers scored worse on the Mini-Mental State Examination (MMSE), the
Trails Making Test Parts A and B, delayed recall of a ten-word list, and the Wechsler
Adult Intelligence Scale Block Design test. Depression scores, gender, and whether or
not an APOE ε4 allele was present did not consistently affect test scores. This work
supports the notion that neuropsychological changes occurring early in AD can be
studied in persons at risk for familial AD and that the changes observed parallel those
seen in sporadic AD. In a large study of members of the Columbian family at risk for
a PS1 mutation, 122 subjects received neuropsychological and genetic testing (Ardila
et al. 2000). When the scores of mutation carriers ($n = 40$) were compared to those of
noncarriers ($n = 82$), no differences were seen except on some measures of intrusions
during verbal memory testing. When the 40 mutation carriers were divided into those
with ($n = 10$) and without ($n = 30$) memory complaints, those with complaints scored
worse on the MMSE, multiple verbal memory tests, and numerous other subtests.

In the study of Ringman et al. (2005), when the subjects were divided into tertiles
depending on their age in relation to the typical age of dementia diagnosis in their
family, only the oldest group that were a mean of 5 years prior to the age of diagnosis
showed cognitive deficits. This differs from the results of a similar study of persons at
risk for frontotemporal dementia by virtue of the P301L *tau* mutation, in which subjects carrying this mutation demonstrated deficits in executive function characteristic
of the disease as early as the second and third decades of life (Geschwind et al. 2001).
As the typical age of onset of clinical disease in this latter family was in the 50s, it
was argued that the early deficits represented a developmental deficiency due to the
tau mutation. The absence of early cognitive differences in PS1 mutation carriers in
the study of Ringman et al. might suggest that despite a potential role of PS1 in
normal development, the mutations have their predominant effect later in life (e.g.,
as beta-amyloid accumulates). In the population studied by Ringman et al., however,

there was a tendency for PS1 mutation carriers to obtain less education overall than noncarriers (Ringman et al. 2007). Therefore, it is still possible that subtle cognitive deficits not detectable with standard neuropsychological testing or psychiatric differences (e.g., depression or reduced motivation; Ringman et al. 2004) in young PS1 mutation carriers might adversely impact academic achievement. Furthermore, taking into account the family-specific age of onset allows the more accurate prediction of decline.

FAD due to mutations in the gene for PS2 are rare with much data coming from studies of different persons with a single mutation that represents a founder effect traced to Germans living in the Volga region of Russia (Bird et al. 1988). PS2 has the oldest (Lippa et al. 2000) and most variable (Sherrington et al. 1996; Ezquerra et al. 2003) age of onset. A neuropsychological study of one family with the M239V substitution in the PS2 gene found anosognosia, visuospatial agnosia, apraxia, and fluent aphasia in the affected proband (Giovagnoli et al. 2006). Of three related preclinical mutation carriers, one was judged to have normal cognition, another had constructive apraxia, and the third had spatial perception and memory deficits. These authors concluded posterior cortical areas were disproportionately involved in this family.

Though there are some clinical differences between FAD and sporadic AD of older onset, the cognitive deficits are similar and any differences present appear to be quantitative in nature rather than qualitative. The study of FAD therefore provides a model for the disease from the molecular level to the clinical level.

Apolipoprotein E

The gene coding for APOE is polymorphic in human populations, with three alleles predominating. The epsilon 3 (ε3) allele is the most common, followed by the ε4, with the ε2 allele being least common. In Caucasian populations, the estimated allele frequencies are 78%, 14%, and 8% respectively (Utermann et al. 1980), though this frequency varies in different ethnic groups (Gamboa et al. 2000). Early studies of APOE function focused on its role in lipid transport (Davignon et al. 1988), and in the early 1990s, an association was observed between the presence of the ε4 allele and increased risk for and decreased onset age of AD (Corder et al. 1993). Furthermore, this effect is dose dependent, with the presence of two copies of the ε4 allele conferring a greater risk than one copy. This effect has been replicated in multiple populations (Murrell et al. 2006), though some studies in non-Caucasian populations either fail to show this effect (Tang et al. 1998; Gureje et al. 2006) or show a weaker effect (Harwood et al. 1999) than is seen in Caucasians. A relatively decreased risk for AD is seen with the ε2 allele. This observation is equally compatible with a "protective" effect of the ε2 allele or the interpretation that the ε2 allele indicates a baseline risk with the ε3 allele conferring an increased risk and the ε4 allele a higher risk still.

The mechanisms by which different APOE isoforms influence the risk of AD is another area of active exploration. The simultaneous presence of an ε4 allele has been shown to decrease the age of onset of dementia in persons carrying PS1 mutations (Pastor et al. 2003), PS2 mutations (Wijsman et al. 2005), and DS (Prasher et al. 1997). Studies in which multivariate statistics were used to study the interactions of APOE genotype, age, gender, education, cognitive status, and various measures of AD pathology suggest that the effect of APOE on clinical status is at least dramatically diminished after accounting for the degree of AD pathology (Bennett et al. 2003; 2005). These authors concluded that the effect of APOE status on dementia risk is mediated in large part through an effect on augmenting AD pathology. However, there is also evidence that the ε4 allele confers a higher risk for cognitive sequelae in head trauma (Jordan et al. 1997), Parkinson's disease (Harhangi et al. 2000), and coronary bypass surgery (Newman et al. 1995), as well as a higher risk of stroke (McCarron et al. 1999) and Parkinson's disease (Li et al. 2004), and is associated with a more aggressive course in amyotrophic lateral sclerosis (Moulard et al. 1996) and multiple sclerosis (Chapman et al. 2001). In control subjects, APOE genotype has been shown to affect cognition (Wetter et al. 2005), focal resting cerebral glucose metabolism (Reiman et al. 2004, Small et al. 1995), and cognitive activation related focal cerebral blood flow as measured with functional magnetic resonance imaging (Bookheimer et al. 2000). The extent to which this reflects incipient AD or some other effect of the APOE ε4 isoform is uncertain. These observations indicate that at least some of the effect of APOE on the clinical manifestations of AD may not be through a direct effect on AD pathology.

Multiple lines of research have suggested pleiotropic roles for the APOE protein in Aβ processing as well as in neuronal growth and repair. Consistent with a putative direct effect of APOE on Aβ processing and neuritic pathology, the degree of brain amyloid deposition in mice transgenic for the V717F APP mutation was dependent on the APOE isoform that they also expressed (Holtzman et al. 2000). Specifically, mice expressing no APOE showed substantially less neuritic degeneration than those with either mouse or human APOE. Furthermore, those expressing human APOE developed fibrillar Aβ deposits and neuritic plaques at a younger age, and those expressing the ε4 isoform had a greater than tenfold increase in fibrillar Aβ deposits. In addition to increasing Aβ deposition, APOE ε4 could also contribute to cognitive deficits by making the brain more susceptible to damage by Aβ. Long-term potentiation (LTP) is a model for learning that can be studied in hippocampal slices in vitro. A group of investigators demonstrated that LTP in such preparations from mice transgenic for human APOE ε4 was more inhibited by exogenously applied oligomeric Aβ$_{42}$ than it was in slices from mice transgenic for ε3 or ε2 (Trommer et al. 2005).

Other studies have demonstrated effects of APOE ε4 that appear to be independent of the Aβ processing pathway. Mice (not transgenic for any human FAD genes and thus not developing amyloid pathology) expressing the APOE ε4 isoform showed learning impairments compared to wild type and those expressing the ε3 isoform (Raber et al. 1998). Other pathways through which the APOE ε4 isoform might contribute to susceptibility of the nervous system to damage is by inducing hyperphosphorylation of tau (Tesseur et al. 2000b) and neurofibrillary pathology (Huang et al. 2001), interfering with axonal transport (Tesseur et al. 2000a) and neurite outgrowth (Nathan et al. 1995), or by increasing sensitivity to excitotoxin-induced injury (Buttini et al. 1999). It has been argued that the tertiary structure of the ε4 isoform allows for interaction of domains that does not occur in the ε3 and ε2 isoforms, and this altered stereochemistry underlies its pathological effects (Mahley et al. 2006). In any case, the APOE ε4 allele seems to contribute to neurological impairment through both AD-related and AD-independent pathways.

Putative Susceptibility Genes

In this chapter and in other writings, AD of onset after age 65 that does not clearly have a fully penetrant autosomal dominant mode of inheritance is frequently referred to as late-onset, "sporadic" AD. However, we have seen that variations in the APOE gene account for, or at least contribute to, many of these apparently sporadic cases. Even when controlling for APOE status, many late-onset cases appear to have a genetic contribution, and it has been estimated that greater than 30% and possibly even greater than 70% of the genetic variance in AD is due to genetic loci that have not yet been identified (Daw et al. 2000). In order to identify these loci, several large studies are currently under way, including the U.S. National Institute on Aging Late-Onset Alzheimer Disease study. To date, many putative linkages with several chromosomal loci have been made including 6p21, 9q22, 10q24, and 11q23 (Bertram and Tanzi 2004), though none are currently as robust and replicable as that for the APOE locus.

In a candidate approach study of polymorphisms in three genes in the 9q22 region, Bertram et al. (2005) identified a single nucleotide polymorphism in an intronic region of the gene coding for ubiquilin 1 (UBQLN1) that was significantly associated with AD in two distinct populations. This alteration, in turn, was associated with a dose-dependent increase in messenger RNA for UBQLN1 that lacked exon 8. A role for UBQLN1 in APP trafficking has recently been reported (Hiltunen et al. 2006). Within the chromosome 10q24 region is the gene coding for insulin degrading enzyme (IDE), which has been demonstrated to function in breaking down Aβ as well as insulin. Some investigators have found associations between specific IDE variants and AD, though others have not (Bertram and Tanzi 2004).

More recently, intronic variants of the gene coding for SORL1, a receptor involved in the intracellular trafficking of APP, have been associated with an increased risk of late-onset AD in multiple populations (Rogaeva et al. 2007). Though the mechanisms of this association are not fully understood, it is thought that the intronic variants lead to differential expression of SORL1 in neurons. Decreased SORL1 expression may lead to increased release of APP into late endosomal pathways where it is subject to Aβ-generating cleavage.

Implications for Clinical Practice

Though much has been revealed about the genetics of AD in the last fifteen years, much remains to be discovered. These findings have elucidated many aspects of the etiology and pathophysiology of AD, but how have they helped us concerning diagnosis and treatment of individual patients? When patients present with a young-onset form of dementia reminiscent of AD, particularly when a family history consistent with autosomal dominant inheritance is present, testing for FAD mutations should be considered. As alterations in PS1 are by far the most common, testing for such mutations should be considered first. Testing for APP and PS2 mutations is now commercially available in the United States as well. Though such results will not necessarily affect the therapeutic interventions implemented in the affected patient, testing can help family members understand the illness and, with appropriate consultation, may augment their ability to plan for and cope with the situation. It is important that family members understand in advance of testing that a positive result for an FAD mutation has important implications for their own risk of the disease.

In persons in whom the diagnosis of AD is clinically suspected, adding APOE genotyping to a comprehensive diagnostic workup can increase specificity, though at a potential cost to sensitivity (Mayeux et al. 1998). It is important, however, that APOE genotyping not be employed as a lone diagnostic test without appropriate ancillary testing (mental status evaluation including assessments for depression, imaging, etc.). Because of the uncertainty regarding whether persons carrying or not carrying the APOE ε4 genotype will ultimately develop AD, APOE genotype in asymptomatic persons is currently not recommended (Greely 1999). The utility of doing so in the future is the topic of the ongoing Risk Evaluation and Education for Alzheimer's Disease study (LaRusse et al. 2005).

Conclusions

Despite our extensive knowledge regarding the genetic underpinnings of AD, creating a transgenic animal that recapitulates the behavioral and pathological manifestations of the illness has proven difficult. It is significant that one of the best animal models of AD, featuring the cognitive decline, amyloid plaques, and neuritic pathology, as well as NFTs and neuronal loss, is the triple transgenic mouse in which pathogenic alterations of the APP, PS1, and tau genes have been introduced (Oddo et al. 2003). This underscores the genetic complexity of AD and suggests that the common form of late-onset AD may similarly arise from a combination of multiple, not yet identified genes. In addition to the genetic contributions to AD discussed above, many environmental risk factors have also been identified (Launer 2006). Like many other illnesses, AD therefore appears to be truly multifactorial in origin. It has emerged as a polygenetic disease that can be considered a model for many other conditions.

Acknowledgments

This work was supported by PHS K08 AG-22228, the Easton Consortium for Biomarker and Drug Discovery in Alzheimer's Disease, California DHS #04-35522, Alzheimer's Disease Research Center Grant P50 AG-16570, an Alzheimer's Disease Research Center of California grant, and the Sidell Kagan Foundation. Dr. Ringman has received honoraria for speaking on behalf of Pfizer, Eisai, Astra-Zenaca, and Novartis Pharmaceuticals as well as Forest Laboratories. He has also received compensation for serving on an advisory board for Avanir Pharmaceuticals. Total compensation from each of these companies totals less than $10,000. Dr. Cummings has provided consultation to Eisai, Janssen, Forest, Lundbeck, Novartis, Merz, and Pfizer pharmaceutical companies relevant to this chapter. Total annual compensation from each of these companies totals less that $10,000.

References

Amir RE, Van den Veyver IB, Wan M, Tran CQ, Francke U, Zoghbi HY (1999). Rett syndrome is caused by mutations in X-linked MECP2, encoding methyl-CpG-binding protein 2. *Nat Genet*, 23:185–8.

Ardila A, Lopera F, Rosselli M, Moreno S, Madrigal L, Arango-Lasprilla JC, et al. (2000). Neuropsychological profile of a large kindred with familial Alzheimer's disease caused by the E280A single presenilin-1 mutation. *Arch Clin Neuropsychol*, 15:515–28.

Arnold SE, Hyman BT, Flory J, Damasio AR, Van Hoesen GW (1991). The topographical and neuroanatomical distribution of neurofibrillary tangles and neuritic plaques in the cerebral cortex of patients with Alzheimer's disease. *Cereb Cortex*, 1:103–16.

Arriagada PV, Marzloff K, Hyman BT (1992). Distribution of Alzheimer-type pathologic changes in nondemented elderly individuals matches the pattern in Alzheimer's disease. *Neurology*, 42:1681–8.

Bennett DA, Schneider JA, Wilson RS, Bienias JL, Berry-Kravis E, Arnold SE (2005). Amyloid mediates the association of apolipoprotein E e4 allele to cognitive function in older people. *J Neurol Neurosurg Psychiatry*, 76:1194–9.

Bennett DA, Wilson RS, Schneider JA, Evans DA, Aggarwal NT, Arnold SE, et al. (2003). Apolipoprotein E epsilon4 allele, AD pathology, and the clinical expression of Alzheimer's disease. *Neurology,* 60:246–52.

Bertram L, Hiltunen M, Parkinson M, Ingelsson M, Lange C, Ramasamy K, et al. (2005). Family-based association between Alzheimer's disease and variants in UBQLN1. *N Engl J Med,* 352:884–94.

Bertram L, Tanzi RE (2004). Alzheimer's disease: one disorder, too many genes? *Hum Mol Genet,* 13 Spec No 1:R135–41.

Bird TD, Lampe TH, Nemens EJ, Miner GW, Sumi SM, Schellenberg GD (1988). Familial Alzheimer's disease in American descendants of the Volga Germans: probable genetic founder effect. *Ann Neurol,* 23:25–31.

Bookheimer SY, Magdalena H, Strojwas BS, Cohen MS, Saunders AM, Pericak-Vance MA, et al. (2000). Patterns of brain activation in people at risk for Alzheimer's disease. *N Engl J Med,* 343:450–6.

Brouwers N, Sleegers K, Engelborghs S, Bogaerts V, Serneels S, Kamali K, et al. (2006). Genetic risk and transcriptional variability of amyloid precursor protein in Alzheimer's disease. *Brain,* 129(Pt 11):2984–91.

Brunkan AL, Goate AM (2005). Presenilin function and gamma-secretase activity. *J Neurochem,* 93:769–92.

Buttini M, Orth M, Bellosta S, Akeefe H, Pitas RE, Wyss-Coray T, et al. (1999). Expression of human apolipoprotein E3 or E4 in the brains of Apoe–/–mice: isoform-specific effects on neurodegeneration. *J Neurosci,* 19:4867–80.

Caballero IM, Hendrich B (2005). MeCP2 in neurons: closing in on the causes of Rett syndrome. *Hum Mol Genet,* 14 Spec No 1:R19–26.

Campion D, Dumanchin C, Hannequin D, Dubois B, Belliard S, Puel M, et al. (1999). Early-onset autosomal dominant Alzheimer disease: prevalence, genetic heterogeneity, and mutation spectrum. *Am J Hum Genet,* 65:664–70.

Cecchi C, Fiorillo C, Sorbi S, Latorraca S, Benedetta N, Bagnoli S, et al. (2002). Oxidative stress and reduced antioxidant defenses in peripheral cells from familial Alzheimer's patients. *Free Radic Biol Med,* 33:1372–9.

Chapman J, Vinokurov S, Achiron A, Karussis DM, Mitosek-Szewczyk K, Birnbaum M, et al. (2001). APOE genotype is a major predictor of long-term progression of disability in MS. *Neurology,* 56:312–6.

Corder EH, Saunders AM, Strittmatter WJ, Schmechel DE, Gaskell PC, Small GW, et al. (1993). Gene dose of apolipoprotein E type 4 allele and the risk of Alzheimer's disease in late onset families. *Science,* 261:921–3.

Crome L, Stern J (1972). The pathology of mental retardation, second edition. Baltimore: Williams & Wilkins.

Davignon J, Gregg RE, Sing CF (1988). Apolipoprotein E polymorphism and atherosclerosis. *Arteriosclerosis*, 8(1):1–21.

Daw EW, Payami H, Nemens EJ, Nochlin D, Bird TD, Schellenberg GD, et al. (2000). The number of trait loci in late-onset Alzheimer disease. *Am J Hum Genet*, 66:196–204.

Diaz-Olavarrieta C, Ostrosky-Solis F, Garcia de la Cadena C, Rodriguez Y, Alonso E (1997). Neuropsychological changes in subjects at risk of inheriting Alzheimer's disease. *Neuroreport*, 8:2449–53.

Doran M, du Plessis DG, Enevoldson TP, Fletcher NA, Ghadiali E, Larner AJ (2003). Pathological heterogeneity of clinically diagnosed corticobasal degeneration. *J Neurol Sci*, 216(1):127–34.

Edwards-Lee T, Ringman JM, Chung J, Werner J, Morgan A, St George Hyslop P, et al. (2005). An African American family with early-onset Alzheimer disease and an APP (T714I) mutation. *Neurology*, 64:377–9.

Ezquerra M, Lleo A, Castellvi M, Queralt R, Santacruz P, Pastor P, et al. (2003). A novel mutation in the PSEN2 gene (T430M) associated with variable expression in a family with early-onset Alzheimer disease. *Arch Neurol*, 60:1149–51.

Farlow M, Murrell J, Ghetti B, Unverzagt F, Zeldenrust S, Benson M (1994). Clinical characteristics in a kindred with early-onset Alzheimer's disease and their linkage to a G to T change at position 2149 of the amyloid precursor protein gene. *Neurology*, 44:105–11.

Fox NC, Kennedy AM, Harvey RJ, Lantos PL, Roques PK, Collinge J, et al. (1997). Clinicopathological features of familial Alzheimer's disease associated with the M139V mutation in the presenilin 1 gene. Pedigree but not mutation specific age at onset provides evidence for a further genetic factor. *Brain*, 120(Pt 3):491–501.

Fox NC, Warrington EK, Seiffer AL, Agnew SK, Rossor MN (1998). Presymptomatic cognitive deficits in individuals at risk of familial Alzheimer's disease: a longitudinal prospective study. *Brain*, 121(Pt 9):1631–9.

Galton CJ, Patterson K, Xuereb JH, Hodges JR (2000). Atypical and typical presentations of Alzheimer's disease: a clinical, neuropsychological, neuroimaging and pathological study of 13 cases. *Brain*, 123(Pt 3):484–98.

Gamboa R, Hernandez-Pacheco G, Hesiquio R, Zuniga J, Masso F, Montano LF, et al. (2000). Apolipoprotein E polymorphism in the Indian and Mestizo populations of Mexico. *Hum Biol*, 72:975–81.

Geschwind DH, Robidoux J, Alarcon M, Miller BL, Wilhelmsen KC, Cummings JL, et al. (2001). Dementia and neurodevelopmental predisposition: cognitive dysfunction in presymptomatic subjects precedes dementia by decades in frontotemporal dementia. *Ann Neurol*, 50:741–6.

Giovagnoli AR, Marcon G, Giaccone G, Confaloni AM, Tagliavini F (2006). Cognitive deficits in familial Alzheimer's disease associated with M239V mutation of presenilin 2. *Dement Geriatr Cogn Disord,* 22(3):238–43.

Goate A, Chartier-Harlin MC, Mullan M, Brown J, Crawford F, Fidani L, et al. (1991). Segregation of a missense mutation in the amyloid precursor protein gene with familial Alzheimer's disease. *Nature,* 349:704–6.

Gomez-Isla T, Hollister R, West H, Mui S, Growdon JH, Petersen RC, et al. (1997). Neuronal loss correlates with but exceeds neurofibrillary tangles in Alzheimer's disease. *Ann Neurol,* 41:17–24.

Gomez-Isla T, Price JL, McKeel DW Jr, Morris JC, Growdon JH, Hyman BT (1996). Profound loss of layer II entorhinal cortex neurons occurs in very mild Alzheimer's disease. *J Neurosci,* 16:4491–500.

Gong Y, Chang L, Viola KL, Lacor PN, Lambert MP, Finch CE, et al. (2003). Alzheimer's disease-affected brain: presence of oligomeric A beta ligands (ADDLs) suggests a molecular basis for reversible memory loss. *Proc Natl Acad Sci USA,* 100:10417–22.

Gonzalez-Alegre P, Afifi AK (2006). Clinical characteristics of childhood-onset (juvenile) Huntington disease: report of 12 patients and review of the literature. *J Child Neurol,* 21:223–9.

Greely HT (1999). Special issues in genetic testing for Alzheimer disease. *Genet Test,* 3(1):115–9.

Gureje O, Ogunniyi A, Baiyewu O, Price B, Unverzagt FW, Evans RM, et al. (2006). APOE epsilon4 is not associated with Alzheimer's disease in elderly Nigerians. *Ann Neurol,* 59:182–5.

Hagberg B, Aicardi J, Dias K, Ramos O (1983). A progressive syndrome of autism, dementia, ataxia, and loss of purposeful hand use in girls: Rett's syndrome: report of 35 cases. *Ann Neurol,* 14:471–9.

Hamilton RL (2000). Lewy bodies in Alzheimer's disease: a neuropathological review of 145 cases using alpha-synuclein immunohistochemistry. *Brain Pathol,* 10:378–84.

Handler M, Yang X, Shen J (2000). Presenilin-1 regulates neuronal differentiation during neurogenesis. *Development,* 127:2593–606.

Harhangi BS, de Rijk MC, van Duijn CM, Van Broeckhoven C, Hofman A, Breteler MM (2000). APOE and the risk of PD with or without dementia in a population-based study. *Neurology,* 54:1272–6.

Harwood DG, Barker WW, Loewenstein DA, Ownby RL, St George-Hyslop P, Mullan M, et al. (1999). A cross-ethnic analysis of risk factors for AD in white Hispanics and white non-Hispanics. *Neurology,* 52:551–6.

Hiltunen M, Lu A, Thomas AV, Romano DM, Kim M, Jones PB, et al. (2006). Ubiquilin 1 modulates amyloid precursor protein trafficking and Abeta secretion. *J Biol Chem,* 281:32240–53.

Holland AJ, Hon J, Huppert FA, Stevens F (2000). Incidence and course of dementia in people with Down's syndrome: findings from a population-based study. *J Intellect Disabil Res,* 44(Pt 2):138–46.

Holland AJ, Hon J, Huppert FA, Stevens F, Watson P (1998). Population-based study of the prevalence and presentation of dementia in adults with Down's syndrome. *Br J Psychiatry*, 172:493–8.

Holtzman DM, Bales KR, Tenkova T, Fagan AM, Parsadanian M, Sartorius LJ, et al. (2000). Apolipoprotein E isoform-dependent amyloid deposition and neuritic degeneration in a mouse model of Alzheimer's disease. *Proc Natl Acad Sci USA*, 97:2892–7.

Hori Y, Hashimoto T, Wakutani Y, Urakami K, Nakashima K, Condron MM, et al. (2007). The Tottori (D7N) and English (H6R) familial Alzheimer disease mutations accelerate Abeta fibril formation without increasing protofibril formation. *J Biol Chem*, 282:4916–23.

Huang Y, Liu XQ, Wyss-Coray T, Brecht WJ, Sanan DA, Mahley RW (2001). Apolipoprotein E fragments present in Alzheimer's disease brains induce neurofibrillary tangle-like intracellular inclusions in neurons. *Proc Natl Acad Sci USA*, 98:8838–43.

Jordan BD, Relkin NR, Ravdin LD, Jacobs AR, Bennett A, Gandy S (1997). Apolipoprotein E epsilon4 associated with chronic traumatic brain injury in boxing. *JAMA*, 278:136–40.

Karlinsky H, Vaula G, Haines JL, Ridgley J, Bergeron C, Mortilla M, et al. (1992). Molecular and prospective phenotypic characterization of a pedigree with familial Alzheimer's disease and a missense mutation in codon 717 of the beta-amyloid precursor protein gene. *Neurology*, 42:1445–53.

Kennedy AM, Newman SK, Frackowiak RS, Cunningham VJ, Roques P, Stevens J, et al. (1995). Chromosome 14 linked familial Alzheimer's disease. A clinico–pathological study of a single pedigree. *Brain*, 118(Pt 1):185–205.

LaRusse S, Roberts JS, Marteau TM, Katzen H, Linnenbringer EL, Barber M, et al. (2005). Genetic susceptibility testing versus family history-based risk assessment: impact on perceived risk of Alzheimer disease. *Genet Med*, 7(1):48–53.

Launer LJ (2006). Prevention of AD: the which, when, and on whom? *Alzheimer Dis Assoc Disord*, 20(3 Suppl 2):S75–8.

Leissring MA, LaFerla FM, Callamaras N, Parker I (2001). Subcellular mechanisms of presenilin-mediated enhancement of calcium signaling. *Neurobiol Dis*, 8:469–78.

Levy E, Carman MD, Fernandez-Madrid IJ, Power MD, Lieberburg I, van Duinen SG, et al. (1990). Mutation of the Alzheimer's disease amyloid gene in hereditary cerebral hemorrhage, Dutch type. *Science*, 248:1124–6.

Li F, Iseki E, Kato M, Adachi Y, Akagi M, Kosaka K (2000). An autopsy case of Alzheimer's disease presenting with primary progressive aphasia: a clinicopathological and immunohistochemical study. *Neuropathology*, 20:239–45.

Li YJ, Hauser MA, Scott WK, Martin ER, Booze MW, Qin XJ, et al. (2004). Apolipoprotein E controls the risk and age at onset of Parkinson disease. *Neurology*, 62:2005–9.

Lippa CF, Swearer JM, Kane KJ, Nochlin D, Bird TD, Ghetti B, et al. (2000). Familial Alzheimer's disease: site of mutation influences clinical phenotype. *Ann Neurol*, 48:376–9.

Lopera F, Ardilla A, Martinez A, Madrigal L, Arango-Viana JC, Lemere CA, et al. (1997). Clinical features of early-onset Alzheimer disease in a large kindred with an E280A presenilin-1 mutation. *JAMA*, 277:793–9.

Lowenberg K, Waggoner RW (1934). Familial organic psychosis (Alzheimer's type). *Archives of Neurology and Psychiatry*, 31:737–54.

Mahley RW, Weisgraber KH, Huang Y (2006). Apolipoprotein E4: a causative factor and therapeutic target in neuropathology, including Alzheimer's disease. *Proc Natl Acad Sci USA*, 103:5644–51.

Mann D (2004). Down's syndrome and Alzheimer's disease. In Esiri MM, Lee VM-Y, Trojanowski JQ, eds. The neuropathology of dementia (pp. 207–26). Cambridge: Cambridge University Press.

Marjaux E, Hartmann D, De Strooper B (2004). Presenilins in memory, Alzheimer's disease, and therapy. *Neuron*, 42(2):189–92.

Martinowich K, Hattori D, Wu H, Fouse S, He F, Hu Y, et al. (2003). DNA methylation-related chromatin remodeling in activity-dependent BDNF gene regulation. *Science*, 302:890–3.

Mayeux R, Saunders AM, Shea S, Mirra S, Evans D, Roses AD, et al. (1998). Utility of the apolipoprotein E genotype in the diagnosis of Alzheimer's disease. Alzheimer's Disease Centers Consortium on Apolipoprotein E and Alzheimer's Disease. *N Engl J Med*, 338:506–11.

McCarron MO, Delong D, Alberts MJ (1999). APOE genotype as a risk factor for ischemic cerebrovascular disease: a meta-analysis. *Neurology*, 53:1308–11.

McKeith IG, Galasko D, Kosaka K, Perry EK, Dickson DW, Hansen LA, et al. (1996). Consensus guidelines for the clinical and pathologic diagnosis of dementia with Lewy bodies (DLB): report of the consortium on DLB international workshop. *Neurology*, 47:1113–24.

Mega MS, Cummings JL, Fiorello T, Gornbein J (1996). The spectrum of behavioral changes in Alzheimer's disease. *Neurology*, 46:130–5.

Moulard B, Sefiani A, Laamri A, Malafosse A, Camu W (1996). Apolipoprotein E genotyping in sporadic amyotrophic lateral sclerosis: evidence for a major influence on the clinical presentation and prognosis. *J Neurol Sci*, 139(Suppl):34–7.

Mullan M, Houlden H, Crawford F, Kennedy A, Rogues P, Rossor M (1993a). Age of onset in familial early onset Alzheimer's disease correlates with genetic aetiology. *Am J Med Genet*, 48:129–30.

Mullan M, Tsuji S, Miki T, Katsuya T, Naruse S, Kaneko K, et al. (1993b). Clinical comparison of Alzheimer's disease in pedigrees with the codon 717 Val → Ile mutation in the amyloid precursor protein gene. *Neurobiol Aging*, 14:407–19.

Murrell JR, Price B, Lane KA, Baiyewu O, Gureje O, Ogunniyi A, et al. (2006). Association of apolipoprotein E genotype and Alzheimer disease in African Americans. *Arch Neurol*, 63:431–4.

Nathan BP, Chang KC, Bellosta S, Brisch E, Ge N, Mahley RW, et al. (1995). The inhibitory effect of apolipoprotein E4 on neurite outgrowth is associated with microtubule depolymerization. *J Biol Chem*, 270:19791–9.

Nelson LD, Orme D, Osann K, Lott IT (2001). Neurological changes and emotional functioning in adults with Down syndrome. *J Intellect Disabil Res*, 45(Pt 5):450–6.

Newman MF, Croughwell ND, Blumenthal JA, Lowry E, White WD, Spillane W, et al. (1995). Predictors of cognitive decline after cardiac operation. *Ann Thorac Surg*, 59:1326–30.

Newman SK, Warrington EK, Kennedy AM, Rossor MN (1994). The earliest cognitive change in a person with familial Alzheimer's disease: presymptomatic neuropsychological features in a pedigree with familial Alzheimer's disease confirmed at necropsy. *J Neurol Neurosurg Psychiatry*, 57:967–72.

Oddo S, Caccamo A, Shepherd JD, Murphy MP, Golde TE, Kayed R, et al. (2003). Triple-transgenic model of Alzheimer's disease with plaques and tangles: intracellular Abeta and synaptic dysfunction. *Neuron*, 39:409–21.

Oddo S, Caccamo A, Tran L, Lambert MP, Glabe CG, Klein WL, et al. (2006). Temporal profile of amyloid-beta (Abeta) oligomerization in an in vivo model of Alzheimer disease: a link between Abeta and tau pathology. *J Biol Chem*, 281:1599–1604.

Oliver C, Crayton L, Holland A, Hall S, Bradbury J (1998). A four year prospective study of age-related cognitive change in adults with Down's syndrome. *Psychol Med*, 28:1365–77.

Pastor P, Roe CM, Villegas A, Bedoya G, Chakraverty S, Garcia G, et al. (2003). Apolipoprotein Eepsilon4 modifies Alzheimer's disease onset in an E280A PS1 kindred. *Ann Neurol*, 54: 163–9.

Petersen RC, Parisi JE, Dickson DW, Johnson KA, Knopman DS, Boeve BF, et al. (2006). Neuropathologic features of amnestic mild cognitive impairment. *Arch Neurol*, 63:665–72.

Prasher VP, Chowdhury TA, Rowe BR, Bain SC (1997). ApoE genotype and Alzheimer's disease in adults with Down syndrome: meta-analysis. *Am J Ment Retard*, 102:103–10.

Prasher VP, Farrer MJ, Kessling AM, Fisher EM, West RJ, Barber PC, et al. (1998). Molecular mapping of Alzheimer-type dementia in Down's syndrome. *Ann Neurol*, 43:380–3.

Raber J, Wong D, Buttini M, Orth M, Bellosta S, Pitas RE, et al. (1998). Isoform-specific effects of human apolipoprotein E on brain function revealed in ApoE knockout mice: increased susceptibility of females. *Proc Natl Acad Sci USA*, 95:10914–9.

Reiman EM, Chen K, Alexander GE, Caselli RJ, Bandy D, Osborne D, et al. (2004). Functional brain abnormalities in young adults at genetic risk for late-onset Alzheimer's dementia. *Proc Natl Acad Sci USA*, 101:284–9.

Renner JA, Burns JM, Hou CE, McKeel DW Jr, Storandt M, Morris JC (2004). Progressive posterior cortical dysfunction: a clinicopathologic series. *Neurology*, 63:1175–80.

Ringman JM, Diaz-Olavarrieta C, Rodriguez Y, Chavez M, Fairbanks L, Paz F, et al. (2005). Neuropsychological function in nondemented carriers of presenilin-1 mutations. *Neurology,* 65:552–8.

Ringman JM, Diaz-Olavarrieta C, Rodriguez Y, Chavez M, Paz F, Murrell J, et al. (2004). Female preclinical presenilin-1 mutation carriers unaware of their genetic status have higher levels of depression than their non-mutation carrying kin. *J Neurol Neurosurg Psychiatry,* 75:500–2.

Ringman JM, Rodriguez Y, Diaz-Olavarrieta C, Chavez M, Thompson M, Fairbanks L, et al. (2007). Performance on MMSE sub-items and education level in presenilin-1 mutation carriers without dementia. *Int Psychogeriatr,* 19:323–32.

Rogaeva E, Meng Y, Lee JH, Gu Y, Kawarai T, Zou F, et al. (2007). The neuronal sortilin-related receptor SORL1 is genetically associated with Alzheimer disease. *Nat Genet,* 39:168–77.

Rogaev EI, Sherrington R, Rogaeva EA, Levesque G, Ikeda M, Liang Y, et al. (1995). Familial Alzheimer's disease in kindreds with missense mutations in a gene on chromosome 1 related to the Alzheimer's disease type 3 gene. *Nature,* 376:775–78.

Ross MH, Galaburda AM, Kemper TL (1984). Down's syndrome: is there a decreased population of neurons? *Neurology,* 34:909–16.

Rosselli MC, Ardila AC, Moreno SC, Standish VC, Arango-Lasprilla JC, Tirado VM, et al. (2000). Cognitive decline in patients with familial Alzheimer's disease associated with E280a presenilin-1 mutation: a longitudinal study. *J Clin Exp Neuropsychol,* 22:483–95.

Rossor MN, Newman S, Frackowiak RS, Lantos P, Kennedy AM (1993). Alzheimer's disease families with amyloid precursor protein mutations. *Ann NY Acad Sci,* 695:198–202.

Rovelet-Lecrux A, Hannequin D, Raux G, Le Meur N, Laquerriere A, Vital A, et al. (2006). APP locus duplication causes autosomal dominant early-onset Alzheimer disease with cerebral amyloid angiopathy. *Nat Genet,* 38:24–6.

Rowe J, Lavender A, Turk V (2006). Cognitive executive function in Down's syndrome. *Br J Clin Psychol,* 45(Pt 1):5–17.

Saura CA, Choi SY, Beglopoulos V, Malkani S, Zhang D, Shankaranarayana Rao BS, et al. (2004). Loss of presenilin function causes impairments of memory and synaptic plasticity followed by age-dependent neurodegeneration. *Neuron,* 42:23–36.

Schellenberg GD, Bird TD, Wijsman EM, Orr HT, Anderson L, Nemens E, et al. (1992). Genetic linkage evidence for a familial Alzheimer's disease locus on chromosome 14. *Science,* 258: 668–71.

Scheuner D, Eckman C, Jensen M, Song X, Citron M, Suzuki N, et al. (1996). Secreted amyloid beta-protein similar to that in the senile plaques of Alzheimer's disease is increased in vivo by the presenilin 1 and 2 and APP mutations linked to familial Alzheimer's disease. *Nat Med,* 2:864–70.

Schupf N, Pang D, Patel BN, Silverman W, Schubert R, Lai F, et al. (2003). Onset of dementia is associated with age at menopause in women with Down's syndrome. *Ann Neurol,* 54:433–8.

Sherrington R, Froelich S, Sorbi S, Campion D, Chi H, Rogaeva EA, et al. (1996). Alzheimer's disease associated with mutations in presenilin 2 is rare and variably penetrant. *Hum Mol Genet,* 5:985–8.

Sherrington R, Rogaev EI, Liang Y, Rogaeva EA, Levesque G, Ikeda M, et al. (1995). Cloning of a gene bearing missense mutations in early-onset familial Alzheimer's disease. *Nature,* 375:754–60.

Small GW, Mazziotta JC, Collins MT, Baxter LR, Phelps ME, Mandelkern MA, et al. (1995). Apolipoprotein E type 4 allele and cerebral glucose metabolism in relatives at risk for familial Alzheimer disease. *JAMA,* 273:942–7.

Snowdon DA (2003). Healthy aging and dementia: findings from the Nun Study. *Ann Intern Med,* 139(5 Pt 2):450–4.

Stern Y (2006). Cognitive reserve and Alzheimer disease. *Alzheimer Dis Assoc Disord,* 20(3 Suppl 2):S69–74.

Swearer JM, O'Donnell BF, Ingram SM, Drachman DA (1996). Rate of progression in familial Alzheimer's disease. *J Geriatr Psychiatry Neurol,* 9(1):22–5.

Tang MX, Stern Y, Marder K, Bell K, Gurland B, Lantigua R, et al. (1998). The APOE-epsilon4 allele and the risk of Alzheimer disease among African Americans, whites, and Hispanics. *JAMA,* 279:751–5.

Takao M, Ghetti B, Murrell JR, Unverzagt FW, Giaccone G, Tagliavini F, et al. (2001). Ectopic white matter neurons, a developmental abnormality that may be caused by the PSEN1 S169L mutation in a case of familial AD with myoclonus and seizures. *J Neuropathol Exp Neurol,* 60:1137–52.

Tesseur I, Van Dorpe J, Bruynseels K, Bronfman F, Sciot R, Van Lommel A, et al. (2000a). Prominent axonopathy and disruption of axonal transport in transgenic mice expressing human apolipoprotein E4 in neurons of brain and spinal cord. *Am J Pathol,* 157:1495–510.

Tesseur I, Van Dorpe J, Spittaels K, Van den Haute C, Moechars D, Van Leuven F (2000b). Expression of human apolipoprotein E4 in neurons causes hyperphosphorylation of protein tau in the brains of transgenic mice. *Am J Pathol,* 156:951–64.

Tokuda T, Fukushima T, Ikeda S, Sekijima Y, Shoji S, Yanagisawa N, et al. (1997). Plasma levels of amyloid beta proteins Abeta1-40 and Abeta1-42(43) are elevated in Down's syndrome. *Ann Neurol,* 41:271–3.

Tournoy J, Bossuyt X, Snellinx A, Regent M, Garmyn M, Serneels L, et al. (2004). Partial loss of presenilins causes seborrheic keratosis and autoimmune disease in mice. *Hum Mol Genet,* 13:1321–31.

Trommer BL, Shah C, Yun SH, Gamkrelidze G, Pasternak ES, Stine WB, et al. (2005). ApoE isoform-specific effects on LTP: blockade by oligomeric amyloid-beta1-42. *Neurobiol Dis,* 18: 75–82.

Utermann G, Langenbeck U, Beisiegel U, Weber W (1980). Genetics of the apolipoprotein E system in man. *Am J Hum Genet,* 32:339–47.

Wakutani Y, Watanabe K, Adachi Y, Wada-Isoe K, Urakami K, Ninomiya H, et al. (2004). Novel amyloid precursor protein gene missense mutation (D678N) in probable familial Alzheimer's disease. *J Neurol Neurosurg Psychiatry,* 75:1039–42.

Wetter SR, Delis DC, Houston WS, Jacobson MW, Lansing A, Cobell K, et al. (2005). Deficits in inhibition and flexibility are associated with the APOE-E4 allele in nondemented older adults. *J Clin Exp Neuropsychol,* 27:943–52.

Wijsman EM, Daw EW, Yu X, Steinbart EJ, Nochlin D, Bird TD, et al. (2005). APOE and other loci affect age-at-onset in Alzheimer's disease families with PS2 mutation. *Am J Med Genet B Neuropsychiatr Genet,* 132(1):14–20.

Wisniewski K, Jervis GA, Moretz RC, Wisniewski HM (1979). Alzheimer neurofibrillary tangles in diseases other than senile and presenile dementia. *Ann Neurol,* 5:288–94.

11 Pharmacogenetic Approaches to Neurocognition in Schizophrenia

Katherine E. Burdick and Anil K. Malhotra

In psychiatry, variable and often incomplete treatment response is a major concern. A significant number of psychiatric patients experience chronic psychotic and affective symptoms that do not completely remit even when taking adequate doses of medication. In addition, intolerable side effects are common in a proportion of patients treated with psychotropic medications, with limited alternative treatments available to control the symptoms of the disease. Moreover, negative symptoms and cognitive impairment are persistent in a majority of patients with schizophrenia, do not respond robustly to medications, and are directly and strongly related to functional disability. The resulting cost to society is enormous, making this a major mental health crisis of critical importance to researchers and clinicians alike (Wyatt et al. 1995).

In schizophrenia, little is known about the correlates of drug response, and patients frequently endure long delays between treatment initiation and clinical efficacy, setting up a "waiting game" without a priori odds of success or failure. The field of pharmacogenetics has emerged with the goal of providing an opportunity to identify biological predictors of treatment response to inform clinical decision making for patients who suffer from these severely debilitating and often inadequately treated illnesses. Additionally, the identification of genetic markers of treatment response or medication intolerability may simultaneously offer new insight into the molecular mechanisms of psychotropic drug action.

There are a number of advantages to using a pharmacogenetics approach in dissecting the heterogeneity of treatment response in psychiatry (Malhotra et al. 2004). These include (1) the stability of genotypic information over the life span and its imperviousness to clinical symptoms, medication exposure, and other environmental or social influences; (2) the recent advancement of molecular genetic technologies, making genotyping relatively cost-efficient, rapid, and accurate, with coverage spanning the entire human genome; and (3) the ease with which DNA samples can be collected in very large samples in the context of clinical trials, allowing for the power to detect underlying genetic differences in smaller subgroups of patients who do or do not respond adequately to a given medication.

Phenotypic Candidates for Pharmacogenetic Studies

To date, there have been a relatively limited number of molecular genetic studies of drug response in patients with schizophrenia. The primary outcome measures of most of these investigations have been related to the clinical efficacy of antipsychotic medications and the development of adverse reactions. In this chapter, rather than reviewing the literature with regard to the pharmacogenetics of antipsychotics, we will turn our focus to the future and to the potential use of pharmacogenetics to predict treatment response to medications that target one of the key intermediate phenotypes of schizophrenia—namely, cognitive impairment.

One of the difficulties inherent in genetic approaches to schizophrenia has been adequately defining the phenotype for examination. For example, there is substantial diagnostic heterogeneity in patients with schizophrenia, which contributes to a weakened signal in genetic studies, and more precise diagnostic subtyping of patients may not be feasible because of power issues related to limitations in sample size. For pharmacogenetics, the definitions for primary outcome measures of treatment response are often arbitrary, and the reliability of the measurement of these phenotypes may be limited. However, unlike clinical symptom efficacy assessments, neurocognitive tests are standardized, reliable instruments that can be readily administered to large samples with relative objectivity. Further, neurocognition represents an ideal treatment target in patients with schizophrenia, as it is extremely prevalent and profound (Keefe et al. 2006). Moreover, cognitive function appears to be globally affected in schizophrenia, and deficits have been shown to directly relate to quality of life by impacting on daily functioning in psychosocial, occupational, and independent living domains (Green 1996).

From the perspective of molecular genetics approaches, cognitive impairment in schizophrenia has emerged as a well-characterized quantitative trait with converging evidence of a strong genetic component (Glahn et al. 2006), which is discussed at length in chapter 9. The underlying etiology of cognitive dysfunction in schizophrenia has not yet been elucidated; however, data support a neurodevelopmental model in which genetic factors play a significant role. Cognitive deficits in patients with schizophrenia are present during the prodromal phase (the period prior to onset of the full syndrome; Lencz et al. 2006), very early in the course of the disease (Bilder et al. 2000), and during remission of clinical symptomatology. Moreover, impaired cognition has been demonstrated to occur in unaffected family members of patients with schizophrenia, supporting a role for a genetic component in the etiology of these deficits (Trandafir et al. 2006).

Recent studies have begun to focus on the critical potential to intervene pharmacologically and to directly target cognitive impairment in patients with schizophrenia. Initial evidence that atypical, or second-generation antipsychotics (SGAs), may significantly improve cognitive function in patients with schizophrenia (Bilder et al. 2002a; Harvey et al. 2003; 2004; 2005; Malhotra et al. 2006) has recently been challenged by data from large-scale clinical trials (Keefe et al. 2007). A recently completed study sponsored by the National Institute of Mental Health, Clinical Antipsychotic Trials of Intervention Effectiveness (CATIE), compared the neurocognitive effects of four SGAs (olanzapine, $n = 211$; risperidone, $n = 183$; quetiapine, $n = 181$; and ziprasidone, $n = 93$) and one typical antipsychotic (perphenazine, $n = 149$) in patients with chronic schizophrenia. Results indicated that all of the antipsychotic treatment groups demonstrated only a small improvement in global neurocognitive function following two months of treatment, with no significant difference between groups. In fact, after eighteen months of treatment, the typical antipsychotic perphenazine demonstrated a slight advantage over the SGAs, with an effect size of approximately one half of a standard deviation improvement, a magnitude of change which is commonly used as a cutoff for clinically significant improvement. These data suggest that while the SGAs are unlikely to negatively impact cognitive performance in patients with schizophrenia, improvement in the group as a whole is modest at best, with effect sizes similar to those reported in subjects receiving a placebo in other controlled trials, suggesting that practice effects, or improvement due to previous exposure to the testing materials, may have confounded early studies (Keefe et al. 2007). These data suggesting an important role for practice effects in studies of neurocognitive function are addressed in two recent studies. In the first study, a putative cognitive enhancer, donepezil, did not demonstrate a significant cognitive advantage over placebo, with marked improvements in neurocognitive test performance in both groups (Keefe et al. 2008). A second study demonstrated no cognitive benefit of olanzapine or risperidone in first-episode patients with schizophrenia, as compared with a control group that also underwent repeated test administration, despite the fact that both groups' cognitive performance improved from baseline (Goldberg et al. 2006).

Of particular interest from a pharmacogenetics perspective, several demographic and clinical factors which may at least in part be genetically influenced contributed to neurocognitive improvement in a subset of CATIE patients. Specifically, poorer neurocognitive performance at baseline and higher estimated premorbid intellect significantly predicted greater cognitive improvement, suggesting that a subgroup of patients who demonstrate a deteriorating course of disease with regard to cognitive function may receive the most cognitive benefit from antipsychotic treatment. Consistent with this, we have recently reported that genetic factors may contribute to deteriorating versus stable cognitive profiles in patients with schizophrenia (Burdick et al. 2007), suggesting a possible genotypically distinct group for potential targeting in cognitive enhancement studies of schizophrenia.

Pharmacogenetics of Cognition: Dopaminergic Agents

As dopaminergic dysfunction is believed to be a primary abnormality in patients with schizophrenia, particularly with regard to executive function and working memory deficits (Weinberger et al. 1988), dopaminergic agents represent one class of drugs that might prove useful in enhancing cognition in schizophrenia. The SGAs are potent dopamine receptor antagonists and may have a modest effect on cognition, at least in some patients. To date, there have been three published studies that have evaluated a molecular genetic predictor of cognitive response to SGAs in patients with schizophrenia (Bertolino et al. 2004; T. W. Weickert et al. 2004; Woodward et al. 2007). In each of these studies, a candidate gene approach was utilized with a focus on the gene that codes for catechol-O-methyltransferase (*COMT*), an enzyme critical in the metabolic pathway of the catecholaminergic neurotransmitters dopamine and norepinephrine. Several studies have demonstrated an association of *COMT* with schizophrenia (Fan et al. 2005) and with cognitive function in patients with schizophrenia (Egan et al. 2001; Bilder et al. 2002b), unaffected relatives of patients with schizophrenia (Rosa et al. 2004), and healthy volunteers (Malhotra et al. 2002; Tsai et al. 2003; Egan et al. 2001).

Bertolino et al. (2004) reported that *COMT* Val158Met genotype predicted working memory performance and dorsolateral prefrontal cortical activation in 20 patients with schizophrenia after treatment with olanzapine. The pattern of results suggested that patients with the 158Met allele, which presumably is associated with increased availability of dopamine in prefrontal cortex (Chen et al. 2004), demonstrated improved performance on the N-back and more efficient prefrontal physiology as compared with 158Val carriers. Consistent with these findings, T. W. Weickert et al. (2004) reported an effect of the same allele (158Met) on working memory in a placebo-controlled, counterbalanced, within-subject study of 20 inpatients with schizophrenia. Specifically, 158Met homozygotes showed a significant improvement in cognitive performance after the administration of both first- and second-generation antipsychotic medications relative to their own performance in a placebo condition. In contrast, 158Val homozygotes showed no such improvement.

More recently, Woodward et al. (2007) described a large-scale prospective study of 86 patients with schizophrenia who were treated with clozapine for six months. Patients were genotyped for *COMT* Val158Met and completed a battery of neurocognitive measures at baseline, six weeks, and six months. Results converge with previous data, with 158Met carriers demonstrating significantly improved cognitive performance on measures of executive function and working memory as compared with

158Val homozygotes after six months of clozapine treatment. Taken together, these data suggest that while the cognitive benefit of the atypical antipsychotic medications may be very modest at the group level, there may exist a molecularly defined subgroup of patients for whom these agents represent efficacious cognitive enhancers.

Information derived from the functionality of the *COMT* Val158Met polymorphism at the neurotransmitter level has been the basis for at least two studies aimed more directly at the COMT effect on cortical dopamine. Mattay et al. (2003) demonstrated that, in healthy control subjects, individuals homozygous for the 158Val allele benefited from the administration of amphetamine, a dopamine–norepinephrine transporter blocker which results in increased dopamine availability at the synapse, on measures of working memory and prefrontal activation parameters, while the performance of 158Met homozygotes did not improve or, in some cases, deteriorated with amphetamine exposure. This is convergent with a genotype effect noted in the opposite direction when patients are administered antipsychotic medications that antagonize dopamine, such that 158Met carriers receive beneficial effects and 158Val carriers do not (Bertolino et al. 2004; T.W. Weickert et al. 2004; Woodward et al. 2007). This is also consistent with a well-described inverted-U functional response curve to manipulating dopamine levels in the prefrontal cortex (Williams and Goldman-Rakic 1995; Goldman-Rakic 1998). These data are consistent with results from follow-up work conducted by the same group, in which tolcapone, a CNS-penetrant COMT inhibitor, was administered to 47 healthy subjects and resulted in improvement on a measure of verbal memory in 158Val carriers. In contrast, 158Met homozygotes' performance tended to worsen after tolcapone exposure (Apud et al. 2006). While there is a potential to utilize novel approaches such as these to enhance cognition in healthy subjects, the cost–benefit ratio has thus far restricted their application in clinical samples. Most problematic, amphetamine may exacerbate psychosis in patients with schizophrenia and in some cases may induce psychosis in unaffected relatives of schizophrenia patients (Abi-Dargham 2004), while tolcapone has serious adverse effects on the liver and thus does not represent an ideal agent for common use.

Pharmacogenetics of Cognition: Glutamatergic Agents

Glutamate is another neurotransmitter that has been a primary focus of cognitive enhancement studies, as there is a substantial body of evidence suggesting that cognitive dysfunction is associated with abnormalities in the glutamatergic system in the brain. The glutamatergic system is mediated by multiple families of ion channels, with the n-methyl-d-aspartate (NMDA) receptor site figuring prominently in synaptic plasticity (Liu et al. 2004). NMDA-receptor-based long-term potentiation is believed to represent the cellular basis of learning and memory (Cotman et al. 1988), and when it is disrupted using NMDA receptor antagonists such as ketamine, learning and memory deficits are prominent in mice and in humans (Malhotra et al. 1996). Taken together, these data suggest that treatments augmenting NMDA-receptor-mediated neurotransmission may improve cognition in patients with schizophrenia.

To date, pharmacological studies investigating pharmacological glutamatergic agents designed to specifically target cognition have been somewhat inconsistent. Preliminary results of placebo-controlled clinical trials with D-serine, an NMDA agonist, provided evidence of its efficacy in schizophrenia. Tsai et al. (1998) assessed the effects of D-serine in a double-blind, placebo-controlled trial in 31 patients with schizophrenia when added to their current antipsychotic regimen, which included both typical and atypical antipsychotics. They reported significant improvement in the D-serine group for positive, negative, and cognitive symptoms, as well as improvement on a measure of executive function. More recently, Heresco-Levy et al. (2005) reported significant improvement in all symptom domains, including cognitive and negative symptoms, when D-serine was added to the commonly prescribed SGAs risperidone or olanzapine in 39 patients with schizophrenia. To date there is one negative study of D-serine, which randomized 65 acutely exacerbated patients to D-serine versus sarcosine (a glycine transporter inhibitor) versus placebo and demonstrated no effect for D-serine, while sarcosine was superior to placebo (Tsai et al. 2004). Finally, in a recently published large-scale study of 157 patients with schizophrenia or schizoaffective disorder, Buchanan and colleagues (2007) compared two other agents with action at the glycine site of the NMDA receptor, D-cycloserine and glycine, with placebo. Results indicated no overall differences on measures of cognition or negative symptoms for either active agent as compared with placebo, suggesting that neither glycine nor D-cycloserine are effective in treating negative and cognitive symptoms of schizophrenia.

Although results are inconsistent, both positive and negative studies suggest that there may be a subset of patients with schizophrenia who benefit from treatment targeting the NMDA receptor. For example, upon further investigation of the statistically significant effects of D-serine versus placebo in the Heresco-Levy et al. (2005) study, only 14 of the 39 patients treated with D-serine demonstrated a clinically meaningful change in symptoms, suggesting that individual clinical response may not be fully represented by analyses at the group level. Genetic factors might explain a proportion of the variance in treatment response to these agents. While there are a number of candidate genes that might be appropriate as potential molecular predictors of response to D-serine, via their impact on the glutamatergic system, dysbindin 1 (*DTNBP1*) represents one of the strongest candidate genes for schizophrenia to date (for review, see Norton et al. 2006) and may also be specifically associated with cognition (Burdick et al. 2006; 2007; Donohoe et al. 2007).

The gene for dysbindin 1 (*DTNBP1*) is located at 6p22.3 and has been significantly associated with schizophrenia in several studies (Norton et al. 2006). While the specific role of DTNBP1 in the CNS is unknown, dysbindin 1 is expressed widely in the brain, including regions in the frontal cortex, temporal cortex, hippocampus, caudate, putamen, nucleus accumbens, amygdala, thalamus, and midbrain (C. S. Weickert et al. 2004). Preliminary data suggest that *DTNBP1* genotype may impact upon the glutamatergic neurotransmitter system through reduced DTNBP1 expression (Bray et al. 2005). Decreased DTNBP1 expression has been demonstrated in patients with schizophrenia in prefrontal cortex and hippocampus, brain regions that have been linked to cognitive symptom pathology (C. S. Weickert et al. 2004). Furthermore, Numakawa and colleagues (2004) recently demonstrated that DTNBP1 is localized to presynaptic glutamatergic terminals in the hippocampus, where it interacts with binding partners to modulate the release of glutamate. These authors further showed that a dysbindin knockdown model resulted in reduced glutamatergic neurotransmission, thought to be caused by suppression of presynaptic proteins involved in intracellular vesicle trafficking. These data suggest that *DTNBP1* may serve as a modulator of treatment response to NMDA receptor agents in patients with schizophrenia.

Further evidence for DTNBP1 as a potential predictor of treatment response in studies of cognitive enhancement is derived from data demonstrating that *DTNBP1* variation influences cognitive performance in patients with schizophrenia (Burdick et al. 2006; 2007; Donohoe et al. 2007) and in healthy subjects (Burdick et al. 2006). In previous work by our group, a six-locus *DTNBP1* haplotype (CTCTAC) was associated with schizophrenia and schizoaffective disorder in Caucasian subjects (Funke et al. 2004). Subsequently, we examined the relationship between this risk haplotype and cognition (Burdick et al. 2006) and found that the risk haplotype was associated with nearly a half standard deviation decrement in general cognitive ability (g) both in patients with schizophrenia and in healthy controls (see figure 11.1). Risk haplotype carriers performed worse than noncarriers in every cognitive domain, including attention, memory, and executive function. Moreover, the risk haplotype was nearly twice as frequent (28.3% frequency vs. 14.4% frequency, respectively) in a "cognitive deficit" group of patients (defined as performance ≥1 standard deviation below the mean of healthy controls) compared to the group of "cognitively spared" patients who did not meet this threshold.

Additionally, in a second study (Burdick et al. 2007), we assessed cognitive decline (change in intellect over the disease course) in 183 Caucasian schizophrenia patients using a proxy measure of premorbid intelligence (IQ) with which current general cognitive ability (g) was compared. We found that schizophrenia patients who carry the CTCTAC risk haplotype demonstrated a significantly greater decline in IQ (residual mean change = 13.5 ± 13.6) as compared with noncarriers.

Our data are consistent with linkage results suggesting that the chromosomal region that encompasses *DTNBP1* is associated with IQ in healthy subjects (Posthuma et al. 2005) and cognitive deficits in schizophrenia (Hallmayer et al. 2005), as well as a

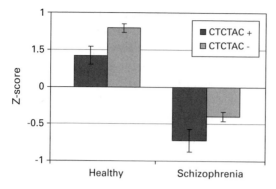

Figure 11.1

DTNBP1 risk haplotype and *g*: global cognitive functioning (*g*) in subjects with and without the *DTNBP1* CTCTAC risk haplotype. Z-scores are standardized using the standardized mean = 0 and standard deviation = 1 from the healthy volunteer sample, such that lower values reflect worse performance. Error bars represent the 95% confidence interval. The overall effect of genotype is significant at p = 0.008, and the subject type by genotype interaction is not significant. (Modified from Burdick et al. 2006)

candidate gene study demonstrating that a protective *DTNBP1* haplotype was associated with higher educational attainment (Williams et al. 2004). Finally, in an Irish cohort, Donohoe et al. (2007) reported that their *DTNBP1* risk haplotype was associated with poorer performance on a measure of spatial working memory in patients with schizophrenia. Taken together, these data suggest that *DTNBP1* influences cognition in a global fashion and may impact upon the severity of intellectual decline in schizophrenia.

A number of other schizophrenia susceptibility genes have been implicated in glutamatergic neurotransmission and may represent future targets for pharmacogenetic studies of neurocognitive function. For example, the candidate gene G72/G30—now known as D-amino acid oxidase activator (*DAOA*)—plays an important role in the activation of D-amino acid oxidase and regulates endogenous D-serine (Chumakov et al. 2002). *DAOA* has also been shown to have an impact on risk for schizophrenia (Detera-Wadleigh and McMahon 2006) and influence working memory and hippocampal activation in patients with schizophrenia (Goldberg et al. 2006), making this another candidate gene of great interest with regard to predicting glutamatergic cognitive enhancement in patients with schizophrenia. In addition, the type II metabotropic glutamate receptor 3 (*GRM3*) gene, located on 7q21.1-q21.2, has been associated with risk for schizophrenia in some (Martie et al. 2002; Fuji et al. 2003; Egan et al. 2004; Chen et al. 2005), but not all (Norton et al. 2005; Schwab et al. 2008), studies to date. Further, in the study by Egan and colleagues (2004), the A allele at the *GRM3* locus rs6465084 was associated not only with increased risk for schizophrenia but also with reductions in in vivo measures of prefrontal N-acetyl aspartate measures, impaired cognition, inefficient activation of dorsolateral prefrontal cortex during working memory, and reduced activation of hippocampus during episodic memory. Additional data from postmortem brain tissue also revealed an association of the A allele with reductions in EAAT2 messenger RNA levels. Taken together with a recent report of an epistatic interaction between *COMT* and *GRM3* (Tan et al. 2007), these data suggest that GRM3 may play a role in both glutamatergic and dopaminergic systems critical to neurocognitive functioning. Indeed, there are currently studies ongoing to assess the efficacy of MGluR2/3 agonists in patients with schizophrenia (Schoepp 2006).

Complications and Confounds

There are several difficulties inherent in molecular genetic studies in psychiatry. At the forefront of these issues remains the somewhat arbitrary definition of the phenotype, specifically with regard to diagnostic categorization. The use of the *Diagnostic and Statistical Manual of Mental Disorders*, fourth edition, categories has proved limiting in the discovery of susceptibility genes to date, with a number of leading candidates crossing diagnostic boundaries (i.e., *Disrupted in Schizophrenia 1, Neuregulin 1, G72, COMT*). This highlights the importance of the identification of, and thorough evaluation of, specific features of disease that either might differentiate illnesses from one another (negative symptoms, cyclicity) or, in contrast, might represent a trait common to more than one diagnostic entity (i.e., cognitive impairment, changes in brain structure and function). The use of intermediate phenotypes in this way may lead to molecular-based strategies for dissecting the heterogeneity of the diagnostic phenotype and might allow for the application of pharmacogenetic strategies that are specific to the traits of the disease that are most debilitating and difficult to treat.

Moreover, as the era of genome-wide association (GWA) has arrived and technology is advancing at an astounding rate, questions regarding the optimal genetic approach to use for studies in psychiatric genetics and pharmacogenetics are ubiquitous. Should single-marker studies be considered a thing of the past? Will whole-genome scans be underpowered by necessity? Should investigations target specific loci with known functional consequences or cast a wide net? As tractable biological pathways are being identified that involve multiple, interacting genes, should our approach be to focus in on the pathways that are involved in the pathophysiology of the disease or are known to be a target for a particular drug of interest, or will this approach limit truly novel findings?

The answers to these questions may be largely dependent on the specific aim of any given study. Pharmacogenetic studies are limited by sample sizes, more so than other types of molecular genetic investigations. While it remains unclear the absolute minimum number of subjects needed to conduct a meaningful whole genome analysis in a complex, polygenic disorder such as schizophrenia, most pharmacogenetics studies include samples on the order of 10× fewer than many case–control association studies, making the GWA approach somewhat less feasible than candidate gene approaches. While candidate gene approaches may fall rapidly out of favor in disease-based studies, this may continue to represent a useful approach in pharmacogenetics. Specifically, as the mechanism of action is known for certain pharmacological agents, an a priori biological target might be more readily established in pharmacogenetic studies as compared with studies aimed at identification of disease susceptibility loci. Moreover, the rapidly emerging data on epistasis and gene pathway mapping is likely to open new doors in pharmacogenetic studies and in samples that are inherently limited by study design.

Looking forward, there are several potential strategies that might help to establish an ideal pharmacogenetics design, although some are more feasible than others. Previous pharmacogenetic efforts have typically focused on samples of convenience (i.e., those from ongoing, large-scale clinical trials). These studies, specifically designed with the hope of generalizability, inherently include heterogeneous samples, making add-on pharmacogenetics aims more difficult to achieve. A priori design of a "model" pharmacogenetic trial would follow along different guidelines than many of the established clinical trials. First, inclusion of a more homogeneous sample would be desired, specifically with regard to factors such as age, sex, race, ethnicity, and any other genetic factors that might influence the outcome measure. Second, a single-arm design for treatment, with a fixed dosing regimen and measurement by precise drug plasma levels, would allow for a clear interpretation of outcome measures. Third, detailed assessment of primary outcome measures, as well as adverse effects of medications, would allow for greater sensitivity, with frequent evaluations scheduled to allow for data analytic strategies beyond last observation carried forward. Specific to cognition as a primary outcome, samples should be matched on baseline IQ, and the issue of practice effects should be considered at the outset of the trial. Ideally, repeated administration of the testing battery prior to treatment would lessen the potential for practice effects during the treatment phase; however, it would also be critical to utilize neurocognitive measures that would be unlikely to result in ceiling effects (optimized performance) in this type of design to ensure that there is room for improvement above and beyond that expected by practice.

Other specific issues to consider in designing pharmacogenetic studies depend largely on the overall aim of the trial. In the case that a specific candidate gene is being targeted for cognition, any previous association to specific cognitive markers should be considered with regard to chosen outcome measures. For example, studies of *COMT* would ideally include several measures sensitive to prefrontal cortical dopamine availability such as the N-back, while a trial focusing on the dopamine receptor

D2 (*DRD2*) gene might preferentially include measures of subcortical dopaminergic function including psychomotor and processing speed tasks such as grooved pegboard or finger tapping. In contrast, more global measures, such as *g* or composite scores, might be considered optimal in a study of the *DTNBP1* gene. Nonetheless, whenever cognition is the primary outcome, it remains important to include "control" measures of cognition to tap into each domain without making too many a priori assumptions about gene function. Finally, in studies designed around a specific marker within a candidate gene, it would be prudent to recruit subjects based on prospective genotyping to provide for optimal power and to limit the need for oversampling.

Advancing technology in genomics and our increasing knowledge of the functional consequences of variation at the genetic level will undoubtedly provide a basis for advancement of our treatment of the clinical symptoms of complex disorders such as schizophrenia. Despite the complications and numerous potential confounds of molecular genetic investigations, pharmacogenetics continues to offer the opportunity for data-driven treatment strategies that may allow for personalized medicine in the not too distant future.

References

Abi-Dargham A (2004). Do we still believe in the dopamine hypothesis? New data bring new evidence. *Int J Neuropsychopharmacol*, 7 (Suppl 1):S1–5.

Apud JA, Mattay V, Chen J, Kolachana BS, Callicott JH, Rasetti R, et al. (2006). Tolcapone improves cognition and cortical information processing in normal human subjects. *Neuropsychopharmacology*, 32:1011–20.

Bertolino A, Caforio G, Blasi G, et al. (2004). Interaction of COMT (Val(108/158)Met) genotype and olanzapine treatment on prefrontal cortical function in patients with schizophrenia. *Am J Psychiatry*, 161:1798–805.

Bilder RM, Goldman RS, Robinson D, et al. (2000). Neuropsychology of first-episode schizophrenia: initial characterization and clinical correlates. *Am J Psychiatry*, 57:549–59.

Bilder RM, Goldman RS, Volavka J, Czobor P, Hoptman M, Sheitman B, et al. (2002a). Neurocognitive effects of clozapine, olanzapine, risperidone, and haloperidol in patients with chronic schizophrenia or schizoaffective disorder. *Am J Psychiatry*, 159:1018–28.

Bilder RM, Volavka J, Czobor P, Malhotra AK, Kennedy JL, Ni X, et al. (2002b). Neurocognitive correlates of the COMT Val(158)Met polymorphism in chronic schizophrenia. *Biol Psychiatry*, 52:701–7.

Buchanan RW, Javitt DC, Marder SR, Schooler NR, Gold JM, McMahon RP, et al. (2007). The Cognitive and Negative Symptoms in Schizophrenia Trial (CONSIST): the efficacy of glutamatergic agents for negative symptoms and cognitive impairments. *Am J Psychiatry*, 164:1593–602.

Burdick KE, Goldberg TE, Funke B, Bates JA, Lencz T, Kucherlapati R, Malhotra AK (2007). DTNBP1 genotype influences cognitive decline in schizophrenia. *Schizophr Res*, 89:169–72.

Burdick KE, Lencz T, Funke B, Finn CT, Szeszko PR, Kane JM, et al. (2006). Genetic variation in DTNBP1 influences general cognitive ability. *Hum Mol Genet*, 15:1563–8.

Chen J, Lipska BK, Halim N, Ma QD, Matsumoto M, Melhem S, et al. (2004). Functional analysis of genetic variation in catechol-O-methyltransferase (COMT): effects on mRNA, protein, and enzyme activity in postmortem human brain. *Am J Hum Genet*, 75:807–21. Epub 2004 September 27. Erratum in *Am J Hum Genet*, 2005, 76:1089.

Chen Q, He G, Chen Q, Wu S, Xu Y, Feng G, et al. (2005). A case–control study of the relationship between the metabotropic glutamate receptor 3 gene and schizophrenia in the Chinese population. *Schizophr Res*, 73:21–6.

Chumakov I, Blumenfeld M, Guerassimenko O, Cavarec L, Palicio M, Abderrahim H, et al. (2002). Genetic and physiological data implicating the new human gene G72 and the gene for D-amino acid oxidase in schizophrenia. *Proc Natl Acad Sci USA*, 99:13675–80.

Cotman CW, Monaghan DT, Ganong AH (1988). Excitatory amino acid neurotransmission: NMDA receptors and Hebb-type synaptic plasticity. *Annu Rev Neurosci*, 11:61–80.

Detera-Wadleigh SD, McMahon FJ (2006). G72/G30 in schizophrenia and bipolar disorder: review and meta-analysis. *Biol Psychiatry*, 60:106–14. Review.

Donohoe G, Morris DW, Clarke S, McGhee KA, Schwaiger S, Nangle JM, et al. (2007). Variance in neurocognitive performance is associated with dysbindin-1 in schizophrenia: a preliminary study. *Neuropsychologia*, 45:454–8.

Egan MF, Goldberg TE, Kolachana BS, Callicott JH, Mazzanti CM, Straub RE, et al. (2001). Effect of COMT Val108/158 Met genotype on frontal lobe function and risk for schizophrenia. *Proc Natl Acad Sci USA*, 98:6917–22.

Egan MF, Straub RE, Goldberg TE, Yakub I, Callicott JH, Hariri AR, et al. (2004). Variation in GRM3 affects cognition, prefrontal glutamate, and risk for schizophrenia. *Proc Natl Acad Sci USA*, 101:12604–9.

Fan JB, Zhang CS, Gu NF, Li XW, Sun WW, Wang HY, et al. (2005). Catechol-O-methyltransferase gene Val/Met functional polymorphism and risk of schizophrenia: a large-scale association study plus meta-analysis. *Biol Psychiatry*, 57:139–44. Review.

Fujii Y, Shibata H, Kikuta R, Makino C, Tani A, Hirata N, et al. (2003). Positive associations of polymorphisms in the metabotropic glutamate receptor type 3 gene (GRM3) with schizophrenia. *Psychiatr Genet*, 13:71–6.

Funke B, Finn CT, Plocik AM, Lake S, DeRosse P, Kane JM, et al. (2004). Association of the DTNBP1 locus with schizophrenia in a U.S. population. *Am J Hum Genet*, 75:891–8.

Glahn DC, Almasy L, Blangero J, Burk GM, Estrada J, Peralta JM, et al. (2006). Adjudicating neurocognitive endophenotypes for schizophrenia. *Am J Med Genet B Neuropsychiatr Genet*, 144(2):242–9.

Green MF (1996). What are the functional consequences of neurocognitive deficits in schizophrenia? *Am J Psychiatry*, 153:321–30.

Goldberg TE, Straub RE, Callicott JH, Hariri A, Mattay VS, Bigelow L, et al. (2006). The G72/G30 gene complex and cognitive abnormalities in schizophrenia. *Neuropsychopharmacology*, 31:2022–32.

Goldman-Rakic PS (1998). The cortical dopamine system: role in memory and cognition. *Adv Pharmacol*, 42:707–11.

Hallmayer JF, Kalaydjieva L, Badcock J, Dragovic M, Howell S, Michie PT, Rock D, Vile D, Williams R, Corder EH, Hollingsworth K, Jablensky A (2005). Genetic evidence for a distinct subtype of schizophrenia characterized by pervasive cognitive deficit. *Am J Hum Genet*, 77(3):468–76.

Harvey PD, Green MF, McGurk SR, Meltzer HY (2003). Changes in cognitive functioning with risperidone and olanzapine treatment: a large-scale, double-blind, randomized study. *Psychopharmacology (Berl)*, 169:404–11.

Harvey PD, Meltzer H, Simpson GM, Potkin SG, Loebel A, Siu C, Romano SJ (2004). Improvement in cognitive function following a switch to ziprasidone from conventional antipsychotics, olanzapine, or risperidone in outpatients with schizophrenia. *Schizophr Res*, 66:101–13.

Harvey PD, Rabinowitz J, Eerdekens M, Davidson M (2005). Treatment of cognitive impairment in early psychosis: a comparison of risperidone and haloperidol in a large long-term trial. *Am J Psychiatry*, 162:1888–95.

Heresco-Levy U, Javitt DC, Ebstein R, Vass A, Lichtenberg P, Bar G, et al. (2005). D-serine efficacy as add-on pharmacotherapy to risperidone and olanzapine for treatment-refractory schizophrenia. *Biol Psychiatry*, 57:577–85.

Keefe RS, Bilder RM, Davis SM, Harvey PD, Palmer BW, Gold JM, et al. (2007). Neurocognitive effects of antipsychotic medications in patients with chronic schizophrenia in the CATIE trial. *Arch Gen Psychiatry*, 64:633–47.

Keefe RS, Bilder RM, Harvey PD, Davis SM, Palmer BW, Gold JM, et al. (2006). Baseline neurocognitive deficits in the CATIE schizophrenia trial. *Neuropsychopharmacology*, 31:2033–46.

Keefe RS, Malhotra AK, Meltzer HY, Kane JM, Buchanan RW, Murthy A, Sovel M, Li C, Goldman R (2008). Efficacy and safety of donepezil in patients with schizophrenia or schizoaffective disorder: significant placebo/practice effects in a 12-week, randomized, double-blind, placebo-controlled trial. *Neuropsychopharmacology*, 33(6):1217–28.

Lencz T, Smith CW, McLaughlin D, Auther A, Nakayama E, Hovey L, et al. (2006). Generalized and specific neurocognitive deficits in prodromal schizophrenia. *Biol Psychiatry*, 59:863–71.

Liu L, Wong TP, Pozza MF, Lingenhoehl K, Wang Y, Sheng M, et al. (2004). Role of NMDA receptor subtypes in governing the direction of hippocampal synaptic plasticity. *Science*, 304:1021–4.

Malhotra AK, Burdick KE, Razi K, Bates JA, Sanders M, Kane JM (2006). Ziprasidone-induced cognitive enhancement in schizophrenia: specificity or pseudospecificity? *Schizophr Res*, 87:181–4.

Malhotra AK, Kestler LJ, Mazzanti C, Bates JA, Goldberg T, Goldman DA (2002). Functional polymorphism in the COMT gene and performance on a test of prefrontal cognition. *Am J Psychiatry*, 159:652–4.

Malhotra AK, Murphy GM Jr, Kennedy JL (2004). Pharmacogenetics of psychotropic drug response. *Am J Psychiatry*, 161:780–96.

Malhotra AK, Pinals DA, Adler CM, Elman I, Clifton A, Pickar D, et al. (1996). NMDA receptor function and human cognition: the effects of ketamine in healthy volunteers. *Neuropsychopharmacology*, 14:301–7.

Martí SB, Cichon S, Propping P, Nöthen M (2002). Metabotropic glutamate receptor 3 (GRM3) gene variation is not associated with schizophrenia or bipolar affective disorder in the German population. *Am J Med Genet*, 114:46–50.

Mattay VS, Goldberg TE, Fera F, Hariri AR, Tessitore A, Egan MF, et al. (2003). Catechol O-methyltransferase val158-met genotype and individual variation in the brain response to amphetamine. *Proc Natl Acad Sci USA*, 100:6186–91.

Norton N, Williams HJ, Dwyer S, Ivanov D, Preece AC, Gerrish A, et al. (2005). No evidence for association between polymorphisms in GRM3 and schizophrenia. *BMC Psychiatry*, 13:5–23.

Norton N, Williams HJ, Owen MJ (2006). An update on the genetics of schizophrenia. *Curr Opin Psychiatry*, 19(2):158–64.

Numakawa T, Yagasaki Y, Ishimoto T, Okada T, Suzuki T, Iwata N, et al. (2004). Evidence of novel neuronal functions of dysbindin, a susceptibility gene for schizophrenia. *Hum Mol Genet*, 13:2699–708.

Posthuma D, Luciano M, de Geus EJ, Wright MJ, Slagboom PE, Montgomery GW, et al. (2005). A genomewide scan for intelligence identifies quantitative trait loci on 2q and 6p. *Am J Hum Genet*, 77:318–26.

Rosa A, Peralta V, Cuesta MJ, Zarzuela A, Serrano F, Martinez-Larrea A, Fananas L (2004). New evidence of association between COMT gene and prefrontal neurocognitive function in healthy individuals from sibling pairs discordant for psychosis. *Am J Psychiatry*, 161:1110–2.

Schoepp DD (2006). New directions in the treatment of schizophrenia: modulators of MGlu2 and/or MGlu3 receptors. *Neuropsychopharmacology*, 31(Supp 1s): S25–6.

Schwab SG, Plummer C, Albus M, Borrmann-Hassenbach M, Lerer B, Trixler M, et al. (2008). DNA sequence variants in the metabotropic glutamate receptor 3 and risk to schizophrenia: an association study. *Psychiatr Genet*, 18:25–30.

Tan HY, Chen Q, Goldberg TE, Mattay VS, Meyer-Lindenberg A, Weinberger DR, Callicott JH (2007). Catechol-O-methyltransferase Val158Met modulation of prefrontal–parietal–striatal brain systems during arithmetic and temporal transformations in working memory. *J Neurosci*, 27:13393–401.

Trandafir A, Meary A, Schurhoff F, et al. (2006). Memory tests in first-degree adult relatives of schizophrenic patients: a meta-analysis. *Schizophr Res*, 81:217–26.

Tsai G, Yang P, Chung LC, Lange N, Coyle JT (1998). D-serine added to antipsychotics for the treatment of schizophrenia. *Biol Psych*, 44:1081–9.

Tsai G, Lane HY, Yang P, Chong MY, Lange N (2004). Glycine transporter I inhibitor, N-methylglycine (sarcosine), added to antipsychotics for the treatment of schizophrenia. *Biol Psychiatry*, 55:452–6.

Tsai SJ, Yu YW, Chen TJ, Chen JY, Liou YJ, Chen MC, Hong CJ (2003). Association study of a functional catechol-O-methyltransferase-gene polymorphism and cognitive function in healthy females. *Neurosci Lett*, 338:123–6.

Weickert CS, Straub RE, McClintock BW, Matsumoto M, Hashimoto R, Hyde TM, et al. (2004). Human dysbindin (DTNBP1) gene expression in normal brain and in schizophrenic prefrontal cortex and midbrain. *Arch Gen Psychiatry*, 61:544–55.

Weickert TW, Goldberg TE, Mishara A, Apud JA, Kolachana BS, Egan MF, Weinberger DR (2004). Catechol-O-methyltransferase val108/158met genotype predicts working memory response to antipsychotic medications. *Biol Psychiatry*, 56:677–82.

Weinberger DR, Berman KF, Illowsky BP (1988). Physiological dysfunction of dorsolateral prefrontal cortex in schizophrenia: III. A new cohort and evidence for a monoaminergic mechanism. *Arch Gen Psychiatry*, 45:609–15.

Williams GV, Goldman-Rakic PS (1995). Modulation of memory fields by dopamine D1 receptors in prefrontal cortex. *Nature*, 376(6541):572–5.

Williams NM, Preece A, Morris DW, Spurlock G, Bray NJ, Stephens M, et al. (2004). Identification in 2 independent samples of a novel schizophrenia risk haplotype of the dystrobrevin binding protein gene (DTNBP1). *Arch Gen Psychiatry*, 61:336–44.

Woodward ND, Jayathilake K, Meltzer HY (2007). COMT val108/158met genotype, cognitive function, and cognitive improvement with clozapine in schizophrenia. *Schizophr Res*, 90:86–96.

Wyatt RJ, Henter I, Leary MC, Taylor E (1995). An economic evaluation of schizophrenia. *Soc Psychiatry Psychiatr Epidemiol*, 30(5):196–205.

Contributors

Kristin L. Bigos, Ph.D.
Genes, Cognition, and Psychosis
Program, National Institute of Mental
Health, Bethesda, Maryland

Katherine E. Burdick, Ph.D.
The Zucker Hillside Hospital, North
Shore-Long Island Jewish Health System
The Feinstein Institute for Medical
Research
Albert Einstein College of Medicine
Glen Oaks, New York

Jingshan Chen, Ph.D.
Genes, Cognition, and Psychosis
Program, National Institutes of Mental
Health, Bethesda, Maryland

Aiden Corvin, Ph.D.
Neuropsychiatric Genetics Research
Group, Department of Psychiatry and
Institute of Molecular Medicine, Trinity
College, Dublin, Ireland

Jeffrey L. Cummings, M.D.
UCLA Alzheimer's Disease Center, Los
Angeles, California

Ian J. Deary, M.D.
Department of Psychology, University of
Edinburgh, Edinburgh, Scotland

Eco J. C. de Geus, Ph.D.
Department of Biological Psychology,
Vrije Universiteit, Amsterdam, The
Netherlands

Gary Donohoe, D.Clin.Psych.
Neuropsychiatric Genetics Research
Group, Department of Psychiatry and
Trinity Institute of Neuroscience, Trinity
College, Dublin, Ireland

Jin Fan, Ph.D.
Department of Psychiatry and Neurosci-
ence, Mount Sinai School of Medicine,
New York, New York

Erika E. Forbes, Ph.D.
Departments of Psychiatry, University of
Pittsburgh Schools of Medicine and
Pharmacy, Pittsburgh, Pennsylvania

John Fossella, Ph.D.
Department of Psychiatry, Mount Sinai
School of Medicine, New York, New
York

Terry E. Goldberg, Ph.D.
Litwin Zucker Alzheimer's Disease
Center and Psychiatry Research
Feinstein Institute, Great Neck, New
York

Ahmad R. Hariri, Ph.D.
Departments of Psychiatry, University of
Pittsburgh Schools of Medicine and
Pharmacy, Pittsburgh, Pennsylvania

Lucas Kempf, M.D.
Genes, Cognition, and Psychosis
Program, National Institute of Mental
Health, Bethesda, Maryland

Anil K. Malhotra, M.D.
The Zucker Hillside Hospital, Feinstein
Institute for Medical Research
Albert Einstein College of Medicine,
Glen Oaks, New York

Venkata S. Mattay, M.D.
Genes, Cognition, and Psychosis
Program, National Institute of Mental
Health, Bethesda, Maryland

Lauren M. McGrath
Department of Psychology, University of
Denver, Denver, Colorado

Kristin K. Nicodemus, Ph.D.
Wellcome Trust Centre for Human
Genetics, University of Oxford, Oxford,
United Kingdom

Clinical Brain Disorders Branch, Genes,
Cognition, and Psychosis Program,
National Institute of Mental Health,
Bethesda, Maryland

Francesco Papaleo, Ph.D.
Clinical Brain Disorders Branch,
National Institute of Mental Health,
Bethesda, Maryland

Bruce F. Pennington, Ph.D.
Department of Psychology, University of
Denver, Denver, Colorado

Michael I. Posner, Ph.D.
Department of Psychology, University of
Oregon, Eugene, Oregon

Danielle Posthuma, Ph.D.
Department of Biological Psychology,
Vrije Universiteit, Amsterdam, The
Netherlands

John M. Ringman, M.D.
Alzheimer Disease Research Center, Los
Angeles, California

Shelley D. Smith, Ph.D.
Department of Psychology, University of
Denver, Denver, Colorado

Daniel R. Weinberger, M.D.
Genes, Cognition, and Psychosis
Program, National Institute of Mental
Health, Bethesda, Maryland

Fengyu Zhang, Ph.D.
Genes, Cognition, and Psychosis
Program, National Institute of Mental
Health, Bethesda, Maryland

Index